Readings for the
21st Century

W9-BBF-477

Readings for the 21st Century

Tomorrow's Issues for Today's Students

Second Edition

William Vesterman
Rutgers University

Josh Ozersky

ALLYN AND BACON

BOSTON   LONDON   TORONTO   SYDNEY   TOKYO   SINGAPORE

Editor in Chief, Humanities: Joseph Opiela
Editorial Assistant: Brenda Conaway
Production Administrator: Rowena Dores
Editorial Production Service: Lauren Green Shafer
Cover Administrator: Linda Dickinson
Manufacturing Buyer: Megan Cochran

Library of Congress Cataloging-in-Publication Data

Readings for the 21st century : tomorrow's issues for today's students
    / [compiled by] William Vesterman, Josh Ozersky.—2nd ed.
        p.   cm.
    Includes indexes.
    ISBN 0-205-15536-7 — ISBN 0-205-15874-9 : free copy
    1. College readers.   2. English language—Rhetoric.
I. Vesterman, William.   II. Ozersky, Josh.   III. Title:
Readings for the twenty-first century.
PE1417.R418   1994
428.6—dc20   93–33503
                                                     CIP

This book is printed on
recycled, acid-free paper.

CREDITS

Angelou, Maya. "The Arc of the Moral Universe Is Long, but It Bends Toward
    Justice," reprinted by permission from *New Perspectives Quarterly,* Winter
    1992.

*Credits continued on page 436, which constitutes an extension of the
copyright page.*

Printed in the United States of America
10 9 8 7 6 5 4 3 2 1   97 96 95 94 93

CONTENTS

v

THE MILLENNIAL MELTING POT
Race and Equality in America's Future

The Past as Prologue

PREFACE

R*eadings for the Twenty-first Century* is a collection of essays grouped around a general theme— –the rapidly approaching twenty-first century. The essays, arranged into ten chapters, focus on various aspects of the future that today's students must face. Each chapter contains essays, usually six in number, that examine a given issue from several perspectives and in several different styles. The authors in each chapter are diversified further by background: Some are professors, some are poets, some distinguished critics, some incisive journalists. All are augurers in one way or another. To balance these predictions, each chapter begins with a classic essay on the theme by a celebrated author: George Orwell commences a chapter on social issues, for example, and Aldous Huxley begins one on technology.

An implicit subtheme in every chapter is "The Future and You," and the critical apparatus of the book invites students to consider themselves in direct relation to the issues and problems that will face their generation in the 1990s and beyond. A brief headnote introduces each author and essay, summarizing its subject. The book also provides questions for each essay on *Themes, Issues, and Ideas* and on *Writing Strategies and Techniques,* along with two *Suggestions for Writing.* At the end of every chapter, *Making Connections* asks students to look critically at two or more essays within the chapter. These questions may form the basis for longer research assignments on chapter themes. A *Rhetorical Index* and an *Index of Authors and Titles* complete the apparatus of the book. With lively classic and contemporary writing addressing a broad spectrum of world and American issues, the book is designed with the hope of helping students to develop thoughtful, informed, articulate views on topics that will define their future.

At the current rate, the 1990s will add a billion more people to the 5.2 billion now inhabiting the earth. Unless those rates diminish, this generation of students may witness a virtual tripling in the earth's population over the next one hundred years. Within this growing world, American power is shrinking. Born into a society that took its economic and political leadership for granted, the Millennial Generation will enter an increasingly powerful global economy. And as it comes to maturity, that generation will face this problem with its many difficult questions. How will the United States deal with a volatile Europe's wars and threats of wars? With the rising status of the Pacific Rim community? With a more powerful Germany, or an ever-changing Middle East? What will be our new relations with Africa, India, and Latin America? Can we deal with a stubbornly high poverty rate at home? How healthy can the population *afford* to be in the year 2000? If people live longer, who will care for them and support them? How will we come to terms with other important social issues facing this country?

Some changes are now in such a state of momentum that they may be considered sure. The United States will become an increasingly older nation with a racial and ethnic mixture whose diversity will be unparalleled in world history. White males will become a minority in the labor force and two-earner households will become the norm. A shortage of skilled technical workers will force government into efforts to improve education at all levels, while adults undergoing career changes may make up the majority of future college applicants.

For several generations now, the year 2000 has symbolized The Future. For all of us, that future will arrive in just a few short years. But it is the Millennial Generation who must lead our country bravely into the twenty-first century. This book is an attempt to help that generation to realize the enormity of their task.

Acknowledgments

Many people have helped to bring this book to its present form. The authors want to thank Kelly Griffin, for research and suggestions, and at Allyn and Bacon, Joe Opiela and (particularly for the second edition) Brenda Conaway and Lauren Green Shafer. For advice in shaping the book we thank teachers at many schools: John Bayer, St. Louis Community College; Kathleen Shine Cain, Merrimack College; Alisa Solomon and Christopher Hallowell of Baruch College (CUNY); William Lutz, Rutgers University–Camden; Jean Reynolds, Polk Community College; Mark Rollins, Ohio State University; Robert Schwegler, University of Rhode Island; and Tom Zaniello, Northern Kentucky University. Finally, for advice and encouragement, we wish to thank Robert Atwan, Louis Naom, Timothy Kunik, Richard Ortlip, and of course Paul Barish.

*Readings for the
21st Century*

CHAPTER ONE

Social Issues for the Twenty-first Century

Human Values in Changing Times

THE PAST AS PROLOGUE

Looking Back on the Spanish War

George Orwell

George Orwell (1903–1950) was the pen name of Eric Blair, one of the great essayists in the English language. Although most famous for his novel 1984, *Orwell spent much of his life writing essays and news reports. It fell to him to chronicle the rise of fascism in the twentieth century, a story he told unflinchingly throughout his career. Born in England and educated at Eton and Oxford, Orwell described himself as a child of the upper-lower-middle-class, and upon graduating began a career as a civil servant in India, then a British colony. Morally disgusted by his work there, he returned to Europe, where he lived as a penniless dishwasher in Paris and as a homeless tramp in England, so as to understand oppression from the other side. The experience stayed with him for the rest of his life, which he spent writing about politics and class in the most realistic way possible. His political education was capped by the Spanish Civil War, in which he fought on the side of the Republicans against the fascist leader Francisco Franco. His book* Homage to Catalonia *provides a fuller record than does the following essay, which was written from greater remove.*

I never think of the Spanish war without two memories coming into my mind. One is of the hospital ward at Lerida and the rather sad voices of the wounded militiamen singing some song with a refrain that ended—

Una resolucion,
Luchar hast' al fin!

Well, they fought to the end all right. For the last eighteen months of the war the Republican armies must have been fighting almost without cigarettes, and with precious little food. Even when I left Spain in the middle of 1937, meat and bread were scarce, tobacco a rarity, coffee and sugar almost unobtainable.

The other memory is the Italian militiaman who shook my hand in the guardroom, the day I joined the militia. I wrote about this man at the beginning of my book on the Spanish war, and do not want to repeat what I said there. When I remember—oh, how vividly!—his shabby uniform and fierce, pathetic, innocent face, the complex side-issues of the war seem to fade away and I see clearly that there was at any rate no doubt as to who was in the right. In spite of power, politics and journalistic lying, the central issue of the war was the attempt of people like this to win the decent life which they knew to be their birthright. It is difficult to think of this particular man's probable end without several kinds of bitterness. Since I met him in the Lenin Barracks he was probably a Trotskyist or an Anarchist, and in the peculiar conditions of our time, when people of that sort are not killed by the Gestapo they are usually killed by the G.P.U. But that does not affect the long-term issues. This man's face, which I saw only for a minute or two, remains with me as a sort of visual reminder of what the war was really about. He symbolises for me the flower of the European working class, harried by the police of all countries, the people who fill the mass graves of the Spanish battlefields and are now, to the tune of several millions, rotting in forced-labour camps.

When one thinks of all the people who support or have supported Fascism, one stands amazed at their diversity. What a crew! Think of a programme which at any rate for a while could bring Hitler, Petain, Montagu Norman, Pavelitch, William Randolph Hearst, Streicher, Buchman, Ezra Pound, Juan March, Cocteau, Thyssen, Father Coughlin, the Mufti of Jerusalem, Arnold Lunn, Antonescu, Spengler, Beverley Nichols, Lady Houston, and Marinetti all into the same boat! But the clue is really very simple. They are all people with something to lose, or people who long for a hierarchical society and dread the prospect of a world of free and equal human beings. Behind all the ballyhoo that is talked about "godless" Russia and the "materialism" of the working class lies the simple intention of those with money or privileges to cling to them. Ditto, though it contains a partial truth, with all the talk about the worthlessness of social reconstruction not accompanied by a "change of heart". The pious ones, from the Pope to the yogis of California, are great on the "change of heart", much more reassuring from their point of view than a change in the economic system. Petain attributes the fall of France to the common people's "love of pleasure". One sees this in its right perspective if one stops to wonder how much pleasure the ordinary French peasant's or workingman's life would contain compared with Petain's own. The damned impertinence of these politicians, priests, literary men, and what-not who lecture the working-class socialist for his "materialism"! All that the working-man demands is what these others would consider the indispensable minimum without which human life cannot be lived at all. Enough to eat, freedom from the haunting terror of unemployment, the knowledge that your children will get a fair chance, a bath once a day, clean linen reasonably often, a roof that doesn't leak, and short enough working hours to leave you with a little energy when the day is done. Not one of those who preach against "materialism" would consider life livable without these things. And how easily that minimum could be attained if we chose to set our minds to it for only twenty years! To raise the standard of living of the whole world to that of Britain would not be a greater undertaking than the war we have just fought. I don't claim, and I don't know who does, that that would solve anything in itself. It is merely that privation and brute labour have to be abolished before the real problems of humanity can be tackled. The major problem of our time is the decay of the belief in personal immortality, and it cannot be dealt with while the average human being is either drudging like an ox or shivering in fear of the secret police. How right the working classes are in their "materialism"! How right they are to realise that the belly comes before the soul, not in the scale of values but in point of time! Understand that, and the long horror that we are enduring becomes at least intelligible. All the considerations that are likely to make one falter—the siren voices of a Petain or of a Gandhi, the inescapable fact that in order to fight one has to degrade oneself, the equivocal moral position of Britain, with its democratic phrases and its coolie empire, the sinister development of Soviet Russia, the squalid farce of left-wing politics—all this fades away and one sees only the struggle of the gradually awakening common people against the lords of property and their hired liars and bumsuckers. The question is very simple. Shall people like that Italian soldier be allowed to live the decent, fully human life which is now technically achievable, or shan't they? Shall the common man be pushed back into the mud, or shall he not? I myself believe, perhaps on insufficient grounds, that the common man will win his fight sooner or later, but I want it to be sooner and not later—some time within the next hundred years, say, and not some time within the next ten thousand years. That was the real issue of the Spanish war, and of the last war, and perhaps of other wars yet to come.

Themes, Issues, and Ideas

1. Orwell ends this selection by saying that the "real issue" of the Spanish war would also be the real issue of wars to come. Does this conclusion seem to be true to you? Does it apply to other wars that you know of?

2. How, according to Orwell, might the "siren voice" of a Gandhi "make one falter?"

3. Orwell makes a list of what he considers "the indispensable minimum without which human life cannot be lived at all." Is there anything that you would add to this list? Anything you would take away?

Writing Strategies and Techniques

1. Orwell's style does not leave much room for disagreement with his ideas. Does this persuade you, or do you feel in some way bullied? Describe your reaction to his style. Then, describe your reaction to the content of his essay.

2. Orwell tends not to get very deeply into facts and figures in his work. What is the effect of this?

3. Often in his writing Orwell will seem to overflow, to rhetorically pound his fist on the desk or slap his forehead. When do such moments occur in the essay, and how do they affect you? How calculated do you think this device is on Orwell's part?

Suggestions for Writing

1. Orwell writes with a very oral, forceful style. What sort of person do you imagine speaking when you read this essay? Describe the views that person might hold on other subjects besides politics.

2. Orwell makes a list of disparate people who supported fascism. Look up these people in an encyclopedia and make a list of their equivalents today. Is there anything that would unite your list?

Crackdown

Treating the Symptoms of the Drug Problem

James Q. Wilson and John J. DiIulio, Jr.

Crime and drugs—two separable but related matters. are among the gravest social issues American society faces in the 1990s. The recent advent of crack—smokable cocaine available in small and relatively low-priced units has intensified national concern. Some aspects of the issues and projections for their future are given in this essay (first published in The New Republic) by two political scientists. The authors also cover the background and many of the arguments, both pro and con, on the growing controversy over legalizing drugs.

James Q. Wilson has long been among the most lucid and frequent commentators on problems of crime in the United States. The author of many articles and books, he is Collins Professor of Management and Public Policy at the University of California at Los Angeles. Recently he has coauthored Crime and Human Nature. John J. DiIulio, Jr., teaches politics at Princeton University. His most recent book is Governing Prisons.

According to the projections, crime was supposed to be under control by now. The postwar baby-boom generation, which moved into its crime-prone years during the early 1960s, has grown up, yielding its place to the (proportionately) less numerous baby-bust generation. With relatively fewer 18-year-olds around, we should all be walking safer streets.

And in fact for most people crime *has* gone down. The Census Bureau's victimization surveys tell us that between 1980 and 1987 the burglary rate declined by 27 percent, the robbery rate by 21 percent. Despite what we hear, 3,000 fewer murders were committed in 1987 than in 1980. Even in some big cities that are in the news for the frequency with which their residents kill each other, the homicide rate has decreased. Take Los Angeles: Despite freeway shootings and gang warfare, there were 261 fewer murders in 1987 than in 1980, a drop of more than 20 percent.

But in specific enclaves the horror stories are all too true. In south central Los Angeles, in much of Newark, in and around the housing projects of Chicago, in the South Bronx and Bedford-Stuyvesant sections of New York, and in parts of Washington, D.C., conditions are not much better than they are in Beirut on a bad day. Drugs, especially crack, are sold openly on street corners; rival gangs shoot at each other from moving automobiles; automatic weapons are carried by teenagers onto school playgrounds; innocent people hide behind double-locked doors and shuttered windows. In Los Angeles there is at least one gang murder every day, Sundays included. A ten-foot-high concrete wall is being built around the junior high school one of us attended, in order, the principal explained, to keep stray bullets from hitting children on the playground.

The problem is drugs and the brutal struggles among competing gangs for control of the lucrative drug markets. The drug of choice is crack (except in Washington, where it is PCP). The crack craze has led to conditions far worse than were found in these same neighborhoods a decade or so ago, when heroin was the preferred drug. The reasons for the change are not reassuring.

Crack is a stimulant; heroin is a sedative. Crack produces exceptional euphoria; heroin produces, after a quick "rush," oblivion. Crack (and PCP) addicts are often stimulated to acts of violence and daring that make them dangerous to themselves as well as to others; heroin addicts are rarely violent when high—the drug even depresses the sexual drive.

Crack is marketed by competitive distribution systems, some of whose members are fighting—literally—to establish monopoly control. Heroin (at least on the East Coast) was marketed in a criminal environment dominated by established monopolies that were well equipped, in muscle and in political connections, to protect their market shares with a minimum of random violence.

Crack users have no attractive chemical alternative. The drug is far more rewarding than any substitute. Heroin users who had progressed to the point where they wanted nothing but relief from the pains of withdrawal and the diseases caused by intravenous injection could take oral methadone. The heroin substitute, though addictive, required no injections, prevented withdrawal pains, and (in the correct dosages) produced little or no "high."

In short, certain neighborhoods of our larger cities are being ravaged by a drug that consumers find more alluring than heroin, that stimulates rather than sedates its users, that suppliers must use violence to sell, and that therapists are at a loss to manage by chemical means.

Attempting to suppress the use of drugs is very costly. Some people therefore conclude that we must eliminate all the costs of law enforcement by repealing the laws that are being enforced. The result would be less crime, fewer and weaker gangs, and an opportunity to address the public health problems in a straightforward manner.

But legalizing drugs would also entail costs. Those costs are hard to measure, in part because they are to a large degree moral and in part because we have so little experience with legalized drugs.

There is an obvious moral reason for attempting to discourage drug use: The heavy consumption of certain drugs ravages human character. These drugs—principally heroin, cocaine, and crack—are for many people powerfully reinforcing. The pleasure or oblivion they produce leads many users to devote their lives to seeking pleasure or oblivion, and to do so regardless of the cost in ordinary human virtues, such as temperance, duty, and sympathy. The dignity, autonomy, and productivity of users is at best impaired, at worst destroyed.

Some people think society has no obligation to form and sustain the character of individuals. Libertarians would leave all adults free to choose their own habits and seek their own destiny so long as their behavior did not cause any direct harm to others. But most people, however willing they may be to tolerate human eccentricities and support civil liberties, act as if they believe that government, as the agent for society, is responsible for helping to instill certain qualities in the citizenry This was the original reason for mandatory schooling. We not only want to train children to be useful, we want to train them to be decent. It is also the reason that virtually every nation that has been confronted by a sharp increase in addiction to any psychoactive substance, including alcohol, has enacted laws designed to regulate or suppress its use.

Great Britain once allowed physicians to prescribe opiates for addicts. The system worked reasonably well so long as the addicts were middle-class people who had become hooked as a consequence of receiving painkillers in hospitals. But when thrill-seeking youth discovered heroin, the number of addicts increased *40-fold,* and so Britain ended the prescription system. It was replaced at first with a system of controlled dispensation from government clinics, and then with a system of substituting methadone for heroin coupled with the stringent enforcement of the laws against the latter.

Even if we were to decide that the government had no responsibility for character formation and should regulate only behavior that hurts other people, we would still have to figure out what to do about drug-dependent people—because such dependency does hurt other people. A heroin addict dreamily enjoying his euphoria, a crack smoker looking for the next high, a cocaine snorter eager for relief from his depression—these users are not likely to be healthy people, productive workers, good parents, reliable neighbors, attentive students, or safe drivers. Moreover, some people are harmed by drugs that they have not chosen to use. The babies of drug-dependent women suffer because of their mothers' habits. We all pay for drug abuse in lowered productivity, more accidents, higher insurance premiums, bigger welfare costs, and less effective classrooms.

The question is whether the costs of drug use are likely to be higher when the drug is illegal or when it is legal. In both cases society must pay the bill. When the drug is illegal, the cost consists of the law enforcement costs (crime, corruption, extensive and intrusive policing), the welfare costs (poorer health, lost wages, higher unemployment benefits, more aid to families with dependent children, and various treatment and prevention programs), and the moral costs (debased and degraded people). If the drug were legal, the bill would consist primarily of the welfare costs and the moral costs. And there would still be law enforcement costs: the costs of enforcing tax collection if the drugs were sold, or of preventing diversion if the drugs were distributed through the health care system, and the costs in either case of keeping the drugs out of the hands, lungs, and veins of minors. Legalization without some form of regulation is inconceivable; the more stringent the regulation, the higher the law enforcement bill.

Which scenario will be costlier? The answer chiefly depends on how many people will use the drug. We have a rough idea of how many people regularly use heroin and cocaine despite its illegality. How many will regularly use it under the legal scenario?

No one really knows, but it will almost surely be many more than now. The free market price of cocaine is probably no more than 5 percent of its present black market price. Even allowing for heavy taxes, Stanford's John Kaplan has estimated that the free market price would be no more than 20 percent of what it now costs. The consumption of a widely desired, pleasure-inducing substance without question will increase dramatically if the price is cut by 80 percent to 95 percent.

Moreover, the true price of the drug is the monetary cost plus the difficulty and inconvenience of the search for it and the risk associated with consuming a product of unknown quality. Though drugs are sold openly on the streets of some communities, for most people—especially for novice, middle-class users—they are hard to come by and often found only in threatening surroundings. Legalization will make the drug more attractive, even if the price actually rises, by reducing the costs of searching for it, negotiating a transaction, and running the risk of ingesting a dangerous substance. The combined effect of lowered market prices and lowered transaction costs will be very great.

Just how great cannot be known without trying it. And one cannot try it experimentally, for there is no way to run a meaningful experiment. The increase in use that would occur if people in one neighborhood or patients at one clinic were allowed to buy the drug at its market cost can give us no reliable information on how many people would use the drug if it were generally available. And the experiment would have irreversible effects. Moreover, as the British experience showed, there is no such thing as "controlled distribution." Inevitably there will be massive leaks of government-supplied drugs into the black market.

We already have the "benefits" of one quasi-experiment. So long as cocaine was available only in its relatively expensive powdered form, its use was pretty much concentrated among more affluent people. But with the invention of crack, which can be sold in single low-priced doses rather than by the high-priced gram, cocaine use increased sharply.

We believe that the moral and welfare costs of heavy drug use are so large that society should continue to enforce the laws against its use for the sake of keeping the number of users as small as possible. But we recognize that by adopting this position, we are placing a heavy burden on those poor communities where drug use is endemic. We are allowing these neighborhoods to be more violent than they would be if the drug were legal. Since we do not live in such communities, we must ask ourselves whether our preferences can be justified to people who do.

The answer to that question is given by the testimony of those who live in the midst of the problem. They want drugs kept illegal. They say so and their representatives in Congress say so. We hope that our libertarian critics will not accuse the people of Watts, Anacostia, and the South Bronx of suffering from false consciousness on this matter. These people know what drug use is and they don't like it.

But if drugs are to be kept illegal, we have a special responsibility to prevent the streets of inner-city neighborhoods from being controlled by those who seek to profit from the trade. We have not done a very good job of this.

In some places there may not be enough police. In others the cops are just badly used, as when the focus is on making a case against "Mr. Big," the local drug kingpin. There are two things wrong with this. First, nothing is easier than replacing Mr. Big; indeed, often the police get evidence on him from tips supplied by his would-be replacement. Meanwhile the distribution of drugs goes on unabated. Second, arresting Mr. Big does nothing to improve the lives of the decent people in the neighborhood who want the drug dealers off the street.

Many cities, notably New York, have recognized this and are concentrating on street-level dealers. The NYPD has wrested control from the drug dealers in parts of the Lower East Side, all of Washington Square Park, much of West 107th Street, and other places. But they have done so at a cost, what Aric Press of *Newsweek* calls the criminal justice equivalent of bulimia. The police go on an arrest binge, and then, "overwhelmed and overfed, the rest of the system—prosecutors, defenders, judges, and jailers—has spent its days in an endless purge, desperately trying to find ways to move its population before it gets hit with another wave tomorrow." The purgatives included granting early release to some inmates and trying to shift other city prisoners to state penitentiaries; pressuring the governor to authorize the appointment of more judges while encouraging faster plea bargaining to clear the crowded dockets; and building "temporary" holding facilities for new arrestees.

The District of Columbia has begun to enter the bulimia phase. The number of people going through the criminal justice system on drug charges has exploded. Between 1983 and 1987 drug arrests increased by 45 percent, drug prosecutions by over 500 percent, drug convictions by over 700 percent. Clearly judges and prosecutors were starting to get tough. But until very recently, the toughness stopped at the jailhouse door. As recently as 1986, only 7 percent of the adults arrested on drug charges—and only 20 percent of those convicted on such charges—were sent to the city's principal correctional facility at Lorton. Then, suddenly, the system lurched into overdrive. Between 1986 and 1987 the number of drug incarcerations more than doubled, so that by the end of the year an adult arrested on a drug charge had a one-in-five chance of going to jail, and one convicted on such a charge had a one-in-two chance of winding up at Lorton.

This means that, until very recently, the price of drug dealing in Washington has been quite low. Those who say that "law enforcement has failed" should remember that until the last two years it was barely tried. Police Chief–designate Isaac Fulwood says that the same dealer may be arrested eight or nine times in the space of a few weeks. The city has been operating a revolving-door criminal justice system.

One reason for the speed with which the door revolves is that in Washington, as in most parts of the country, the prisons are jammed full. Another factor is that professional drug dealers know they can get a favorable plea bargain if they threaten to make the system give them a full trial, replete with every conceivable motion. The mere threat of such a demand is ordinarily enough to ensure that an attractive bargain is offered.

How can an overtaxed system help protect people in the drug-ridden neighborhoods? Building more conventional prisons is part of the answer, but that takes a lot of time, and no one wants them in their back yard. The goal is to take drug dealers off the streets for a longer period than the time it takes to be booked and released. One step is to ensure that no good arrest is washed out for want of prosecution because of a shortage of judges, prosecutors, and public defenders. These are not cheap, but candidates for these posts are more readily available than vacant lots on which to build jails.

Nevertheless, prisons are still needed and can be had, provided we are willing to think of alternatives to conventional holding tanks. One is to reserve regular prison space for major traffickers and to use parts of present (or all of former) military camps as boot camps for lower-level dealers. At these minimum-security camps, inmates would receive physical training, military discipline, and drug-abuse treatment, all under the direction of military personnel and with the aim of preparing them for a life that would combine, to the extent possible, the requirement of regular drug tests and the opportunity for gainful employment.

Meanwhile, the chances of released inmates rejoining old gangs can perhaps be reduced by enforcing a law, such as the one recently passed in California, that makes mere membership in certain gangs illegal and attaches civil or criminal penalties to parents who knowingly allow their children to join them.

Critics of punishment object that (1) incarceration is not a deterrent, either because young drug dealers are not "rational" or because drug trafficking is so lucrative as to make short stays behind a fence worth it; and that (2) the only true solution to the drug problem is to reduce the demand for drugs by education and treatment. We are tempted to respond to these views by pointing out that, insofar as we can tell, each is wrong in whole or in substantial part. Instead, let's assume that these views are entirely correct. They are also irrelevant.

At this stage, we are not trying to deter drug sales or reduce drug use. All we wish to do is to reassert lawful public control over public spaces. Everything else we may wish to achieve—reducing the demand for drugs, curing the users of drugs, deterring the sale of drugs—can only be done after the public and the police, not the dealers and the gangs, are in charge of the neighborhoods. In the short run, this can be done by repeatedly arresting every suspected dealer and user and sending them through the revolving door. If we cannot increase the severity of the penalties they face, we can at least increase the frequency with which they bear them. In police terms, we want to roust the bad guys.

After the bad guys find they are making repeated trips to the same prison camps, the decent people of the neighborhood must form organizations willing and able to work with the police to keep the bad guys from regaining control of the streets. The Kenilworth-Parkside area of Washington shows what can be done. A few years ago this neighborhood, the site of a public housing project, was an open-air drug market that spawned all manner of crime. In 1982 a tenants' committee led by Kimi Gray formed a corporation and assumed control of the housing project. Though the residents were primarily unwed mothers living on welfare, over the next five years their association collected the rents, ran the buildings, enforced school attendance on the children, and got rid of the addicts. In 1988 the association signed a contract to purchase the project from the government.

A key to the Kenilworth-Parkside group's accomplishment lies in its cooperation with the police. Gray and her colleagues set up neighborhood watch groups, held police-community meetings, and helped the police find and arrest drug dealers and street criminals.

Much is made these days of "community-oriented" policing. Both of us have written favorably about it and the problem-solving, police-neighborhood collaboration that lies at its heart. But the success stories are always in communities in which the people are willing to step forward and the police are willing to meet them halfway. Where open-air drug markets operate every night, where Uzi-toting thugs shoot rivals and bystanders alike, it is a brave or foolhardy resident who will even testify against a criminal, much less lead an anticrime crusade. But once the police have shown that they can control the streets, even if the dealers they have chased off spend only brief (albeit frequent) periods in prison camp, there is an opportunity to build new partnerships.

The drugs-crime problem ultimately will be solved only when the demand for drugs is dramatically reduced. Though it is necessary to make major investments in overseas crop eradication, the interdiction of international drug shipments, and the control of our borders, there is scarcely an experienced law enforcement officer in the country who does not believe that controlling the sources of supply is much more than a holding operation.

How do we reduce demand? We do not know. Realizing that is the beginning of wisdom. The greatest mischief is to assume that the demand for drugs will decline only when there is less racism and poverty, better schools and more jobs, more religion, and better-quality television.

Recall how the heroin epidemic finally ended. At one time the number of new addicts seemed to be rising exponentially despite the ending of the Turkish supply of illicit opium and the breaking up of the French processing laboratories. Now we have a fairly stable number of confirmed addicts whose ranks seem not to be increasing and may be decreasing. This was accomplished by three things: death, testing, and methadone.

Youngsters who were ready to ignore the lectures of their teachers or the blandishments of public-service television commercials were not so ready to ignore the testimony of their everyday experiences. Heroin addicts were dying from drug overdoses, dirty needles, and personal neglect. Doing heroin no longer seemed as glamorous as it did when one first heard about it from jazz musicians and big-time crooks.

The military began a rigorous program of testing, which continues to this day. There were sanctions attached to being found out— often a delay in being returned home, possibly military punishment, and probably a dishonorable discharge. Drug use in the military dropped dramatically, and has stayed low.

Heroin addicts who were burned out by their long and increasingly unsatisfying bout with the drug often turned to methadone as a way of easing the pain and stabilizing their lives. If they stayed with it, they had a good chance of benefiting from the counseling and training programs made available to them.

These three prevention measures are not likely to be as effective with cocaine and crack addicts. Some users are dying from these drugs, but smoking crack still seems to many users to be far more exciting and much less dangerous than injecting heroin. In time, enough people will ruin their lives so that even the fantastic high that crack produces will begin to seem unattractive to potential users. But that time is not here yet.

Testing works, but only if it is done rigorously and with real consequences, ranging from immediate counseling to discharge or punishment. As yet few civilian institutions seem prepared (or able) to do what the armed forces did. It is hard enough for private employers to test, and they are not subject to the search-and-seizure provisions of the Fourth Amendment. Opposition from employee groups and civil libertarians shows little sign of abating. Some government agencies are testing, but they are doing so gingerly, usually by limiting tests to workers such as prison guards and customs agents, who are in obviously sensitive positions. It is hard to imagine many schools adopting a testing program, though some are trying.

And there is no cocaine equivalent for methadone, though science may yet find one.

That doesn't leave much: some school-based drug-education programs that look promising but have not (as yet) proved their efficacy, and many treatment programs that can have some success—provided the patient is willing to stay in them.

"Willing": That is the key. Heavy drug use is an addiction about which we have, in other contexts, already learned a great deal. Fifty years ago we knew as little about dealing with alcoholism as we now know about cocaine abuse. Today we know enough about alcoholism to realize the key steps to coping with it.

First and foremost: Addicts will not get better until they first confront the fact that they are addicts. Alcoholics Anonymous knows this full well, making it the cornerstone of its Twelve Steps. The families of alcoholics are taught that they did not cause and can neither control nor cure the addictive behavior—the disease—of the alcoholic. The deaths of others and an inescapable testing program can help provoke among drug users what the destruction of the lives of alcoholics sometimes stimulates—a recognition that they are powerless in the face of the drug and that they need the help of others like themselves.

Among the heroin treatment programs that have worked, even without methadone, are those that have involved some aspect of confrontation. Therapeutic communities provide this, but they tend to reach relatively few people. The civil commitment program (technically, Civil Addict Program) in California reached more. It worked this way: An addict (usually arrested by the police) was incarcerated for a brief period, followed by release into the community under instructions to report regularly for a urine test. A parolee with a dirty urine test was reincarcerated on the original charge.

Douglas Anglin and William McGlothlin at UCLA were able to compare the drug use of two similar groups—one that had been sent through the Civil Addict Program and another that had been sent to it but was quickly released from its testing requirements through some legal error made in the commitment proceedings. Those who went through the full program reduced their narcotic use and criminality over a five-year–follow-up period at a rate three times greater than the control group.

This raises the possibility that frequent drug testing, backed up by the revocation of parole or of probation for those who fail, may help produce (out of either fear or growing self-awareness) that willingness to confront the fact of addiction that is the prerequisite of successful treatment. Though experts disagree about the role of coercion in treatment programs, an impressive number of studies suggest that cocaine-using arrestees will rarely volunteer for treatment unless they are subject to considerable legal pressure.

Harry Wexler and Douglas Lipton, two experienced drug researchers, have summarized what they have learned about intervening with drug offenders this way: "The criminal justice system must frequently and systematically supervise cocaine-heroin users so that they have less time for crime and drug use." This means urine testing as a condition of probation or parole.

The advocates of treatment and prevention sometimes argue as if these programs can be made to work under wholly voluntary arrangements, provided enough treatment slots are available. Indeed, the helping atmosphere makes treatment seem preferable to the callous toughness of law enforcement strategies. This is sometimes true, but for the majority of addicts it is a serious error, akin to thinking that alcoholics will follow their doctors' advice, if there are enough doctors around. Alcoholics need some measure of coercion; AA supplies it, through the peer pressure generated at regular meetings of other alcoholics. Cocaine users will require even more pressure because coke is far more pleasure-giving than alcohol.

Much of what we have said here will seem pointless to those who still believe that every social problem must be viewed as an indictment of society and its failure to eliminate the "root causes" of its ills. But when it comes to addictive behaviors, the symptoms *are* the causes. We do not know why some people try cocaine and then drop it, others try it and abuse it, and still others do not try it at all.

We do not know the answers to those questions with respect to alcohol abuse either, and we have been studying that "symptom" pretty seriously for the last half century. What we do know is that addiction is a self-sustaining reaction that spreads as the addictive drug becomes more easily available.

We must begin with the facts, not with theories. The facts are these: Some parts of our cities are being destroyed by gangs competing for the right to destroy lives by selling drugs. Those gangs have to be defeated, even if it means hiring more judges and building more correctional facilities. After that we can help communities reorganize themselves so that the good people control the streets and the teachers, doctors, and scientists have a chance to find out what will prevent another addictive epidemic from breaking out when some chemist discovers a drug that is even cheaper and more euphoria-inducing than crack. And that last event, we can be certain, will happen.

Themes, Issues, and Ideas

1. Besides the cost of drugs to users, the authors are also concerned with the costs society incurs when drug abuse is prevalent. What are the three kinds of costs mentioned? Would these costs increase or decrease with legalization?

2. Are the authors of this essay more concerned with helping addicts toward recovery or with helping neighborhoods become safer? How do they defend their position? Do you agree? Explain your answer.

3. The authors claim that people who live among drug users are against legalization and that "since we do not live in such communities, we must ask ourselves whether our preferences can be justified to people who do." What do you think of this argument? What might the authors say to the objection that if public opinion decides the issue, we need polltakers rather than policy experts?

Writing Strategies and Techniques

1. The authors speculate on two remedies for the drug problem: legalization and law enforcement. In what differing ways do they organize their arguments on each topic? In what way is each method of organization similar?

2. How do the authors deal with the objection that these remedies only cure the "symptoms" and not the "root causes" of the problem?

Suggestions for Writing

1. Where do you stand on the issue of legalizing drugs? Write an essay in which you express your views, being sure to take into account the evidence and arguments Wilson and DiIulio offer.

2. Write an essay in which you analyze the differing ways Wilson and DiIulio address the two issues of helping addicts and helping neighborhoods.

Invasion of the Body Snatchers

Fetal Rights vs. Mothers' Rights

Ronni Sandroff

Abortion is one of the issues that have been raised as a result of the clash between the constantly improving technology available to modern medicine and the slowly changing traditional views of human rights. What happens to human rights originally formulated to safeguard human "individuals" in the case of pregnant women, who may be viewed as physically representing more than one individual? Society continues to agonize over this general question and its growing number of particular implications.

In an essay originally published in Vogue *magazine, Ronni Sandroff takes us through part of the legal and ethical maze by reporting on both the case histories of ordinary people and the arguments marshaled by experts who often disagree among themselves.*

The baby and mother were almost certain to die unless a cesarean section was performed. But the mother was part of a small fundamentalist sect that prohibited surgery. And she was surrounded by family members who told her, "You can't have a cesarean section. Even if the baby dies, it's OK."

It was not OK with the doctor in charge, Mary Jo O'Sullivan, M.D., professor of obstetrics and gynecology at the University of Miami School of Medicine. "The baby's head was way too large. Without a c-section the only way to get the baby out would be to wait until it died and take it apart, piece by piece. I just couldn't do that. Nor was anyone else at the hospital willing to do it."

Dr. O'Sullivan finally took the matter to court, petitioning for the right to override the mother's decision. The court ordered a cesarean, but Dr. O'Sullivan was still uncomfortable about forcing surgery.

"To my surprise, when I showed the patient the court order, she seemed relieved that the decision was out of her hands," says Dr. O'Sullivan.

The story had a happy ending—mother, baby, and doctor are doing fine—but cases like this are causing alarm among civil libertarians and feminists. "The courts have no business in the delivery room," insists George Annas, professor of Health Law at Boston University School of Public Health. "Competent adults have the right to refuse even lifesaving treatment."

And it's irrelevant that, in this case, the mother turned out to be grateful to have the court decide, says Nancy Milliken, M.D., who recently cowrote a critique of cases of court-ordered surgery in the *Journal of the American Medical Association:* "Individuals can't have it both ways. We can't say: we want the right to make our own health decisions and then turn around and expect the doctor to *make us* do what's good for us."

Though the number of court-ordered cesareans is small, each one symbolizes a disturbing trend—the encroachment on the rights of the pregnant woman; the view of her as the "jar" or "container" of the next generation. In Wisconsin, for example, a sixteen-year-old pregnant girl was held in detention for her "lack [of] motivation or ability to seek prenatal care." In Michigan and Illinois, courts have permitted the child to sue its mother for damaging it during pregnancy. And, in a number of states, legislation has been introduced to expand the laws on child abuse to cover the fetus. This would permit after-the-fact prosecution of women who do anything during pregnancy (smoke, drink, use drugs, refuse treatment) that damages the offspring.

Public support for measures of this kind is surprisingly strong. A recent Gallup poll found that almost half of those surveyed agreed that a woman should be legally liable for damaging her child by drinking or smoking during pregnancy. People were about equally split on whether a woman should be held liable for refusing a cesarean.

Doctors are no more in agreement than the general public. The reason for the dissension is that our technological prowess has leapt ahead of our ethical and legal thinking. In the past, obstetricians had one patient: the mother. But new technology has opened up a much greater window on what's going on with the fetus throughout gestation.

"We're now taking care of premature infants at twenty-six, twenty-seven, twenty-eight weeks," explains Dr. Milliken. "So we're starting to devise treatments for fetuses as separate patients."

But the interests of the fetus are sometimes in conflict with the interests or desires of the mother—if a mother disagrees with medical advice or is reckless about how her actions affect the unborn child. In these cases, who is to defend the "rights" of the fetus?

Most experts hold that its physical location makes it impossible for a fetus to have rights: An unborn child cannot be treated without invading the body of its mother and severely affecting her freedom of movement, privacy, and health. Until a baby is born, they argue, it has no more independent rights than any other organ in the mother's body.

"On the one hand the interest in fetal rights is new," says Lynn Paltrow, staff counsel for the American Civil Liberties Union Reproductive Freedom Project. "On the other, it is simply a reflection of a historical trend to limit women's rights based on their reproductive ability."

Today, the question is whether our new understanding of gestation creates a need for special legislation to protect the interests of the fetus. The legions of infants born deformed, mentally retarded, or addicted to drugs are a burden to society as a whole as well as the individual parents.

John A. Robertson, a law professor at the University of Texas at Austin who did some of the earliest ethical work on fetal blood transfusions, believes we can take a stance against prenatal injury of a child who will be carried to term without diminishing a woman's right to abortion: "The rights of the actual offspring to be free of prenatally caused harm, rather than the right of the fetus to complete gestation, is at question."

Dr. Milliken, however, believes that the whole concept of fetal rights is unnecessary and has terrific potential for harm: "My impression is that there are very few women who do not undertake tremendous sacrifice for their fetuses."

New York City Civil Court Judge Margaret Taylor confesses she never thought about having to intervene in the interests of the fetus until 1980, when doctors at St. Vincent's Hospital petitioned her for a c-section order for a thirty-year-old, indigent woman who had borne nine children. The doctors had found that the umbilical cord was wrapped around the fetus's neck and felt it was in danger of being born brain-damaged.

Judge Taylor visited the patient in the hospital to hear her side of the story. "She was a poor woman and women in her neighborhood had not done well after cesarean sections. The hospital was trying to pressure her. I tried to tell her that if she had a brain-damaged child, her whole family would suffer. She said that nature makes these choices. I couldn't convince her. I couldn't see subjecting her to possible death for someone who's not even born yet. It's been held unreasonable to subject an accused criminal to surgery to find a bullet for evidence. If that's unreasonable, this certainly is."

Judge Taylor refused to grant the order, then spent "the worst two hours of my life," waiting for the child to be born. To the doctors', but not the mother's, surprise, the vaginal birth resulted in a healthy baby.

Outcomes where the mother's decision proves correct are not rare. In six of eleven cases of requests for court-ordered cesareans, the women went on to successful vaginal births, according to a study by lawyer Janet Gallagher. Many critics accuse doctors of favoring cesarean deliveries because they generate higher fees and reduce the likelihood of malpractice suits.

Even when medical decisions are made solely for clinical reasons, they often involve playing the odds—and losing. In the 1950s, doctors urged many women to take diethylstilbestrol (DES) to prevent miscarriages. The resulting daughters have since been found to have a higher risk of cervical cancer. "Now we know that the women who refused treatment were wiser," says Lynn Paltrow. "We have to let decision-making rest with the woman. If someone is going to make a mistake, it has to be her. The real conflict is not over fetal rights, but doctors' rights—they think they should be the ones to decide."

A frightening example of what can happen when the fetus's rights are put over the mother's is the case of Pamela Stewart, a poor California woman who was arrested in San Diego months after she bore a severely brain-damaged infant who died about six weeks after birth. The deputy district attorney said Stewart was responsible since "she didn't follow through on medical advice." The charge was based on a California statute that makes it a crime to "willfully omit" necessary support, including medical care, for a child or fetus.

Stewart had been through a dangerous pregnancy, marked by placenta previa, a condition that can threaten the life of the mother and fetus. Her doctor told her to seek attention immediately if she started to hemorrhage, but Stewart allegedly bled for several hours before going to the hospital. She also violated medical advice during pregnancy by having sexual intercourse with her husband, smoking marijuana, and taking amphetamines.

But Stewart's living conditions were exceedingly difficult. She lived with her two children and husband first in a single hotel room and then with her mother-in-law in a mobile home. Neighbors said the police had been called ten to fifteen times in one year to control the husband's beatings of his wife and mother.

All of this, plus reports on Stewart's sexual life, were reviewed in great detail in the media, causing public outrage and debate. The charges against her were dismissed in February 1987. The court found that the California child-support statute did not apply, but it left open the future enactment of such a law.

A potent argument against forcing women to do what the doctor says is right for their unborn children is that such measures will be used almost exclusively against poor and minority women. As Judge Taylor puts it: "Who would ask a judge to order Happy Rockefeller to have a cesarean?" Fear of prosecution might encourage poor and drug-addicted women to avoid prenatal care altogether.

"There's a terrible irony in mandating the mother's actions surrounding birth while not offering money for prenatal care for poor women, or child care, housing, and health care for poor children after birth," Judge Taylor says.

Some experts do support prosecution of women who damage their offspring: Let them make their decisions, the argument goes, but hold them responsible for reckless behavior. "When a woman chooses to carry the baby, rather than abort, society can take the position that she should abide by certain standards during her pregnancy," says ethicist John Robertson. The standards, presumably, will be set by medical experts.

The turmoil over forced cesareans is likely to subside as physicians and the public become more accustomed to making decisions amid the wealth of new knowledge about fetal development. But in the meantime, pregnant women are being bullied—by everyone from waiters who question a request for a glass of wine to employers who want to decide if it's in the best interests of the fetus for mothers not to work during pregnancy.

The absurdity of letting future parenthood infringe on an individual's freedom becomes clearest if we imagine applying it to men. There's some evidence, for example, that fathers who drink heavily during the month of conception have children with lower birth weights, regardless of whether or not the mother drinks. And it's possible that a father's smoking or drug use also influences the baby's condition at birth. Does this mean we should consider preventive detention, or sterilization, of men who persist in bad habits? Should we create a pregnancy police to visit the bedrooms of prospective parents? Insist that prospective parents be examined and licensed before having a child?

The alternative is to rely on education and parental good will, and accept the fact that parents are no more perfect than doctors, judges, and the rest of society. As law clerk and ethicist Dawn

Johnsen puts it: "The state should not try to transform pregnant women into ideal baby-making machines."

Themes, Issues, and Ideas

1. In Sandroff's article, four "participants" in the debate claim to have certain rights that should be protected. Who are they? For each participant, find at least one passage in the essay that defends her rights. Whose rights does Sandroff seem most interested in defending? Explain.

2. According to Sandroff, "fetal rights" were not an issue in the past. What does she identify as the cause of this new concern for protecting the fetus? Who, according to Sandroff, would be most affected by fetal legislation? Why? Explain Judge Taylor's remarks on the "terrible irony" in such legislation.

3. What differing assumptions does the essay present on the relations between "rights" and "laws?" For example, do laws establish or protect rights? If laws only protect rights, who decides what they are?

Writing Strategies and Techniques

1. The way in which statistics are presented can affect the impression they give the reader. Sandroff says: "Public support for measures of this kind is surprisingly strong. A recent Gallup poll found that almost half of those surveyed agreed that a woman should be legally liable for damaging her child by drinking or smoking during pregnancy." If the second sentence were changed to read that "fewer than half of those surveyed agreed" (a correct formulation, according to the statistics), what impression would it then make on the reader? Would the first sentence, about strong public support, still seem accurate?

2. How often does Sandroff use a sentence form *other* than the declarative? What effects does her style create? How, for example, would you characterize her tone of voice?

Suggestions for Writing

1. Where do you stand on the issue of fetal rights versus mothers' rights? Write an essay that expresses your views, being sure to take into account all the views and arguments in Sandroff's essay.

2. Write an essay in the form of a letter from you to Ronni Sandroff, praising or blaming her treatment of the delicate subject of abortion. Be sure to use examples.

On AIDS

Susan Sontag

Susan Sontag has been one of the most respected and influential American intellectuals for over twenty years. She was born in New York City in 1933, raised in Arizona, and attended the University of California at Berkeley and then the University of Chicago, where she earned a bachelor's degree at eighteen. In 1966, she burst onto the literary scene with essays like "Against Interpretation," "On Style," and the now-classic "Notes on Camp." Sontag's essays were characterized by an original, freewheeling style that then, as now, resembled the writings of few other intellectuals or social critics. "Camp," which has now entered the American lexicon, for example, was first defined and seriously discussed by Susan Sontag.

Sontag has been a major presence in American letters since the 1960s. This essay was taken from her 1988 book AIDS and Its Metaphors.

Just as one might predict for a disease that is not yet fully understood as well as extremely recalcitrant to treatment, the advent of this terrifying new disease, new at least in its epidemic form, has provided a large-scale occasion for the metaphorizing of illness.

Strictly speaking, AIDS—acquired immune deficiency syndrome— is not the name of an illness at all. It is the name of a medical condition, whose consequences are a spectrum of illnesses. In contrast to syphilis and cancer, which provide prototypes for most of the images and metaphors attached to AIDS, the very definition of AIDS requires the presence of other illnesses, so-called opportunistic infections and malignancies. But though not in *that* sense a single disease, AIDS lends itself to being regarded as one—in part because, unlike cancer and like syphilis, it is thought to have a single cause.

AIDS has a dual metaphoric genealogy. As a microprocess, it is described as cancer is: an invasion. When the focus is transmission of the disease, an older metaphor, reminiscent of syphilis, is invoked: pollution. (One gets it from the blood or sexual fluids of infected

people or from contaminated blood products.) But the military metaphors used to describe AIDS have a somewhat different focus from
those used in describing cancer. With cancer, the metaphor scants the
issue of causality (still a murky topic in cancer research) and picks up
at the point at which rogue cells inside the body mutate, eventually
moving out from an original site or organ to overrun other organs or
systems—a domestic subversion. In the description of AIDS the enemy is what causes the disease, an infectious agent that comes from
the outside:

> The invader is tiny, about one sixteen-thousandth the size of the
> head of a pin. . . . Scouts of the body's immune system, large cells
> called macrophages, sense the presence of the diminutive foreigner
> and promptly alert the immune system. It begins to mobilize an
> array of cells that, among other things, produce antibodies to deal
> with the threat. Single-mindedly, the AIDS virus ignores many of
> the blood cells in its path, evades the rapidly advancing defenders
> and homes in on the master coordinator of the immune system, a
> helper T cell. . . .

This is the language of political paranoia, with its characteristic distrust of a pluralistic world. A defense system consisting of cells "that,
among other things, produce antibodies to deal with the threat" is,
predictably, no match for an invader who advances "single-mind-
edly." And the science-fiction flavor, already present in cancer talk, is
even more pungent in accounts of AIDS—this one comes from *Time*
magazine in late 1986—with infection described like the high-tech warfare for which we are being prepared (and inured) by the fantasies of our
leaders and by video entertainments. In the era of Star Wars and Space
Invaders, AIDS has proved an ideally comprehensible illness:

> On the surface of that cell, it finds a receptor into which one of its
> envelope proteins fits perfectly, like a key into a lock. Docking
> with the cell, the virus penetrates the cell membrane and is
> stripped of its protective shell in the process. . . .

Next the invader takes up permanent residence, by a form of alien
takeover familiar in science-fiction narratives. The body's own cells
become the invader. With the help of an enzyme the virus carries with
it,

> the naked AIDS virus converts its RNA into . . . DNA, the master
> molecule of life. The molecule then penetrates the cell nucleus,

inserts itself into a chromosome and takes over part of the cellular machinery, directing it to produce more AIDS viruses. Eventually, overcome by its alien product, the cell swells and dies, releasing a flood of new viruses to attack other cells. . . .

As viruses attack other cells, runs the metaphor, so "a host of opportunistic diseases, normally warded off by a healthy immune system, attacks the body," whose integrity and vigor have been sapped by the sheer replication of "alien product" that follows the collapse of its immunological defenses. "Gradually weakened by the onslaught, the AIDS victim dies, sometimes in months, but almost always within a few years of the first symptoms." Those who have not already succumbed are described as "under assault, showing the telltale symptoms of the disease," while millions of others "harbor the virus, vulnerable at any time to a final, all-out attack."

Cancer makes cells proliferate; in AIDS, cells die. Even as this original model of AIDS (the mirror image of leukemia) has been altered, descriptions of how the virus does its work continue to echo the way the illness is perceived as infiltrating the society. "AIDS Virus Found to Hide in Cells, Eluding Detection by Normal Tests" was the headline of a recent front-page story in *The New York Times* announcing the discovery that the virus can "lurk" for years in the macrophages--disrupting their disease-fighting function without killing them, "even when the macrophages are filled almost to bursting with virus," and without producing antibodies, the chemicals the body makes in response to "invading agents" and whose presence has been regarded as an infallible marker of the syndrome. That the virus isn't lethal for *all* the cells where it takes up residence, as is now thought, only increases the illness-foe's reputation for wiliness and invincibility.

What makes the viral assault so terrifying is that contamination, and therefore vulnerability, is understood as permanent. Even if someone infected were never to develop any symptoms—that is, the infection remained, or could by medical intervention be rendered, inactive—the viral enemy would be forever within. In fact, so it is believed, it is just a matter of time before something awakens ("triggers") it, before the appearance of "the telltale symptoms." Like syphilis, known to generations of doctors as "the great masquerader," AIDS is a clinical construction, an inference. It takes its identity from the presence of *some* among a long, and lengthening, roster of symptoms (no one has everything that AIDS could be), symptoms which "mean" that what the patient has is this illness. The construction of the illness rests on the invention not only of AIDS as a clinical entity but of a kind of junior AIDS, called AIDS-related complex (ARC), to which people are assigned if they show "early" and often intermittent symptoms of immunological deficit such as fevers, weight loss, fungal infections, and swollen lymph glands. AIDS is progressive, a disease of time. Once a certain density of symptoms is attained, the course of the illness can be swift, and brings atrocious suffering. Besides the commonest "presenting" illnesses (some hitherto unusual, at least in a fatal form, such as a rare skin cancer and a rare form of pneumonia), a plethora of disabling, disfiguring, and humiliating symptoms make the AIDS patient steadily more infirm, helpless, and unable to control or take care of basic functions and needs.

The sense in which AIDS is a slow disease makes it more like syphilis, which is characterized in terms of "stages," than like cancer. Thinking in terms of "stages" is essential to discourse about AIDS. Syphilis in its most dreaded form is "tertiary syphilis," syphilis in its third stage. What is called AIDS is generally understood as the last of three stages—the first of which is infection with a human immunodeficiency virus (HIV) and early evidence of inroads on the immune system—with a long latency period between infection and the onset of the "telltale" symptoms. (Apparently not as long as syphilis, in which the latency period between secondary and tertiary illness might be decades. But it is worth noting that when syphilis first appeared in epidemic form in Europe at the end of the fifteenth century, it was a rapid disease, of an unexplained virulence that is unknown today, in which death often occurred in the second stage, sometimes within months or a few years.) Cancer *grows* slowly: it is not thought to be, for a long time, latent. (A convincing account of a process in terms of "stages" seems invariably to include the notion of a normative delay or halt in the process, such as is supplied by the notion of latency.) True, a cancer is "staged." This is a principal tool of diagnosis, which means classifying it according to its gravity, determining how "advanced" it is. But it is mostly a spatial notion: that the cancer advances through the body, traveling or migrating along predictable routes. Cancer is first of all a disease of the body's geography, in contrast to syphilis and AIDS, whose definition depends on constructing a temporal sequence of stages.

Themes, Issues, and Ideas

1. Sontag suggests that AIDS has been metaphorized as an enemy agent or an attacking invader. How might this perception affect public response to AIDS?

2. Sontag compares AIDS to other diseases and the metaphors by which those diseases are commonly described. What do such metaphors imply? Do you think of these diseases the way Sontag does?

3. Most people, it is safe to say, do not think about AIDS or any other disease in terms of the complex metaphors Sontag elaborates. Why is the way we talk about disease important? Give examples besides AIDS.

Writing Strategies and Techniques

1. Like many intellectuals, Sontag writes with a style that may be somewhat off-putting (e.g., "AIDS has a dual metaphoric genealogy"). Does this style help Sontag communicate more precisely with her audience, or does it impose a "braininess-barrier" between writer and reader? Give examples.

2. Of one passage about AIDS, Sontag writes: "This is the language of political paranoia, with its characteristic distrust of a pluralistic world." What language does Sontag write in?

Suggestions for Writing

1. Write a list of ten possible metaphors for diseases, other than the ones Sontag mentions.

2. Write an essay discussing your own image of the AIDS virus.

Not in My Backyard!

The Waste-Disposal Crisis

Ted Peters

As the twenty-first century approaches, the population of the United States continues to grow; technology and the production it fosters continue to grow; the volume of industrial waste continues to grow; but sites for waste disposal are shrinking in number. Some of the reasons for this shrinkage are not physical but ethical, as an expert on ethics points out in this essay (first published in The Christian Century).*

Ted Peters is Professor of Systematic Theology at Pacific Lutheran Seminary in Berkeley, California. Trained in the rigorous examination of both ethics and the language by which ethics are defined and argued, Peters investigates a clash between individual self-interest and social self-interest that has environmental implications for the kind of country today's students will live in tomorrow.

In government circles it's called the "NIMBY problem." Whether the proposal is for AIDS clinics, halfway houses for prison parolees or dumps for toxic and nuclear waste, it is usually met by the opposition of citizens' groups who shout NIMBY—"not in my backyard!"

Yet these components of modern life must exist in somebody's backyard. As James Wall pointed out in "Storing Nuclear Waste: My Backyard or Yours?", "What to do with nuclear waste is a problem that requires a moral examination precisely because it is so filled with uncertainty that we dare not resolve it without some sense of a higher purpose at stake." Without determining a higher purpose, we will never overcome the NIMBY obstacle.

NIMBY expresses our desire for self-preservation. People perceive the location of hazardous-waste landfill in their neighborhoods as a threat to their own and their families' health. Also, most people do not trust industrial or governmental leaders. History supports this suspicion. From 1980 to 1985 the U.S. Environmental Protection Agency recorded 6,928 accidents—an average of five per day—involving toxic chemicals and radioactive materials at American plants. A congressional research team in April 1985 concluded that nearly half of the 1,246 hazardous-waste dumps it surveyed showed signs of polluting nearby groundwater. The Office of Technology Assessment estimates that at least 10,000 hazardous waste sites in the U.S. now pose a serious threat to public health and are in dire need of cleaning up. During the 1970s, leakage from steel drums holding low-level nuclear waste brought about the closing of disposal sites in West Valley, New York; Sheffield, Illinois; and Maxey Flats, Kentucky. One could recite a lengthy litany of foul-ups, safety violations and instances of mismanagement, stupidity, and cost cutting. All this has diminished public confidence in government and business leaders. Motivated by fear and distrust, people join citizens' action campaigns, hire lawyers to file class-action suits, and even take to the streets to protest the apparent threat to their safety and health. This seems the democratic thing to do, the right thing to do.

But is it? Our perspective changes quickly when we try to view NIMBY in light of the needs of society as a whole. We need waste dumps just as we need prisons and halfway houses. Our society as a whole needs somebody's backyard. Yet in an age in which public participation is becoming integral to decision making, we find that virtually no one wants to make a backyard available. NIMBY is becoming NIABY—"not in anybody's backyard!"

Over the next decade our nation will face increased pressure to find a home for toxic refuse. The people's mood, however, is one of refusal. Many states will run out of landfill sites in the early 1990s, but voter referendums are turning down new site proposals. Standards have now been set for disposal of hazardous wastes, but local citizens' groups have petitioned to block the construction even of sites that would meet those standards. The Federal Nuclear Waste Policy Act has mandated that deep-mine disposal of high-level radioactive effluent and spent fuel rods from nuclear reactors commence by 1998, but states with proposed geological sites are screaming foul. What we have is a standoff: Government agencies are instructed to establish dump sites, while local citizens' groups prevent those agencies from performing their task.

We need ethical reflection on the situation. There have been two approaches to NIMBY that could be dubbed "ethical." In the case of the already alluded to defend-the-underdog approach, we assume that government agencies and associated industries conspire to exploit citizens by dumping toxic garbage on a community to the financial benefit of some power elite. The local citizens are the underdogs. The ethical thing to do seems to be championing the underdogs' cause against the monolith of governmental and industrial power.

Although defending the defenseless is laudable, as a general rule this policy has two weaknesses. First, government and industry are not always marshaled against the people. Quite frequently government-agency employees who set and enforce policy are very conscientious and are simply doing the best they can, given their mandate from the legislature. Second, the defend-the-underdog approach looks after the interests of only a particular community; it does not take into account the good of the whole society.

A second approach concerns the wider issue of environmental protection. I call it the constipate-the-system strategy. This approach assumes that if all communities take the NIMBY attitude, government agencies will not be able to find any backyard in which to dump toxic chemicals and nuclear waste, and the system will become plugged. To relieve this constipation, we must consume less—and to that end, nuclear power generators must shut down. This would force that industry out of business and perhaps even reduce our dependence on nonbiodegradable petrochemicals. However, regardless of one's position on the desirability of nuclear power or of petrochemicals, the toxic and radioactive waste cannot be wished out of existence. We still must find a place for waste that has already been generated, and the longer we postpone dealing with it directly, the more we increase the danger of contamination.

Let me suggest a third ethical approach to NIMBY that would not supplant as much as supplement the defend-the-underdog and constipate-the-system proposals: whole-part ethics. Whole-part ethics assumes a built-in connection between individuals and the global human community, between the present generation and our future progeny. It attempts to discern the good of the whole society, the commonweal, and to establish constructive reciprocity between the individual person or individual community and the society as a whole. We must acknowledge that our society has produced toxic waste and will continue to do so into the foreseeable future, and that it is in the best interests of the commonweal to handle that waste properly so as to protect human health and the natural environment. This means that, when all is said and done, it will have to go in somebody's backyard.

The process of determining just whose backyard will play host will undoubtedly raise questions of justice. For precedents we may look to past experience with public works projects in general, such as dam construction. Here we can borrow a bit from John Rawls's *A Theory of Justice* and assume that justice may be done even if the dam's location causes some individuals the inconvenience of having to move their residence. In these cases, the ethics of justice make two demands: that the negative impact on the environment and on certain people will be offset by a clear benefit to the larger society, and that individuals and communities suffering adverse effects are offered a means of redress and are duly compensated. These criteria of justice can also apply to waste-dumping disputes.

The goal of redress and compensation will be impossible to achieve completely, however, because future generations, though among those to be affected by toxic waste storage, obviously cannot take part in negotiations about where to place that waste today. Once a hazardous-waste landfill has been filled and covered, it remains dangerous for decades. Certain nuclear wastes are extremely long-lasting in their toxicity. Some repositories may remain dangerous for thousands of years. The Department of Energy estimates that it generally takes 1,500 years for the relative biohazard index of high-level wastes to arrive at that of the ore from which it was made. For spent fuel it takes 10,000. And a site that contains plutonium 239 will be a threat for 250,000 or even 500,000 years. Our planet and its life-forms will inherit certain risks and, unless we make plans, they will inherit none of the benefits of waste disposal. A responsible ethic demands that we consider the good of the whole of society, temporally as well as geographically.

With this in mind, I propose some principles to help us translate the abstract whole-part dialectic into public policy regarding waste disposal.

First, our basic criteria should be safety and permanence. Waste-disposal methods should not threaten the safety of those who live near disposal sites. Chemical toxicity and radioactivity levels should be kept as low as reasonably achievable in order to protect the biosphere. And we need to be confident that future generations will enjoy the same protections we wish for ourselves. These two criteria imply that we are responsible for developing the technology to secure permanent safety, or at least keep our waste in monitored retrievable storage.

Second, locations for hazardous-waste facilities should be determined primarily by technical ability to preserve safety and permanence. Some places make better hosts for waste facilities than others. For example, a chemical-waste landfill should be placed in an area that does not flood more often than once a century. The soil beneath should be heavy so as to resist the flow of water. The best sites have a thick natural layer of clay. Much more care needs to be taken in choosing locations for deep-mine repositories for high-level radioactive waste. A suitable disposal site for mined geologic waste must include the following characteristics: The rock mass's previous geologic history should indicate probable stability for the next 10,000 years or more; it should be relatively isolated from circulating ground water; it must be capable of containing waste without losing its desirable properties; and it must be amenable to technical analysis.

Third, as mentioned above, the location of a waste facility is just if the repository can be reasonably expected to contribute to the good of the whole society, and if those persons and communities suffering adverse effects have a means of redress and are duly compensated. Sometimes businesses or the government attempt to buy a community's compliance by offering more than appropriate or just compensation. They may offer a host community money to build a new town swimming pool or rebuild roads, and in general infuse the economy with outside wealth. The DOE, for example, offered the state of Nevada $10 million per year to relinquish its legal right to object to hosting a high-level nuclear repository, and $20 million per year if the site were to be chosen. Such over-compensation is extortion if demanded by the host community, bribery if offered by the authorities.

Extortion and bribery neglect two important considerations. Such a practice reduces the government's motivation to apply its best technology and most vigilant management to the safekeeping of waste; it assumes that the right to increase the risks to public health and the environment can be purchased. Second, it contracts only with the present generation and ignores the future. Those living today increase their wealth, but those who come after us inherit only the toxic threat.

Compensation could be ethical if it addressed the first criterion mentioned above—namely, the projected benefit to the commonweal. This requires a mutual relationship between part and whole: The good of the whole society benefits the individual person or community, while the achievements of the individual or community benefit the whole. Justifiable compensation (to the degree that it could be accurately calculated) would pay for actual damages or loss, including decreased property value or loss of environmental beauty and tranquillity. The difference between overpayment or bribes and ethical compensation will be very difficult to determine. The disruption of a host community's quality of life cannot be easily measured in terms of dollars and cents; therefore rectification of known error should lean toward overpayment rather than underpayment.

In some cases the roles are reversed, which clouds the issue of redress. The EPA is now offering $50,000 grants to citizens' groups that commission evaluations from experts of their own choice. Some communities, seeking financial income to offset high unemployment, decide on the basis of their findings to invite waste facilities into their backyard. The Alabama-Coushatta tribe of native Americans in East Texas, for example, has proposed building a waste incinerator on its land. The people of Chenois, Missouri, have asked for a hazardous-waste dump and received a permit, leading surrounding communities to lodge a legal protest. We may in the distant future have to reassess the ethics of this kind of practice, because we might wake up some day to find that we have dumped all our toxic refuse in poorer communities—that the rich have exploited the poor once again.

Fourth, we should not ask residents near a disposal site to do anything we would not be willing to do if we were in their situation. Not all community residents will wish to sell their property and relocate if a waste facility is planned for their area. The repositories should be made as safe as possible for those remaining in the neighborhood. One test of such safety would be the willingness of those most in the know to live on site.

Fifth, we owe our progeny knowledge of the hazard. Withholding knowledge from future generations excludes them from our ethical community. At minimum we owe them an on-site warning that explains the dump's contents. If possible, we should compile and make available a complete description of the landfill or repository holdings. We should also take all feasible measures to ensure the site against vandalism or sabotage.

This leads directly to a sixth principle: The user should plan for future facility management and accident indemnification. The generation enjoying the benefits of producing chemical and radioactive waste should consider investing a portion of today's profits in an endowment fund, gathered perhaps from a pollution tax. This endowment fund could support site management for decades, if not centuries. Some of the interest could be drawn for maintenance expenses, while the bulk of the principal would create an accident insurance fund. Interest over a 100- or 1,000-year period might grow to quite a sum. Barring unforeseeable circumstances, the fund could eventually provide a fortuitous compensation for the welfare of the future.

Finally, we need to employ our best technology and best management with painstaking care. No matter how ethically conscientious our vision, execution may fail to provide the greatest safety and permanence possible. We must encourage the highest quality of workmanship over the long haul. Financial constraints may tempt us to cut corners on quality. Because of the long-term and perhaps even boring nature of the work, we may slacken our concentration. But commitment to safety requires that we muster our best technology, and commitment to permanence requires that we be vigilant in establishing long-term management policies. All of us have an interest in solving the NIMBY problem. We should solve it justly. We will not be able to move beyond our current impasse until individual communities begin to work together with government agencies while sharing a vision of the good of society as a whole.

Themes, Issues, and Ideas

1. In discussing the ethics of waste-disposal policies, Peters identifies two ethical approaches taken in the past. Briefly describe each of these. What criticisms does Peters level at these approaches? Where do you stand?

2. The issue of adequate compensation is important to Peters's "whole-part" ethics. What two reasons does Peters give for his belief that overcompensation is unethical? What criteria does he suggest using to determine adequate compensation? Do you think that money can repair the damage to one's physical well-being or replace the scenic landscape lost when a waste-disposal site is established in one's "backyard"?

3. Peters's "whole-part" ethics is an attempt to reconcile the needs and wishes of the individual, the community, and society in recommending a solution to the NIMBY obstacle. Because of the lasting effects of waste disposal, however, one population is left out of the negotiations. What population is this? How does Peters propose that we ensure that this population is also compensated and its safety guarded?

Writing Strategies and Techniques

1. Peters's essay is written in the first person plural. He speaks often of what "we" must do and what "we" desire. Do you think this approach is justified? What does it presume about the relationship among members of society? Do you think this assumption is valid? Find a sentence in Peters's essay written in the first person plural with which some of "us" might disagree. Rewrite it from this perspective.

2. Peters uses the acronym NIMBY throughout his essay. Do you think it is an effective technique? Do you risk offending readers if you use this technique?

Suggestions for Writing

1. What do you think of Peters's arguments? Write an essay in which you attack, defend, or modify his analysis and proposals.

2. What do you think of one proposal that has been hotly debated: namely, that states "running out" of landfill sites ship their waste to those with more area? Write an essay in which you argue on one side of this issue or the other.

Tribes and Tribulations

Jennifer Juarez Robles

Jennifer Juarez Robles was born in 1957 in Emporia, Kansas. After graduating from the University of Kansas in 1986, she became an editorial writer for the Minneapolis Star-Tribune, *writing about urban affairs and issues involving race and poverty. Of her desire to write this piece, which originally appeared in 1992 in the gay journal* The Advocate, *she says, "it had to do with the 500th anniversary of Columbus's arrival in the New World. It put to light the treatment of indigenous peoples by the Europeans, and how that struggle continues to this day. The religious element of the conquest tore apart Indian culture, and made gay people separate in a way they were not before. That is an element of Columbus's legacy."*

Like all such civic events, this year's Columbus Day parade in Chicago was led by a phalanx of community leaders, government officials, and political candidates. And, in keeping with the country's anti-incumbent mood, the huge crowd lining the route booed and jeered as soon as they saw the familiar faces. But when the onlookers spied the next parade entry, they fell silent.

Pressured by activists and politicians, parade organizers had invited the local American Indian Center to march in the event commemorating Columbus's stumbling upon Indian lands 500 years ago. And the indigenous delegation—small and proud—marched unsmilingly the full route.

It was a curious sight, and the group's participation was a bit of an anomaly in terms of Native American response to Columbus Day this year. But in its way it symbolized the diversity of responses to the quincentennial among American Indian groups—responses nearly as varied as Native American attitudes toward native gays. This year gay men and lesbians in the native community were integral to the October protests throughout the nation. In San Francisco, for example, a prominent American Indian lesbian community leader was the kickoff speaker at the city's main demonstration.

Native groups declared this year a time of unity across tribal and state boundaries and even across differences of sexual orientation. Benito Torres, spokesman for the League of Indigenous Sovereign Nations, an international native rights organization, says that in his group's demonstration at the United Nations building in New York, "there were gay groups working together with us from the beginning. I'm sure there were other gay and lesbian people who were present and in solidarity. We're all in the same boat."

For many Native Americans, this seemed only natural. By tradition, some Native American tribes have accorded positions of spiritual leadership to "two spirits"—the indigenous term for gays, meaning people with male and female spirits. For others, especially those who have experienced Native American homophobia in rural areas and on reservations, these anti-Columbus collaborations served as a sign of hope that they may yet have a place as open gays in their ethnic communities.

"All our people have been greatly involved in quincentennial efforts working side by side, but you won't see a banner that says GAY AND LESBIAN," says Angukcuaq (also known as Richard LaFortune), a two-spirit activist and director of training at the National Native American AIDS Prevention Center in Oakland, Calif. "Gay and lesbian Native Americans are doing quiet work within our communities because the communities are very homophobic."

Curtis Harris, a member of WeWah and BarCheAmpe, a New York two-spirit group, is more blunt. "In terms of educating the native community, we have a long way to go," he says. "There were factions of Native American groups [at Columbus Day demonstrations] who excluded our involvement. We know that many of the folks involved in these organizations have been virulently homophobic in the past. I find that oftentimes as a gay Indian man I'm rebuffed by Native Americans."

Angukcuaq says that because many Native Americans experience a mixture of both traditional values and Anglo teachings, attitudes toward gays and lesbians may be widely divergent from one community to the next. "There are men and women who are cross-dressing and raising children and occupying positions of power, and everyone knows about it," he explains. "There are 500 discrete native nations and cultures on this continent. There are many common denominators, and there are many differences. It's going to be harder in redneck Wisconsin to be openly two-spirit on a reservation. It depends on the community and the pressure for assimilation."

U.S. representative Ben Nighthorse Campbell (D-Colo.), the only Native American in Congress, has found his cosponsorship of the federal gay rights bill to be controversial among Native American constituents. Campbell's support is unusual: Three of the most prominent native civil rights groups—the American Indian Movement's International Indian Treaty Council, the Native American Rights Fund, and the National Congress of American Indians, which represents about 25% of the Indian and native Alaskan population—have no policy statement on gay rights.

Campbell spokeswoman Carol Knight says the representative "has taken some heat from tribal leaders who oppose gay rights," which, she says, is often based on ignorance about AIDS. "I'd venture to guess that gay Native Americans are just now experiencing the backlash that white gay males felt in the early 1980s. We see a lot of hostility toward gay natives because of AIDS."

In an August meeting of the Navajo Nation council in Window Rock, Ariz., Larry Curley, executive director of Navajo Nation health services, drew fire when he proposed quarantining people with AIDS to protect the general Navajo population, citing the Cuban policy of forcing people with HIV, the virus believed to lead to AIDS, to live in restricted areas. Curley later retracted his comments under pressure from the president of the Navajo Nation, which is one of the largest tribal nations in the United States, comprising 200,000 people.

Melvin Harrison, president of the Navajo Nation AIDS Network, a nonprofit educational and lobbying group, says, "Curley's comments raised consciousness about AIDS and got people talking about the issues. We still have a lot of work to be done. There's still a lot of denial and bigotry out there."

Probably the most difficult place for Native Americans to be openly gay is on reservations in rural areas. Susan Beaver, a Mohawk lesbian who is executive director of Two-Spirited People of the First Nations, a Toronto support and education group, testified in June about discrimination on reservations before the Royal Commission on Aboriginal Peoples, a Canadian government council. "We often grow up without a language to describe ourselves: *Lesbian, gay,* or *queer* are used as curses and insults," Beaver said. "With the influence of the church and Europeans, two spirit is a tradition pushed so far away, only a few remember it, and even fewer honor it.

"Women are expected to marry a man or suffer the consequences of our willfulness," Beaver continued. "Two-spirited men know there is no room for their lives on the reserve. Your sexuality is not tolerated, and many men leave to find urban centers where they can express themselves. Many men live a dual life: Bisexuality on the reserve is more common than many think. If you are strong enough to be who you are, you are ridiculed, harassed, and only sometimes understood as again being 'different.' "

Tom Ledo, a Tlingit and Filipino gay man, knows firsthand the danger on reservations. Though openly gay in his job as HIV coordinator for San Diego's Indian Health Council, he isn't open about his sexuality when he visits reservations, about 50 miles north of San Diego.

"I've had tribal leaders tell me that they don't appreciate being around 'faggots,' " says Ledo, who heads the San Diego group Two-Spirited Nations of the Four Directions. "They tell me that if [gays] got AIDS, they deserve it. I'm outspoken about queer issues outside the reservation. But to be effective in my work, I need to talk to people about AIDS and their behavior. That's my priority. I try to work on their homophobia, but it's very hard."

"Unfortunately, there is a lot of hatred and ignorance about AIDS and two-spirited people," adds Avis Little Eagle, associate editor of the Rapid City, S.D., paper *Indian Country Today,* formerly the *Lakota Times.* Little Eagle concedes that many tribal leaders, particularly those in rural areas, often refuse to believe that homosexuality exists among their people. "They say they don't have any homosexuals in their tribes because they are traditional people," says Little Eagle. "We are from more isolated communities, so [gay issues] haven't hit us except in isolated incidents."

One of the incidents that Little Eagle recalls is the murder last fall of a gay man on the Pine Ridge reservation in southwestern South Dakota. Patrick Red Elk, a 30-year-old member of the Oglala tribe, was attacked on the reservation by three men who beat him with a football helmet and kicked him to death. The attackers were convicted of second-degree murder and sent to federal prison.

Assistant attorney general Robert Mandel, who handled the Pine Ridge case, remembers another assault there a few years ago in which two men attacked a gay man, fracturing his jaw. The assailants were convicted and sent to prison.

Mandel points out that the number of assaults generally on the reservation, where more than 15,000 people live, is significantly higher than that of South Dakota on the whole. "We get many assaults and murders there," he says, estimating that his office, which handles the Pine Ridge reservation exclusively, prosecutes about a hundred felonies per year.

"I have no doubt that there is violence and gay bashing on reservations," says Angukcuaq. "When you have a whole generation of people raised in Catholic boarding schools and you have homophobia inculcated in the community, then you put those people on reserva-tions—which are very close-knit—there is going to be violence. Our people are being taught today that it's OK to beat up gays and lesbi-ans.

"But violence on reservations and in urban communities is not confined to gay, lesbian, and bisexual people," Angukcuaq adds. "We cannot escape the violence."

Ironically, antigay attitudes aren't traditional, many two-spirit people argue. "Before, in our culture, two-spirited people were re-spected and honored, not ridiculed," says Little Eagle. "It's new now to see the younger generation ridicule gay people. Actually, it's for-eign to our nation."

"In most native cultures, gay men and lesbians held positions as healers, visionaries, and teachers," explains Beaver. "They were the doctors and lawyers of native societies before the Europeans came. Tolerance used to be indigenous to our culture. We try to reclaim, against opposition from our own people, that we were the holy peo-ple, the special people."

In the clash between traditional acceptance and homophobia, many two spirits hope to lead tribal nations to greater cooperation and unity, seeing their role as a conduit of traditional Indian values.

"I've gone to the White River Apache reservation in Arizona to speak about homophobia," says Erna Pahe, a member of Gay Ameri-can Indians, a San Francisco group, and the vice chair of the city's Board of Urban Indian Health. "They need Indians to go there and educate people. We have to tell them that we can't just throw away our kids if they're two-spirit. We can't afford to throw them off the reservations.

"Two spirits need to speak up and talk about ourselves," urges Pahe, who grew up on Navajo and Apache reservations in Arizona. "We can't afford to let the younger generation grow up thinking there's a group of people—two spirits—who don't know who they are or don't have anything to offer the tribe. That's the only way our people will understand. Two spirits have something to offer our people."

Themes, Issues, and Ideas

1. There is a long history of problems facing Native Americans. Does Robles address these problems? What is not said—but implied—in her essay that a foreigner might miss?

2. According to some of the sources Robles quotes, "two spirits" were revered by many tribes. Do all of Robles's sources agree? How would you describe the range of opinion here about "two spirits?"

3. Gay people in white American society face many of the same problems as the gay Native Americans Robles describes. What do you think are the differences in the problems the two groups face?

Writing Strategies and Techniques

1. Although this piece involves a great deal of reportage, it is clearly not "objective" journalism. How does the fact that it is written for a magazine called *The Advocate* inform its readers?

2. Robles uses the Native American entry in a Columbus Day parade to begin her story. How is this anecdote meaningful? Can you think of a better opening?

Suggestions for Writing

1. Every ethnic group has a different attitude toward gays. Write an essay describing your own group's response. If you are Native American, write an essay responding to Robles's article.

2. Write an essay in which you take the view of one of the people in the piece who is described as being antigay. Discuss some of the problems you face as a heterosexual Native American. Try to keep the voice sane and sympathetic; don't impersonate a bigot.

MAKING CONNECTIONS

1. George Orwell describes what he sees as "the real issue of the Spanish War, and of the last war [WWII], and of other wars yet to come." What do the other authors in this chapter think is the root cause of the social issues they discuss? Do they find any root cause? How does having or not having an Orwellian sense of "the big picture" help a writer?

2. What might Susan Sontag make of some of the metaphors in "Crackdown" and "Body Snatchers?" What do the writers in this chapter have in common as writers? How, for instance, do the different writers make use of "expert" opinion? How does expert opinion help or hurt their work? Explain.

3. Would George Orwell have enjoyed Susan Sontag's "On AIDS?" How would he have viewed Sandroff or Peters? What seems to set Sontag's essay apart from all the others in this chapter? What is your own feeling about this quality?

4. This chapter includes essays that discuss public policy, private thoughts and decisions, and politics on an international scale. How do these planes intersect in the different essays, and how might they continue to intersect as the twenty-first century approaches? Give examples of such intersections from the essays, as well as any outside examples that might suggest themselves to you.

5. Some of the authors in this chapter seem to stress moral responsibility more than others. Their reasons for doing so, however, are very different. Identify the authors whom you think are most concerned with what Orwell calls "a change of heart" and tell why you think this is the case. Also give reasons why you think the other writers have not stressed this concept.

CHAPTER TWO

Feminine Gender—Future Tense

Women's Issues for the Nineties and Beyond

THE
PAST AS
PROLOGUE

Sisterhood

Gloria Steinem

Gloria Steinem was born in Toledo, Ohio, in 1934. After moving to New York she became a highly successful journalist and publisher, helping to found New York *magazine in 1968 and founding* Ms. *magazine in 1971. In 1972,* McCall's *magazine named her Woman of the Year.*

In this classic essay, which first appeared in Ms. *in 1972, Steinem makes a strong statement for the feminist cause in the midst of the growing resurgence of the twentieth-century feminist movement. Using her personal history, Steinem traces the "great sea-change in women's views" of themselves, and lays out the issues for men and women that continue to be important as topics of debate.*

A very, very long time ago (about three or four years), I took a certain secure and righteous pleasure in saying the things that women are supposed to say. I remember with pain—

"My work won't interfere with marriage. After all, I can always keep my typewriter at home." Or:

"I don't want to write about women's stuff. I want to write about foreign policy." Or:

"Black families were forced into matriarchy, so I see why black women have to step back and let their men get ahead." Or:

"I know we're helping Chicano groups that are tough on women, but *that's their culture.*" Or:
"Who would want to join a women's group? I've never been a joiner, have you?" Or (when bragging):
"He says I write like a man."

I suppose it's obvious from the kinds of statements I chose that I was secretly nonconforming. I wasn't married. I was earning a living at a profession I cared about. I had basically—if quietly—opted out of the "feminine" role. But that made it all the more necessary to repeat the conventional wisdom, even to look as conventional as I could manage, if I was to avoid some of the punishments reserved by society for women who don't do as society says. I therefore learned to Uncle Tom with subtlety, logic, and humor. Sometimes, I even believed it myself.

If it weren't for the women's movement, I might still be dissembling away. But the ideas of this great sea-change in women's view of ourselves are contagious and irresistible. They hit women like a revelation, as if we had left a dark room and walked into the sun.

At first my discoveries seemed personal. In fact, they were the same ones so many millions of women have made and are continuing to make. Greatly simplified, they go like this: Women are human beings first, with minor differences from men that apply largely to the single act of reproduction. We share the dreams, capabilities, and weaknesses of all human beings, but our occasional pregnancies and other visible differences have been used—even more pervasively, if less brutally, than racial differences have been used—to create an "inferior" group and an elaborate division of labor. The division is continued for a clear if often unconscious reason: the economic and social profit of males as a group.

Once this feminist realization dawned, I reacted in what turned out to be predictable ways. First, I was amazed at the simplicity and obviousness of a realization that made sense, at last, of my life experience. I couldn't figure out why I hadn't seen it before. Second, I realized how far that new vision of life was from the system around us, and how tough it would be to explain this feminist realization at all, much less to get people (especially, though not only, men) to accept so drastic a change.

But I tried to explain. God knows (*she* knows) that women try. We make analogies with other groups that have been marked for subservient roles in order to assist blocked imaginations. We supply endless facts and statistics of injustice, reeling them off until we feel like human information-retrieval machines. We lean heavily on the device of reversal. (If there is a male reader to whom all my *pre*realization statements seem perfectly logical, for instance, let him read each sentence with "men" substituted for "women"—or himself for me—and see how he feels: "My work won't interfere with marriage. . . ."; ". . . Chicano groups that are tough on men. . . ." You get the idea.)

We even use logic. If a woman spends a year bearing and nursing a child, for instance, she is supposed to have the primary responsibility for raising that child to adulthood. That's logic by the male definition, but it often makes women feel children are their only function, keeps them from doing any other kind of work, or discourages them from being mothers at all. Wouldn't it be just as logical to say that the child has two parents, therefore both are equally responsible for child rearing, and the father should compensate for that extra year by spending *more* than half the time caring for the child? Logic is in the eye of the logician.

Occasionally, these efforts at explaining actually succeed. More often, I get the feeling that most women are speaking Urdu and most men are speaking Pali.

Whether joyful or painful, both kinds of reactions to our discovery have a great reward. They give birth to sisterhood.

First, we share the exhilaration of growth and self-discovery, the sensation of having the scales fall from our eyes. Whether we are giving other women this new knowledge or receiving it from them, the pleasure for all concerned is enormous. And very moving.

In the second stage, when we're exhausted from dredging up facts and arguments for the men whom we had previously thought advanced and intelligent, we make another simple discovery: women understand. We may share experiences, make jokes, paint pictures, and describe humiliations that mean little to men, but *women understand*.

The odd thing about these deep and personal connections among women is that they often leap barriers of age, economics, worldly experience, race, culture—all the barriers that, in male or mixed society, seem so impossible to cross.

I remember meeting with a group of women in Missouri who, because they had come in equal numbers from the small town and from its nearby campus, seemed to be split between wives with white gloves welded to their wrists and students with boots who used words like "imperialism" and "oppression." Planning for a child-care center had brought them together, but the meeting seemed hopeless until three of the booted young women began to argue among themselves about a young male professor. The leader of the radicals on campus, he accused all women unwilling to run mimeograph machines of not being sufficiently devoted to the cause. As for child-care centers, he felt their effect of allowing women to compete with men for jobs was part of a dreaded "feminization" of the American male and American culture.

"He sounds just like my husband," said one of the white-gloved women. "He wants me to have bake sales and collect door-to-door for his Republican party."

The young women had sense enough to take it from there. What difference did boots or white gloves make if they were all getting treated like servants and children? Before they broke up, they were discussing some subjects that affected them all (like the myth of the vaginal orgasm) and planning to meet every week. "Men think we're whatever it is we do for men," explained one of the housewives. "It's only by getting together with other women that we'll ever find out who we are."

Even racial barriers become a little less formidable once we discover this mutuality of our life experiences as women. At a meeting run by black women domestics who had formed a job cooperative in Alabama, a white housewife asked me about the consciousness-raising sessions or "rap groups" that are often an organic path to feminism. I explained that while men, even minority men, usually had some-place—a neighborhood, a bar, a street corner, something—where they could get together and be themselves, women were isolated in their houses and families; isolated from other females. We had no street corners, no bars, no offices, no territory that was recognized as ours. Rap groups were an effort to create something of our own, a free place—an occasional chance for total honesty and support from our sisters.

As I talked about isolation, about the feeling that there must be something wrong with us if we aren't content to be housekeepers and mothers, tears began to stream down the cheeks of this dignified woman—clearly as much of a surprise to her as to us. For the black women, some distance was bridged by seeing this white woman cry.

"He does it to us both, honey," said the black woman next to her, putting an arm around her shoulders. "If it's your own kitchen or somebody else's, you still don't get treated like people. Women's work just doesn't count."

The meeting ended with the housewife organizing a support group of white women who would extract from their husbands a living wage for domestic workers and help them fight the local authorities who opposed any pay raises; a support group without which the domestic workers felt their small and brave cooperative could not survive.

As for the "matriarchal" argument that I swallowed in prefeminist days, I now understand why many black women resent it and feel it's the white sociologists' way of encouraging the black community to imitate a white suburban life-style. "If I end up cooking grits for revolutionaries," explained a black woman poet from Chicago, "it isn't my revolution. Black men and women need to work together: You can't have liberation for half a race." In fact, some black women wonder if criticism of the strength they were forced to develop isn't a way to keep half the black community working at lowered capacity and lowered pay, as well as to attribute some of black men's sufferings to black women, instead of to their real source—white racism. I wonder with them.

Looking back at all those male-approved things I used to say, the basic hang-up seems clear—a lack of esteem for women, whatever our race, and for myself.

This is the most tragic punishment that society inflicts on any second-class group. Ultimately the brainwashing works, and we ourselves come to believe our group is inferior. Even if we achieve a little success in the world and think of ourselves as "different," we don't want to associate with our group. We want to identify up, not down (clearly my problem in not wanting to join women's groups). We want to be the only woman in the office, or the only black family on the block, or the only Jew in the club.

The pain of looking back at wasted, imitative years is enormous. Trying to write like men. Valuing myself and other women according to the degree of our acceptance by men—socially, in politics, and in our professions. It's as painful as it is now to hear two grown-up female human beings competing with each other on the basis of their husband's status, like servants whose identity rests on the wealth or accomplishments of their employers.

And this lack of esteem that makes us put each other down is still the major enemy of sisterhood. Women who are conforming to society's expectations view the nonconformists with justifiable alarm. *Those noisy, unfeminine women,* they say to themselves. *They will only make trouble for us all.* Women who are quietly nonconforming, hoping nobody will notice, are even more alarmed because they have more to lose. And that makes sense, too.

The status quo protects itself by punishing all challengers, especially women whose rebellion strikes at the most fundamental social organization: the sex roles that convince half the population that its identity depends on being first in work or in war, and the other half that it must serve as docile, unpaid, or underpaid labor.

In fact, there seems to be no punishment inside the white male club that quite equals the ridicule and personal viciousness reserved for women who rebel. Attractive or young women who act forcefully are assumed to be either unnatural or male-controlled. If they succeed, it could only have been sexually, through men. Old women or women considered unattractive by male standards are accused of acting out of bitterness, because they could not get a man. Any woman who chooses to behave like a full human being should be warned that the armies of the status quo will treat her as something of a dirty joke. That's their natural and first weapon. She will *need* sisterhood.

All of that is meant to be a warning but not a discouragement. There are more rewards than punishments.

For myself, I can now admit anger and use it constructively, where once I would have submerged it and let it fester into guilt or collect for some destructive explosion.

I have met brave women who are exploring the outer edge of human possibility, with no history to guide them, and with a courage to make themselves vulnerable that I find moving beyond the words to express it.

I no longer think that I do not exist, which was my version of that lack of self-esteem afflicting many women. (If male standards weren't natural to me, and they were the only standards, how could I exist?) This means that I am less likely to need male values and approval and am less vulnerable to classic arguments. ("If you don't like me, you're not a real woman"—said by a man who is coming on. "If you don't like me, you can't relate to other people, you're not a real person"—said by anyone who understands blackmail as an art.)

I can sometimes deal with men as equals and therefore can afford to like them for the first time.

I have discovered politics that are not intellectual or superimposed. They are organic. I finally understand why for years I inexplicably identified with "out" groups: I belong to one, too. And I know it will take a coalition of such groups to achieve a society in which, at a minimum, no one is born into a second-class role because of visible difference, because of race or of sex.

I no longer feel strange by myself or with a group of women in public. I feel just fine.

I am continually moved to discover I have sisters.

I am beginning, just beginning, to find out who I am.

Themes, Issues, and Ideas

1. In the beginning of the essay Steinem lists some remarks she used to make and uses them to head topics in the rest of her essay. How would you label these topics? For example, the first issue might be called "Women and Careers." What other issues are outlined?

2. Steinem says that her personal feeling of isolation was a common one for women until they began "consciousness-raising sessions," because women formerly lacked the occasions and locations for meetings. In her essay, how does she show these sessions to be effective? Is personal isolation overcome? Where and how?

3. In making her point about shared child care, Steinem seems to assume that a two-parent family is typical. How do you think Steinem might address the issue of child care in broken homes or single-parent families?

Writing Strategies and Techniques

1. The length of Steinem's paragraphs varies enormously. What seem to be her principles of paragraphing? In what ways do you find the varying use of length effective?

2. Steinem interweaves her personal testimony with descriptions of other women that include dialogue. In what ways does she make sure that the style and content of the dialogue are reflective of the particular speaker?

Suggestions for Writing

1. Write an essay on your personal experience as a man or a woman that begins like Steinem's essay, with quotations you no longer believe in.

2. Write an essay analyzing the form of Steinem's argument with particular regard to the end. In what ways does or does not the end of her essay form a conclusion?

Jobs for Women in the Nineties

Julie Bailey

More women are working in the American workforce than ever before and still more are on the way to joining it. How the numbers translate into opportunities and problems is the subject of this essay, first published in Ms. *magazine in 1988. Polling long-range planners in the private and public sectors of the economy, along with interested parties from unions, management, and education, the journalist Julie Bailey predicts some ways in which the American economy will develop and how women might best prepare for those developments.*

The American job market of the 1990s will be a turbulent place, and women workers can expect to claim a larger share of the best opportunities. In just 12 years between now and the year 2000, the resilient U.S. economy will spin off 21 million new jobs for a work force that will grow at less than two-thirds the rate of the last decade. Since these new jobs will tend to demand more skills, planning is needed now to make sure there are people trained to fill them.

"The tremendous changes that will be forced upon the American workplace are still largely unappreciated," says Pamela Flaherty, personnel director for Citicorp:

- Two of every three new workers will be women.

- Women, together with minorities and recent immigrants, will add 19 million new workers to the labor force, which will reach 139 million by the turn of the century.

- White, non-Hispanic men, the majority of the U.S. labor force, will represent less than 10 percent of all incoming workers.

Women already make up about 45 percent of the labor force, and the pressure that today exists for employers, labor unions, and legislators to improve women's access to jobs by addressing a range of issues will increase as that share grows. These include affordable child care and flexible working schedules as well as attention to the persistent "glass ceiling" faced by upwardly mobile women managers and professionals as women increasingly occupy traditionally male occupations, especially those that require advanced education. In addition, there will be pressure to upgrade the low-level service and clerical jobs dominated by women, particularly if policymakers hope to move poor women and their children from welfare rolls into sustaining jobs.

But employment will be less stable. It is the smaller, more precarious companies of less than 100 employees that are expected to create the major number of new jobs by the year 2000. The National Association of Women Business Owners estimates that two of every three of these are started by women. But new companies can just as quickly disappear. Throughout the economy in the 1990s, job security for both sexes will become a relic of the past: Automation, swifter product obsolescence, cutthroat competition from abroad, and the much ballyhooed need for even the largest, most stable corporations to become leaner will mean many of today's jobs will disappear. "Workforce 2000," a study commissioned by the U.S. Department of Labor from the Hudson Institute, a nonprofit social and economic think tank, estimates that employees will change jobs an average of five or six times.

According to the study, 52 percent of all new jobs being created over the next 12 years will require some education beyond high school. Today, only 44 percent do. The surest ticket to the safest occupational havens of the 1990s, then, will be a college degree and, increasingly, specialized graduate training.

How will American women fare in the workplace as we move toward the twenty-first century? *Ms.* asked that question of almost 100 well-informed labor force observers, including economists and educators, businesspeople and labor leaders, sociologists and women's rights advocates. Here is what they told us.

Women will benefit as employers strive to accommodate different gender, ethnic, and cultural work styles in the workplace of the 1990s, eventually transforming the old, white, male-dominated American corporate culture.

"Valuing diversity" will be the catchword of progressive managers of the 1990s. A number of companies have already launched new programs designed to prepare both managers and staff for a diverse workplace, sometimes under the direction of a Multicultural Manager, a hot new job category typically occupied by a woman, often black or Asian.

"We've always expected workers who are different to 'blend in' with the majority, but the old melting pot theory may no longer be the best approach," says Daisy Chin-Lor, who was Avon's director of Multicultural Planning and Design. Today, emphasis is on acceptance of heterogeneity, and it's not only women and blacks who are being positioned to move up the corporate ladder, but Asians, Hispanics, and other ethnic groups as well. "Under equal opportunity, such efforts were legally driven, but they're now becoming company-driven," says King-Ming Young, project manager of Hewlett-Packard's Managing Diversity Program.

What's behind the big push? Nurturing diversity in the workplace makes good business sense, says Lennie Copeland, a San Francisco consultant and partner in Lewis Griggs Productions, who produced a straight-talking video series, "Valuing Diversity," on dealing with gender and ethnic differences and stereotyping. The series was financed by 30 *Fortune* 500 corporations including Aetna, Honeywell, Weyerhauser, and Xerox. "Management teams consisting exclusively of white, male clones won't be able to come up with the most creative ways of reaching the ethnically diverse U.S. marketplace of today and the future," she says.

Programs to change the corporate culture can take from three to five years to make an impact, says consultant Judith Katz of Cincinnati-based Kaleel Jamison Associates. Meanwhile, firms are using outside experts and inside mentors to help valued women and minority employees decode "a foreign, uncomfortable culture," says Avon's Chin-Lor.

As more women and minorities move into senior corporate positions in the 1990s, changes will take place in the way companies are run. Marilyn Loden, organizational consultant and author of *Feminine Leadership or How to Succeed in Business Without Being One of the Boys* (Times Books), sees greater acceptance of what she calls "the natural management style of women." Women, she says, prefer a team approach that favors consensus-building, in contrast to the traditional "paramilitary model of the tough, competitive, impersonal American male leader." A consensus style should be well suited to the most entrepreneurial American companies of the 1990s where the old hierarchical layers are replaced by close-knit teams of workers with greater autonomy for making decisions, akin to widely touted Japanese management techniques.

Although the emphasis in the 1990s will be on getting along in a multicultural environment, whenever the stakes are high and opportunities limited, there will be the potential for conflict. Earlier this year, a federal regulation reclassified women as minorities for the awarding of highway construction contracts. There was bitter resentment among black contractors when competing firms headed by white women won three times as many contracts in Illinois.

Employers and legislators will expand efforts to accommodate such workers as disadvantaged minorities who need training and parents who require child care—but will control costs carefully.

As the baby-boom workers age and children of the baby bust enter the work force by the 1990s, only two-thirds as many workers as the 2.4 million who joined the labor force each year during the 1970s will be around to take up new jobs. Already, a drastic shortage of entry-level workers, ages sixteen to twenty-four, is giving headaches to employers ranging from fast food operators to law firm messenger supervisors. More and more of this group will be disadvantaged black and minority youths. They'll be hitting the job market often undereducated and underskilled, but they will find companies more willing than ever before to hire and train them.

Despite the massive efforts now under way to reform the nation's public school system, employers recognize that for the foreseeable future, they will have to fill part of the gap themselves with on-the-job remedial education as well as basic skills training for disadvantaged workers. Such programs will increase throughout the 1990s. "We're faced with a colossal skills mismatch," says labor economist Richard Belous of the Conference Board.

For most employers, a more controversial issue is what portion of the national child-care bill they should pay. In fact, barely 3,000 of the nation's six million employers seem to dispense any help at all, and many of these offer only referral assistance.

But pressure on these employers will increase. "Subsidized day care is the kind of benefit our workers expect us to bring routinely to the negotiating table," says Pat Scarcelli, international vice president and director of women's affairs for the 1.3 million-member United Food and Commercial Workers International Union. About one-third of the union's members have children under 13, and agreements, such as a recent one with Philadelphia's Acme Supermarkets to set aside $15 a month for each of its 2,600 unionized workers for child-care referral services, may become commonplace.

"But there's a limit on how far employers will go. We can no longer afford the world's highest-cost labor force," says Pamela Flaherty of Citicorp. The likely compromise: "Cafeteria" packages, which ask employees to select the benefits mix they prefer up to a predetermined dollar limit from a broad menu, including child care as well as such things as dental and pension coverage. Or employees may be required to shoulder more of the expense by paying incremental costs for benefits beyond those included in a standard package. "Tough choices will have to be made," says Flaherty.

What child-care help can parents expect from the government in the 1990s? The bill for quality child care for all eligible children of mothers in the work force would be as much as $100 billion annually, or 10 percent of total federal expenditures, according to preschool programs authority Edward Zigler. A more realistic annual contribution from the government will probably range from $1 billion to $4 billion a year, predicts Douglas Besharov, of the conservative American Enterprise Institute. He criticizes Democratic Senator Christopher Dodd's Act for Better Child Care Services (ABC), presently before Congress and itself with a price tag of $2.5 billion a year, on grounds its income limit for parents exceeding the median income level of $34,000 defines it as just another middle-class entitlement.

Yet for ardent supporters of an expanded federal role like Helen Blank of the Children's Defense Fund, federal support is urgently needed by state and local governments to "rationalize the present patchwork day-care system and set up licensing and regulatory standards." Working parents can expect better child-care options in the 1990s and some additional help from employers and the state. But they'll still be digging into their pockets for most of the cost.

Demand for flexible work schedules will increase, and unions and women's rights advocates will press for greater protection of temps and part-timers. Distinctions between part- and full-time work will blur.

In four decades, the de facto U.S. workweek has dropped on the average from 40 hours to less than 35. According to "Workforce 2000," it will continue to plummet, perhaps all the way to 30 by the end of the century. Retail clerks already average just 29 hours. As the workweek shrinks, differences between part- and full-time employment will become less clear.

Flextime—including such options as compressed workweeks, job sharing, and through telecommuting, work-at-home arrangements—is currently available to 12 percent of the U.S. work force. "The technology exists now to expand flextime. However, our corporate culture questions the commitment of any middle or top manager who doesn't want to be in the office full-time," says John Fernandez, an AT&T

human resources specialist and author of *Childcare and Corporate Productivity* (Lexington Books).

Jack Nilles of the Center for Effective Organizations estimates that more than 500,000 managerial and professional employees now work from home—an arrangement that can benefit both company and worker. An especially successful program, according to Kathleen Christensen, director of the National Project on Home-Based Work, involves 126 J. C. Penney customer service representatives, most of them women, who handle customer queries on company-supplied telephone-linked home-based computer terminals. At peak demand times, J. C. Penney can mobilize extra employees almost instantly. "What makes this work is the employer's commitment to giving at-home workers the same wages and benefits as office employees," emphasizes Christensen.

Whether or not the number of American women working as part-timers is expanding or declining is a matter of debate. Bureau of Labor Statistics (BLS) data show part-timers falling from just under 25 percent of all working women to just over 20 percent between 1976 and 1986. Yet as BLS Commissioner Janet Norwood recently pointed out, many workers counted as full-timers are really temps, hired on a permanent basis. They are paid less and receive fewer benefits than regular full-timers and can be fired at a moment's notice. "Just-in-time workers," Audrey Freedman of the Conference Board calls them; "disposable workers" is the label used by her colleague Richard Belous.

For a growing number of labor economists and union leaders, this is the troubling underside to part-time or "contingent" work. "We're in danger of creating a two-tier work force," asserts a worried Karen Nussbaum, executive director of 9to5, National Association of Working Women. BLS statistics show that over 5 million part-timers would rather be working full-time, and almost 5 percent of all women workers held two or more jobs during the first half of the 1980s— giving as their principal reason the need to earn more money. Yet no one doubts that many women, particularly mothers, prefer the flexible working schedules offered by part-time jobs.

However, women who choose part-time work need a better deal, emphasizes Karen Nussbaum. "In return for short-term flexibility, they're sacrificing a full-timer's benefits and opportunities for training and advancement," she says. Efforts by many unions to close the compensation and opportunities gap between part- and full-timers will increase throughout the 1990s.

Despite clear advances in the work force and more access to education, women throughout the 1990s will remain underrepresented in upper echelons of

the professions and overrepresented in the lower ranks. Technology may rein-
force "pink-collar ghettos."

Although the average female salary is now 70 percent of the
average man's salary and will still lag at 74 percent in the year 2000,
women are capturing a greater share of higher paying jobs than in the
past. In the mid-1970s, for example, women claimed about one-fifth
of executive, managerial, and administrative jobs. A decade later, they
had garnered over one-third. By the early 1980s, women accounted
for 36 percent of all computer science majors and 42 percent of business
majors; they earned 36 percent of law degrees and 45 percent of
accountancy degrees.

But the real picture may be less sanguine. One out of every three
law associates in the country's largest law firms is a woman, but only
one in every 13 partners. Eight of every ten women employed in the
computer industry are clerical workers while slightly more than one
of every ten is a manager. "We're discouraged," admits Cynthia Marano,
executive director of the Washington, D C –based Wider Opportuni
ties for Women. "Even in what will be the fastest-growing occupations
of the 1990s, women appear to be concentrated in the lower ranks."

Nowhere are women more overrepresented at the lower echelons
of the professional working world than in the clerical field: According
to 9to5, almost one of every three American women workers is a
clerical worker, 14.6 million, compared to one of every 17 men.

"Back office" clerical staffers in these "pink-collar ghettos" are
increasingly separated from the "front office" sales personnel, technicians, and managers. Moreover, as technology automates and fragments their tasks, they are more isolated from other workers and their
work is seen as demanding fewer skills. The result: Such jobs no longer
represent logical stepping-stones to more desirable positions.

"Natural career ladders are disappearing for these women," says
Susan Christopherson, an authority on contingent workers and assistant
professor at Cornell University's City and Regional Planning Department. She emphasizes that the only escape hatch from such dead-end
jobs in the 1990s will be advanced training. "But there is too little
emphasis on the direct relationship between the personal investment
in education and career advancement," Christopherson says. Her contention is borne out by the experience of Manpower, Inc., the nation's
largest employer of temps: Many women temps are initially less interested than men temps in learning computer applications like spread-
sheeting.

According to "Workforce 2000," the skill level of the U.S. economy will move inexorably upward. For example, there is a proposal
in New York City to require that both male and female police rookies

have two to four years of college to qualify for promotions. Low-paying, low-to-medium-skill occupations such as waitress, retail, and administrative clerk will represent the new "bottom" of the U.S. job skills curve of the 1990s, according to "Workforce 2000" director William Johnston. And to keep jobs with upward potential over a working lifetime will require what the nonprofit Work in America Institute calls "continuous learning" or skills upgrading that is spread out over the worker's career.

As the U.S. becomes a virtual service economy, unions will turn their sights on service workers, particularly women and minorities.
The flood of low-income jobs brought by the expanding service sector, expected to represent 75 percent of the U.S. economy by the year 2000, is often blamed for the first drop in median U.S. family income since the 1930s. Average wages, adjusted for inflation, simply stopped growing after 1973.

The numbers of women and youth willing to work for low wages in service jobs in fields like health care, retail trade, education, and government services in the 1970s meant employers had little incentive to adopt the kinds of labor-saving technology that promote productivity gains. Today, however, with a worsening labor shortage, that has changed. "Workforce 2000" projects a burst of productivity gains during the 1990s, and with it, probable salary gains.

But unions will have their work cut out for them, even though sizable pockets of unorganized workers with comparatively low salaries exist throughout the exploding service sector. Union membership has declined from over one-third of the U.S. work force in the 1950s to less than one-fifth today, and less than 10 percent of the service sector is unionized. Old-line unions like the United Auto Workers (UAW) are making increasing efforts to branch out from manufacturing industries. "We're looking at just about any group that's interested," says Barbara Rahke, Coordinator of Organizing for the UAW's fast-growing Technical, Office, and Professional Department. That has meant government employees, university clerks and lab technicians, legal aid attorneys and health insurance clerks.

While the service sector affords unions a tempting target, formidable obstacles await any group attempting to organize service workers. Workplaces are typically small and more dispersed than in the shrinking manufacturing sector. They have fewer workers, so organizing costs can be astronomical; workers also move more frequently from job to job. In New York City, for example, efforts to contain salary costs in Medicaid's $700 million home-care program for the elderly poor and convalescent resulted in thousands of women home-care attendants subsisting on typical salaries of $5,000 to $6,000 a year. It took an unusual cooperative effort of two unions—Local 1199 of the Drug, Hospital and Health Care Employees Union, and District Council 1707 of the American Federation of State, County, and Municipal Employees—to organize the attendants, winning an 85-cent wage hike to $5 an hour, basic health benefits, and more generous weekend pay. The home-care workers were particularly difficult to organize since they are dispersed over thousands of different work sites.

Women part-timers and temps are also tough to organize. "They don't perceive themselves as ever working for very long. Then suddenly, they've retired and have nothing," says the United Food and Commercial Workers' Scarcelli.

According to Dallas Salisbury, director of the Employee Benefit Research Institute, there is a de facto swing in collective bargaining for contingent workers to temp agencies like Manpower, Inc., which are increasingly demanding and getting better pay, benefits, and even pensions for many of their workers. "Human resource managers are already calling them the unions of tomorrow," says Salisbury.

What can we expect for the work force of the year 2000? Some trends are clear. For example, to live as well as our parents means both partners will have to work throughout the 1990s. Most single parents can expect a tough time keeping up with two-earner families. One of the great social challenges of the coming decade will be assisting families headed by a single earner, particularly young black women who are high school dropouts, into economic self-sufficiency in the mainstream job market. For them as for so many women workers, education will be the ticket of admission. As Patricia Albjerg Graham, dean of the Graduate School of Education at Harvard, puts it: "The increasing gap between bottom- and top-level jobs is what we should worry about as we approach the year 2000."

Themes, Issues, and Ideas

1. Bailey makes an important point in the first paragraph: "Since these new jobs will tend to demand more skills, planning is needed now to make sure there are people trained to fill them." Whose job is it to do this planning? List the types of planners Bailey covers and tell how and why women fit into their plans.

2. " 'Valuing diversity,' " Bailey says, "will be the catchword of progressive managers of the 1990s." What values does she show such managers finding in diversity? How will the values benefit workers?

How will they benefit corporations? According to Bailey, why haven't they always been seen as valuable?

3. Education is one of the essay's subthemes. Where do college-educated women fit into the projections? What does Bailey imply and conclude about the importance of higher education?

Writing Strategies and Techniques

1. Bailey often adopts a good news/bad news method of organization. What other techniques does she use in the essay as a whole and within its sections to organize her topic?

2. Given the nature of the essay's subject, many of its facts are presented in numerical form. In what ways does the author attempt to keep the numbers from overwhelming the reader's attention?

Suggestions for Writing

1. "But there's a limit on how far employers will go," Bailey reports. Using her facts, write an essay describing what the limit should be on accommodating the needs of women.

2. Bailey's essay ends with a quotation that directly states a theme implicit in much of the factual data she supplies: "The increasing gap between bottom- and top-level jobs is what we should worry about as we approach the year 2000." Write an essay in which you argue that this worry is or is not a pertinent one to women.

Why Mothers Should Stay Home

Deborah Fallows

> In this essay Deborah Fallows uses the evidence of
> her own life to argue for "the radical middle" position on
> the issue of working versus full-time mothers. Fallows be-
> lieves that "the choice is not to be either a career woman or
> a dumb housewife." She attempts to show how neither
> stereotype does justice to the possibilities available for
> women who want to raise their own children
>
> Deborah Fallows was raised in Ohio and educated at
> Radcliffe College and the University of Texas, where she
> earned a doctorate in linguistics. She worked as a research
> linguist and as an assistant dean at Georgetown University
> before deciding to stay at home with her two children. She
> describes the reasons for making her choice in an essay first
> published in Washington Monthly magazine.

About eighteen months ago, when our first son was
three years old and our second was about to be born, I decided to
stop working and stay at home with our children. At the time, I
wrote an article about the myth of the superwoman, saying that
contrary to the prevailing notion of the day, it was not possible to
be both a full-time career woman and a full-fledged mother. I said
that while everyone recognizes the costs a stay-at-home mother
pays in terms of power, prestige, money, and advancement in traditional careers, we are not always aware of or do not so readily
admit what a full-time working woman loses and gives up in terms
of mothering.

I've been at home with our children for almost a year and a
half now, and I've learned a number of things about my choice. My
convictions about the importance of mothering, which were based
more on intuition than experience at the time, run even deeper and

stronger. Nothing means more to me now than the hours I spend with my children, but I find myself coping with a problem I hadn't fully foreseen. It is the task of regearing my life, of learning to live as a full-time mother without a professional career but still with many of the interests and ambitions that I had before I had children. And this is the hard part. It means unraveling those long-held life plans for a certain kind of career and deciding which elements are possible to keep and which I must discard. Perhaps even more important, it means changing the way I've been taught to think about myself and value the progress of my life.

My mother became a mother in 1946; she had gone to college, studied music, and worked for a year at her father's office. Then she married and had my sister by the time she was twenty-two. She wasn't expected to have a career outside the home, and she didn't. When I was growing up, the only mothers who worked were those who, as we whispered, "had to." Even the high-school teachers, who we recognized probably weren't doing it just for the money, were slightly suspect.

But between my mother's time and our own, the climate of opportunity and expectations for women started to change. Betty Friedan and *The Feminine Mystique* came between all of those mothers and all of us daughters. The small town in northern Ohio where I grew up was not exactly a hotbed of feminist activity, but even there the signals for young women were changing in the mid-sixties. We were raised with a curious mixture of hope of becoming homecoming queen and pressure to run for student council president. When I was eleven, the mothers in our neighborhood bundled off their awkward, preadolescent daughters to Saturday morning charm classes, where we learned how to walk on a straight line, one foot directly in front of the other, and the proper way to don a coat. We all felt a little funny and humiliated, but we didn't say anything. By the time we were seventeen, we were May Queens, princesses, head drum majorettes, and cheerleaders, but we were also class valedictorians, editors of the school paper and yearbook, student directors of the school band, and candidates for six-year medical programs, Seven Sisters colleges, and honors programs at the Big Ten universities. I admit with some embarrassment that my two most thrilling moments in high school were being chosen for the homecoming court and being named first-chair trumpet in the concert band.

This was the way we were supposed to achieve—to be both beautiful and brilliant, charming and accomplished. It was one step beyond what our mothers did: We were aiming to be class presidents, not class secretaries; for medical school, not nursing school; we were building careers, not just jobs to tide us over before we landed husbands and started raising babies.

When I made my decision to stop working and stay home with our children, it was with a mixture of feelings. Part was defiance of the background I've just described—how could feminism dare tell me that I couldn't choose, with *pride,* motherhood alone? Part was anxiety—how could I keep some grasp on my extra-mothering self, on the things I had really enjoyed doing before I had children? I didn't want to become what the world kept telling me housewives are— ladies whose interests are confined to soap operas and the laundry. Certainly I knew from my own mother and from other women who had spent their middle years as full-time mothers that it was possible to be a thoughtful and sensitive person and still be a mother. But I didn't know how, and I didn't know where to turn to ask. Even my mother didn't have the answers. She was surprised when I told her I wanted to stop working and stay home with my kids. "You young women seem to handle everything so easily, so smoothly," she told me. "I never knew you were so torn between being a mother and being a professional."

The arrival of children in a woman's late twenties or early thirties can be handy, of course, because it means you can finish your education and start a career before taking "time out" to start your family. But it's also awkward.

At my tenth college reunion last June, I found that many of my friends had just become partner or vice-president of one thing or another, doctor-in-charge of some ward, tenured professor, editor-in-chief, and so forth. In these moments, I feel as if everyone is growing up around me. My reactions, though human, are not altogether pretty. I feel sorry for myself—there but for two small children go I. I feel frustrated in being passed over for things I know I could handle as well as or better than the next person. I feel anxious, wondering if I am going to "lose my touch," get rusty, boring, old, trivial too quickly. And I am afraid that in putting aside my professional ambitions just now, I may be putting aside forever the chance to attain the levels I once set for myself.

All of us, I think, spend time once in a while pondering the "what ifs" of our lives, and we all experience momentary pangs of self-pity over the course we've taken. I know I'm not an exception to this, but I also know that when I add up the pluses and minuses my choice was right for me, and it might be right for other women.

The Importance of "Quantity" Time

The first adjustment on that first morning that I dressed for motherhood rather than for success was to believe intellectually in what I felt emotionally: that it was as important, as worthy for me to spend my time with my small children as to study, do research, try cases, or invest a bank's money. Furthermore, I had to believe it was worth it to the children to have me—not someone else—there most of the time. There are a thousand small instances I have witnessed over the past year and a half that illustrate this feeling. One that stays in my mind happened last summer.

I had just dropped off our older son at the morning play camp at the neighborhood school. I was about to drive off when a little boy about eight years old burst out of the school and ran down the front steps in tears. His mother was on her way down the walk and of course she saw him. She led him over to the steps, took his hands in hers, looked him directly in the eyes, and talked with him softly but deliberately for a few minutes, calming him down so he could go back inside happily and she could go on her way. What I recognized in that instant was something I'd been trying to put my finger on for months. I'd witnessed dozens of similar events, and when a child was simply overwhelmed by something, and I knew there was a difference—a distinct difference in the way parents respond at such moments from the way I had seen baby-sitters or maids act, however loving and competent they may have been. Parents seem to have some combination of self-assurance, completeness, deliberateness, and consistency. If that boy had been my son, I would have wanted to be with him, too.

Perhaps this one episode was no more important than the many reprimands or comforts I give my children during the day. But the more I'm around my children, the more such instances I happen to see and deal with. Perhaps a thousand of these episodes add up to the values and security I want to give my children.

I spend a lot of time with my children at playgrounds. We often go out on nice afternoons when our older son gets home from school, sampling new ones or returning to old favorites. I particularly like playgrounds because of the balance they afford: They encourage the kids to strike out on their own but let me be there as a fallback. I've watched my older son in his share of small fistfights and scuffles, and I have been able to let him fight without intervening. He knows I'm there and runs back as often for protection as for nice things like a "Mom, see what I can do." Or our younger son toddles toward the big slide and needs me to follow him up and hold him as we slide down together. After so many hours, we've developed a style of play. I think my children know what to expect of me and I have learned their limits. I've watched the styles of many mothers and children, and you often can see, after a time, a microcosm of their lives together. I've also seen plenty of children there with full-time maids. The maids have their own styles, which usually are different from the mothers'. I've never seen a maid slide down a slide with her small charge, but I have seen plenty scold children for climbing too high on the jungle gym, and I've seen plenty step in to stop the sandfights before anyone gets dirty or hurt. There's a reason for this, of course: A maid has a lot to explain if a youngster arrives home with a bloody nose, but a mother doesn't. Sometimes, I think, the nose is worth the lesson learned from it, yet that is something only a parent—not a maid or baby-sitter—can take the responsibility to decide.

It has taken me a few years to realize I have very high standards for my role as a mother. I don't have to be a supermom who makes my children's clothes (I really can't sew), who does all the volunteer work at school (I do my share), or who cooks gourmet meals (we eat a lot of hamburgers). But I have to be around my children—a lot. I have to know them as well as I possibly can and see them in as many different environments and moods as possible in order to know best how to help them grow up—by comforting them, letting them alone, disciplining and enjoying them, being dependable but not stifling. What I need with them is time—in quantity, not quality.

I'm not talking about being with my children every minute of the day. From the time they were several months old, we sent them out for short periods to the favorite neighborhood baby-sitter's. By the time he was two and a half, our older son was in a co-op nursery school (my husband and I would take turns doing parent duty for the seventeen kids); now he's in pre-kindergarten for a full school day. These periods away from me are clearly important for my sanity, as well as for my children's socialization, their development of trust in people, and their ability to experience other ways of living. But there is a big difference between using childcare from 8 to 6, Monday through Friday, and using a baby-sitter or a nursery school three mornings a week.

I realize that not everyone enjoys the luxury of choice. Some of my female friends work because it's the only way to make ends meet. But I think a lot of people pretend they have less room for choice than they really do. For some women, the reason may be the feeling—which is widespread among men—that their dignity and success are related to how much money they earn. For others, there is a sense of independence that comes with earning money that is hard to give up.

(I know that I felt freer to buy things, especially for myself, or spend money on baby-sitters when I was contributing to the family income.) And still others define "necessities" in an expensive way: I've heard more than one woman say she "has to work" to keep up payments on the second house. Such a woman is the parallel to the government appointee who "has to resign" from his post to return to his former profession because he "can no longer afford government service."

Even though some women do have a choice, I am not suggesting that all the responsibility for home and children should lie with the mother. While my husband and I are an example of a more traditional family, with a bread-winning father, a full-time mother, and two children, he shares with me many of the family responsibilities: night-tending, diapering, bathing, cooking, and playtime. A woman's decision to stay home or work is, at worst, a decision made by herself and, at best, a decision made with her spouse.

But with all these qualifications noted, I still know that my own choice is to stay with my children. Why does this seem to be at odds with the climate of the times, especially among certain feminists? I think it is because of a confused sense of ambition—based, in turn, on a mistaken understanding of what being a housewife or mother actually means.

While the world's idea of the comparative importance of career and motherhood may have changed a good deal since my mother's time, the general understanding of what motherhood means for those who choose it has not changed or advanced. And that may be the real problem for many women of my generation: Who can blame them for shying away from a commitment to full-time motherhood if they're told, despite raising children, that motherhood is a vapid life of chores, routines, and TV? I couldn't stand motherhood myself if that were true. One of my many discoveries as a mother is that motherhood requires not the renunciation of my former ambitions but rather their refinement.

Even for those who intend to rush straight back to work, motherhood involves some interruption in the normal career plan. Separating people, even temporarily, from their professional identities, can help them see the difference between the ambition to *be*—to have an impressive job title to drop at cocktail parties—and the ambition to *do* specific things that seem satisfying and rewarding. The ambition to be is often a casualty of motherhood; the ambition to do need not be.

I see many of my friends intensely driven to keep doing things, to keep involved in their former interests, or to develop entirely new ones that they can learn from and grow with. In the free time they manage to set aside—thanks to baby-sitters, co-op babycare, naptimes, grandmothers' help, and husbands like mine who spend a lot of time with the children—they are thinking and doing.

Women I have talked to have described how, after some months or years of settling into motherhood, their sense of what work is worth, and what they're looking for in work, has greatly changed. They are less tolerant, more selective, more demanding in what they do. One woman said that before she had children she would focus on a "cause," and was willing to do just about anything as her job toward that cause. Now she's still interested in advancing the cause, but she has no patience for busywork. In the limited time she can spare from her family, she wants to do things that really count, work in areas where her efforts make a difference. I'm not suggesting narcissism here but a clearer focus on a search for some long-range goal, some tangible accomplishment, a feeling so necessary during the season of child raising when survival from one end of the day to the other is often the only achievement.

Each one's search is different, depending on factors like her husband's job (if she has a husband) and the extent of his role as a caretaker, her children's needs, her family's financial situation, and her personal lifestyle.

One of my friends had taught English in public high schools for the last ten years. She was the kind of teacher you remember fondly from your own childhood and hope your kids are lucky enough to have because she's dedicated, demanding, and creative. She expanded her subject to include other humanities, keeping herself several steps ahead of her students by reading and studying on her own, traveling to see museums and exhibits firsthand, collecting slides and books as she goes. She has a new baby daughter now and has stopped working to stay home with her child. She's decided to go back to school next fall, taking one or two courses at a time, to pursue a master's in fine arts—a chance to study formally what she's mostly taught herself and to return to her job someday with an even better background and more ideas for her teaching.

Going to school can be perfect for new mothers, as many in my own mother's generation found. It requires very little time away from home, which means cutting down on time away from the children as well as on child-care costs. It can be cheap, as with my friend, who can attend a virtually tuition-free state university. You can pace your work to suit demands at home by carefully choosing the number of courses you take and the type of work required. And it's physically easy but intellectually challenging—the complement to the other demands of the early years of mothering.

Other mothers I know do different things with their time. One friend, formerly a practicing lawyer and now a full-time mother, volunteers some of her time to advising the League of Women Voters on legal matters. Another, formerly a producer at a big radio station, now produces her own shows, albeit at a slower pace. A third quit her job to raise her daughter but spends a lot of time on artistic projects, which she sells.

But if there's no real blueprint for what a modern mother should be, you wouldn't know it from what comes through in the media. On the "Today Show" last summer, for instance, Jane Pauley interviewed Felice Schwartz, the president of Catalyst, an organization that promotes career development for women. They were discussing women's changing life-styles. Ms. Schwartz said that now women are going back to work full-time four months after having children, while fifteen years ago they were taking twenty years off to have them. "Isn't that fantastic progress?" she said. Fantastic it certainly is; progress it is not, except toward the narrowest and least generous notion of what achievement means for women or for humanity. Progress such as this is a step not toward "liberation" but toward the enslavement to career that has been the least attractive aspect of masculine success.

What it is really like to be a mother today seems to be a secret that's kept from even my contemporaries who may be considering motherhood themselves. At a dinner recently, I sat near a young woman about my age, a New York television producer and recently appointed White House fellow. She and my husband and I were having a conversation about bureaucracy and what she found new or interesting or surprising about it in her new position. After several minutes, she turned away from my husband to me directly and said, "And how old are your children, Debbie?" It wasn't the question—not at all—but the tone that was revealing, the unattractive, condescending tone I've heard many older people use with youngsters, or doctors with patients. If I'd had her pegged as a fast-track superachiever, she had me pegged as little mother and lady of the house.

Hurt and anger were the wrong feelings at a moment like that, although I felt them. Instead, I should have felt sorry for her, not because of her own choice but because she had no sense that a choice exists—waiting to be made by women like her and like me. The choice is *not* to be either a career woman or a dumb housewife. The issue is one that she, a woman at the age when careers take off and childbearing ability nears its eleventh hour, should be sensitive to and think about.

Themes, Issues, and Ideas

1. Fallows says that her decision to stay at home was made with mixed feelings. What are these feelings and how does she describe coming to terms with them?

2. What does Fallows see as the principal difference between her life as a mother and her mother's life?

3. What does Fallows mean by "quantity time"? What other reasons does she give in favoring part-time work over part-time mothering?

Writing Strategies and Techniques

1. How does Fallows confront the points of view of those who have not made her decision? How does she blend reasoned arguments with anecdotes from her own life?

2. Whom does Fallows seem to be addressing? That is, where does she seem to be addressing young women who have perhaps not yet formed an opinion on the issue, and where does she seem to speak to women who already have careers and children? How do you decide on her imagined audience in each case?

Suggestions for Writing

1. Write a response to Fallows as it might be written by one of the types of women she imagines in her essay; for example, the "fast-track superachiever."

2. Write an essay describing your own views as a man or a woman on the proper role for mothers of young children.

The New Feminine Mystique

Betty Friedan

Betty Friedan is one of the founders of modern Ameri-can feminism. The publication of her book The Feminine Mystique *in 1963 marks one of the mileposts in the struggle of American women for equality, and also serves as a defin-ing moment in American culture. What Friedan called the "feminine mystique" in 1963 was the tendency of men to marginalize women by putting them on male-built pedestals. In this essay from 1991, Friedan addresses a world changed in many ways, but one in which women are still being mar-ginalized.*

Friedan is currently Visiting Distinguished Professor at both the University of Southern California and New York University.

T*he problem lay buried, unspoken, for many years in the minds of American women. It was a strange stirring, a sense of dis-satisfaction, a yearning that women suffered in the middle of the 20th century in the United States. Each suburban wife struggled with it alone. As she made the beds, shopped for groceries, matched slip-cover material, ate peanut butter sandwiches with her children, chauffeured Cub Scouts and Brownies, lay beside her husband at night, she was afraid to ask, even of herself, the silent question—"Is this all?"*

—The Feminine Mystique, *W.W. Norton, 1963.*

I was that suburban housewife. I had been living some years in Rock-land County outside of New York City with three little kids and rather surreptitiously writing for magazines like *McCall's*. I was the only woman in my suburb, in those years of the station wagon dream life, who was "working" (although, of course, we all worked inside the home) and I hid it, the way you would secret drinking in the morning.

Of course, most of us, after the deprivation of the wartime years, wanted very much to be wives and mothers, to have the home and the furnishings and the appliances and the station wagon. But strangely, each woman thought she was alone if she also wanted to be more than B.J.'s wife, Junior's mother and the servicer of the house—that hers was some unique guilt or shame. I called this secret longing, "the problem that has no name," and I attributed it to the feminine mystique, which returned us to the home after World War II, limiting and distorting our very definition of women. This image of a woman who was less than fully human, who was defined only in terms of her relationship to men and babies and home, was so pervasive that it actually blotted out of women's own consciousness—and the national consciousness as well— the 100-year battle for women's rights that ended with winning the vote in 1920.

By now we've had a quarter of a century of women's movement. We have won for our daughters their personhood as women, their entitlement to equal opportunity, to education and to participate in the mainstream of society.

But now I see this revolution, this great life-enhancing revolution, still not finished, but having enormously changed the possibilities for all women—and therefore for men and children too—stalled, stuck, stopped in its tracks. It has been slowed to a halt by the general reversal of social progress in America in the dozen years of the Reagan and Bush administrations. All the rights that women have won in the past 20 years are in grave danger.

I have been aware of the warning signals of this new feminine mystique for three or four years now, and it fills me with fear. I fear for our daughters and granddaughters who have grown up taking for granted what we have won.

In the past few years *having it all* has become almost a pejorative phrase. It has been made to seem as if women are greedily asking for too much, reaching for too much. Newsmagazine covers have shown women in those dress-for-success suits putting down their briefcases and picking up unhappy babies.

So now we see the creation of a new feminine mystique. Here are some of the danger signs, straws in the wind that, taken together, pose an ominous threat.

The Happy Housewife and the Pretty Woman

There is today a virtual fade-out in movies and television of the image of strong, active, independent women taking control of their lives. In the '60s, while women's roles were expanding in everyday life, television moved from *I Love Lucy* to *Maude* and Mary Tyler Moore and Carol Burnett. Then came programs like *Cagney & Lacey, L.A. Law, Designing Women* and *Golden Girls. Cagney & Lacey* and a host of other shows are gone now, and the only new independent, feisty character of the past few years is Murphy Brown. In fact, according to a recent study of television characters by the National Commission on Working Women, the most common female job is clerical work, and the number of full-time housewives on television has "notably increased" in the past few seasons.

Do you remember the strong sort of character that Meryl Streep used to play. Now Streep has publicly complained there are no good roles for women. When you think about movies of the past few years, you come up mainly with violent films where women are victims and *Pretty Woman,* which celebrates the hooker and says that all you need is a rich sugar daddy to buy you clothes. The very shock of *Thelma and Louise* and the killer women of last summer's films shows how far we have strayed from autonomous, independent women in control of their lives, the old kind of zestful woman that used to be played by Katherine Hepburn, Barbara Stanwyck, Myrna Loy and Bette Davis.

The fade-out of strong women in movies and television is accompanied by an even more frightening annihilation of the image and even the mention of women in newspapers and broadcast news. In my "Men, Women and Media" project at the University of Southern California, we did a simple count of all the women quoted, cited or pictured on the front pages of 20 newspapers across the country and a month's monitoring of all three networks plus Fox news. Women accounted for a mere 15 percent. Men, who make up slightly less than half the population, not only still dominate print and broadcast news, but occupy 85 percent of the space.

"Go Home!"

Increasingly we are hearing obliquely or head-on that women should go home again. I am interviewed once or twice a week by newsmagazines and women's magazines on what I think about women wishing to go home, their supposed repudiation of jobs and careers, and their return to a "new traditionalism."

Of course, women don't wish to go home again; economically they can't afford to and psychologically they would be worse off than the mothers I interviewed for *The Feminine Mystique*. Still, seizing on the real problems of carrying two jobs at once, the "go home" message grows more and more insidious.

The New Perfection

When we don't want women to move in the mainstream of society, we proliferate the details of running a perfect home and raising perfect children. And, in the '50s, the women's magazines did just that.

In *The Feminine Mystique* I wrote, "Fulfillment as a woman had only one definition for American women after 1949—the housewife-mother. Only one out of three heroines in the women's magazines was a career woman and she was shown in the act of renouncing her career and discovering that what she really wanted to be was a housewife. In 1958 and again in 1959, I went through issue after issue of the three major women's magazines [*McCall's, Good Housekeeping, Ladies' Home Journal*] without finding a single heroine who had a career, a commitment to any work, art, profession or mission in the world other than 'Occupation: Housewife.' Only one in 100 heroines had a job; even the young unmarried heroines no longer worked except at snaring a husband." I added that in such a milieu, "housework expands to fill the time available."

Well, we can't make women worry any longer about ring-around-the-collar. You can't play on the elementary housewife guilt anymore. Magazines like *McCall's*, whose evolution I've been so proud of as they have broken through and beyond the mother-housewife image to the complex, diverse life of women today, no longer devote themselves to spring cleaning.

But other magazines and books are burgeoning that can conjure up more elaborate guilt about, say, something like entertaining, which, like housework, can expand to fill the time available. There is nothing wrong with *Martha Stewart Living* or with a magazine like *Victoria*, except that they set standards so high that, willy nilly, they are asking and expecting women to devote themselves to these pursuits, to the exclusion of the richer, fuller, busier life of today's woman.

The Motherhood Choice

The very basic right of women to decide when and how many and whether to have children is in dire jeopardy. Out of Washington comes the ultimate feminine-mystique message: Biology is destiny; motherhood is not to be chosen; if you are a woman it chooses you.

A most liberating factor in the lives of our daughters was The Pill. But we are decades behind other nations in birth control, and birth-control research in this country has been brought to a virtual standstill. At the same time forces are now violently blocking women's access to abortion. The threatened reversal of *Roe* v. *Wade* and the even more pernicious and dangerous Supreme Court decision holding that doctors in federally funded clinics cannot even advise poor women that abortion is a *possibility* are not only a blow to women but a dangerous attack on freedom of speech in our country.

When I speak, as I do, to high school or college students and, increasingly, to the new networks of professional women in every field—younger women—I know they take the battle for women's rights and the battle for equality for granted. If they're aware of it at all, they think it's history.

And so, right off, I ask, "How many of you have ever worn a girdle?" I say to them, "Not so long ago, when your mothers were your age, no woman left her house in the morning—not so long ago most women didn't necessarily leave their house in the morning!—without enclosing her flesh in rigid plastic sausage casing. It didn't matter whether she weighed 120 pounds or 220 pounds. She wasn't supposed to notice that this casing made it difficult for her to move and breathe. She wasn't supposed to notice that it left red welts on her belly when she came home at night and took it off. She didn't ask why she wore the girdle. It was what being a woman meant. Did it make her more attractive to men to look like a sausage?"

I say to these young woman, "How can I expect you to know what it felt like when being a woman meant you wore a girdle, when you have never worn anything under your blue jeans except pantyhose or a bikini brief or nothing at all? How can I expect you to know what it felt like when being a woman meant you wore a girdle over your mind, you wore a girdle over your heart, to say nothing of that girdle you wore down below.

"We who took that girdle off know the difference: to be able to know what you know, to see what you see, to feel what you feel and to say what you think and feel—and to move, to move freely in this society. You can never sell us that girdle again, that feminine mystique. That was the girdle we took off.

"But you, who have never worn it, they are trying to sell it to you again. They are actually selling some of you that old confining girdle. The question is: Why would you buy it? Why would women buy it again?"

The fact of the matter is that it is not easy for women to put all the forces of their lives together. The women's revolution was stopped before we could restructure the workplace and our homes to take into account the fact that we are still the ones who give birth to children. The places where women work and the homes to which they return each night are still organized in terms of the experience of the men of the past, whose wives took care of all the details of life. We haven't been able to reach the next step, which would allow women to have real choices: to have their children if they wish and still keep their jobs and sustain their careers as men do.

Women are still expected to take primary responsibility for children and home, and I'm not sure they want to give that up completely. But they need a basic restructuring of the workplace and of the home, and innovative services from community and society—from the corporations and businesses where they work, from their husbands at home and, above all, from government.

In countries as diverse as France, Australia and Israel, it is a matter of national pride that the majority of two- and three-year-old children attend free, public nursery schools. It is obscene that this, the United States of America, the great, rich nation, is the only industrialized nation besides South Africa without national policies of child care and parental leave.

Can women solve their problems by going home again and waiting for a man to take care of them and their numerous children for the rest of their lives? Of course not. It would be worse for them than for their mothers, for they have had a taste of freedom.

I tell the young people I talk to today: "I know you say, 'I'm not a feminist. I'm not a feminist but I want to be an astronaut. I'm not a feminist but I'm going to law school and maybe I'll be a senator or a judge. Sure I'll get married when I get around to it and have a successful husband but he won't have to be that successful because I will be—and I'll have my 1.3 children . . . ,' and so on."

And then I always tell them—because I want to jolt them out of their complacency—"You are going to have to say, 'I am a feminist' and say it loud and clear or you're not going to have those rights that you take for granted. The either/or choices you are being offered today—home and family or job and career—won't even solve your personal dilemmas for long. You really can't go home again. You have to march politically anew, to save your very possibility of expanded choices and the larger dream of our democracy."

Themes, Issues, and Ideas

1. Friedan describes "a virtual fade-out" of independent women images. She gives several examples. Do you agree with her assessment? Give examples, other than the ones Friedan uses, to support your claim.

2. Friedan rejects the idea that a woman has to choose between home and family. This idea is at odds with Deborah Fallows's essay "Why Mothers Should Stay Home." Which writer makes a more persuasive argument? Which one describes more realistically the situation as you have experienced it?

Writing Strategies and Techniques

1. By beginning with a personal note, Friedan seeks to make an emotional bond with the reader. Do you find this device more or less persuasive than the style used by Steinem or Bailey? What is Friedan's purpose in using the first person throughout her essay?

2. By describing what women of her generation endured by wearing a girdle, what does Friedan hope to accomplish? Does she succeed? Discuss the shift in style from direct quotation back to essay narrative.

3. In the closing part of her essay, Friedan recounts what she considers a typical speech by young people. Do you think the speech is typical of how young people speak about this issue? If so, why? If not, write a more accurate speech that can still function in Friedan's essay.

Suggestions for Writing

1. Write a response to Friedan as a member of the generation she addresses at the end of her essay. What would you point out to her that she might have missed about you?

2. Friedan writes, "The women's revolution was stopped before we could restructure the workplace and our homes to take into account the fact that we are still the ones who give birth to children." Write a proposal for a workplace or a home that might take this fact into account.

It's a Jungle Out There, So Get Used to It!

Camille Paglia

Camille Paglia was until a few years ago an unknown professor of art history at the Philadelphia College of Art. Then, in 1990 her book Sexual Personae: Art and Decadence from Nefertiti to Emily Dickinson *was published, and she achieved instant notoriety. Paglia's ideas, which are always controversial and incendiary, center around the natural sexual forces she believes are part of the human condition, and which are controlled and expressed through popular and serious art.*

In "It's a Jungle Out There, So Get Used to It!" Paglia leaves her home ground of art history, and considers a much thornier question: What is rape, and what can be done about it? Paglia has alienated many feminists by her staunch opposition to the feminist critique of rape and sexuality. Here, she examines what she sees as the dynamics of campus rape, and how young women have been made vulnerable by misinformation.

Rape is an outrage that cannot be tolerated in civilized society. Yet feminism, which has waged a crusade for rape to be taken more seriously, has put young women in danger by hiding the truth about sex from them.

In dramatizing the pervasiveness of rape, feminists have told young women that before they have sex with a man, they must give consent as explicit as a legal contract's. In this way, young women have been convinced that they have been the victims of rape. On elite campuses in the Northeast and on the West Coast, they have held consciousness-raising sessions, petitioned administrations, demanded inquests. At Brown University, outraged, panicky "victims" have scrawled the names of alleged attackers on the walls of women's rest rooms. What marital rape was to the '70s, "date rape" is to the '90s.

The incidence and seriousness of rape do not require this kind of exaggeration. Real acquaintance rape is nothing new. It has been a horrible problem for women for all of recorded history. Once fathers and brothers protected women from rape. Once the penalty for rape was death. I come from a fierce Italian tradition where, not so long ago in the motherland, a rapist would end up knifed, castrated, and hung out to dry.

But the old clans and small rural communities have broken down. In our cities, on our campuses far from home, young women are vulnerable and defenseless. Feminism has not prepared them for this. Feminism keeps saying the sexes are the same. It keeps telling women they can do anything, go anywhere, say anything, wear anything. No, they can't. Women will always be in sexual danger.

One of my male students recently slept overnight with a friend in a passageway of the Great Pyramid in Egypt. He described the moon and sand, the ancient silence and eerie echoes. I will never experience that. I am a woman. I am not stupid enough to believe I could ever be safe there. There is a world of solitary adventure I will never have. Women have always known these somber truths. But feminism, with its pie-in-the-sky fantasies about the perfect world, keeps young women from seeing life as it is.

We must remedy social injustice whenever we can. But there are some things we cannot change. There are sexual differences that are based in biology. Academic feminism is lost in a fog of social constructionism. It believes we are totally the product of our environment. This idea was invented by Rousseau. He was wrong. Emboldened by dumb French language theory, academic feminists repeat the same hollow slogans over and over to each other. Their view of sex is naive and prudish. Leaving sex to the feminists is like letting your dog vacation at the taxidermist's.

The sexes are at war. Men must struggle for identity against the overwhelming power of their mothers. Women have menstruation to tell them they are women. Men must do or risk something to be men. Men become masculine only when other men say they are. Having sex with a woman is one way a boy becomes a man.

College men are at their hormonal peak. They have just left their mothers and are questing for their male identity. In groups, they are dangerous. A woman going to a fraternity party is walking into Testosterone Flats, full of prickly cacti and blazing guns. If she goes, she should be armed with resolute alertness. She should arrive with girlfriends and leave with them. A girl who lets herself get dead drunk at a fraternity party is a fool. A girl who goes upstairs alone with a brother at a fraternity party is an idiot. Feminists call this "blaming the victim." I call it common sense.

For a decade, feminists have drilled their disciples to say, "Rape is a crime of violence but not of sex." This sugar-coated Shirley Temple nonsense has exposed young women to disaster. Misled by feminism, they do not expect rape from the nice boys from good homes who sit next to them in class.

Aggression and eroticism are deeply intertwined. Hunt, pursuit, and capture are biologically programmed into male sexuality. Generation after generation, men must be educated, refined, and ethically persuaded away from their tendency toward anarchy and brutishness. Society is not the enemy, as feminism ignorantly claims. Society is woman's protection against rape. Feminism, with its solemn Carry Nation repressiveness, does not see what is for men the eroticism or fun element in rape, especially the wild, infectious delirium of gang rape. Women who do not understand rape cannot defend themselves against it.

The date-rape controversy shows feminism hitting the wall of its own broken promises. The women of my '60s generation were the first respectable girls in history to swear like sailors, get drunk, stay out all night—in short, to act like men. We sought total sexual freedom and equality. But as time passed, we woke up to cold reality. The old double standard protected women. When anything goes, it's women who lose.

Today's young women don't know what they want. They see that feminism has not brought sexual happiness. The theatrics of public rage over date rape are their way of restoring the old sexual rules that were shattered by my generation. Because nothing about the sexes has really changed. The comic film *Where the Boys Are* (1960), the ultimate expression of '50s man-chasing, still speaks directly to our time. It shows smart, lively women skillfully anticipating and fending off the dozens of strategies with which horny men try to get them into bed. The agonizing date-rape subplot and climax are brilliantly done. The victim, Yvette Mimieux, makes mistake after mistake, obvious to the other girls. She allows herself to be lured away from her girlfriends and into isolation with boys whose character and intentions she misreads. *Where the Boys Are* tells the truth. It shows courtship as a dangerous game in which the signals are not verbal but subliminal.

Neither militant feminism, which is obsessed with politically correct language, nor academic feminism, which believes that knowledge and experience are "constituted by" language, can understand pre-verbal or non-verbal communication. Feminism, focusing on sexual politics, cannot see that sex exists in and through the body. Sexual desire and arousal cannot be fully translated into verbal terms. This is why men and women misunderstand each other.

Trying to remake the future, feminism cut itself off from sexual history. It discarded and suppressed the sexual myths of literature, art, and religion. Those myths show us the turbulence, the mysteries and passions of sex. In mythology we see men's sexual anxiety, their fear of women's dominance. Much sexual violence is rooted in men's sense of psychological weakness toward women. It takes many men to deal with one woman. Woman's voracity is a persistent motif. Clara Bow, it was rumored, took on the USC football team on weekends. Marilyn Monroe, singing "Diamonds Are a Girl's Best Friend," rules a conga line of men in tuxes. Half-clad Cher, in the video for "If I Could Turn Back Time," deranges a battleship of screaming sailors and straddles a pink-lit cannon. Feminism, coveting social power, is blind to woman's cosmic sexual power.

To understand rape, you must study the past. There never was and never will be sexual harmony. Every woman must take personal responsibility for her sexuality, which is nature's red flame. She must be prudent and cautious about where she goes and with whom. When she makes a mistake, she must accept the consequences and, through self-criticism, resolve never to make that mistake again. Running to Mommy and Daddy on the campus grievance committee is unworthy of strong women. Posting lists of guilty men in the toilet is cowardly, infantile stuff.

The Italian philosophy of life espouses high-energy confrontation. A male student makes a vulgar remark about your breasts? Don't slink off to whimper and simper with the campus shrinking violets. Deal with it. On the spot. Say, "Shut up, you jerk! And crawl back to the barnyard where you belong!" In general, women who project this take-charge attitude toward life get harassed less often. I see too many dopey, immature, self-pitying women walking around like melting sticks of butter. It's the Yvette Mimieux syndrome: Make me happy. And listen to me weep when I'm not.

The date-rape debate is already smothering in propaganda churned out by the expensive Northeastern colleges and universities, with their overconcentration of boring, uptight academic feminists and spoiled, affluent students. Beware of the deep manipulativeness of rich students who were neglected by their parents. They love to turn the campus into hysterical psychodramas of sexual transgression, followed by assertions of parental authority and concern. And don't look for sexual enlightenment from academe, which spews out mountains of books but never looks at life directly.

As a fan of football and rock music, I see in the simple, swaggering masculinity of the jock and in the noisy posturing of the heavy-metal guitarist certain fundamental, unchanging truths about sex. Masculinity is aggressive, unstable, combustible. It is also the most creative cultural force in history. Women must reorient themselves toward the elemental powers of sex, which can strengthen or destroy.

The only solution to date rape is female self-awareness and self-control. A woman's number one line of defense is herself. When a real rape occurs, she should report it to the police. Complaining to college committees because the courts "take too long" is ridiculous. College administrations are not a branch of the judiciary. They are not equipped or trained for legal inquiry. Colleges must alert incoming students to the problems and dangers of adulthood. Then colleges must stand back and get out of the sex game.

Themes, Issues, and Ideas

1. What does Paglia say is the primary cause of rape? What, according to her, do feminists say is?

2. According to Paglia, "[w]omen who do not understand rape cannot defend themselves against it." Why should this be true? Explain your answer.

3. Common sense, prudence and caution, and self-awareness and self-control are what women need, according to Paglia, not "dumb French language theory" and "running to Mommy and Daddy on the campus grievance committee." What are the merits of this line of reasoning? What are its flaws? Write a balanced essay in which you neither support nor deny Paglia's points, but rather consider them in an objective way.

Writing Strategies and Techniques

1. What does Paglia accomplish by saying "dumb French language theory" instead of "post-structuralist discourse"?

2. What is the effect of Paglia's first sentence? Do you feel when you are reading the essay that Paglia is really concerned with rape as a danger?

Suggestions for Writing

1. Write an essay in which you reply to Paglia without using or referring to any of the arguments she brings up in this reading.

2. Write an essay agreeing or disagreeing with Paglia's description of men. Use examples from your own experience.

Feminism—It's a Black Thang!

bell hooks

During the 1960s, two major social movements were at work: women's liberation and the civil rights struggle. As Gloria Steinem's essay suggested, however, there was little overlap between the two causes and often some friction. To this day, bell hooks suggests, the progress of the two movements has stayed separate. In "Feminism—It's a Black Thang!" she suggests some good reasons for changing the status quo.

bell hooks is a cultural critic who is based in Ohio. Her books include Black Looks: Race and Representation *(1992) and* Ain't I a Woman: Black Women and Feminism *(1981), among many others.*

It is obvious that most Black men are not in positions that allow them to exert the kind of institutionalized patriarchal power and control over Black women's lives that privileged white men do in this society. But it is undeniable that they do exert a lot of power over Black women and children in everyday life. Most of us are, however, reluctant to admit that male domination causes much of the gender conflict and pain experienced in Black women's lives.

Whether a man demands that "his" woman turn her signed paycheck over to him or forces his female companion to do the "wild thing" without a condom (because "the condom hurts" him), such assertions of power are sexist and abusive. And even if Black women do not have to face the sexist threats of male domination in the home, all too often when we walk down the streets, it is the brothers, not white men, who address us with sexual taunts. And if we do not respond, they become hostile and scream epithets at us like "Bitch, you think you too good to speak to me?" And when sexist incidents like this occur, Black women feel afraid—afraid that we may be hit, raped, robbed or some combination of the above.

Yet in spite of the fact that thousands of Black women are assaulted by Black males on the street or in the home every day, in most of these cases our male offenders do not believe that they've done anything wrong. Note recent conversations among Black folks about the Tyson case, where, by and large, men and women tend to see the woman as guilty, even though Tyson's own public history reveals him to be a man who has consistently abused women.

It is also no comfort to any of us that so much Black popular music—especially the growing subgenre of woman-hating rap—encourages Black males and every other listener to think there is nothing wrong with abusing women in general, and Black women in particular. That a Black male rap group like N.W.A. can become richer and even more famous than they already are by pushing woman-bashing lyrics is a sign of how dangerous these times are for women. And if any of us should think the boys are just having a little fun at our expense, we should take note of the fact that one of the group members is being sued for assaulting Black female television host Dee Barnes in an L.A. club. He has responded by bragging in *Rolling Stone:* "It ain't no big thing—I just threw her through a door." Let's face it, abusive Black male domination of Black women and children is so much a regular part of everyday Black life that most Black folks do not take it seriously.

Every Black person concerned about our collective survival must acknowledge that sexism is a destructive force in Black life that cannot be effectively addressed without an organized political movement to change consciousness, behavior and institutions. What we need is a feminist revolution in Black life. But to have such a revolution, we must first have a feminist movement.

Many Black folks do not know what the word *feminism* means. They may think of it only as something having to do with white women's desire to share equal rights with white men. In reality, feminism is a movement to end *all* sexism and sexist oppression. The strategies necessary to achieve that end are many. We need to find ways to address the specific forms that sexism takes in our diverse communities. We must start by educating our communities—at the grass-roots level—as to what sexism is, how it is expressed in daily life and why it creates problems.

Today many Black women and men are afraid that if we say that we support feminist movements, we will either be seen as traitors to the race or be privately or publicly humiliated by other Black people. In the past few months I have talked at colleges around the country where young Black men are physically threatening and even assaulting Black female students for criticizing and resisting Black male sexism, for starting Black female consciousness-raising support groups and even for taking women's studies classes.

A feminist movement that addresses the needs of Black women, men and children can strengthen our bonds with one another, deepen our sense of community and further Black liberation. We must not be afraid to create such a movement.

Themes, Issues, and Ideas

1. The abuse that hooks describes black women as taking from black men is very dramatic and obvious. Why do you think it would need to be addressed only now, thirty years after the women's movement began to change American life?

2. Hooks talks about creating a "feminist movement that addresses the needs of black women, men and children." What goals might such a movement have?

Writing Strategies and Techniques

1. The essay begins with hooks speaking about black women and black men. Then she begins to use the first person ("Most of us . . ."). What purpose does this technique serve?

2. Throughout hooks's essay, "Black" is capitalized. What impact does this have, grammatically and politically?

3. Throughout her essay, hooks mixes an academic style ("The strategies necessary to achieve that end are many") with more down-to-earth idioms ("Let's face it . . . most Black folks do not take [abuse] seriously.") Why does she do this?

Suggestions for Writing

1. Write an essay discussing some sexist elements of your own ethnic heritage, and how they might be addressed.

2. Do you think hooks is fair to black culture? Write an essay from the perspective of someone defending black culture.

MAKING CONNECTIONS

1. Gloria Steinem's awareness of the women's movement seems to have come about more dramatically than Betty Friedan's. What is the difference between both women's discoveries of the women's liberation movement?

2. For bell hooks, feminism is an empowering tool long resisted by black women. Would Camille Paglia agree with this interpretation? What is the difference between Paglia's and hooks's views of black womanhood? What are their differences concerning empowerment?

3. All the writers in this chapter in one way or another look toward the future. Write an essay that describes your own views on what women's lot might be in the twenty-first century.

4. Which of the authors in this chapter do you most admire as a writer? Which as a thinker? Compare two of the authors as writers and thinkers.

5. Who do you think does more for women: an idealistic feminist like Gloria Steinem or Betty Friedan, or a practical writer like Deborah Fallows or Camille Paglia? Explain your answer.

CHAPTER THREE

The Millennial Melting Pot

Race and Equality in America's Future

THE PAST AS PROLOGUE

I Have a Dream

Martin Luther King, Jr.

Martin Luther King, Jr. (1929–1968) was born in Atlanta, Georgia, and educated at Morehouse College, Crozer Theological Seminary, and Boston University. By 1954 he had begun to receive national attention for his civil rights policy of passive resistance. In 1964 he was awarded the Nobel Peace Prize. Four years later he was assassinated in Memphis, Tennessee.

King delivered "I Have a Dream" from the steps of the Lincoln Memorial in Washington, D.C., in 1963, the hundredth anniversary of the Emancipation Proclamation. The audience, over 200,000 people, had come to Washington to demonstrate for civil rights.

I am happy to join with you today in what will go down in history as the greatest demonstration for freedom in the history of our nation.

Five score years ago, a great American, in whose symbolic shadow we stand today, signed the Emancipation Proclamation. This momentous decree came as a great beacon light of hope to millions of Negro slaves who had been seared in the flames of withering injustice. It came as a joyous daybreak to end the long night of their captivity. But one hundred years later, the Negro still is not free. One hundred years later, the life of the Negro is still sadly crippled by the manacles of segregation and the chains of discrimination. One hundred years later, the Negro lives on a lonely island of poverty in the midst of a vast ocean of material prosperity. One hundred years later, the Negro is still anguished in the corners of American society and finds himself in exile in his own land. And so we have come here today to dramatize a shameful condition.

In a sense we have come to our nation's capital to cash a check. When the architects of our republic wrote the magnificent words of the Constitution and the Declaration of Independence, they were signing a promissory note to which every American was to fall heir. This note was the promise that all men— yes, black men as well as white men—would be guaranteed the inalienable rights of life, liberty, and the pursuit of happiness.

It is obvious today that America has defaulted on this promissory note insofar as her citizens of color are concerned. Instead of honoring this sacred obligation, America has given the Negro people a bad check, a check which has come back marked "insufficient funds." But we refuse to believe that the bank of justice is bankrupt. We refuse to believe that there are insufficient funds in the great vaults of opportunity of this nation; and so we have come to cash this check, a check that will give us upon demand the riches of freedom and the security of justice.

We have also come to this hallowed spot to remind America of the fierce urgency of *now*. This is no time to engage in the luxury of cooling off or to take the tranquilizing drug of gradualism. *Now* is the time to make real the promises of democracy. *Now* is the time to rise from the dark and desolate valley of segregation to the sunlit path of racial justice. *Now* is the time to lift our nation from the quicksands of racial injustice to the solid rock of brotherhood. *Now* is the time to make justice a reality for all of God's children.

It would be fatal for the nation to overlook the urgency of the moment. This sweltering summer of the Negro's legitimate discontent will not pass until there is an invigorating autumn of freedom and equality. Nineteen sixty-three is not an end, but a beginning. And those who hope that the Negro needed to blow off steam and will now be content will have a rude awakening if the nation returns to business as usual. There will be neither rest nor tranquility in America until the Negro is granted his citizenship rights. The whirlwinds of revolt will continue to shake the foundations of our nation until the bright day of justice emerges.

But there is something that I must say to my people who stand on the warm threshold which leads into the palace of justice. In the process of gaining our rightful place, we must not be guilty of wrongful deeds. Let us not seek to satisfy our thirst for freedom by drinking from the cup of bitterness and hatred. We must forever conduct our struggle on the high plane of dignity and discipline. We must not allow our creative protest to degenerate into physical violence. Again and again we must rise to the majestic heights of meeting physical force with soul force. And the marvelous new militancy which has engulfed the Negro community must not lead us to a distrust of all white people; for many of our white brothers, as evidenced by their presence here today, have come to realize that their destiny is tied up with our destiny, and they have come to realize that their freedom is inextricably bound to our freedom.

We cannot walk alone. And as we walk we must make the pledge that we shall always march ahead. We cannot turn back. There are those who are asking the devotees of civil rights, "When will you be satisfied?" We can never be satisfied as long as the Negro is the victim of the unspeakable horrors of police brutality. We can never be satisfied as long as our bodies, heavy with the fatigue of travel, cannot gain lodging in the motels of the highways and the hotels of the cities. We cannot be satisfied as long as the Negro's basic mobility is from a smaller ghetto to a larger one. We can never be satisfied as long as our children are stripped of their selfhood and robbed of their dignity by signs stating "For Whites Only." We cannot be satisfied as long as the Negro in Mississippi cannot vote and a Negro in New York believes he has nothing for which to vote. No, no, we are not satisfied, and we will not be satisfied until justice rolls down like waters and righteousness like a mighty stream.

I am not unmindful that some of you have come here out of great trials and tribulations. Some of you have come fresh from narrow jail cells. Some of you have come from areas where your quest for freedom left you battered by the storms of persecution and staggered by the winds of police brutality. You have been the veterans of creative suffering. Continue to work with the faith that unearned suffering is redemptive.

Go back to Mississippi, and go back to Alabama. Go back to South Carolina. Go back to Georgia. Go back to Louisiana. Go back to the slums and ghettos of our Northern cities, knowing that somehow this situation can and will be changed. Let us not wallow in the valley of despair.

I say to you today, my friends, even though we face the difficulties of today and tomorrow, I still have a dream. It is a dream deeply rooted in the American dream. I have a dream that one day this nation will rise up and live out the true meaning of its creed: "We hold these truths to be self-evident, that all men are created equal." I have a dream that one day, on the red hills of Georgia, sons of former slaves and the sons of former slave owners will be able to sit down together at the table of brotherhood. I have a dream that one day even the state of Mississippi, a state sweltering with the heat of injustice, sweltering with the heat of oppression, will be transformed into an oasis of freedom and justice. I have a dream that my four little children will one day live in a nation where they will not be judged by the color of their skin, but by the content of their character.

I have a dream today. I have a dream that one day down in Alabama—with its vicious racists, with its governor's lips dripping with the words of interposition and nullification—one day right there in Alabama, little black boys and black girls will be able to join hands with little white boys and white girls as sisters and brothers.

I have a dream today. I have a dream that one day every valley shall be exalted and every hill and mountain shall be made low, the rough places will be made plain and the crooked places will be made straight, and the glory of the Lord shall be revealed, and all flesh shall see it together.

This is our hope. This is the faith that I go back to the South with. And with this faith we will be able to hew out of the mountain of despair a stone of hope. With this faith we will be able to transform the jangling discords of our nation into a beautiful symphony of brotherhood. With this faith we will be able to work together, to play together, to struggle together, to go to jail together, to stand up for freedom together, knowing that we will be free one day.

And this will be the day—this will be the day when all of God's children will be able to sing with new meaning:

> My country, 'tis of thee,
> Sweet land of liberty,
>   Of thee I sing;
> Land where my fathers died,
> Land of the Pilgrims' pride,
> From every mountainside
>   Let freedom ring.

And if America is to be a great nation, this must become true.

And so let freedom ring from the prodigious hilltops of New Hampshire. Let freedom ring from the mighty mountains of New York. Let freedom ring from the heightening Alleghenies of Pennsylvania. Let freedom ring from the snow-capped Rockies of Colorado. Let freedom ring from the curvaceous slopes of California.

But not only that. Let freedom ring from Stone Mountain of Georgia. Let freedom ring from Lookout Mountain of Tennessee. Let freedom ring from every hill and molehill of Mississippi. "From every mountainside let freedom ring."

And when it happens—when we allow freedom to ring, when we let it ring from every village and every hamlet, from every state and every city—we will be able to speed up that day when all of God's children, black men and white men, Jews and Gentiles, Protestants and Catholics, will be able to join hands and sing in the words of the old Negro spiritual: "Free at last! Free at last! Thank God Almighty. We are free at last!"

Themes, Issues, and Ideas

1. Where and how does King allude to Abraham Lincoln in his speech? What effects are created by the allusions?

2. King's speech stirs the emotions, but it also employs reasoning and argumentation. How does King argue against resorting to physical violence, for example?

3. Where and how does King combine appeals to patriotism with criticism of his country? What kind of language expresses the patriotic themes? What kind of language expresses his criticism?

Writing Strategies and Techniques

1. In his speech King deals with the past, the present, and the future. What portion of his attention does he direct to each?

2. King often repeats words or phrases in succeeding sentences. When do the repetitions occur and how are they related to the content? Try rewriting a section to avoid repetition, then compare the effects.

Suggestions for Writing

1. King's speech often refers to other writing, such as the Emancipation Proclamation and a patriotic song. Write an essay describing how and why King uses these examples to make his points.

2. Write an essay describing how relevant you think King's speech will be at the turn of this century.

The Ballot or the Bullet

Malcolm X

Malcolm X was born Malcolm Little in 1925 in Omaha, Nebraska. After dropping out of high school, he was convicted of burglary at the age of 21 and sent to prison. There, he taught himself to read by copying the entire dictionary in longhand. While in prison he also converted to Islam, and upon his release adopted the name X to protest his legal status as the descendant of slaves. Malcolm X became a firebrand, and rivaled Martin Luther King, Jr., as a black leader. Militant and lucid, Malcolm possessed the religious austerity and conviction of a devoted Muslim. His appreciation of Islam as a world religion, among other things, led to his break with the Black Muslims, a radical organization. He was assassinated at the Audubon Ballroom in New York's Harlem on February 21, 1965

The following excerpt is from Malcolm X's speech "The Ballot or the Bullet" which he delivered in early 1964.

If we don't do something real soon, I think you'll have to agree that we're going to be forced either to use the ballot or the bullet. It's one or the other in 1964. It isn't that time is running out—time has run out! 1964 threatens to be the most explosive year America has ever witnessed. The most explosive year. Why? It's also a political year. It's the year when all of the white politicians will be back in the so-called Negro community jiving you and me for some votes. The year when all of the white political crooks will be right back in your and my community with their false promises, building up our hopes for a letdown, with their trickery and their treachery, with their false promises which they don't intend to keep. As they nourish these dissatisfactions, it can only lead to one thing, an explosion; and now we have the type of black man on the scene in America today—I'm sorry, Brother Lomax—who just doesn't intend to turn the other cheek any longer.

Don't let anybody tell you anything about the odds are against you. If they draft you, they send you to Korea and make you face 800 million Chinese. If you can be brave over there, you can be brave right here. These odds aren't as great as those odds. And if you fight here, you will at least know what you're fighting for.

I'm not a politician, not even a student of politics; in fact, I'm not a student of much of anything. I'm not a Democrat, I'm not a Republican, and I don't even consider myself an American. If you and I were Americans, there'd be no problem. Those Hunkies that just got off the boat, they're already Americans; Polacks are already Americans; the Italian refugees are already Americans. Everything that came out of Europe, every blue-eyed thing, is already an American. And as long as you and I have been over here, we aren't Americans yet.

Well, I am one who doesn't believe in deluding myself. I'm not going to sit at your table and watch you eat, with nothing on my plate, and call myself a diner. Sitting at the table doesn't make you a diner, unless you eat some of what's on that plate. Being here in America doesn't make you an American. Being born here in America doesn't make you an American. Why, if birth made you American, you wouldn't need any legislation, you wouldn't need any amendments to the Constitution, you wouldn't be faced with civil-rights filibustering in Washington, D.C., right now. They don't have to pass civil-rights legislation to make a Polack an American.

No, I'm not an American. I'm one of the 22 million black people who are the victims of Americanism. One of the 22 million black people who are the victims of democracy, nothing but disguised hypocrisy. So, I'm not standing here speaking to you as an American, or a patriot, or a flag-saluter, or a flag-waver—no, not I. I'm speaking as a victim of this American system. And I see America through the eyes of the victim. I don't see any American dream; I see an American nightmare. . . .

Last but not least, I must say this concerning the great controversy over rifles and shotguns. The only thing that I've ever said is that in areas where the government has proven itself either unwilling or unable to defend the lives and the property of Negroes, it's time for Negroes to defend themselves. Article number two of the constitutional amendments provides you and me the right to own a rifle or a shotgun. It is constitutionally legal to own a shotgun or a rifle. This doesn't mean you're going to get a rifle and form battalions and go out looking for white folks, although you'd be within your rights—I mean, you'd be justified; but that would be illegal and we don't do anything illegal. If the white man doesn't want the black man buying rifles and shotguns, then let the government do its job. That's all. And don't let the white man come to you and ask you what you think about what Malcolm says—why, you old Uncle Tom. He would never ask you if he thought you were going to say, "Amen!" No, he is making a Tom out of you.

So, this doesn't mean forming rifle clubs and going out looking for people, but it is time, in 1964, if you are a man, to let that man know. If he's not going to do his job in running the government and providing you and me with the protection that our taxes are supposed to be for, since he spends all those billions for his defense budget, he certainly can't begrudge you and me spending $12 or $15 for a single-shot, or double-action. I hope you understand. Don't go out shooting people, but any time, brothers and sisters, and especially the men in this audience—some of you wearing Congressional Medals of Honor, with shoulders this wide, chests this big, muscles that big—any time you and I sit around and read where they bomb a church and murder in cold blood, not some grownups, but four little girls while they were praying to the same god the white man taught them to pray to, and you and I see the government go down and can't find who did it.

Why, this man—he can find Eichmann hiding down in Argentina somewhere. Let two or three American soldiers, who are minding somebody else's business way over in South Vietnam, get killed, and he'll send battleships, sticking his nose in their business. He wanted to send troops down to Cuba and make them have what he calls free elections—this old cracker who doesn't have free elections in his own country. No, if you never see me another time in your life, if I die in the morning, I'll die saying one thing: the ballot or the bullet, the ballot or the bullet.

If a Negro in 1964 has to sit around and wait for some cracker senator to filibuster when it comes to the rights of black people, why, you and I should hang our heads in shame. You talk about a march on Washington in 1963, you haven't seen anything. There's some more going down in '64. And this time they're not going like they went last year. They're not going singing "We Shall Overcome." They're not going with white friends. They're not going with placards already painted for them. They're not going with round-trip tickets. They're going with one-way tickets.

And if they don't want that non-nonviolent army going down there, tell them to bring the filibuster to a halt. The black nationalists aren't going to wait. Lyndon B. Johnson is the head of the Democratic Party. If he's for civil rights, let him go into the Senate next week and declare himself. Let him go in there right now and declare himself. Let him go in there and denounce the Southern branch of his party. Let him go in there right now and take a moral stand—right now, not later. Tell him, don't wait until election time. If he waits too long, brothers and sisters, he will be responsible for letting a condition develop in this country which will create a climate that will bring seeds up out of the ground with vegetation on the end of them looking like something these people never dreamed of. In 1964, it's the ballot or the bullet. Thank you.

Themes, Issues, and Ideas

1. What is Malcolm X's attitude toward government and society?

2. What is the point of the phrase "the ballot or the bullet?" Why does Malcolm X repeat it several times throughout this selection?

3. Compare and contrast Malcolm X's view with Martin Luther King, Jr.'s.

Writing Strategies and Techniques

1. This reading, like Dr. King's, was taken from a speech. How can you tell that this selection was meant for oral recitation?

2. Where Martin Luther King, Jr., speaks of a dream, Malcolm X speaks of a nightmare. How do their styles reflect a dream and a nightmare, respectively?

Suggestions for Writing

1. Write an essay comparing "The Ballot or the Bullet" and "I Have a Dream." Without choosing sides, answer the following questions: Which speech is more effective? Which was more relevant at the time of writing? Which means more to you? Which has more relevance to the twenty-first century?

2. Do you consider yourself an American? What do you hold as the minimum definition of an "American?"

The Arc of the Moral Universe Is Long, but It Bends Toward Justice

Maya Angelou

Maya Angelou is a poet, playwright, and author of several autobiographical works including I Know Why the Caged Bird Sings *and* The Heart of a Woman. *President Clinton selected her to compose a poem for his inaugura-tion, which she read at the ceremony in January of 1993. She is currently the Z. Smith Reynolds Professor of Ameri-can Studies at Wake Forest University and continues to maintain a place as one of the most celebrated women in American letters.*

This essay was taken from a special issue of New Perspectives Quarterly, *in which a number of noted black intellectuals were asked to comment on the racial climate of our times.*

Look at two fragments of American history: Selma 1965 and Los Angeles 1991. After the successful Selma march, President Johnson and key congressional leaders assured Dr. Martin Luther King that a strong voting rights bill would be enacted quickly. But first, marchers had to suffer the infamous attack by the police and state troopers at the Edmund Pettus Bridge, and bear the murders of several of their fellow civil rights marchers.

In the 26 years that have passed since Selma, one salient step has been taken: American politicians are no longer attacking black Amer-ica by supporting discriminatory laws or heinous crimes like lynching or other types of murder. Today, the number of politicians who openly attack blacks seems to have diminished.

This is an enormous change, particularly when one considers that the actions of politicians reflect the desires of the people. I agree with philosophers from Euripides to Locke who say that people deserve the leaders they have. Americans deserved the politicians that gave them the police and state troopers in Selma. And we must see hope in the fact that those photographs coming out of Selma—of the police dog leaping toward the genitalia of the young black man—horrified a nation and provoked a change. Americans could have heard about the police brutality in Selma and not been so moved, but seeing it really embarrassed a large portion of the population—not all, but a large portion.

That event changed America, and the politicians that refused to change were taken out of office.

Visual Aid: Fighting our Invisibility

For the most part, white Americans before Selma were not unlike Germans during the 1930s—both could still turn their heads and pretend not to see what was going on in their country. Jews and blacks were invisible, beaten members of society. By the 1940s in Germany, however, I don't believe any German was unaware of what was happening. In the US, until as late as 1957, for the most part, blacks were invisible and the cruelties foisted upon them were absolutely ignorable. Whites who did not consider themselves prejudiced did not think anything of sitting in the front of the bus and seeing the majority of people standing in the back because they were black.

Blacks in the US are no longer invisible. They have emerged, though not always positively, into the vision of whites. I say "not always positively" in the sense that a number of whites now see blacks, but only as a threat to their safety or their jobs. But at least they see them.

The young man who captured the beating of Rodney King on videotape is an embryonic historian. He, like the photographers in Selma, helped keep our plight in view; helped us fight our invisibility. The bestiality captured on film has affected all who would like to claim themselves apart from those baton-wielding police.

Without the film, we might have been able to deny our own bestiality, but seeing it allowed us to face our barbarism and run from it; to seek shelter in the horror we felt viewing that scene; to come closer to our own humanity.

Slow vs. Fast Temperament

There is a natural, slow temperament in the body of those who are not themselves being harassed, imprisoned, segregated or abused.

And there is a rapid temperament which inhabits those who are aware of social and political discrepancies, whether those discrepancies affect their own conditions or not. The fact that people become heros and sheroes can be credited to their ability to identify and empathize with "the other." These men and women could continue to live quite comfortably with their slow temperament, but they chose not to. They make the decision to be conscious of the other—the homeless and the hopeless, the downtrodden and oppressed. Heroism has nothing to do with skin color or social status. It is a state of mind and a willingness to act for what is right and just.

If we don't say enough about these heroes—those who went before us and acted in a heartful way—our young people will be discouraged from trying to do what is right. It is important to claim as part of our heritage the good actions and the victories they engendered.

Young black men and women in this country must see and understand that there have been changes since Selma or they will be hell-bent on their own suicide mission. We must have an answer when they say, "you mean to tell me that with the sacrifice of Martin Luther King and Malcolm X and Medgar Evers there *still* have been no changes? Well, then why the hell am I fighting?"

To contend that there have been no changes is as stultifying and crippling as saying that racism no longer exists and that if you're suffering, it's your fault.

An American Martyr

I sympathize with Rodney King. But I will say this: Someone had to be Rodney King. Someone had to force us to begin the next phase of our national morality play. We have always needed martyrs. I am just sorry it was Rodney King.

However, I will not go so far as to say that this incident will herald a new era of national introspection. Unfortunately, we Americans do high-wire walking much better than we engage in introspection. Yet the distinct and powerful stench this incident has released over our collective self-image will not diminish quickly. It might even have the power to hold some of our viciousness, our bestiality, in check for a while.

Rodney King's isn't a story of an individual American being denied basic human rights but the story of America. It is the story of black and white and Asian and native American. The violence, the secret, furtive, collective, cave-man, good-old-boy, sexual—not just sensual, but sexual—violence is America.

When one notes that 57 percent of the white residents of Los Angeles polled responded that they were in support of the Los Angeles chief of police, they were responding in self-defense. These whites were not saying they were *for* the beating; they were saying they were for their protector. There is a difference. Their answer indicates that they are afraid to give away their mercenary. And Chief Gates, for them, is their mercenary. He is the person they have entrusted to protect their streets, their homes. Their response has nothing to do with perfidy. It has everything to do with self-defense.

I have little hope for any splendid, rapid rapprochement between the races. There is a large percentage of middle-class blacks and whites who are able to speak enough of the same language to communicate and even love each other. However, I am sorry to say that the unworking and working class of both races have not had the advantages of learning the language that could afford them the possibility of exchanging dialogue. Those unworking and working-class whites who think all they have is their skin color—no future, no career, no pride in past, no pride in present—will find the back of a black man or woman to give them a boost up. And a black man who has seen no kindness from whites and no effort from whites and no effort to include him in the larger polity will say, "there's nothing a white man can do but show me how far below him the black man is." This is the beginning of silence; a long and dangerous silence.

Themes, Issues, and Ideas

1. What do you think Angelou means by slow and fast temperaments? Is this phrase a descriptive one? What do "slow" and "fast" refer to?

2. Angelou says that "I am sorry to say the unworking and working class of both races have not had the advantages of learning the language that could afford them the possibility of exchanging dialogue." What language is it that Angelou is thinking of? Do you accept her statement that miscommunication is at the heart of racism?

3. "The violence, the secret, furtive, collective, cave-man, good-old-boy, sexual—not just sensual, but sexual—violence is America." What does this phrase mean? What are its basic premises? Do you agree?

Writing Strategies and Techniques

1. The title of this essay is long and poetic. Do you think it fits the subject? What might an alternative title be? Do you think this essay would be served better by a brief, succinct title, or by a long poetic one such as the one Angelou has given it?

2. Angelou credits photojournalism with making America aware of its "bestiality." Can prose such as Angelou's help to accomplish the same task? Why or why not? What are some other artistic styles that might accomplish this?

Suggestions for Writing

1. Write an essay in which you discuss the same issues as Angelou, but from a different perspective and in a different style. Imagine that your essay will be appearing next to hers in a national magazine.

2. Compare Maya Angelou's perspective to Malcolm X's. Which do you find more appealing? Which more accurate?

Mother Tongue

Amy Tan

As different races mix and collide in the American melting pot, one of the most important issues is bound to be language. Traditionally, English has been the first mode of assimilation for immigrants in America, and in this reading Amy Tan describes some of the differences between a first- and second-generation Chinese-American's use of English. Is there really only one English, the English of the SATs? Tan suggests otherwise in "Mother Tongue."

Tan, born in 1952, is the author of The Joy Luck Club, The Kitchen God's Wife, *and other stories of Chinese-American life.*

I am not a scholar of English or literature. I cannot give you much more than personal opinions on the English language and its variations in this country or others.

I am a writer. And by that definition, I am someone who has always loved language. I am fascinated by language in daily life. I spend a great deal of my time thinking about the power of language—the way it can evoke an emotion, a visual image, a complex idea, or a simple truth. Language is the tool of my trade. And I use them all—all the Englishes I grew up with.

Recently, I was made keenly aware of the different Englishes I do use. I was giving a talk to a large group of people, the same talk I had already given to half a dozen other groups. The nature of the talk was about my writing, my life, and my book, *The Joy Luck Club.* The talk was going along well enough, until I remembered one major difference that made the whole talk sound wrong. My mother was in the room. And it was perhaps the first time she had heard me give a lengthy speech, using the kind of English I had never used with her. I was saying things like, "The intersection of memory upon imagination" and "There is an aspect of my fiction that relates to thus-and-thus"—a speech filled with carefully wrought grammatical phrases, burdened, it suddenly seemed to me, with nominalized forms, past perfect tenses, conditional phrases, all the forms of standard English I did not use at home with my mother.

Just last week, I was walking down the street with my mother, and I again found myself conscious of the English I was using, the English I do use with her. We were talking about the price of new and used furniture and I heard myself saying this: "Not waste money that way." My husband was with us as well, and he didn't notice any switch in my English. And then I realized why. It's because over the twenty years we've been together I've often used that same kind of English with him, and sometimes he even uses it with me. It has become our language of intimacy, a different sort of English that relates to family talk, the language I grew up with.

So you'll have some idea of what this family talk I heard sounds like, I'll quote what my mother said during a recent conversation which I videotaped and then transcribed. During this conversation, my mother was talking about a political gangster in Shanghai who had the same last name as her family's, Du, and how the gangster in his early years wanted to be adopted by her family, which was rich by comparison. Later, the gangster became more powerful, far richer than my mother's family, and one day showed up at my mother's wedding to pay his respects. Here's what she said in part:

"Du Yusong having business like fruit stand. Like off the street kind. He is Du like Du Zong—but not Tsung-ming Island people. The local people call putong, the river east side, he belong to that side local people. That man want to ask Zu Dong father take him in like become own family. Du Zong father wasn't look down on him, but didn't take seriously, until that man big like become a mafia. Now important person, very hard to inviting him. Chinese way, came only to show respect, don't stay for dinner. Respect for making big celebration, he shows up. Mean gives lots of respect. Chinese custom. Chinese social life that way. If too important won't have to stay too long. He come to my wedding. I didn't see, I heard it. I gone to boy's side, they have YMCA dinner. Chinese age I was nineteen."

You should know that my mother's expressive command of English belies how much she actually understands. She reads the *Forbes* report, listens to *Wall Street Week,* converses daily with her stockbroker, reads all of Shirley MacLaine's books with ease—all kinds of things I can't begin to understand. Yet some of my friends tell me they understand 50 percent of what my mother says. Some say they understand 80 or 90 percent. Some say they understand none of it, as if she were speaking pure Chinese. But to me, my mother's English is perfectly clear, perfectly natural. It's my mother's tongue. Her language, as I hear it, is vivid, direct, full of observation and imagery. That was the language that helped shape the way I saw things, expressed things, made sense of the world.

Lately, I've been giving more thought to the kind of English my mother speaks. Like others, I have described it to people as "broken" or "fractured" English. But I wince when I say that. It has always bothered me that I can think of no other way to describe it other than "broken," as if it were damaged and needed to be fixed, as if it lacked a certain wholeness and soundness. I've heard other terms used, "limited English," for example. But they seem just as bad, as if everything is limited, including people's perceptions of the limited English speaker.

I know this for a fact, because when I was growing up, my mother's "limited" English limited *my* perception of her. I was ashamed of her English. I believed that her English reflected the quality of what she had to say. That is, because she expressed them imperfectly her thoughts were imperfect. And I had plenty of empirical evidence to support me: the fact that people in department stores, at banks, and at restaurants did not take her seriously, did not give her good service, pretended not to understand her, or even acted as if they did not hear her.

My mother has long realized the limitations of her English as well. When I was fifteen, she used to have me call people on the phone to pretend I was she. In this guise, I was forced to ask for information or even to complain and yell at people who had been rude to her. One time it was a call to her stockbroker in New York. She had cashed out her small portfolio and it just so happened we were going to go to New York the next week, our very first trip outside California. I had to get on the phone and say in an adolescent voice that was not very convincing, "This is Mrs. Tan."

And my mother was standing in the back whispering loudly, "Why he don't send me check, already two weeks late. So mad he lie to me, losing me money."

And then I said in perfect English, "Yes, I'm getting rather concerned. You had agreed to send the check two weeks ago, but it hasn't arrived."

Then she began to talk more loudly. "What he want, I come to New York tell him front of his boss, you cheating me?"And I was trying to calm her down, make her be quiet, while telling the stockbroker, "I can't tolerate any more excuses. If I don't receive the check immediately, I am going to have to speak to your manager when I'm in New York next week." And sure enough, the following week there we were in front of this astonished stockbroker, and I was sitting there red-faced and quiet, and my mother, the real Mrs. Tan, was shouting at his boss in her impeccable broken English.

We used a similar routine just five days ago, for a situation that was far less humorous. My mother had gone to the hospital for an appointment, to find out about a benign brain tumor a CAT scan had revealed a month ago. She said she had spoken very good English, her best English, no mistakes. Still, she said, the hospital did not apologize when they said they had lost the CAT scan and she had come for nothing. She said they did not seem to have any sympathy when she told them she was anxious to know the exact diagnosis, since her husband and son had both died of brain tumors. She said they would not give her any more information until the next time and she would have to make another appointment for that. So she said she would not leave until the doctor called her daughter. She wouldn't budge. And when the doctor finally called her daughter, me, who spoke in perfect English—lo and behold—we had assurances the CAT scan would be found, promises that a conference call on Monday would be held, and apologies for any suffering my mother had gone through for a most regrettable mistake.

I think my mother's English almost had an effect on limiting my possibilities in life as well. Sociologists and linguists probably will tell you that a person's developing language skills are more influenced by peers. But I do think that the language spoken in the family, especially in immigrant families which are more insular, plays a large role in shaping the language of the child. And I believe that it affected my results on achievement tests, IQ tests, and the SAT. While my English skills were never judged as poor, compared to math, English could not be considered my strong suit. In grade school I did moderately well, getting perhaps B's, sometimes B-pluses, in English and scoring perhaps in the sixtieth or seventieth percentile on achievement tests. But those scores were not good enough to override the opinion that my true abilities lay in math and science, because in those areas I achieved A's and scored in the ninetieth percentile or higher.

This was understandable. Math is precise; there is only one correct answer. Whereas, for me at least, the answers on English tests were always a judgment call, a matter of opinion and personal experience. Those tests were constructed around items like fill-in-the-blank sentence completion, such as, "Even though Tom was _____, Mary thought he was _____." And the correct answer always seemed to be the most bland combination of thoughts, for example, "Even though Tom was shy, Mary thought he was charming," with the grammatical structure "even though" limiting the correct answer to some sort of semantic opposites, so you wouldn't get answers like, "Even though Tom was foolish, Mary thought he was ridiculous." Well, according to my mother, there were very few limitations as to what Tom could have been and what Mary might have thought of him. So I never did well on tests like that.

The same was true with word analogies, pairs of words in which you were supposed to find some sort of logical, semantic relationship—for example, "*Sunset* is to *nightfall* as _____ is to _____." And here you would be presented with a list of four possible pairs, one of which showed the same kind of relationship: *red* is to *stoplight, bus* is to *arrival, chills* is to *fever, yawn* is to *boring*. Well, I could never think that way. I knew what the tests were asking, but I could not block out of my mind the images already created by the first pair, "*sunset* is to *nightfall*"—and I would see a burst of colors against a darkening sky, the moon rising, the lowering of a curtain of stars. And all the other pairs of words—red, bus, stoplight, boring—just threw up a mass of confusing images, making it impossible for me to sort out something as logical as saying: "A sunset precedes nightfall" is the same as "a chill precedes a fever." The only way I would have gotten that answer right would have been to imagine an associative situation, for example, my being disobedient and staying out past sunset, catching a chill at night, which turns into feverish pneumonia as punishment, which indeed did happen to me.

I have been thinking about all this lately, about my mother's English, about achievement tests. Because lately I've been asked, as a writer, why there are not more Asian Americans represented in American literature. Why are there few Asian Americans enrolled in creative writing programs? Why do so many Chinese students go into engineering? Well, these are broad sociological questions I can't begin to answer. But I have noticed in surveys—in fact, just last week— that Asian students, as a whole, always do significantly better on math achievement tests than in English. And this makes me think that there are other Asian-American students whose English spoken in the home might also be described as "broken" or "limited." And perhaps they also have teachers who are steering them away from writing and into math and science, which is what happened to me.

Fortunately, I happen to be rebellious in nature and enjoy the challenge of disproving assumptions made about me. I became an English major my first year in college, after being enrolled as premed. I started writing nonfiction as a freelancer the week after I was told by my former boss that writing was my worst skill and I should hone my talents toward account management.

But it wasn't until 1985 that I finally began to write fiction. And at first I wrote using what I thought to be wittily crafted sentences, sentences that would finally prove I had mastery over the English language. Here's an example from the first draft of a story that later made its way into *The Joy Luck Club,* but without this line: "That was my mental quandary in its nascent state." A terrible line, which I can barely pronounce.

Fortunately, for reasons I won't get into today, I later decided I should envision a reader for the stories I would write. And the reader I decided upon was my mother, because these were stories about mothers. So with this reader in mind—and in fact she did read my early drafts—I began to write stories using all the Englishes I grew up with: the English I spoke to my mother, which for lack of a better term might be described as "simple"; the English she used with me, which for lack of a better term might be described as "broken"; my translation of her Chinese, which could certainly be described as "watered down"; and what I imagined to be her translation of her Chinese if she could speak in perfect English, her internal language, and for that I sought to preserve the essence, but neither an English nor a Chinese structure. I wanted to capture what language ability tests can never reveal: her intent, her passion, her imagery, the rhythms of her speech and the nature of her thoughts.

Apart from what any critic had to say about my writing, I knew I had succeeded where it counted when my mother finished reading my book and gave me her verdict: "So easy to read."

Themes, Issues, and Ideas

1. Why does Tan think of her mother as a model reader? Do you think of a family member as a model reader? Do you have any model reader at all?

2. How many different kinds of English do you use in your daily life? What are the different strengths and weaknesses of these Englishes?

3. Is Tan's mother's English really as rich as Tan maintains, or is she being merely loyal and sentimental? Support your opinion with specific examples from the text and your own experience.

Writing Strategies and Techniques

1. Why does Tan begin the way she does? Is her opening statement borne out by her essay? Describe the effect her prose has on her argument.

2. Describe the use of humor in "Mother Tongue."

Suggestions for Writing

1. Write an essay about a friend or relative of yours who speaks in "broken" or "diluted" English.

2. Rewrite Tan's mother's story in three separate types of English, such as academic/intellectual English, "deadhead" English, black English, etc.

Barrio Boy

Ernesto Galarza

Part of ethnic identity comes from the areas immigrants live in: The more concentrated and isolated the area, the more cultural barriers arise. In "Barrio Boy," Ernesto Galarza describes what it was like to live in the Sacramento barrio, or ghetto, where he grew up.

Galarza graduated from Stanford and Columbia Universities in 1944, and then spent many years as a union organizer fighting for the rights of migrant workers. He taught elementary school and established some of the earliest programs in bilingual education. He published his autobiography in 1971, from which this reading is taken.

We found Americans as strange in their customs as they probably found us. Immediately we discovered that there were no *mercados* and that when shopping you did not put the groceries in a *chiquihuite*. Instead everything was in cans or in cardboard boxes or each item was put in a brown paper bag. There were neighborhood grocery stores at the corners and some big ones uptown, but no *mercado*. The grocers did not give children a *pilón*, they did not stand at the door and coax you to come in and buy, as they did in Mazatlán. The fruits and vegetables were displayed on counters instead of being piled up on the floor. The stores smelled of fly spray and oiled floors, not of fresh pineapple and limes.

Neither was there a plaza, only parks which had no bandstands, no concerts every Thursday, no Judases exploding on Holy Week, and no promenades of boys going one way and girls the other. There were no parks in the *barrio;* and the ones uptown were cold and rainy in winter, and in summer there was no place to sit except on the grass. When there were celebrations nobody set off rockets in the parks, much less on the street in front of your house to announce to the neighborhood that a wedding or a baptism was taking place. Sacramento did not have a *mercado* and a plaza with the cathedral to one side and the Palacio de Gobierno on another to make it obvious that there and nowhere else was the center of town.

It was just as puzzling that the Americans did not live in *vecindades,* like our block on Leandro Valle. Even in the alleys, where people knew one another better, the houses were fenced apart, without central courts to wash clothes, talk and play with the other children. Like the city, the Sacramento *barrio* did not have a place which was the middle of things for everyone.

In more personal ways we had to get used to the Americans. They did not listen if you did not speak loudly, as they always did. In the Mexican style, people would know that you were enjoying their jokes tremendously if you merely smiled and shook a little, as if you were trying to swallow your mirth. In the American style there was little difference between a laugh and a roar, and until you got used to them you could hardly tell whether the boisterous Americans were roaming mad or roaring happy. . . .

The older people of the *barrio,* except in those things which they had to do like the Americans because they had no choice, remained Mexican. Their language at home was Spanish. They were continuously taking up collections to pay somebody's funeral expenses or to help someone who had had a serious accident. Cards were sent to you to attend a burial where you would throw a handful of dirt on top of the coffin and listen to tearful speeches at the graveside. At every baptism a new *compadre* and a new *comadre* joined the family circle. New Year greeting cards were exchanged, showing angels and cherubs in bright colors sprinkled with grains of mica so that they glistened like gold dust. At the family parties the huge pot of steaming tamales was still the center of attention, the *atole* served on the side with chunks of brown sugar for sucking and crunching. If the party lasted long enough, someone produced a guitar, the men took over and the singing of *corridos* began.

In the *barrio* there were no individuals who had official titles or who were otherwise recognized by everybody as important people. The reason must have been that there was no place in the public business of the city of Sacramento for the Mexican immigrants. We only rented a corner of the city and as long as we paid the rent on time everything else was decided at City Hall or the County Court House, where Mexicans went only when they were in trouble. Nobody from the *barrio* ever ran for mayor or city councilman. For us the most important public officials were the policemen who walked their beats, stopped fights, and hauled drunks to jail in a paddy wagon we called *La Julia.*

The one institution we had that gave the *colonia* some kind of image was the *Comisión Honorífica,* a committee picked by the Mexican Consul in San Francisco to organize the celebration of the *Cinco de Mayo* and the Sixteenth of September, the anniversaries of the battle of Puebla and the beginning of our War of Independence. These were the two events which stirred everyone in the *barrio,* for what we were celebrating was not only the heroes of Mexico but also the feeling that we were still Mexicans ourselves. On these occasions there was a dance preceded by speeches and a concert. For both the *cinco* and the sixteenth queens were elected to preside over the ceremonies.

Between celebrations neither the politicians uptown nor the *Comisión Honorífica* attended to the daily needs of the *barrio.* This was done by volunteers—the ones who knew enough English to interpret in court, on a visit to the doctor, a call at the county hospital, and who could help make out a postal money order. By the time I had finished the third grade at the Lincoln School I was one of these volunteers. My services were not professional but they were free, except for the IOU's I accumulated from families who always thanked me with "God will pay you for it."

My clients were not *pochos,* Mexicans who had grown up in California, probably had even been born in the United States. They had learned to speak English of sorts and could still speak Spanish, also of sorts. They knew much more about the Americans than we did, and much less about us. The *chicanos* and the *pochos* had certain feelings about one another. Concerning the *pochos,* the *chicanos* suspected that they considered themselves too good for the *barrio* but were not, for some reason, good enough for the Americans. Toward the *chicanos,* the *pochos* acted superior, amused at our confusions but not especially interested in explaining them to us. In our family when I forgot my manners, my mother would ask me if I was turning *pochito.*

Turning *pocho* was a half-step toward turning American. And America was all around us, in and out of the *barrio.* Abruptly we had to forget the ways of shopping in a *mercado* and learn those of shopping in a corner grocery or in a department store. The Americans paid no attention to the Sixteenth of September, but they made a great commotion about the Fourth of July. In Mazatlán Don Salvador had told us, saluting and marching as he talked to our class, that the *Cinco de Mayo* was the most glorious date in human history. The Americans had not even heard about it.

Themes, Issues, and Ideas

1. What are some of the differences between Masatlán and Sacramento? How do the physical differences between the two cities reveal their differing cultural values?

2. Why do residents of the *barrio* feel isolated and alienated from the American culture around them?

3. What is the difference between *chicanos* and *pochos*? What seems to be the relationship between the two groups? What about the relationship between each group and the native Sacramentoans?

Writing Strategies and Techniques

1. How do you feel about the narrator of this essay? Is his a sympathetic voice? Give examples to support your view.

2. Galarza uses the words "we" and "they" very often throughout his essay. To which group does he seem to assume his reader belongs?

Suggestions for Writing

1. Write an essay about an experience in your childhood comparable to one in Galarza's. Have you ever experienced a cultural dislocation?

2. Respond to the implicit accusation that ends the essay.

Twice an Outsider: On Being Jewish and a Woman

Vivian Gornick

Vivian Gornick (b. 1935) has worked as a journalist for more than twenty years. Her articles and reviews have appeared in The Nation, The Village Voice, The Washington Post, The Atlantic, *and many other magazines and newspapers. She has also written five books, among them* Women in Science: Portraits from a World in Transition *(1983) and* Fierce Attachments: A Memoir *(1987).*

In "Twice an Outsider: On Being Jewish and a Woman," Gornick describes the discovery of her Jewishness, and then the gradual overshadowing of her Jewishness by her womanhood. Does being a minority take precedence over being a woman, or vice versa? Can both identities exist side by side? Gornick describes her answer to this question in the autobiographical essay below.

When I was growing up, the whole world was Jewish. The heroes were Jewish and the villains were Jewish. The landlord, the doctor, the grocer, your best friend, the village idiot, the neighborhood bully: all Jewish. We were working-class and immigrant as well, but that just came with the territory. Essentially, we were Jews on the streets of New York. We learned to be kind, cruel, smart, and feeling in a mixture of language and gesture that was part street slang, part grade-school English, part kitchen Yiddish. We learned about politics and society in much the same way: down the block were a few Orthodox Jews, up the block a few Zionists, in between a sprinkling of socialists. For the most part, people had no politics at all, only a cautious appetite for the goods of life. It was a small, tight, hyphenated world that we occupied, but I didn't know that; I thought it *was* the world.

One Sunday evening when I was eight years old my parents and I were riding in the back seat of my rich uncle's Buick. We had been out for a drive and now we were back in the Bronx, headed for home. Suddenly, another car sideswiped us. My mother and my aunt shrieked. My uncle swore softly. My father, in whose lap I was sitting, said out the window at the speeding car, "That's all right. Nothing but a bunch of kikes in here." In an instant I knew everything. I knew there was a world beyond our streets, and in that world my father was a humiliated man, without power or standing. By extension, we were all vulnerable out there; but *we* didn't matter so much. It was my father, my handsome, gentle father, who mattered. My heart burned for him. I burrowed closer in his lap, pressed myself against his chest. I wanted to warm the place in him that I was sure had grown cold when he called himself a kike.

That was in the middle of the Second World War—*the* watershed event for the men and women of my generation. No matter what your social condition, if you were a child growing up in the early 1940s you entered the decade destined for one kind of life and came out of it headed for another. For those of us who had gone into the war the children of intimidated inner-city Jews, 1945 signified an astonishing change in the atmosphere. The end of the war brought frozen food and nuclear fission, laundromats and anticommunists, Levittown and the breakup of the college quota system. The trolley tracks were torn up, and the streets paved over. Buses took you not only to other parts of the Bronx but into Manhattan as well. When my brother graduated from the Bronx High School of Science in 1947 my father said, "Now you can become a salesman." But my cousin Joey had been a bombardier in the Pacific and was now one of the elite: a returned GI at City College. My brother sat down with my father and explained that even though he was not a genius he had to go to college. It was his right and his obligation. My father stared at his son. Now we were in the new world.

When I was sixteen a girl in the next building had her nose straightened; we all trooped in to see Selma Shapiro lying in state, swathed in bandages from which would emerge a person fit for life beyond the block. Three buildings away a boy went downtown for a job, and on his application he wrote "Arnold Brown" instead of "Arnold Braunowitz." The news swept through the neighborhood like wildfire. A nose job? A name change? What was happening here? It was awful; it was wonderful. It was frightening; it was delicious. Whatever it was, it wasn't stasis. Things felt lively and active. Chutzpah was on the rise, passivity on the wane. We were going to run the gauntlet. That's what it meant to be in the new world. For the first time we could *imagine* ourselves out there.

But who exactly do I mean when I say we? I mean Arnie, not Selma. I mean my brother, not me. I mean the boys, not the girls. My mother stood behind me, pushing me forward. "The girl goes to college, too," she said. And I did. But my going to college would not mean the same thing as my brother's going to college, and we all knew it. For my brother, college meant getting from the Bronx to Manhattan. But for me? From the time I was fourteen I yearned to get out of the Bronx, but get out into *what?* I did not actually imagine myself a working person alone in Manhattan and nobody else did either. What I did imagine was that I would marry, and that the man I married would get me downtown. He would brave the perils of class and race, and somehow I'd be there alongside him.

The greater chain of social being obtained. Selma straightened her nose so that she could marry upward into the Jewish middle class. Arnie changed his name so that he could wedge himself into the Christian world. It was the boys who would be out there facing down the terrors of the word "kike," not the girls. The boys would run the gauntlet, for themselves and for us. We would be standing not beside them but behind them, egging them on. And because we knew we'd be behind them, we—the girls—never experienced ourselves directly as Jews. I never shivered inside with the fear of being called a kike. I remember that. Somehow I knew that if I were insulted in that way I might feel stunned, but the fear and shame would be once removed. I knew I'd run home to Arnie, and I'd say, "Arnie, they called me a kike," and he'd look miserable, and I'd say, "Do something!" and the whole matter would be out of my hands the minute I said "Do something." It was Arnie who'd have to stand up to the world, search his soul, test his feelings, discover his capacity for courage or action. Not me. And that is why Arnie grew up to become William Paley, and the other boys on the block—the ones who sneered and raged and trembled, who knew they'd have to run that gauntlet, get into that new world like it or not, and were smart and sensitive, and hated and feared and longed for it all—they grew up to become Philip Roth and Woody Allen. Me and Selma? We grew up to become women.

The confusion is historic; the distinction is crucial.

Woody Allen is exactly my age. I remember as though it were yesterday listening to Allen's first standup comic monologues in the late fifties at the Bitter End Café. We were all in our twenties, my friends and I and Allen. It was as though someone on the block had suddenly found it in himself to say to a world beyond the street, "Listen. You wanna know how it is? This is how it is," and with more courage than anxiety he had shaped our experience. This wasn't Milton Berle or Henny Youngman up there, a Borscht Belt comic speaking half Yiddish, half English, half outsiderness. No, this was one of us, describing how it felt to be our age and in our place: on the street, at a party, in the subway, at home in the Bronx or Brooklyn, and then out there, downtown, in the city. Half in, half out.

Philip Roth, of course, cut closer to the bone. His sentence structure deepened the experience, drove home better than Allen could the pain and the excitement, the intelligence and the anguish, the hilarity and the madness of getting so close you could touch it and *still* you weren't inside.

Behind Allen and Roth stood Saul Bellow, who made the words "manic" and "Jewish" synonymous, whose work glittered with a wild flood of feeling that poured from a river of language, all pent-up brilliance, the intelligence driven to an edge of hysteria that resembled Mel Brooks as much as it did Philip Roth. Although Bellow had been writing since the forties, it was only now in the fifties and sixties that his work and its meaning traveled down from a small community of intellectual readers to the reading populace at large. Here was a street-smart writing Jew who was actually extending the American language, using us—our lives, our idiom—to say something about American life that had not been said before. In the process, he gave us—me and my contemporaries—the equipment to define ourselves, and therefore become ourselves.

These men are on a continuum. From Milton Berle and Mel Brooks to Saul Bellow, Philip Roth, and Woody Allen—the subtle alterations of tone and voice among them constitute a piece of social history, chart a progress of the way Jews felt about themselves in America, embody a fine calibration of rage, resentment, and hunger.

My mother hated Milton Berle, and I understood why—he was hard to take. But I laughed against my will, and I knew he was the real thing. To see the idiom of your life coming back at you, shaped and enlarged by a line of humorous intelligence as compelling as a poem in the sustained nature of its thesis and context, was to experience one of life's deepest satisfactions. When that famous chord of recognition strikes, it is healing—illuminating and healing.

Milton Berle was my first experience of an artist's work applied to the grosser materials of my own environment. Berle, operating at a lower level of genius, was just as sinister as the Marx brothers. It was the wildness of his humor and the no-holds-barred atmosphere that it generated. Berle was coarse and vulgar, fast and furious, frightening in the speed of his cunning and his rage. My mother was repelled. She knew this was Jewish self-hatred at its most vicious.

Mel Brooks was more of the same, only ten years younger, and the ten years made a difference. A few years ago Brooks reminisced about how, when he began writing for Sid Caesar, his mother asked him how much money he was making, and he told her sixty dollars a week. He knew if he told her what he was really making she'd have a heart attack. "The heart," he said. "It would attack her." That story was for us: Woody Allen built on it. Brooks—also marked by a Borscht Belt coarseness that spoke to an uneducated sense of America, a lack of conversance with the larger culture—was still the shrewd, wild Jew talking, but his tone was a bit sadder, a bit quieter than Milton Berle's, less defended against the fears that dominated our lives. The lessened defense was the sign of change.

With Woody Allen, we passed through into a crucial stage of development. Allen built a persona, an identity, a body of work out of the idea of the mousy Jew who makes a fool of the gentile rather than of another Jew. This had not happened before. Its meaning was unmistakable.

The Woody Allen character is obsessed with getting laid. Every one else does it; he alone can't do it. Everywhere he goes—in the street, on the subway, at a party—he gazes mournfully at the golden shiksas all around him, always beyond reach. It's not a Jewish girl he's trying to get into bed; it's Diane Keaton. The Jewish girl is Brooklyn; Annie Hall is Manhattan.

And what does sexual success mean? It means everything. It means the defeat of all that life bitterly withholds, already characterized by the fact that one has been born a Jew instead of Humphrey Bogart. If Allen can just get that blue-eyed beauty into bed. He wants it so bad he's going to die of it. He's going to expire from this hunger right there before your eyes.

The humor turns on Allen's extraordinary ability to mock himself. He's as brilliant as Charlie Chaplin at making wonderful his own smallness. And he's as successful as Chaplin at making a hero of the little man, and a fool of the withholding world in the person of the pretty girl. When Diane Keaton wrings her hands and moans, "I can't," and Allen blinks like a rabbit and says, "Why? Because I'm Jewish?"—he accomplishes a minor miracle on the screen. The beautiful woman is made ridiculous. The golden shiksa has become absurd, inept, incapable: the insincere and the foolish cut down to size so that Allen can come up to size.

When was the first time I saw it? Which movie was it? I can't remember. I remember only that at one of them, in the early seventies, I suddenly found myself listening to the audience laugh hysterically while Allen made a dreadful fool of the girl on the screen, and I realized that he had to make a fool of her, that he would always have to make a fool of her, because she was the foil: the instrument of his unholy deprivation, the exasperating source of life's mean indifference. I said to myself, "This is dis-*gust*-ing," and as I said it I knew I'd been feeling this way all my life: from Milton Berle to Saul Bellow to Woody Allen. I had always laughed, but deep inside I'd frozen up, and now I saw why. Milton Berle with his mother-in-law jokes, Saul Bellow with the mistresses who hold out and the wives who do him in, Mel Brooks and Woody Allen with the girl always and only the carrot at the end of the stick. Every last one of them was trashing women. Using women to savage the withholding world. Using us. Their mothers, their sisters, their wives. To them, we weren't friends or comrades. We weren't even Jews or gentiles. We were just girls.

At that moment I knew that I would never again feel myself more of a Jew than a woman. I had never suffered as men did for being a Jew in a Christian world because, as a Jew, I had not known that I wanted the world. Now, as a woman, I knew I wanted the world and I suffered.

Hannah Arendt, watching the Nazis rise to power in Germany, had denied the meaning of her own Jewishness for a long time. When she acknowledged it, she did so by saying, "When one is attacked as a Jew, one must defend oneself *as a Jew.* Not as a German, not as a world-citizen, not as an upholder of the Rights of Man [emphasis in original]." I read that and I was ready to change the sentences to read, "When one is attacked as a woman, one must defend oneself *as a woman.* Not as a Jew, not as a member of the working class, not as a child of immigrants."

My father had to be Jewish; he had no choice. When he went downtown he heard "kike." I live downtown, and I do not hear "kike." Maybe it's there to be heard and I'm not tuned in, but it can't be there all that much if I don't hear it. I'm out in the world, and this is what I *do* hear:

I walk down the street. A working-class man puts his lips together and makes a sucking noise at me.

I enter a hardware store to purchase a lock. I choose one, and the man behind the counter shakes his head at me. "Women don't know how to use that lock," he says.

I go to a party in a university town. A man asks me what I do. I tell him I'm a journalist. He asks if I run a cooking page. Two minutes later someone asks me not if I have a husband but what my husband does.

I go to another party, a dinner party on New York's Upper West Side. I'm the only woman at the table who is not there as a wife. I speak a few sentences on the subject under discussion. I am not responded to. A minute later my thought is rephrased by one of the men. Two other men immediately address it.

Outsiderness is the daily infliction of social invisibility. From low-grade humiliation to life-threatening aggression, its power lies in the way one is seen, and how that in turn affects the way one sees oneself. When my father heard the word "kike" the life force within him shriveled. When a man on the street makes animallike noises at me, or when a man at a dinner table does not hear what I say, the same thing happens to me. This is what makes the heart pound and the head fill with blood. This is how the separation between world and self occurs. This is outsiderness alive in the daily way. It is here, on the issue of being a woman, not a Jew, that I must make my stand and hold my ground.

A few years ago I taught at a state university in a small Western town. One night at a faculty party a member of the department I was working in, a man of modest intelligence, said of another teacher who had aroused strong feeling in the department, "He's a smart Jew crashing about in all directions." I stared at this man, thinking, "How interesting. You *look* civilized." Then I said, quite calmly, "What a quaint phrase. In New York we don't hear ourselves described as smart Jews any more. Is that still current out here?" The man turned dull red, and the exchange was at an end.

A few weeks later at another party I saw this same man engaged in conversation with another member of the department, a woman. I knew this woman, and in my view her gifts of mind and spirit were comparable to the man's. She was not a scholar and he was not a scholar. She was not intellectual and neither was he. They were both hard-working university teachers. I watched the two standing together, talking. The woman gestured widely as she spoke, smiled inordinately, fingered her hair. Her eyes were bright; her tone was eager. She exclaimed; she enthused; she performed. The man stood there, pulling at a pipe, silent, motionless, his body slack, his face immobile, his entire being unreadable except for his eyes and his mouth: in them an expression of mockery and patronage as the woman grew ever more frantic in her need to gain a response. It was clear that the harder she tried, the more secure he felt. At a certain point it became obvious that he was deliberately withholding what he knew she needed. I was watching a ritual exchange of petition and denial predicated on a power structure that in this instance turned wholly on his maleness and her femaleness.

I watched these two for a long time, and as I watched I felt my throat tighten, my arms and legs begin to tingle, a kind of sick feeling spread through my chest and belly. I wanted to put her up against the wall, but I wanted to put him through the wall. I realized I'd been absorbing this kind of thing twenty times a day in this department, in this university, in this town; and it was making me ill.

This daily feeling, this awareness of the subtle ways in institutional life that the most ordinary men accord each other the simplest of recognitions and withhold these recognitions from the equally ordinary women with whom they work, is palpable, and it burns inside every woman who experiences it—whether she is aware of what is happening or has numbed herself to what is happening.

When I hear an anti-Semitic remark I am hurt, I am angered, but I am not frightened. I do not fear for my life or my livelihood or my right to pursue the open expression of my convictions. When I hear a sexist remark I feel all of the above. I feel that stomach-churning rage and pain that tells me that I am in trouble, that I am up against threat and wipeout. I am in the presence of something virulent in the social scheme directed against me not because of what I actually am but because of an immutable condition of birth. Something I might once have experienced as a Jew but today can feel only as a woman.

Bellow, Roth, Allen: these are writers who have had only the taste of their own lives as the stimulus for creative work—and a rich, lively taste it has been: tart and smart, full of bite and wisdom. But these writers were allowed to become so fabulously successful precisely because the stigma of Jewishness was fading even as they were recording it. When Bellow wrote *Herzog,* being Jewish was no longer the open wound it had been when he wrote *The Victim;* and by the time Allen and Roth were coming into their own they were far more integrated into the larger world than their work suggested. Therefore, for Allen or Roth to go on making the golden shiksa the foil, or for Bellow to keep portraying the Jewish intellectual who can't arrive as his foil, is tiresome and unpersuasive. It does not speak to the lives that any of us are now living. Such work strikes no chord of recognition; it strikes only chords of memory and sentiment. The thing about outsiderness is that one feels it in the flesh every day; one feels oneself invisible in the ordinary social way. These are requirements of the condition.

This invisibility once made Jews manic and blacks murderous. It works on women in a variety of ways:

I leaned across the counter in the hardware store and said to the man who had told me women didn't know how to use the lock I'd chosen, "Would you say that to me if I were black?" He stared lightly at me for a long moment. Then he nodded, "Gotcha," he said.

To the man at the university party I explained my work in great and careful detail. The man, a sixty-year-old Ivy Leaguer, was frankly puzzled at why I spoke of something fairly simple at such excessive length. I knew this was the first time he had heard what I was *really* saying, and I didn't expect it to sink in. What I did expect was that the next time he heard a woman speak these words, they would begin to take hold.

At the dinner party in New York I made a scene. I brought harmless sociability to an end. I insisted that everyone see that the little social murders committed between men and women were the real subtext of the evening, and that civilized converse was no longer possible unless this underlying truth was addressed. I did this because these were liberal intellectuals. They had heard it all before, many times, and *still* they did not get it. It was as terrible for me to go home that evening with the taste of ashes in my mouth as it was for everyone else—we had all come expecting the warm pleasures of good food and good conversation—but I couldn't have lived with myself that night if I hadn't spoken up. Just as I would have had to speak up if the conversation had suddenly turned politely anti-Semitic. Which it would not have in this company.

The Jewishness inside me is an education. I see more clearly, can think more inventively, because I can think analogously about "them" and "us." That particular knowledge of being one among the many is mine twice over. I have watched masters respond to "them" and "us," and I have learned. I wouldn't have missed being Jewish for the world. It lives in me as a vital subculture, enriching my life as a writer, as an American, and certainly as a woman.

Themes, Issues, and Ideas

1. Gornick begins her essay with a discovery. Is this discovery like the other ones she mentions later on? What makes it important enough to begin her essay with?

2. Gornick says she is "twice an outsider." Is this a fair description of her feelings as she articulates them here? What is her attitude toward those outside her position?

3. How would you characterize Gornick's resentment? What does it mean to be an "outsider?" Do you think her feelings are justified?

Writing Strategies and Techniques

1. Does Gornick impress you as being a likable person? What do you make of her offhand remarks about "shiksas," blacks, Jewish men, and people who cross her in public?

2. How do Gornick's descriptions of her physical sensations (". . . a sick feeling spread throughout my chest and belly," etc.) affect you as a reader?

Suggestions for Writing

1. Write a short script dramatizing one of the scenes from the reading.

2. Write an essay taking other male minority entertainers as examples of "outsider humor."

America as a Collage

Ryzsard Kapuscinski

Ryzsard Kapuscinski has spent most of the post–World War II years reporting on war and revolution in Africa, the Middle East, and Latin America. He has written a trilogy on dictators that covers Haile Selassie I of Ethiopia, Idi Amin of Uganda, and the last Shah of Iran. Being away from the United States frequently and being acquainted with social, ethnic, and racial conflicts in many cultures has given Kapuscinski a broader perspective on the social pressures facing the United States in the future. In this essay, commissioned by The New Perspectives Quarterly, *Kapuscinski finds the changing composition of the American melting pot not a source of social problems but a sign of a positive future and of the continuing vitality of the democratic experiment represented by the people and the government of the United States.*

The mere fact that America still attracts millions of people is evidence that it is not in decline. People aren't attracted to a place of decline. Signs of decline are sure to be found in a place as complex as America: debt, crime, the homeless, drugs, dropouts. But the main characteristic of America, the first and most enduring impression, is dynamism, energy, aggressiveness, forward movement.

It is so hard to think of this nation in decline when you know that there are vast regions of the planet which are absolutely paralyzed, incapable of any improvement at all.

It is difficult for me to agree with Paul Kennedy's thesis in *The Rise and Fall of Great Powers* that America must inevitably follow historical precedent. That's the way history used to be—all powerful nations declined and gave way to other empires. But maybe there is another way to look at what is happening. I have a sense that what is going on here concerns much more than the fate of a nation.

It may be that the Euro-centered American nation is declining as it gives way to a new Pacific civilization that will include, but not be limited to, America. Historically speaking, America may not decline, but instead fuse with the Pacific culture to create a kind of vast Pacific collage, a mix of Hispanic and Asian cultures linked through the most modern communication technologies.

Traditional history has been a history of nations. But here, for the first time since the Roman Empire, there is the possibility of creating the history of a civilization. Now is the first chance on a new basis with new technologies to create a civilization of unprecedented openness and pluralism. A civilization of the polycentric mind. A civilization that leaves behind forever the ethnocentric, tribal mentality. The mentality of destruction.

Los Angeles is a premonition of this new civilization.

Linked more to the Third World and Asia than to the Europe of America's racial and cultural roots, Los Angeles and southern California will enter the twenty-first century as a multiracial and multicultural society. This is absolutely new. There is no previous example of a civilization that is being simultaneously created by so many races, nationalities, and cultures. This new type of cultural pluralism is completely unknown in the history of mankind.

America is becoming more plural every day because of the unbelievable facility of the new Third World immigrants to put a piece of their original culture inside of American culture. The notion of a "dominant" American culture is changing every moment. It is incredible coming to America to find you are somewhere else—in Seoul, in Taipei, in Mexico City. You can travel inside this Korean culture right on the streets of Los Angeles. Inhabitants of this vast city become internal tourists in the place of their own residence.

There are large communities of Laotians, Vietnamese, Cambodians, Mexicans, Salvadorans, Guatemalans, Iranians, Japanese, Koreans, Armenians, Chinese. We find here Little Taipei, Little Saigon, Little Tokyo, Koreatown, Little Central America, the Iranian neighborhood in Westwood, the Armenian community in Hollywood, and the vast Mexican-American areas of East Los Angeles. Eighty-one languages, few of them European, are spoken in the elementary school system of the city of Los Angeles.

This transformation of American culture anticipates the general trend in the composition of mankind. Ninety percent of the immigrants to this city are from the Third World. At the beginning of the twenty-first century, 90 percent of the world's population will be dark-skinned; the white race will be no more than 11 percent of all human beings living on our planet.

Something that can only be seen in America: In the manicured, landscaped, ultraclean high-technology parks of northern Orange County there is a personal computer company that seven years ago did not exist. There were only strawberry fields where the plant is. Now, there is a $500 million company with factories in Hong Kong and Taiwan as well.

The company was founded by three young immigrants—a Pakistani Muslim and two Chinese from Hong Kong. They only became citizens in 1984. Each individual is now probably worth $30 million.

Walking through this company we see only young, dark faces—Vietnamese, Cambodians, Laotians, Mexicans—and the most advanced technology. The culture of the work force is a mix of Hispanic-Catholic family values and Asian-Confucian group loyalty. Employment notices are never posted; hiring is done through the network of families that live in southern California. Not infrequently, employees ask to work an extra twenty hours a week to earn enough money to help members of their extended family buy their first home.

In Los Angeles, traditional Third World cultures are, for the first time, fusing with the most modern mentalities and technologies.

After decades of covering war and revolution in the Third World, I carry in my mind an image of crowds, tension, crisis. My experience has always been of social activity that leads to destruction, to trouble, to unhappiness. People are always trying to do something, but they are unable to. The intentions of people trying to make revolution are just and good, but suddenly, something goes wrong. There is disorganization, unending problems. The weight of the past. They cannot fulfill their objectives.

Usually, the contact between developed and underdeveloped worlds has the character of exploitation—just taking people's labor and resources and giving them nothing. And the border between races has usually been a border of tension, of crisis. Here we see a revolution that is constructive.

This Pacific Rim civilization being created is a new relationship between development and underdevelopment. Here, there is openness. There is hope. And a future. There is a multicultural crowd. But it is not fighting. It is cooperating, peacefully competing, building. For the first time in four hundred years of relations between the nonwhite Western world and the white Western world, the general character of the relationship is cooperation and construction, not exploitation, not destruction.

Unlike any other place on the planet, Los Angeles shows us the potential of development once the Third World mentality merges with an open sense of possibility, a culture of organization, a Western conception of time.

For the destructive, paralyzed world where I have spent most of my life, it is important, simply, that such a possibility as Los Angeles exists.

To adjust the concept of time is the most difficult thing. It is a key revolution of development.

Western culture is a culture of arithmetical time. Time is organized by the clock. In non-Western culture, time is a measure between events. We arrange a meeting at nine o'clock but the man doesn't show up. We become anxious, offended. He doesn't understand our anxiety because for him, the moment he arrives is the measure of time. He is on time when he arrives.

In 1924, the Mexican philosopher José Vasconcelos wrote a book entitled *La Raza Cosmica*. He dreamt of the possibility that, in the future, mankind would create one human race, a *mestizo* race. All races on the planet would merge into one type of man. *La raza cosmica* is being borne in Los Angeles, in the cultural sense if not the anthropological sense. A vast mosaic of different races, cultures, religions, and moral habits are working toward one common aim. From the perspective of a world submerged in religious, ethnic and racial conflict, this harmonious cooperation is something unbelievable. It is truly striking.

What is the common aim that harmonizes competing cultures in one place?

It is not only the better living standard. What attracts immigrants to America is the essential characteristic of American culture: the chance to try. There is a combination of two things that are important: culture and space. The culture allows you to try to be somebody—to find yourself, your place, your status. And there is space not only in a geographical sense, but in the sense of opportunity, of social mobility. In societies that are in crisis and in societies which are stagnant—or even in those which are stable—there is no chance to try. You are defined in advance. Destiny has already sentenced you.

Other countries, even if they are open like Great Britain or France, don't have this dynamic of development. There is no space for development. This is what unites the diverse races and cultures in America. If the immigrant to America at first fails, he always thinks, "I will try again." If he had failed in the old society, he would be discouraged and pessimistic, accepting the place that was given to him. In America, he's thinking, "I will have another chance, I will try again." That keeps him going. He's full of hope.

Themes, Issues, and Ideas

1. Kapuscinski says that traditional history is the history of nations. What does he see as different about history in the future and how does he see America as uniquely suited to that future?

2. According to the author, Los Angeles is a symbol of the future. How does your knowledge of the Los Angeles riots of 1992, which took place after this essay was written, affect your reading of Kapuscinski's ideas?

3. How and why does the author distinguish between the social problems of other countries and those of the United States?

Writing Strategies and Techniques

1. The author talks about large and complex issues in a causal and informal style. How is that style achieved? Point to some techniques; for example, word choice.

2. Los Angeles becomes a symbol of the future in the essay. What other symbols does the author evoke and what do they stand for?

Suggestions for Writing

1. Do you think it likely that the America of the future will be more influenced by Asia than by Europe? Write an essay in which you defend or disagree with the author on this issue.

2. Pick something other than a city that symbolizes the American future for you. Using Kapuscinski's essay as a model, sketch out your views.

MAKING CONNECTIONS

1. Martin Luther King, Jr. and Malcolm X represent very different approaches to the problem of minority rights. Which man's approach is more appealing on an emotional level? Which on a practical level? Which on a political level?

2. What are some differences between Amy Tan's and Vivian Gornick's writing styles? How do some of these differences help or hinder each writer's argument?

3. Write an essay describing the contributions your own ethnic or racial group will make in the next century and what problems it might face.

4. Which do you find more suited to addressing the problem of racial inequality: an anecdotal essay like Amy Tan's or Ernesto Galarza's, or an ideological essay like Maya Angelou's? Why?

5. After reading these selections, do you feel more optimistic or pessimistic about race relations in the twenty-first century? Explain your answer.

CHAPTER FOUR

American Education for the Twenty-first Century

The Academy and the Workplace

THE PAST AS PROLOGUE

Some Very Modest Proposals for the Improvement of American Education

Nathan Glazer

Nathan Glazer, a well-known professor of education and sociology at Harvard University, was born in New York City in 1923. Over the years he has authored and co-authored many influential and controversial books, including The Lonely Crowd *in 1950 (with David Riesman and Reuel Denny);* Beyond the Melting Pot *in 1970 (with Daniel Patrick Moynihan);* Ethnic Dilemmas: 1964–1982 *in 1983; and* The Fulbright Experience and Academic Exchanges *in 1987. He has long been an editor of* The Public Interest *magazine.*

This essay first appeared in Daedalus, *an interdisciplinary magazine sponsored by the American Academy of Arts and Sciences. Although Glazer's title alludes to the famous satire by Jonathan Swift, each author gives the word* modest *a different ironic twist.*

That we can do a great deal for the sorry state of American education with more money is generally accepted. Even apparently modest proposals will, however, cost a great deal of money. Consider something as simple as increasing the average compensation of American teachers—who are generally considered underpaid—by $2,000 a year each. The bill would come to five billion dollars a year. A similar figure is reached by the report of the highly qualified Twentieth Century Task Force on Federal, Elementary, and Secondary Educational Policy, which proposes fellowships and additional compensation for master teachers. Reducing class size 10 percent, or increasing the number of teachers by the same percentage would cost another five billion dollars. With present-day federal deficits, these look like small sums, but since education is paid for almost entirely by states and local government, these modest proposals would lead to substantial and painful tax increases. (I leave aside for the moment the views of skeptics who believe that none of these changes would matter.)

But the occasional visitor to American schools will note some changes that would cost much less, nothing at all, or even save money – and yet would improve at least the educational *environment* in American schools (once again, we ignore those skeptics who would insist that even a better educational environment cannot be guaranteed to improve educational achievement). In the spirit of evoking further cheap proposals, here is a small list of suggestions that, to my mind at least—and the mind I believe of any adult who visits American public schools—would mean a clear plus for American education:

1. *Disconnect all loudspeaker systems in American schools—or at least reserve them, like the hotline between Moscow and Washington, for only the gravest emergencies.* The American classroom—and the American teacher and his or her charges—is continually interrupted by announcements from central headquarters over the loudspeaker system. These remind teachers to bring in some form or other; or students to bring in some form or other; or students engaged in some activity to remember to come to practice or rehearsal; or they announce a change of time for some activity. There is nothing so unnerving to a teacher engaged in trying to explain something, or a student engaged in trying to understand something, as the crackle of the loudspeaker prepared to issue an announcement, and the harsh and gravelly voice (the systems are not obviously of the highest grade) of the announcement itself.

Aside from questions of personal taste, why would this be a good idea? As I have suggested, one reason is that the loudspeaker interrupts efforts to communicate complicated material that requires undivided attention. Second, it demeans the teacher as professional: Every announcement tells her whatever she is doing is not very important and can be interrupted at any time. Third, it accentuates the notion of hierarchy in education—the principal and assistant principal are the most important people, and command time and attention even in the midst of instruction. Perhaps I have been softened by too many years as a college teacher, but it would be unimaginable that a loudspeaker, if one existed, would ever interrupt a college class except under conditions of the gravest and most immediate threat to life and limb. One way of showing students that education is important is not to interrupt it for band-rehearsal announcements.

2. *Disarm the school.* One of the most depressing aspects of the urban school in the United States is the degree of security manifest within it, and that seems to me quite contradictory to what a school should be. Outer doors are locked. Security guards are present in the corridors. Internal doors are locked. Passes are necessary to enter the school or move within it, for outsiders and for students. Students are marched in groups from classroom to classroom, under the eye of the teachers. It is understandable that given the conditions in lower-class areas in our large cities—and not only lower-class areas—some degree of security-mindedness is necessary. There is valuable equipment— typewriters, computers, audio-visual equipment—that can be stolen; vandalism is a serious concern; marauders can enter the school in search for equipment, or teachers' pocketbooks, or to threaten directly personal safety in search of money or sex, and so on. School integration and busing, at least in their initial stages, have contributed to increased interracial tensions in schools and have in part severed the link between community and school. The difference in ethnic and racial composition of faculty, other staff, administrators, and students contributes to the same end.

Having acknowledged all this, I still believe the school should feel less like a prison than it does. One should examine to what extent outside doors must be closed; to what extent the security guard cannot be replaced by local parents, volunteer or paid; the degree to which the endless bells indicating "stop" and "go" are really necessary. I suspect that now that the most difficult period of school integration has passed, now that teachers and administrators and staff more closely parallel in race and ethnic background students and community owing to the increase in black and Hispanic teachers and administrators, we may be saddled with more security than we need. Here we come to the sticky problem of *removing* security measures whose need has decreased. What school board will open itself to suit or to public criticism by deliberately providing *less* security? And yet one must consider the atmosphere of the school and a school's primary objective as a teaching agent: Can this be reconciled with a condition of maximum security? Perhaps there are lessons to be learned from colleges and community colleges in older urban areas, which in my experience do seem to manage with less security. One reason is that there are more adults around in such institutions. Is that a hint as to how we could manage better in our public schools?

3. *Enlist the children in keeping the school clean.* Occasionally we see a practice abroad that suggests possible transfer to the American scene. In Japan, the children clean the school. There is a time of day when mops and pails and brooms come out, and the children sweep up and wash up. This does, I am sure, suggest to the children that this is *their* school, that it is not simply a matter of being forced to go to a foreign institution that imposes alien demands upon them. I can imagine some obstacles in the way of instituting regular student cleanup in American schools—custodians' unions, for example, might object. But they can be reassured that children don't do that good a job, and they will still be needed. Once again, as in the case of the security problem, one wants to create in the school, if at all possible, a common enterprise of teachers and students, without the latter being bored and resistant, the former, in response, becoming equally indifferent. The school should be seen as everyone's workplace—and participation in cleaning the school will help.

4. *Save old schools.* Build fewer new ones. It has often surprised me that while in schools such as Eton and Oxford—and indeed well-known private schools and colleges in the United States—old buildings are prized, in so many communities older public schools are torn down when to the naked eye they have many virtues that would warrant their maintenance and use. Only a few blocks from where I live, an excellent example of late nineteenth-century fine brickwork and carved stonework that served as the Cambridge Latin School came down for a remodeling. The carved elements are still displayed about the re-modeled school, but why a building of such character should have deserved demolition escaped my understanding, particularly since one can take it almost as a given that a school building put up before the 1940s will be built of heavier and sturdier materials than one constructed today. Even the inconveniences of the old can possess a charm that makes them worthwhile. And indeed many of the reforms that seemed to require new buildings (for example, classrooms without walls, concentrated around activities centers in large open rooms) have

turned out, on use, to be not so desirable. Our aim should be to give each school a history, a character, something that at least some students respond to. The pressures for new buildings are enormous, and sometimes perfectly legitimate (as when communities expand), but often illegitimate, as when builders and building-trades workers and contract-givers seek an opportunity or when state aid makes it appear as if a new building won't cost anything.

5. *Look on new hardware with a skeptical eye.* I think it likely that the passion for the new in the way of teaching-hardware not only does not contribute to higher education achievement but may well serve as a temporary means to evade the real and hard tasks of teaching—which really require almost no hardware at all, besides textbooks, blackboard, and chalk. Admittedly, when one comes to high-school science, something more is called for. And yet our tendency is to always find cover behind new hardware. It's *fun* to get new audio-visual equipment, new rooms equipped with them in which all kinds of things can be done by flicking a switch or twisting a dial, or, as is now the case, to decide what kind of personal computers and software are necessary for a good educational program. Once again, foreign experience can be enlightening. When Japanese education was already well ahead of American, most Japanese schools were in prewar wooden buildings. (They are now as up-to-date as ours, but neither their age nor up-to-datedness has much to do with their good record of achievement.) Resisting the appeal of new hardware not only saves money, and provides less in the way of saleable goods to burglarize, but it also prevents distraction from the principal tasks of reading, writing, and calculating. When it turns out that computers and new software are shown to do a better job at these key tasks—I am skeptical as to whether this will ever be the case—there will be time enough to splurge on new equipment. The teacher, alone, up front, explaining, encouraging, guiding, is the heart of the matter—the rest is fun, and very helpful to corporate income, and gives an inflated headquarters staff something new to do. But students will have time enough to learn about computers when they get to college, and getting there will depend almost not at all on what they can do with computers, but how well they understand words and sentences, and how well they do at simple mathematics.

There is nothing wrong with old textbooks, too. Recently, reviewing some recent high-school American history texts, I was astonished to discover they come out in new editions every two years or so, and not because the main body of the text is improved, but because the textbook wants to be able to claim it covers the very last presidential campaign, and the events of the last few years. This is a waste of time and energy and money. There is enough to teach in American history up to 1950 or 1960 not to worry about whether the text includes Reagan's tax cuts. I suspect many new texts in other areas also offer little advantage over the older ones. There is also a virtue in a teacher becoming acquainted with a particular textbook. When I read that a school is disadvantaged because its textbooks are old, I am always mystified. Even the newest advances in physics and biology might well be reserved for college.

   6. *Expand the pool from which we draw good teachers.* This general heading covers a number of simple and concrete things, such as: If a teacher is considered qualified to teach at a good private school, that teacher should be considered qualified to teach at a public school. It has always seemed to me ridiculous that teachers accepted at the best private schools in New York City or top preparatory schools in the country would not be allowed to teach in the public school system of New York or Boston. Often, they are willing— after all, the pay is better in public schools and there are greater fringe benefits. They might, it is true, be driven out of those schools by the challenge of lower- and working-class children. But when they are willing, it seems unbelievable that the teacher qualified (or so Brearley thinks) for Brearley will not be allowed to teach at P.S. 122.* Greater use of part-time teachers might also be able to draw upon people with qualities that we are told the average teacher unfortunately doesn't possess— such as a higher level of competence in writing and mathematics.

   Our recurrent concern with foreign-language teaching should lead us to recruit foreign-born teachers. There are problems in getting teaching jobs today in Germany and France—yet teachers there are typically drawn from pools of students with higher academic skills than is the case in this country. Paradoxically, we make it easy for teachers of Spanish-language background to get jobs owing to the expansion of bilingual programs—but then their teaching is confined to children whose Spanish accent doesn't need improvement. It would make more sense to expose children of foreign-language background more to teachers with native English—and children from English-speaking families to teachers who speak French, German, Spanish, and, why not, Japanese, and Chinese natively. This would mean that rules requiring that a teacher must be a citizen, or must speak English without an accent, should be lifted for special teachers with special tasks. Perhaps we

*Brearley: a private school in New York City.

could make the most of the oversupply of teachers in some foreign countries by using them to teach mathematics—a subject where accent doesn't count. The school system in Georgia is already recruiting from Germany. Colleges often use teaching assistants whose English is not native and far from perfect, including Asians from Korea and China, to assist in science and mathematics courses. (There are many state laws which would not permit them to teach in elementary and secondary schools.)

All the suggestions above eschew any involvement with some great issues of education—tradition or reform, the teaching of values, the role of religion in the schools—that have in the past dominated arguments over education and still do today. But I add one more proposal that is still, I am afraid, somewhat controversial:

7. *Let students, within reason, pick their schools, or let parents choose them for them.* All those informed on school issues will sense the heaving depths of controversy under this apparently modest proposal. Does this mean they might choose parochial schools, without being required to pay tuition out of their own pockets? Or does this mean black children would be allowed to attend schools in black areas, and whites in white areas, or the reverse if each is so inclined? As we all know, the two great issues of religion and race stand in the way of any such simple and commonsensical arrangement. Students are regularly bused from one section of a city to another because of their race, and students cannot without financial penalty attend that substantial sector of schools—30 percent or so in most northern and midwestern cities—that are called "private." I ignore the question of whether, holding all factors constant, students do "better" in private or public schools, in racially well-mixed or hardly mixed schools. The evidence will always be uncertain. What is perhaps less arguable is that students will do better in a school that forms a community, in which teachers, parents, and students all agree that *that* is the school they want to teach in, to attend, to send their children to. I would guess that this is the kind of school most of the readers of this article have attended; it is the kind of school, alas, that our complex racial and religious history makes it harder and harder for those of minority race or of lower- and working-class status to attend.

I have eschewed the grand proposals—for curriculum change, for improving the quality of entering teachers, for checking on the competence of teachers in service, for establishing national standards for achievement in different levels of education—all of which now form the agenda for many state commissions of educational reform, and all of which seem reasonable to me. Rather, I have concentrated on a variety of other things that serve to remove distraction, to open the school to those of quality who would be willing to enter it to improve it, to concentrate on the essentials of teaching and learning as I (and many others) have experienced it. It would be possible to propose larger changes in the same direction: for example, reduce the size of the bureaucracies in urban school systems. Some of my modest proposals are insidiously intended to do this—if there were less effort devoted to building new schools, buying new equipment, evaluating new textbooks, or busing children, there would be no need to maintain quite so many people at headquarters. Or so I would hope.

In the meantime, why not disconnect the loudspeakers?

Themes, Issues, and Ideas

1. Glazer claims that all of his proposals are modest, but he gives prominence to the issue of loudspeakers. Why do you think he does so? Which proposal do you think most important, and why?

2. Glazer sees a potential pool of instruction among the foreign born and suggests that they teach mathematics as foreign graduate assistants and professors do in college, since mathematics is "a subject where accent doesn't count." Do you agree with the proposal and with the reasoning? Explain.

3. What do you think about one of the major issues that Glazer skirts— greater interaction of public, private, and parochial schools?

Writing Strategies and Techniques

1. How are Glazer's first two paragraphs like his last two? How are they different? What would be the effect of switching their places?

2. Glazer is a college teacher who admits to the easy environment his classes provide. What other techniques does he use to avoid seeming condescending to public-school teachers in his proposals?

Suggestions for Writing

1. As a student, you have some expertise for judging Glazer's proposals. Write an essay agreeing or disagreeing with Glazer on the basis of your own educational experience.

2. Surely Glazer has not exhausted the possibilities of improvements for the environment and morale of public education in the United States. Make a modest proposal or two of your own and support your reasoning in an essay.

2001

The World Our Students Will Enter

Louis Harris

Louis Harris was born in 1919. He founded the famous national polling organization Louis Harris Associates, of which he is now chairman and chief executive officer. As he recounts in this essay (originally published in The College Board Review), years of public opinion sampling have led him to feel close to the thinking of the American people on the issues he raises for the future of the United States and of its students. Harris attempts a qualitative analysis of the quantitative trends he sees affecting the nation's economy in the 1990s and beyond. He bases his suggestions for educational improvements on the conclusion that America needs "a labor force that can think for itself." To that end he proposes what he calls "design standards."

In the 1990s, the configuration of the world will change dramatically. By 1992, Western Europe will form a new economic entity which will make the United States the world's number two economic power. Indeed, by the year 2001, we might well be the number three economic power, behind a southeastern sphere of influence headed by Japan, but excluding China, which will likely be a closer ally of ours than of Japan. The Soviet sphere will still exist, but will rank far down economically from the three economic superpowers. But the mark of these new configurations will be that they will command upon all economic activity that it think globally or not survive.

Ford Motor Company today is the prototype of what major American companies will be like by the year 2001. Ford will produce 40 percent of its cars in the Far East, 40 percent in the United States, and 20 percent in Europe. All the planning, conceptualization, production, marketing, and servicing will be done in five separate and self-contained centers with two each located in Asia and the United States and the other in Europe.

Ford will still be an American company, but it will operate on a truly global basis. However, the ground rules that will exist in the newly integrated Europe will be different from Asia or the United States. To qualify for work in this new global economy, the young person of 2001 will have to have a global perspective, an intimate knowledge of what the world outside the United States is really like. While today most young people are just plain illiterate about world geography, cross-cultural comprehension and understanding will be not only the mark of an educated person, but a requisite for tomorrow's economic survival. Why? Simply because the jobs young people will be aspiring to will be intimately related to how well that young person comprehends and relates in a global perspective. This will mean not only being language-proficient but culturally sophisticated. This will mean understanding what common economic practices might be universal—practices that are tempered by subtle, national cultural differences.

But this is only half of the global story. The other half can affect the basic personal living standards of nearly every human being. Because they are becoming industrialized almost overnight, nations such as Mexico, Brazil, Korea, Singapore, Taiwan, China, and many others can produce many basic products at wages of no more than three to four dollars an hour. In addition, if Japan is their role model, they are going to rapidly raise their real incomes along with their productivity. As this trend continues to the end of the century, America will face rising living standards in emerging industrial nations around the globe, produced by work forces that have out-competed our own.

This will pose some terrible dilemmas for American society. One solution that will be dismissed out of hand is that labor in this country work for much lower rates, such as four or five dollars an hour. Yet another is to create a two-tier labor force—one that pays twelve to sixteen dollars an hour for skilled, craft labor, as has been the tradition here for a long time, and then pay less trained Americans from poverty settings, or even immigrants from Latin America, Asia, or the Middle East, a competitive four to six dollars an hour. Of course, this would violate the fair labor standards law, as it reads today. Indeed, there will be some who suggest that the United States would be opting for a variation of the South African model.

But there is another option for the United States and that is to educate, train, and use a labor force that the world has never seen before—one that would be difficult for other nations to duplicate: A pool of people trained to think creatively for themselves and to know where to get information when they do not know answers. By training a labor force of this kind, the United States could also develop whole new industries and businesses that would be the envy of the rest of the world. They would be service industries. They would range from hi-tech to finance, health, education, and computers, to cite a few. The singular mark of such an economy would be not its technology or methodology, but its distinctive *labor force*. Ironically, while twentieth-century American technology has remained dominant, we have consistently found ourselves out-produced when our technology is employed by much cheaper or more dedicated labor. If we cannot compete in this labor market, our standard of living will surely fall.

Just a reminder: We have gone close to a decade in this country without real income going up. It could be that we are poised to see real income decline, and, with it, the standard of living that has been our continuing pride. Obviously, if we are to increase our real wages and our standard of living, then we must effect increases in productivity by a labor force that is far superior to that of the rest of the world—the only labor force that can *think for itself*.

Within the United States, some of the greatest changes will be demographic, and not necessarily the ones that have been so widely advertised. For example, there are sure signs now that marriages are on the rise, divorces have topped out, and families will stick together more than had been predicted a decade ago. However, the nature and configuration of the family will change virtually beyond recognition. For example, the number of traditional mothers who stay home and raise children, now only 24 percent of all adult women, will shrink even further to less than 10 percent. Assuming that 10 percent will be having babies or be chronically ill or out of the labor force for other reasons, it is sound to predict that eight in ten adult women will be working by the year 2001, as compared with 64 percent today. Working will be viewed as an accepted fact of life. Indeed, there will be almost as many working women as men. In addition, a basic change will have taken place among the elderly. The impetus will be the new legislation outlawing mandatory retirement, which will take full hold by 1992.

In the 1990s, as much as one-third to one-half of the elderly retired will reenter the labor force because of what will be a demand for labor in a period of shortage. They will, of course, need to be reeducated and retrained. But their motivation and powers of application will be extraordinarily high.

The third leg of the tripod in this rather unorthodox scenario will be the minorities—blacks, Hispanics, Asians, and others whom the country will also need to meet work-force shortages over the next decade. Over a third of the entire population of this country will be nonwhite minority by the turn of the century. If population trends continue, it is not inconceivable that close to a majority of the children under eighteen will be nonwhite minority group members. These statistics reveal the essence of the challenge of survival America faces. To put it bluntly and categorically: By the end of the next decade, the United States will have either succeeded or failed on the pivotal issue of how to open the doors of opportunity to minority young people.

If we succeed in learning how to make productive citizens out of minorities, if we can find ways to make them creative, thinking workers, as must happen with young whites, then surely we will have created a strongly competitive America that will be the envy of the world. But, if we fail, then *all* other bets are off, simply because we will be mired in a system in which the baggage we will have to carry in unproductive human beings, mainly the minorities and the disabled, will be too heavy and will condemn us to second-tier economic status.

The irony, of course, is that if we properly utilize the elderly, women, and the minorities, we will no doubt have solved the social security and medicare funding crises, and will have reduced the welfare rolls dramatically. We also will have proven to the world that the United States, which has long attracted the masses of underprivileged, will have acquired the most enviable reputation of being the land of true *equal* opportunity. Why? Not because of bleeding-heart motives, but instead because of self-interest, the basic will to survive.

I am an optimist. By the nature of my work, I feel close to the people and where they live. Fundamentally, I agree with Thornton Wilder that survival is humankind's basic instinct, and we will survive— by the skin of our teeth. Thus, I genuinely think that we will be well on our way toward solving the question of how to bring minorities into the mainstream of American life and to allow them to blossom and to thrive as productive members of the new labor force.

There will then be other consequences in our politics and public agenda. For example, it is not hard to predict that by the year 2001, with Hispanics and blacks part of the mainstream, the two largest states of the Union, California and Texas, will have a majority of the electorate who are Hispanic and black. The major office holders of those states will reflect this bedrock political fact. Presidential candidates will find it well nigh impossible to forfeit the two biggest states and hope to win the White House.

When this happens, our country will enjoy one of the greatest feelings of community in our entire history. We will likely look back on the 1980s as historians now look at the golden 1920s—as a time of wanton escapism, when buccaneer fortunes were made, when government was virtually invisible, because it operated on the assumption that whatever the private sector did must have been either divined by God or, in the end, was sure to be the "right" thing, even if millions of people went right down the drain in the process. Government itself will not be the cure-all and the dominant initiating force as in the New Deal era. Nevertheless, with the deep recession that is sure to take place between now and the year 2001, government will have to take a much more decisive role in the rebuilding of the economy than it has in the 1980s. Government will serve in quite another role, additionally, as the scrupulous monitor of the public interest, of the community interest, as the fearless rooter out of excesses in the system that do not let it function at its full potential.

Now what does all this mean for the educational system? As my colleague Marc Tucker at the National Center for Education and the Economy—on whose board I sit—has repeatedly pointed out, the problem in education here in America is *not* that we have slipped from some standard we *used* to meet. If that were so, then all we would have to do is put old policies back into place. Actually, over the past two decades, performance at the secondary school level has slipped some, while elementary-school performance, especially for minorities, has gone up.

The hard truth is that there have been few substantial changes in education in the United States, but almost the entire world around us has changed radically. Instead of simply finding ways to keep a marginal lead on the rest of the world, we now have terrible and even radical challenges and changes to make. In short, we have to become a nation that thinks for a living. The key for education lies in the standards that must be adopted and strongly enforced. The difference, Tucker and others point out, is the distinction between a design standard and performance standard.

Design standards are put together on the assumption that there are certain set ingredients in a system that are configured in some preordained way. Everyone in the system is expected to adhere to the design. A performance standard, by contrast, is constructed with certain clear-cut criteria and objectives and *must* be achieved, no matter what. But you leave it up to the people who build the system, and then operate it, to *creatively* build the system. This performance standard will consistently yield higher quality at a much lower price—*provided* incentives and penalties are built into the system.

If those vested with the responsibility make it work, they will be rewarded as other professionals are—handsomely, in every way. If they fail, then they will no longer be part of the system. Unfortunately, the education system has been geared to design standards. The people on top tell those below them precisely what to do, and then they tell those below them in greater detail how to do it, until the whole weight of the process falls on the principal and the teachers. It just does *not* work, but everyone says, "All I did was precisely what I was supposed to do, just as I was told."

Real accountability is obviously missing. By contrast, people must be told, "Here is the performance standard. You must figure out how to carry it out in your community, with your students."

Our current system has minimum standards. Part of the problem is that parents are worried that if the standards are too tough, their kids will fail, so they opt for more modest standards. Educators complain that if you raise the standards too high, then the kids who are already at the bottom of the ladder will give up on the system and drop out.

I am suggesting that we must reach for a higher standard to prepare kids to think for themselves and to think globally. And we must do this at a time when many parents and educators are seeking to lower standards because they have lost faith in our schools and our children. The key does *not* lie in setting up minimum standards or moderate standards or even stringently high standards. Instead, the key obviously lies in setting up proper incentives, where the principals and the teachers are told the higher the performance of your students, the higher your own rewards will be. Thus, they are always striving to meet a higher, not a minimum, standard. And then, when they attain that standard, they will want to strive to achieve still higher goals.

There remains the question of just what kinds of standards there ought to be. Today, the parents in suburban schools demand performance that should be measured by the rates of college admission, by performance on SATs. In the cities, performance is measured in terms of tests of basic skills. Thus, inner-city children are measured by mind-numbing exercises. It is no surprise at all that they get bored and drop out. Sadly, the by-rote exercises they experience leave them little or no time to learn how to think for themselves. *That* is a foreign experience for them. There are still others who believe in the notion that you have to have basic skills before you acquire higher-order skills. That is just not the case. I know how to write and I teach people how to write.

The way you do *that* is to get them to write, and, as they acquire the taste for writing, they then get interested in grammar and spelling; *not* the other way around. We are educating a whole generation of young people who have basic skills, yet who will be largely unemployable. We are stamping out the last vestiges of hope for those inner-city kids. They desperately need to be saved. If they are not brought into the mainstream, then our entire educational and economic system will be placed in dire jeopardy.

I think I know what the environment will be in 2001. I think I have a clue to what it *can* be by 2001. But, if we simply wait for it to happen, if we go on about our business of patching and filling, then we are doomed to a fate worse than has been described up to now. If we are prepared to bite the bullet, then we can have a new day. But we must act soon and act with passion and dispatch, before it is too late. I remember what Archibald MacLeish wrote when I was a young man, "America is promises for those who take them." We must take them now and take them boldly. Our future lies in the balance.

Themes, Issues, and Ideas

1. Harris says that the changes soon to come will "pose some terrible dilemmas for American society." What are those dilemmas? What solutions does Harris see? Which alternative solution does he favor?

2. Harris claims that "the United States will have either succeeded or failed on the pivotal issue of how to open the doors of opportunity to minority young people." What arguments and evidence does he bring to support this claim? Do you agree with Harris's judgment that this issue is of crucial importance? Why, or why not?

3. Harris cites a distinction by his colleague Marc Tucker between two educational standards—a "design" standard and a "performance" standard. What is the difference? On which standard do you think your own education has been formed? Use examples to support your answers.

Writing Strategies and Techniques

1. Harris stresses that writing is a skill that stimulates thought. What is his own writing like? Pick a paragraph and analyze the strengths and weaknesses of his expository style.

2. Harris often uses the words "I" and "we." What does he seem to imagine his audience to be like? What other techniques give you a sense of who he is addressing?

Suggestions for Writing

1. Harris, attempting to refute the notion that basic skills and rote learning lead to higher-level skills, uses writing as an example. Do you agree? Use writing or another example in an essay in which you attack, defend, or modify Harris's position.

2. What do you think of the ideas for "design standards?" Write an essay arguing how design standards would or would not be an effective way of achieving educational goals.

The Future of Work

Robert B. Reich

This essay provides a detailed survey on the future of those activities that your education will presumably prepare you for. Robert B. Reich takes you on a more in-depth tour of occupations than Louis Harris did in the preceding essay. Some occupations will expand in the future, others will almost disappear. Reich lays out the costs and benefits that each general career area provides. One drawback to planning, as the author establishes early in the essay, is that what is best known is what one should definitely not do to prepare for the work of tomorrow.

Reich wrote this essay for Harper's *magazine while he was a professor of Political Economy at the John F. Kennedy School of Government at Harvard University. He is currently the U.S. Secretary of Labor.*

It's easy to predict what jobs you *shouldn't* prepare for. Thanks to the wonders of fluoride, America, in the future, will need fewer dentists. Nor is there much of a future in farming. The federal government probably won't provide long-term employment unless you aspire to work in the Pentagon or the Veterans Administration (the only two departments accounting for new federal jobs in the last decade). And think twice before plunging into higher education. The real wages of university professors have been declining for some time, the hours are bad, and all you get are complaints.

Moreover, as the American economy merges with the rest of the world's, anyone doing relatively unskilled work that could be done more cheaply elsewhere is unlikely to prosper for long. Imports and exports now constitute 26 percent of our gross national product (up from 9 percent in 1950), and barring a new round of protectionism, the portion will move steadily upward. Meanwhile, ten thousand people are added to the world's population every hour, most of whom, eventually, will happily work for a small fraction of today's average American wage.

This is good news for most of you, because it means that you'll be able to buy all sorts of things far more cheaply than you could if they were made here (provided, of course, that what your generation does instead produces even more value). The resulting benefits from trade will help offset the drain on your income resulting from paying the interest on the nation's foreign debt and financing the retirement of aging baby boomers like me. The bad news, at least for some of you, is that most of America's traditional, routinized manufacturing jobs will disappear. So will routinized service jobs that can be done from remote locations, like keypunching of data transmitted by satellite. Instead, you will be engaged in one of two broad categories of work: either complex services, some of which will be sold to the rest of the world to pay for whatever Americans want to buy from the rest of the world, or person-to-person services, which foreigners can't provide for us because (apart from new immigrants and illegal aliens) they aren't here to provide them.

Complex services involve the manipulation of data and abstract symbols. Included in this category are insurance, engineering, law, finance, computer programming, and advertising. Such activities now account for almost 25 percent of our GNP, up from 13 percent in 1950. They already have surpassed manufacturing (down to about 20 percent of GNP). Even *within* the manufacturing sector, executive, managerial, and engineering positions are increasing at a rate almost three times that of total manufacturing employment. Most of these jobs, too, involve manipulating symbols.

Such endeavors will constitute America's major contribution to the rest of the world in the decades ahead. You and your classmates will be exporting engineering designs, financial services, advertising and communications advice, statistical analyses, musical scores and film scripts, and other creative and problem-solving products. How many of you undertake these sorts of jobs, and how well you do at them, will determine what goods and services America can summon from the rest of the world in return, and thus—to some extent—your generation's standard of living.

You say you plan to become an investment banker? A lawyer? I grant you that these vocations have been among the fastest growing and most lucrative during the past decade. The securities industry in particular has burgeoned. Between 1977 and 1987, securities-industry employment nearly doubled, rising 10 percent a year, compared with the average yearly job growth of 1.9 percent in the rest of the economy. The crash of October 1987 temporarily stemmed the growth, but by mid-1988 happy days were here again. Nor have securities workers had particular difficulty making ends meet. Their average income grew 21 percent over the decade, compared with a 1 percent rise in the income of everyone else. (But be careful with these numbers; relatively few securities workers enjoyed such majestic compensation. The high average is partly due to the audacity of people such as Henry Kravis and George Roberts, each of whom takes home a tidy $70 million per year.)

Work involving securities and corporate law has been claiming one-quarter of all new private sector jobs in New York City and more than a third of all the new office space in that industrious town. Other major cities are not too far behind. A simple extrapolation of the present trend suggests that by 2020 one out of every three American college graduates will be an investment banker or a lawyer. Of course, this is unlikely. Long before that milestone could be achieved, the nation's economy will have dried up like a raisin, as financiers and lawyers squeeze out every ounce of creative, productive juice. Thus my advice: Even if you could bear spending your life in such meaningless but lucrative work, at least consider the fate of the nation before deciding to do so.

Person-to-person services will claim everyone else. Many of these jobs will not require much skill, as is true of their forerunners today. Among the fastest growing in recent years: custodians and security guards, restaurant and retail workers, day-care providers. Secretaries and clerical workers will be as numerous as now, but they'll spend more of their time behind and around electronic machines (imported from Asia) and have fancier titles, such as "paratechnical assistant" and "executive paralegal operations manager."

Teachers will be needed (we'll be losing more than a third of our entire corps of elementary- and high-school teachers through attrition over the next seven years), but don't expect their real pay to rise very much. Years of public breast-beating about the quality of American education notwithstanding, the average teacher today earns $28,000—only 3.4 percent more, in constant dollars, than he or she earned fifteen years ago.

Count on many jobs catering to Americans at play—hotel workers, recreation directors, television and film technicians, aerobics instructors (or whatever their twenty-first century equivalents will call themselves). But note that Americans will have less leisure time to enjoy these pursuits. The average American's free time has been shrinking for more than fifteen years, as women move into the work force (and so spend more of their free time doing household chores) and as all wage earners are forced to work harder just to maintain their standard of living. Expect the trend to continue.

The most interesting and important person-to-person jobs will be in what is now unpretentiously dubbed "sales." Decades from now most salespeople won't be just filling orders. Salespeople will be helping customers define their needs, then working with design and production engineers to customize products and services in order to address those needs. This is because standardized (you can have it in any color as long as it's black) products will be long gone. Flexible manufacturing and the new information technologies will allow a more tailored fit—whether it's a car, machine tool, insurance policy, or even a college education. Those of you who will be dealing directly with customers will thus play a pivotal role in the innovation process, and your wages and prestige will rise accordingly.

But the largest number of personal-service jobs will involve health care, which already consumes about 12 percent of our GNP, and that portion is rising. Because every new medical technology with the potential to extend life is infinitely valuable to those whose lives might be extended—even for a few months or weeks—society is paying huge sums to stave off death. By the second decade of the next century, when my generation of baby boomers will have begun to decay, the bill will be much higher. Millions of corroding bodies will need doctors, nurses, nursing-home operators, hospital administrators, technicians who operate and maintain all the fancy machines that will measure and temporarily halt the deterioration, hospice directors, home-care specialists, directors of outpatient clinics, and euthanasia specialists, among many others.

Most of these jobs won't pay very much because they don't require much skill. Right now the fastest growing job categories in the health sector are nurse's aides, orderlies, and attendants, which compose about 40 percent of the health-care work force. The majority are women; a large percentage are minorities. But even doctors' real earnings show signs of slipping. As malpractice insurance rates skyrocket, many doctors go on salary in investor-owned hospitals, and their duties are gradually taken over by physician "extenders" such as nurse practitioners and midwives.

What's the best preparation for one of these careers?

Advice here is simple: You won't be embarking on a career, at least as we currently define the term, because few of the activities I've mentioned will proceed along well-defined paths to progressively higher levels of responsibility. As the economy evolves toward services tailored to the particular needs of clients and customers, hands-on experience will count for more than formal rank. As technologies and markets rapidly evolve, moreover, the best preparation will be through cumulative learning on the job rather than formal training completed years before.

This means that academic degrees and professional credentials will count for less; on-the-job training, for more. American students have it backwards. The courses to which you now gravitate—finance, law, accounting, management, and other practical arts—may be helpful to understand how a particular job is *now* done (or, more accurately, how your instructors did it years ago when they held such jobs or studied the people who held them), but irrelevant to how such a job *will* be done. The intellectual equipment needed for the job of the future is an ability to define problems, quickly assimilate relevant data, conceptualize and reorganize the information, make deductive and inductive leaps with it, ask hard questions about it, discuss findings with colleagues, work collaboratively to find solutions, and then convince others. And *these* sorts of skills can't be learned in career-training courses. To the extent they can be found in universities at all, they're more likely to be found in subjects such as history, literature, philosophy, and anthropology—in which students can witness how others have grappled for centuries with the challenge of living good and productive lives. Tolstoy and Thucydides are far more relevant to the management jobs of the future, for example, than are Hersey and Blanchard (*Management of Organizational Behavior,* Prentice Hall, 5th Edition, 1988).

Themes, Issues, and Ideas

1. Many writers whose subject is the future have talked about the dangers of population increase to human well-being. Why does Reich conditionally say that the increase is *good* news? What are the conditions that will make the news good?

2. What type of occupations does Reich say will constitute America's major economic contribution to the world in the years to come? How many of the occupations he surveys fall into this area?

3. Reich says that among the most interesting and important jobs will be those now generally called "sales." What reasons does he give for this opinion? Do you agree with his view of "sales?" Why, or why not?

Writing Strategies and Techniques

1. Reich addresses students directly. What writing techniques does he use to maintain the sense of a specific and an immediate audience for his predictions?

2. Much of Reich's information is necessarily mathematical in form. How does he use humor to lighten the burden of factual content?

Suggestions for Writing

1. Many people have shied away from sales and need to be sold on the idea as a career path. How does Reich sell his idea that sales will be a very important part of the future economy? Write an essay analyzing his persuasive techniques.

2. Though his subject is careers of the future, Reich deprecates the possibility or usefulness of any direct career training. Do you agree? Write an essay in which you attack, defend, or modify Reich's suggestions for an education suitable to the American future.

Will America Choose High Skills or Low Wages?

Ira Magaziner and Hillary Rodham Clinton

Ira Magaziner, at the time this essay was written, was president of SJS Inc., a public policy consulting firm. As this book goes to press, he is President Clinton's senior policy advisor on domestic affairs. Hillary Rodham Clinton, of course, is the wife of the President of the United States as well as a longtime advocate of progressive public policy. In this proposal, Magaziner and Clinton point out some of the shortcomings of our current labor policy and go on to explain how they may be remedied. "High performance" workers are the key, they claim, and the sooner we can produce a better, more highly motivated, highly skilled work force the sooner we will be able to compete with our international rivals.

During the past two decades, the United States has watched as Singapore, Taiwan, and Korea grew from run-down Third World outposts to world premier exporters; as Germany, with one quarter of our population, almost equaled us in exports; as Japan became the world's economic juggernaut. During these transformations, America became the world's biggest borrower.

We have heard the excuses: The countries we beat in World War II are simply regaining their former places in the world. The Europeans and the Japanese are exploiting their low wages. Our competitors are class-ridden countries.

The truth is otherwise: Our former adversaries are doing far better in relation to us then they did before the war. A dozen nations now pay wages above ours. Our distribution of income is more skewed than any of our major competitors, and our poverty rate is much higher.

Our education statistics are as disappointing as our trade statistics. Our children rank at the bottom on most international tests—behind children in Europe and East Asia. Again, we heard the excuses: They have elite systems, but we educate everyone. They compare a small number of their best to our much larger average. The facts are otherwise: Many of the countries with the highest test scores have more of their students in school than we do.

We are not facing the facts about our future. What we are facing is an economic cliff—and the frontline working people of America are about to fall off.

A Drop in Productivity

From the 1950s to the 1970s, America's productivity grew at a healthy pace. The nation was getting richer, and workers lived better on what they earned. Since then, the rate of increase in productivity has dropped dramatically. The distribution of income in the United States has been worsening. Those with college degrees are prospering, but frontline workers have seen the buying power of their paychecks shrink year after year. Since 1969, real average weekly earnings in the United States have fallen by more than 12 percent. And, during the past two decades, our productivity growth has slowed to a crawl. It now takes nearly three years to achieve the same productivity improvement we used to achieve in one year.

If productivity continues to falter, we can expect one of two futures. Either the top 30 percent of our population will grow wealthier while the bottom 70 percent becomes progressively poorer, or we all slide into relative poverty together.

If we are to avert catastrophe, we must make drastic improvements in our rate of productivity growth. But we cannot grow simply by putting more people to work. We must grow by having every American worker produce more. If we do not, our incomes will go into a free-fall with no end in sight.

Going High Performance

We must work more productively and be more competitive. We cannot do this simply by using better machinery, because low-wage countries can use the same machines and still sell their products more cheaply than we can. Nor can we continue to organize work by breaking complex jobs into myriad simple rote tasks, because the world's best companies now use new high-performance work organizations, unleashing major advances in productivity, quality, variety, and speed of new product introductions.

Because most American employers organize work in a way that does not require high skills, they foresee no shortage of people who have such skills. With some exceptions, the education and skill levels of American workers roughly match the demands of their jobs. But if we want to compete more effectively in the global economy, we will have to move to high-performance work organizations.

To do this we must mobilize our most vital asset, the skills of our people—not just the skills of the 30 percent who will graduate with baccalaureate degrees from college, but those of the frontline workers—the bank tellers, farm workers, truck drivers, retail clerks, data entry operators, laborers, and factory workers.

We can do this only by reorganizing the way we work in our stores and factories, in our warehouses, insurance offices, government agencies, and hospitals. We can give our frontline workers much more responsibility, educate them well, and train them to do more highly skilled jobs.

If we do this, we can streamline work. We will need fewer supervisors, fewer quality checkers, fewer production schedulers, and fewer maintenance people, so organizations will become more efficient. Because they will be more efficient, they will be able to sell more. Because they will sell more, they can expand. Because they can expand, they can employ more people. Although each operation will require fewer people, society as a whole can increase employment and wages can go up.

The Commission on the Skills of the American Workforce

With hopes of steering a new course for the U.S. before we face a crisis, the Commission on the Skills of the American Workforce came together in June 1989 to analyze the interplay between economic trends and population dynamics. The Commission included a research team of 23 loaned executives from companies, unions, industry associations, and the U.S. Department of Labor.

The team probed into several industries both in the United States and abroad and concentrated on major markets of several states. In total, the team interviewed more than 2,000 people at 550 firms and agencies and analyzed many government and private reports.

The Commission's findings on American industry, labor policy, and education pointed in one direction: Americans are unwittingly making a choice that most of us would not make were we aware of its consequences. It is a choice that will lead to an America where over 70 percent of our people will see their dreams slip away.

This choice is being made by companies that cut wages to remain competitive. It is being made by public school officials who fail to prepare our children to be productive workers. Ultimately, we are all making the choice by silently accepting this course.

We still have time to make the other choice, one that will lead us to a more prosperous future: we can opt for high skills rather than low wages. But to make this choice we must fundamentally change our approach to work and education.

Problems and Solutions

The Commission set out to both identify the problems America faces and recommend feasible solutions. Based on its research, the Commission made several key recommendations for an education and training system.

Problem 1: Two factors stand in the way of producing a highly educated work force—we lack a clear standard of achievement and few students are motivated to work hard in school. One reason that students going right to work after school have little motivation to study hard is that they see little or no relationship between how well they do in school and what kind of job they can get after school.

Recommendation: A new educational performance standard should be set for all students, to be met at or around age 16. This standard should be established nationally and benchmarked to the highest in the world.

Students passing a series of performance-based assessments that incorporate this new standard would be awarded a Certificate of Initial Mastery. Possession of the certificate would qualify the student to choose among going to work, entering a college preparatory program, or studying for a Technological and Professional Certificate, described below.

Problem 2: More than 20 percent of our students drop out of high school—almost 50 percent in many of our inner cities. These dropouts go on to make up more than a third of our frontline work force. Turning our backs on those dropouts, as we do now, is tantamount to turning our backs on our future work force.

Recommendation: The states should take responsibility for assuring that virtually all students achieve the Certificate of Initial Mastery. Through new local employment and training boards, states, with federal assistance, should create and fund alternative learning environments for those who cannot attain the Certificate of Initial Mastery in regular schools.

All students should be guaranteed the educational attention necessary to attain the Certificate of Initial Mastery by age 16, or as soon as possible thereafter. Youth Centers should be established to enroll school dropouts and help them reach that standard.

Problem 3: Other industrial nations have multiyear career-oriented educational programs that prepare students to operate at a professional level in the workplace. America prepares only a tiny fraction of its non-college bound students for work. As a result, most flounder in the labor market, moving from low paying job to low-paying job until their mid-20s, never being seriously trained.

Recommendation: A comprehensive system of technical and professional certificates should be created for students and adult workers who do not pursue a baccalaureate degree.

Technical and professional certificates would be offered across the entire range of service and manufacturing occupations. A student could earn the entry-level occupation certificate after completing a two- to four-year program of combined work and study. A sequence of advanced certificates could be obtained throughout one's career.

National committees of business, labor, education, and public representatives should be convened to define certification standards for two- to four year programs of professional preparation in a broad range of occupations. These programs should combine general education with specific occupational skills and should include a significant work component.

Problem 4: The vast majority of American employers are not moving to high-performance work organizations, nor are they investing in training their nonmanagerial employees for these new forms of work organization. The movement to high-performance work organizations is more widespread in other nations, and training of frontline workers is commonplace.

Recommendation: We propose a system whereby all employers will invest at least 1 percent of their payroll for the education and training of their workers. We further recommend that public technical assistance be provided to companies, particularly small businesses, to assist them in moving to higher-performance work organizations.

Problem 5: The United States is not well organized to provide the highly skilled workers needed to support the emerging high-performance work organizations. The training system is fragmented with respect to policies, administration, and service delivery.

Recommendation: A system of employment and training boards should be established by federal and state governments, together with local leadership, to organize and oversee the new school-to-work transition programs and training systems.

We envision a new, more comprehensive system where skills development and upgrading for the majority of our workers becomes a central aim of public policy. The key to accomplishing these goals is finding a way to enable the leaders of our communities to take responsibility for building a comprehensive system that meets their needs. The local employment and training boards would serve as the vehicles for oversight and management of training and school-to-work transition programs, Youth Centers, and job information services.

Implementing America's Choice

Since the release of the report in June 1990, the Commission has promoted awareness of the report's recommendations through speeches and briefing sessions with educators, business and labor leaders, government officials, and advocacy groups. As the report's findings have been disseminated, interest in implementing its recommendations has become widespread.

On the national level, key members of Congress, both Democrats and Republicans, have introduced the High Skills, Competitive Workforce Act of 1991 based on the Commission's recommendations. Without creating a needless new bureaucracy, this legislation (H.R. 3470 and S. 1790) goes a long way toward ensuring that U.S. businesses will remain competitive in the global marketplace and that American workers will continue to enjoy a high standard of living. The act supports national education and job-skill standards benchmarked to world-class standards. It provides grants to local communities to establish Youth Opportunity Centers aimed at bringing high school dropouts back into the education system to ensure that they, too, meet world-class standards. And the bill provides technical assistance to employers to help them train their frontline workers and make the shift to high-performance work organizations. To finance the training, the bill requires employers to invest at least 1 percent of payroll in training frontline workers or contribute to a national trust fund earmarked for training.

More than 20 states have expressed an interest in working with the Commission on implementation strategies. Oregon, Washington, New York, and Minnesota have already created legislative initiatives to implement the Commission's recommendations. And education groups are moving to do the same.

New Standards for the Schools

Key national groups, including the President's Advisory Committee on Education, the governing board of the National Assessment of Educational Progress, and the National Education Goals Panel, have begun to advocate the development of an examination system consistent with the creation of a Certificate of Initial Mastery.

And recently, President Bush, in his education initiative, "America 2000," announced the development of a national examination system for the nation's K-12 school system. Numerous groups, including the New Standards Project, a partnership of the National Center on Education and the Economy and the Learning Research and Development Center of the University of Pittsburgh, have begun to develop a new student performance assessment system, putting into place the first steps to making this new system a reality.

Recovering Our Dropouts

It will do no good to raise academic standards for school leavers if large numbers of high school students cannot meet them. The idea of Youth Centers, the Commission's strategy for recovering school dropouts and bringing them up to a high academic standard, is an essential component of the whole strategy for national human resource development.

The Commission is working closely with the William T. Grant Foundation's Commission on Work, Family, and Citizenship and others to develop a national network of Youth Centers. A bill has been submitted to the New York State legislature to create Youth Centers in that state. The Commission is also working to make information available to other states on the characteristics of successful alternative education programs for dropouts.

Preparing Frontline Workers

Most employers in this country have never been seriously involved in setting industry standards for entry-level employment and have no established mechanisms for doing so. Neither do they have a tradition of offering formal, multiyear, on-the-job training programs to high school graduates.

Efforts are currently under way to change American employer attitudes and practices toward work force education. The U.S. Departments of Labor and Education are focusing on work force training and vocational education. The Department of Labor's Commission on Work-Based Learning serves as an advisory commission on workplace training and high-performance work organization.

The Commission on the Skills of the American Workforce plans to work with industry associations and key national business organizations to develop certification standards for their industries. This past summer, the Commission participated with the National Governor's Association and the National Council on Vocational Education in an NGA-sponsored conference on new forms of technical and professional preparation programs.

Reorganizing Work

Setting standards must go hand-in-glove with a strategy to reorganize work. Under current forms of work organization, employers do not demand highly skilled workers. It is unlikely that this country will do what must be done about workers' skills unless there is a strong demand from business and industry for people with those skills. That will not happen until employers see the need to embrace high-performance forms of work organization.

The Commission has met with national business groups to begin a concerted campaign to promote an understanding of high-performance work organization. Plans are under way to develop an industry-led technical assistance network to help companies make the transition. Some companies will have the international resources to develop the necessary training programs to upgrade worker skills, while others will need outside consultation.

Building a Comprehensive System

Without a coherent labor market system that embraces national, state, and local government, the Commission's other recommendations will be less effective. Therefore, the Commission has put forth a legislative proposal that we believe is a first step toward uniting disparate pieces of the nation's existing labor market programs. In addition, we plan to publish papers on the elements of the system we believe should be put in place—from postsecondary data systems to a reborn employment service. Then, we hope to convene a working group of state, federal, and national government leaders with business, labor, and education leaders to begin discussions in implementation.

Leaping Ahead

The system we propose provides a uniquely American solution. Boldly executed, it has the potential not simply to put us on an equal footing with our competitors, but to allow us to leap ahead, to build the world's premier work force. In doing so, we will create a formidable competitive advantage.

The status quo is not an option. The choice is between becoming a nation of high skills or one of low wages. The choice is ours. It should be clear. It must be made.

Themes, Issues, and Ideas

1. The logic of this essay is very tight, but does it allow for many obstacles? What stumbling blocks other than the ones mentioned might prevent American companies from adopting the authors' plan?

2. According to Magaziner and Clinton, by training its workers better and paying them more, America can turn its labor force around. Do you think this is true based on your own experience? Explain.

3. Is this essay directed only toward businesspeople, or does it have any importance for college students such as yourself? Explain your answer.

Writing Strategies and Techniques

1. What can you say about the style that Magaziner and Clinton use? Does it fit the subject matter? Why do you think it was chosen by the authors.

2. The authors of this essay talk about training "frontline" workers better. Why do you think they use this term? What images does it suggest?

Suggestions for Writing

1. Write a proposal for lower wages, written in as close an imitation of Magaziner and Clinton's style as you can manage.

2. Write an essay discussing the differences between abstract policy and actual reform, using this essay as an example.

Blowing Up the Tracks

Patricia Kean

> The practice of public school "tracking"—setting up
> classes for gifted, intermediate, and remedial students—has
> been around for the better part of a century. But according
> to Patricia Kean, tracking isn't all it's cracked up to be: It
> keeps "slower" students from receiving better grades, bet-
> ter education, and ultimately better jobs. Is there anything
> that can be done about tracking? What are its advantages,
> anyway? Patricia Kean, in an essay taken from the Wash-
> ington Monthly, takes a fresh look at an old practice—and
> gives it an F.
>
> Kean taught grade school in Manhattan during the
> 1980s. She is now writing about education full-time.

I t's morning in New York, and some seventh graders are
more equal than others.

Class 7-16 files slowly into the room, prodded by hard-faced
men whose walkie-talkies crackle with static. A pleasant looking
woman shouts over the din, "What's rule number one?" No reply. She
writes on the board. "Rule One: Sit down."

Rule number two seems to be an unwritten law: Speak slowly.
Each of Mrs. H's syllables hangs in the air a second longer than
necessary. In fact, the entire class seems to be conducted at 16 RPM.
Books come out gradually. Kids wander about the room aimlessly.
Twelve minutes into class, we settle down and begin to play "O.
Henry Jeopardy," a game which requires students to supply one-word
answers to questions like: "O. Henry moved from North Carolina to
what state—Andy? Find the word on the page."

The class takes out a vocabulary sheet. Some of the words they
are expected to find difficult include popular, ranch, suitcase, arrested, recipe, tricky, ordinary, humorous, and grand jury.

Thirty minutes pass. Bells ring, doors slam.

Class 7-1 marches in unescorted, mindful of rule number one.
Paperbacks of Poe smack sharply on desks, notebooks rustle, and kids

lean forward expectantly, waiting for Mrs. H to fire the first question. What did we learn about the writer?

Hands shoot into the air. Though Edgar Allen Poe ends up sounding a lot like Jerry Lee Lewis—a booze-hound who married his 13-year-old cousin—these kids speak confidently, in paragraphs. Absolutely no looking at the book allowed.

We also have a vocabulary sheet, drawn from "The Tell-Tale Heart," containing words like audacity, dissimulation, sagacity, stealthy, anxiety, derision, agony and supposition.

As I sit in the back of the classroom watching these two very different groups of seventh graders, my previous life as an English teacher allows me to make an educated guess and a chilling prediction. With the best of intentions, Mrs. H is teaching the first group, otherwise known as the "slow kids," as though they are fourth graders, and the second, the honors group, as though they are high school freshmen. Given the odds of finding a word like "ordinary" on the SAT's, the children of 7-16 have a better chance of standing before a "grand jury" than making it to college.

Tracking, the practice of placing students in "ability groups" based on a host of ill-defined criteria—everything from test scores to behavior to how much of a fuss a mother can be counted on to make— encourages even well-meaning teachers and administrators to turn out generation after generation of self-fulfilling prophecies. "These kids know they're no Einsteins," Mrs. H said of her low-track class when we sat together in the teacher's lounge. "They know they don't read well. This way I can go really slowly with them."

With his grades, however, young Albert would probably be hanging right here with the rest of lunch table 7-16. That's where I discover that while their school may think they're dumb, these kids are anything but stupid. "That teacher," sniffs a pretty girl wearing lots of purple lipstick. "She talks so slow. She thinks we're babies. She takes a year to do anything." "What about the other one?" a girl named Ingrid asks, referring to their once-a-week student teacher. "He comes in and goes like this: Rail (pauses) road. Rail (pauses) road. Like we don't know what a railroad means!" The table breaks up laughing.

Outside the walls of the schools across the country, it's slowly become an open secret that enforced homogeneity benefits no one. The work of researchers like Jeannie Oakes of UCLA and Robert Slavin of Johns Hopkins has proven that tracking does not merely reflect differences—it causes them. Over time, slow kids get slower, while those in the middle and in the so-called "gifted and talented" top tracks fail to gain from isolation. Along the way, the practice resegregates the nation's schools, dividing the middle from the lower classes, white from black and brown. As the evidence piles up, everyone from the Carnegie Corporation to the National Governors Association has called for change.

Though some fashionably progressive schools have begun to reform, tracking persists. Parent groups, school boards, teachers, and administrators who hold the power within schools cling to the myths and wax apocalyptic about the horrors of heterogeneity. On their side is the most potent force known to man: bureaucratic inertia. Because tracking puts kids in boxes, keeps the lid on, and shifts responsibility for mediocrity and failure away from the schools themselves, there is little incentive to change a nearly century-old tradition. "Research is research," the principal told me that day, "This is practice."

Back Track

Tracking has been around since just after the turn of the century. It was then, as cities teemed with immigrants and industry, that education reformers like John Franklin Bobbitt began to argue that the school and the factory shared a common mission, to "work up the raw material into that finished product for which it was best adapted." By the twenties, the scientific principles that ruled the factory floor had been applied to the classroom. They believed the IQ test—which had just become popular—allowed pure science, not the whims of birth or class, to determine whether a child received the type of education appropriate for a future manager or a future laborer.

It hasn't quite worked out that way. Driven by standardized tests, the descendants of the old IQ tests, tracking has evolved into a kind of educational triage premised on the notion that only the least wounded can be saved. Yet when the classroom operates like a battleground, society's casualties mount, and the results begin to seem absurd: Kids who enter school needing more get less, while the already enriched get, well, enricher. Then, too, the low-track graduates of 70 years ago held a distinct advantage over their modern counterparts: If tracking prepared them for mindless jobs, at least those jobs existed.

The sifting and winnowing starts as early as pre-K. Three-year old Ebony and her classmates have won the highly prized "gifted and talented" label after enduring a battery of IQ and psychological tests. There's nothing wrong with the "regular" class in this Harlem public school. But high expectations for Ebony and her new friends bring tangible rewards like a weekly field trip and music and computer lessons.

Meanwhile, regular kids move on to regular kindergartens where they too will be tested, and where it will be determined that some children need more help, perhaps a "pre-first grade" developmental year. So by the time they're ready for first grade reading groups, certain six-year-olds have already been marked as "sparrows"—the low performers in the class.

In the beginning, it doesn't seem to matter so much, because the other reading groups—the robins and the eagles—are just a few feet away and the class is together for most of the day. Trouble is, as they toil over basic drill sheets, the sparrows are slipping farther behind. The robins are gathering more challenging vocabulary words, and the eagles soaring on to critical thinking skills.

Though policies vary, by fourth grade many of these groups have flown into completely separate classrooms, turning an innocent three-tier reading system into three increasingly rigid academic tracks—honors, regular, and remedial—by middle school.

Unless middle school principals take heroic measures like buying expensive software or crafting daily schedules by hand, it often becomes a lot easier to sort everybody by reading scores. So kids who do well on reading tests can land in the high track for math, science, social studies, even lunch, and move together as a self-contained unit all day. Friendships form, attitudes harden. Kids on top study together, kids in the middle console themselves by making fun of the "nerds" above and the "dummies" below, and kids on the bottom develop behavioral problems and get plenty of negative reinforcement.

By high school, many low-track students are locked out of what Jeannie Oakes calls "gatekeeper courses," the science, math, and foreign language classes that hold the key to life after twelfth grade. Doors to college are slamming shut, though the kids themselves are often the last to know. When researcher Anne Wheelock interviewed students in Boston's public schools, they'd all insist they were going to become architects, teachers, and the like. What courses were they taking? "Oh, Keyboarding II, Earth Science, Consumer Math. This would be junior year and I'd ask, 'Are you taking Algebra?' and they'd say no."

Black Marks

A funny thing can happen to minority students on the way to being tracked. Even when minority children score high, they often find themselves placed in lower tracks where counselors and principals assume they belong.

In Paula Hart's travels for The Achievement Council, a Los Angeles-based educational advocacy group, she comes across district after district where black and Latino kids score in the 75th percentile for math, yet never quite make it into Algebra I, the classic gatekeeper course. A strange phenomenon occurs in inner city areas with large minority populations—high track classes shrink, and low track classes expand to fit humble expectations for the entire school population.

A few years ago, Dr. Norward Roussell's curiosity got the better of him. As Selma, Alabama's first black school superintendent, he couldn't help but notice that "gifted and talented" tracks were nearly lily white in a district that was 70 percent black. When he looked for answers in the files of high school students, he discovered that a surprising number of low track minority kids had actually scored higher than their white top track counterparts.

Parents of gifted and talented students staged a full-scale revolt against Roussell's subsequent efforts to establish logical standards for placement. In four days of public hearings, speaker after speaker said the same thing: We're going to lose a lot of our students to other schools. To Roussell, their meaning was clear: Put black kids in the high tracks and we pull white kids out of the system. More blacks and more low-income whites did make it to the top under the new criteria, but Roussell himself was left behind. The majority-white school board chose not to renew his contract, and he's now superintendent in Macon County, Alabama, a district that is overwhelmingly black.

Race and class divisions usually play themselves out in a more subtle fashion. Talk to teachers about how their high track kids differ from their low track kids and most speak not of intelligence, but of motivation and "family." It seems that being gifted and talented is hereditary after all, largely a matter of having parents who read to you, who take you to museums and concerts, and who know how to work the system. Placement is often a matter of who's connected. Jennifer P., a teacher in a Brooklyn elementary school saw a pattern in her class. "The principal put all the kids whose parents were in the PTA in the top tracks no matter what their scores were. He figures that if his PTA's happy, he's happy."

Once the offspring of the brightest and the best connected have been skimmed off in honors or regular tracks, low tracks begin to fill up with children whose parents are not likely to complain. These kids get less homework, spend less class time learning, and are often taught by the least experienced teachers, because avoiding them can become a reward for seniority in a profession where perks are few.

With the courts reluctant to get involved, even when tracking leads to racial segregation and at least the appearance of civil rights violations, changing the system becomes an arduous local battle fought school by school. Those who undertake the delicate process of untracking need nerves of steel and should be prepared to find resistance from every quarter, since, as Slavin notes, parents of high-achieving kids will fight this to the death. One-time guidance counselor Hart learned this lesson more than a decade ago when she and two colleagues struggled to introduce a now-thriving college curriculum program at Los Angeles' Banning High. Their efforts to open top-track classes to all students prompted death threats from an unlikely source—their fellow teachers.

Off Track Betting

Anne Wheelock's new book, *Crossing the Tracks,* tells the stories of schools that have successfully untracked or never tracked at all. Schools that make the transition often achieve dramatic results. True to its name, Pioneer Valley Regional school in Northfield, Massachusetts was one of the first in the nation to untrack. Since 1983, the number of Pioneer Valley seniors going on to higher education jumped from 37 to 80 percent. But, the author says, urban schools continue to lag behind. "We're talking about unequal distribution of reform," Wheelock declares. "Change is taking place in areas like Wellesley, Massachusetts and Jericho, Long Island. It's easier to untrack when kids are closer to one another to begin with."

It's also easier for educators to tinker with programs and make cosmetic adjustments than it is to ask them to do what bureaucrats hate most: give up one method of doing things without having another to put in its place. Tracking is a system; untracking is a leap of faith. When difficult kids can no longer be dumped in low tracks, new ways must be found to deal with disruptive behavior: early intervention, intensive work with families, and lots of tutoring. Untracking may also entail new instructional techniques like cooperative group learning and peer tutoring, but what it really demands is flexibility and improvisation.

It also demands that schools—and the rest of us—admit that some kids will be so disruptive or violent that a solution for dealing with them must be found *outside* of the regular public school system. New York City seems close to such a conclusion. Schools Chancellor Joseph Fernandez is moving forward with a voluntary "academy" program, planning separate schools designed to meet the needs of chronic troublemakers. One of them, the Wildcat Academy, run by a non-profit group of the same name, plans to enroll 150 students by the end of the year. Wildcat kids will attend classes from nine to five, wear uniforms, hold part-time jobs, and be matched with mentors from professional fields. Districts in Florida and California are conducting similar experiments.

Moving away from tracking is not about taking away from the gifted and talented and giving to the poor. That, as Wheelock notes, is "political suicide." It's not even about placing more black and Latino kids in their midst, a kind of pre-K affirmative action. Rather, it's about raising expectations for everyone. Or, as Slavin puts it: "You can maintain your tracking system. Just put everyone into the top track."

That's not as quixotic as it sounds. In fact, it's long been standard practice in the nation's Catholic schools, a system so backward it's actually progressive. When I taught in an untracked parochial high school, one size fit all—with the exception of the few we expelled for poor grades or behavior. My students, who differed widely in ability, interest, and background, nevertheless got Shakespeare, Thoreau, and Langston Hughes at the same pace, at the same time—and lived to tell the tale. Their survival came, in part, because my colleagues and I could decide if the cost of keeping a certain student around was too high and we had the option of sending him or her elsewhere if expulsion was warranted.

The result was that my honor students wrote elegant essays and made it to Ivy League schools, right on schedule. And far from being held back by their "regular" and "irregular" counterparts, straight-A students were more likely to be challenged by questions they would never dream of asking. "Why are we studying this?" a big-haired girl snapping gum in the back of the room wondered aloud one day. Her question led to a discussion that turned into the best class I ever taught.

In four years, I never saw a single standardized test score. But time after time I watched my students climb out of whatever mental category I had put them in. Tracking sees to it that they never get that chance. Flying directly in the face of Yogi Berra's Rule Number One, it tells kids it's over before it's even begun. For ultimately, tracking stunts the opportunity for growth, the one area in which all children are naturally gifted.

Themes, Issues, and Ideas

1. Did you attend a school where tracking was used? If so, does Kean's critique seem true? If not, do you think your school would have been helped or hindered by tracking?

2. Public versus private education is a controversial issue now. Does this reading shed light on this issue for you? How so?

3. What are some benefits to tracking for students? What are some disadvantages? Answer the question for both "gifted" and "backward" students.

Writing Strategies and Techniques

1. How does Kean get the reader on her side in the essay? What does she do, and not do, to persuade the reader?

2. What does Kean assume about the reader? Does your response, as a reader, justify these assumptions?

Suggestions for Writing

1. Write an essay describing how tracking might work in another setting: college, home, work, etc.

2. Write an essay describing your own experience with the tracking system. Does it cause you to agree or disagree with Kean? Explain.

Education—
Less of It!

Tertius Chandler

The preceding essays in this chapter present wide-ranging disagreements, but they all share the view that more and perhaps different formal education is needed to meet the life awaiting us in the twenty-first century. The author of this essay has a different estimation of the benefits and limits of higher education. Although he acknowledges the common faith people place in education, he says, "I venture to wonder why."

Tertius Chandler was born near Boston in 1915 and graduated from Harvard University in 1937. He did graduate work at the University of California at Berkeley and has both given and taken courses throughout his lifetime. He has also washed "a few million dishes," edited two magazines, and run for Congress twice. This essay was first published in The College Board Review.

Will Durant in his *Lessons of History* claimed that the greatest hope of the human race is increased education.

I venture to wonder why? School is unfree, rather like a jail with a term lasting twenty years, if you're able to stick the course. Childhood and youth are sacred times when innate curiosity is intense and health and zest tend to be strong. Those years are too important to be frittered away memorizing irrelevant trivia in herded mobs under the heavy hand of compulsion. Ben Franklin had just two years in school and flunked both times—yet he went on to make himself the ablest and best-rounded leader in our history. Pascal and Petrie had no schooling at all. So learning can occur outside school as well as in—perhaps even better, and especially now, when there are fine libraries open to all as well as television, bookstores, newspapers, and magazines. Think of the *National Geographic!*

Here on the other hand are arguments for education:

1. *Older people know more, so the young can learn from them.* Parental teaching might be preferable (and does increasingly occur), but in many families both parents are away at work. Anyway, teachers are specialists in particular subjects. These arguments are valid, and, it must be conceded, some learning does occur in schools.

2. *Money!* A school diploma is virtually useless on the job market, and so is a college degree. But school prepares for college, which prepares for postgraduate school, which prepares for entry into well-paid professions. In 1981 the average high school graduate made $18,138, whereas the average for those with five or more years of college was $32,887. Lifetime earnings for the high school graduates averaged $845,000, compared with $1,503,000 for five-year collegians.[1] Yet an underlying flaw vitiates the comparison, for college draws people of higher intelligence and those from richer families. Their lifelong earnings largely reflect these particular factors.

3. *The rah-rah spirit.* A person likes to say he or she has been to such-and-such college. It's the "in" thing.

4. *High ambition.* In this country of open opportunity parents naturally push their children all they can. It is refreshing to recall, however, that Washington, Lincoln, and Truman were among those who made it to president without going to college—and they were unusually good presidents.

5. *Culture.* The claim is often made that if culture wasn't rammed into the young, they would never come to appreciate literature, art, and fine music. Frankly, that's ridiculous.

6. *Meeting friends.* There are, of course, other places to meet people, and most of them allow more leisure to enjoy the friendship. Nevertheless it must be said that college is a fine place to make interesting acquaintances. Students are easily met in the dining halls and on campus. Eventually one may make friends even among the professors.

To sum up, education does pass on some learning and introduces a person to many out-of-town folks, while being the only way to enter some professions. But it takes a long, long time!

Conditioned Robots

Raymond Moore observes that: "The biggest shortcoming of mass education is the fact that students end up completely turned off to learning."[2] Or as Bertrand Russell ruefully concluded: "We are faced with the paradox that education has become one of the chief obstacles of intelligence and freedom of thought."

The educational profession has become geared to the College Board examinations, which give it an awesome amount of rigidity. As a result, elective courses are rather few, and are becoming fewer even in college.

The number of school years is also prescribed. If a child masters mathematics in one year, so much the worse for him. Conversely, someone of low IQ has to suffer year after year with subjects that baffle him. Insofar as school is adjusted to anybody, it is adjusted to the mediocre student, and he, hopelessly unable to lead the class or win any prize, just drones on, loathing the whole procedure.

All that keeps the system from destroying the students altogether is that most of them instinctively rebel inwardly against it and cooperate only enough to get by, reserving as much energy and time as they can manage for other activities. Indeed, the most unruly boys in class sometimes tend to do better later on in life. Unfortunately some rebellious activities, such as smoking, heavy drinking, and fast driving, are not healthy, yet by a discreet degree of rebelliousness and shirking a boy can remain spiritually alive.

As Agatha Christie put it: "I suppose it is because nearly all children go to school nowadays, and have things arranged for them, that they seem so forlornly unable to produce their own ideas."[3]

Kahlil Gibran's great passage is relevant here: "Your children are not your children. They are the sons and daughters of life's longing for itself . . . you may give them your love but not your thoughts, for they have their own thoughts. You may house their bodies but not their souls. Their souls dwell in the house of tomorrow, which you may not visit, even in your dreams."

Gibran was not looking for conditioned robots.

A Shorter School Year

Some sadist must have written the law requiring 180 annual school days. They begin in August, when berries are still ripening, and last into the sweltering heat of June. Fall and spring, by their nature gorgeous seasons, become fixed in young minds as symbols of the agony of school.

It was when I was about halfway through prep school that teachers thought up a way to cut into the summer vacation—our only prolonged free time. They began assigning compulsory reading of novels. This was a grief and an indignity I will not easily forget. I had been reading the finest sort of literature on my own in the summers. After that I read the minimum—and hated it. Liberty dies hard in the human soul.

Change should be in the other direction: toward less schooling.

How Early?

Jean Piaget noticed stages in children's capacity to learn. To impose reading and mathematics on them before their minds are ready is to puzzle and torment them. School by its nature is force-feeding and, when children are very young, not only their bodies but also their feelings are very tender. To separate them from their parents and to inflict cold drill in seemingly pointless subjects on them can drive their feelings inward and make them feel unwanted and lonely, even in a crowded room. All this Piaget understood. Indeed, it is perfectly obvious.

But, Piaget added, give the students those same subjects a few years later, and they can grasp them rather quickly, because their minds have become equal to the techniques needed and because they have reached the stage where they can see a purpose in what they are doing.

Raymond Moore in his book *School Can Wait*[4] suggests delaying school to the age of eight or ten and in a recently published letter[5] opposes giving any exams before the age of ten. The idea is not new. A century ago Robert Owen withheld books from children in his famous school until their tenth year. Montessori, likewise, set the young to playing games. These are the real heroes for the cause of children.

Puberty

School treats pupils alike year after year. Yet somewhere in their teens boys notice girls. They are never the same again. School carries on as if the children were still just that. In the school where I went, aside from a warning to "stay pure," nothing changed. The hard drill on useless scholasticism to get us into college continued. We were to think college and nothing but college so that success in life would be automatic.

I got the message. When I was seventeen I met a girl I liked on a ski trip. I deliberately dropped her and by a hard effort, managed to forget her, since I still had five years before I'd be clear of college (actually nine, but I didn't know about postgraduate study then). That was a romance that should have gotten off the ground and didn't. Looking back, I see that I could probably have worked in the girl's father's factory. The father and mother liked me. I was past the compulsory school-age, which was then sixteen in my state—but nobody told me things like that. College was a fixation for my parents and my teachers, and therefore for me, too.

I was not unique. Bernard DeVoto told us in a talk at Harvard around 1935, "No one marries his first love." He meant among the highly educated, for of course some dropouts do marry their first choice. It was, anyway, a chilling remark, an unpleasant commentary on how the educational system impacts on youth. The trade-off of love for a series of degrees is a poor deal.

Lately, private schools have done a sudden about-face and flung the boys and girls together. They are aroused to love earlier and so have longer to agonize. Education and puberty thus now clash head-on, but they still haven't come to terms.

On Teaching English

English can be dropped altogether. Charles W. Eliot of Harvard and others put English into our schools in 1900 by making it a requirement for the College Board Examinations. Eliot's idea was that pupils can be compelled to present ideas clearly and to enjoy literature. He would drill these skills into them. The sheer quantity of disciplined effort would get results and turn our 18-year-olds into incisive, clear, witty writers.

The result of all this massive drill over nearly a century has been to make our youths somewhat duller than before. Our few famous writers now are notable for their gloom, their insobriety, and their utter inability to come up with answers to our problems. It would seem that English was made a required subject to no purpose whatsoever.

The correct way to teach English fundamentals—grammar, spelling, sentence structure—is to teach them as a part of other subjects. That way, English has a chance of being interesting. Just in this way, one teaches the use of a hammer in the process of teaching carpentry; one does not take a special course in hammering. It would be fiendishly dull if one did.

Mathematics

Ever since the Russians put Sputnik into orbit in 1957 there have been spasmodic efforts to increase the mathematics load of *all* U.S. schoolchildren, including future janitors, nurses, maids, and ditch diggers. While I respect those occupations, they do not require higher mathematics. Actually any useful computations for war or business will be made by a very few experts—perhaps by one-hundredth of 1 percent of the population—and they will be using computers.

Underwood Dudley of DePauw University, himself a mathematics teacher, believes that we teach mathematics not to solve problems or inculcate logical thinking but simply because we always have done so. As he puts it: "Practical? When was the last time you had to solve a quadratic equation? Was it just last week that you needed to find the volume of a cone? Isn't it a fact that you never need any mathematics beyond arithmetic? . . . Algebra? Good heavens! Almost all people never use algebra, ever, outside of a classroom."[6]

He rightly adds that mathematical talent is very easy to spot early in life. Surely he is right that a special annual test should be held to see which students should be allowed to take mathematics beyond arithmetic—as an honor, not a requirement! The motivated proud few would then accomplish more than the slave-driven multitude.

Any School at All?

Once the need for school was clear. Back around 1800 schools were few and didn't take long, only four to six years. They taught basics and were almost the only place for the young to get books. Nowadays, alternative means of learning are plentiful. As already mentioned, they include public libraries, television, bookstores, newspapers, and magazines. These actually represent an overabundance.

If some state dropped schooling altogether, I wouldn't oppose it. (I would not wish this change to be imposed by the federal government however.)

Self-Reliance

Adult life calls for decision making and responsibility. These arise naturally at home but not in the educational system, where teachers make the decisions. A student, moreover, is competing against all the others, a self-centered attitude he will have to drop when he goes on to a job or into marriage.

Required Reading

In British colleges (but not schools!) the students pick their own reading. Here in the United States, students are told what to read and when to read it. Recoiling against this conformity, Professor Carl Sauer told us in his class at the University of California in 1939: "The required book list defeats its own purpose. Books should enable you to meet ideas, meet other personalities, if you like, appropriating from them what you can use, what you need. I don't think I remember a single thing I had to read as required reading for any professor in college. I think if I had had any share in the discovery of something, a few ideas would have stuck. . . . Doing things for instructors is basically not doing anything at all."

Do Universities Broaden Minds?

Does university training help or hinder in developing intellectual capacity to do highly original work? Among highly creative modern thinkers the following were formally educated: Montesquieu, Jefferson, Goethe, Macaulay, Marx, Freud, Schweitzer, Proskouriakoff, Champollion, and Gandhi. These did not go to college: Voltaire, Hume, Owen, Austen, Balzac, Jairazbhoy, Gibran, Tolstoy, Twain, and Shaw.

Bright people can teach themselves. As Henry Adams said, "No one can educate anyone else. You have to do it for yourself." There should, of course, be equivalency exams for the self-taught, as well as on-the-job training, for most professions.

Some would claim that if the youthful were encouraged to act freely, their initiative would be too great; that they would go berserk. But I think not: Most would marry, others would travel, invent, and carry on original work on all sorts of lines. Early marriage could balance many of them so they could work better. It is worth remembering in this connection that among the young, idealism and faith are uncommonly strong.

Those destined for ordinary jobs don't need to learn anything taught in college, and many of them know it. They attend college because it's the thing to do. They tend to take "snaps" such as English literature or sociology. I see no objection to letting them enjoy themselves at private colleges if they want to.

Public universities should, I think, confine themselves to serious training. The number entering should be preset as in Sweden, so as to train the quantity of people needed to fit the estimated number of openings in each profession, always allowing for the rise of some persons via equivalency exams.

College represents now too much of a good thing. There are too many learned professors and section leaders to adjust to, too many books to hasten through at a set speed, too many years to plod away on the treadmill. A Ph.D. in history is now expected to take four to eight years—on top of the twelve in school and four in college. Perhaps, worst of all, the Ph.D. subject is deliberately kept small, so that the student will be able to claim mastery of something. Four to eight years of deliberate narrowing can have the effect of incapacitating him from ever taking a broad view of anything. The result of all this mental drill tends to be a mashed human, an eviscerated person. Only a very sturdy soul, such as a Freud or a Schweitzer, can come through all this and still retain the ability to think for himself. University study could, with no intrinsic loss, be shortened from eight years to four, and school could be limited to ages ten to fifteen.

These suggested reductions in compulsory education would have another powerful advantage: They might set our people's minds largely free, a result surely to be wished.

References

1. *Digest of Education Statistics.* Washington, D.C.: National Center for Education Statistics, 1982. P. 181–82.
2. Raymond Moore, *Parent Educator & Family Report,* August 1984. P. 6.
3. Agatha Christie, *Autobiography.* New York: Doubleday, 1978.   P. 59.
4. Raymond Moore, *School Can Wait.*
5. Raymond Moore, correspondence cited in *Parent Educator & Family Report,* January 24, 1985.
6. Underwood Dudley, article in *San Francisco Chronicle,* April 28, 1984.

Themes, Issues, and Ideas

1. Chandler says of the years we normally spend in education: "Those years are too important to be frittered away memorizing irrelevant trivia in herded mobs under the heavy hand of compulsion." What examples and arguments does he offer to support his views?

2. How has your own education equipped you to judge Chandler's essay? Does your experience support or refute Chandler's claims?

3. Chandler argues that English courses should be dropped altogether. How do you feel about this? What arguments would you use to defend or refute Chandler on this issue?

Writing Strategies and Techniques

1. How many famous people without formal education does Chandler name? How does he use them as examples? Does he suggest, for instance, that *not* going to school will make you famous?

2. Chandler lists six reasons in favor of education in the beginning of his essay. What would have been the effect if he had made his own points first?

Suggestions for Writing

1. Beginning with a list of Chandler's arguments against formal education, write an essay defending education, using Chandler's essay as a model.

2. Write an essay that sketches out the ideal education for students (as Chandler would see it) from the time they begin school up to the age of twenty-one.

MAKING CONNECTIONS

1. Robert Reich, Hillary Rodham Clinton, and Ira Magaziner are, unlike most of the authors in this book, now in a position to implement some of their ideas. Does this give their essays added weight? How does the fact that they may influence national policy change the way you read their work?

2. How might Patricia Kean respond to Clinton and Magaziner's or Chandler's views of education? How does the idea of tracking appear in some of the other essays in this chapter?

3. Describe a typical school day as it might exist if each of the writers in this chapter had his or her way.

4. Do you think writers such as Nathan Glazer or Tertius Chandler really seem to know what it's like to go to school in the 1990s? What could you tell them they missed in their essays? Would your comments radically change the point of their essays?

5. After reading these essays, combine the best ideas in each of them to create your own master plan for revitalizing American education. Support your selections with quotations from the readings and solid reasoning of your own.

CHAPTER FIVE

American Policy for the Twenty-first Century

The Nation's Place in a Changing World

THE PAST AS PROLOGUE

Inaugural Address

John Fitzgerald Kennedy

Nominated on the first ballot at the Democratic Convention, Senator John Fitzgerald Kennedy (1917–1963) won the 1960 presidential election by the narrow popular margin of 118,000 votes (though he gained a substantial majority in the electoral college) and became the youngest president in the history of the United States. Kennedy served in World War II and succeeded President Dwight D. Eisenhower, who led the Allied armies in Europe during that war. As Kennedy's speech shows, he took office during a time when America's confidence in its military, economic, and moral powers was at its height, though those powers were felt to be threatened by the global expansion of communism. Kennedy delivered his inaugural address on January 20, 1961.

Vice-President Johnson, Mr. Speaker, Mr. Chief Justice, President Eisenhower, Vice-President Nixon, President Truman, Reverend Clergy, Fellow Citizens:

We observe today not a victory of party but a celebration of freedom—symbolizing an end as well as a beginning—signifying renewal as well as change. For I have sworn before you and Almighty God the same solemn oath our forebearers prescribed nearly a century and three-quarters ago.

The world is very different now. For man holds in his mortal hands the power to abolish all forms of human poverty and all forms of human life. And yet the same revolutionary beliefs for which our forebearers fought are still at issue around the globe—the belief that the rights of man come not from the generosity of the state but from the hand of God.

We dare not forget today that we are the heirs of that first revolution. Let the word go forth from this time and place, to friend and foe alike, that the torch has been passed to a new generation of Americans—born in this century, tempered by war, disciplined by a hard and bitter peace, proud of our ancient heritage—and unwilling to witness or permit the slow undoing of those human rights to which this nation has always been committed, and to which we are committed today at home and around the world.

Let every nation know, whether it wishes us well or ill, that we shall pay any price, bear any burden, meet any hardship, support any friend, oppose any foe to assure the survival and the success of liberty.

This much we pledge—and more.

To those old allies whose cultural and spiritual origins we share, we pledge the loyalty of faithful friends. United, there is little we cannot do in a host of cooperative ventures. Divided, there is little we can do—for we dare not meet a powerful challenge at odds and split asunder.

To those new states whom we welcome to the ranks of the free, we pledge our word that one form of colonial control shall not have passed away merely to be replaced by a far more iron tyranny. We shall not always expect to find them supporting our view. But we shall always hope to find them strongly supporting their own freedom—and to remember that, in the past, those who foolishly sought power by riding the back of the tiger ended up inside.

To those people in the huts and villages of half the globe struggling to break the bonds of mass misery, we pledge our best efforts to help them help themselves, for whatever period is required—not because the Communists may be doing it, not because we seek their votes, but because it is right. If a free society cannot help the many who are poor, it cannot save the few who are rich.

To our sister republics south of our border, we offer a special pledge—to convert our good words into good deeds—in a new alliance for progress—to assist free men and free governments in casting off the chains of poverty. But this peaceful revolution of hope cannot become the prey of hostile powers. Let all our neighbors know that we shall join with them to oppose aggression or subversion anywhere in the Americas. And let every other power know that this hemisphere intends to remain the master of its own house.

To that world assembly of sovereign states, the United Nations, our last best hope in an age where the instruments of war have far outpaced the instruments of peace, we renew our pledge of support—to prevent it from becoming merely a forum for invective—to strengthen its shield of the new and the weak—and to enlarge the area in which its writ may run.

Finally, to those nations who would make themselves our adversary, we offer not a pledge but a request: that both sides begin anew the quest for peace, before the dark powers of destruction unleashed by science engulf all humanity in planned or accidental self-destruction.

We dare not tempt them with weakness. For only when our arms are sufficient beyond doubt can we be certain beyond doubt that they will never be employed.

But neither can two great and powerful groups of nations take comfort from our present course—both sides overburdened by the cost of modern weapons, both rightly alarmed by the steady spread of the deadly atom, yet both racing to alter that uncertain balance of terror that stays the hand of mankind's final war.

So let us begin anew—remembering on both sides that civility is not a sign of weakness, and sincerity is always subject to proof. Let us never negotiate out of fear. But let us never fear to negotiate.

Let both sides explore what problems unite us instead of belaboring those problems which divide us.

Let both sides, for the first time, formulate serious and precise proposals for the inspection and control of arms—and bring the absolute power to destroy other nations under the absolute control of all nations.

Let both sides seek to invoke the wonders of science instead of its terrors. Together let us explore the stars, conquer the deserts, eradicate disease, tap the ocean depths, and encourage the arts and commerce.

Let both sides unite to heed in all corners of the earth the command of Isaiah—to "undo the heavy burdens . . . [and] let the oppressed go free."

And if a beachhead of cooperation may push back the jungle of suspicion, let both sides join in creating a new endeavor, not a new balance of power, but a new world of law, where the strong are just and the weak secure and the peace preserved.

All this will not be finished in the first one hundred days. Nor will it be finished in the first one thousand days, nor in the life of this administration, nor even perhaps in our lifetime on this planet. But let us begin.

In your hands, my fellow citizens, more than mine, will rest the final success or failure of our course. Since this country was founded, each generation of Americans has been summoned to give testimony to its national loyalty. The graves of young Americans who answered the call to service surround the globe.

Now the trumpet summons us again—not as a call to bear arms, though arms we need—not as a call to battle, though embattled we are—but a call to bear the burden of a long twilight struggle, year in and year out, "rejoicing in hope, patient in tribulation"—a struggle against the common enemies of man: tyranny, poverty, disease, and war itself.

Can we forge against these enemies a grand and global alliance, North and South, East and West, that can assure a more fruitful life for all mankind? Will you join in that historic effort?

In the long history of the world, only a few generations have been granted the role of defending freedom in its hour of maximum danger. I do not shrink from this responsibility—I welcome it. I do not believe that any of us would exchange places with any other people or any other generation. The energy, the faith, the devotion which we bring to this endeavor will light our country and all who serve it—and the glow from that fire can truly light the world.

And so, my fellow Americans: Ask not what your country can do for you—ask what you can do for your country.

My fellow citizens of the world: Ask not what America will do for you, but what together we can do for the freedom of man.

Finally, whether you are citizens of America or citizens of the world, ask of us here the same high standards of strength and sacrifice which we ask of you. With a good conscience our only sure reward, with history the final judge of our deeds, let us go forth to lead the land we love, asking His blessing and His help, but knowing that here on earth God's work must truly be our own.

Themes, Issues, and Ideas

1. According to President Kennedy, what are the main differences in the United States between the time of the American Revolution and 1961?

2. What similarities does he see between Revolutionary times and his own era?

3. "Power" and "peace" are two themes that run throughout the speech. How and where does the language of power express the theme of peace? What is the effect of this combination?

Writing Strategies and Techniques

1. In his first paragraph, President Kennedy begins using a series of antitheses that organize many of the sentences throughout his speech: "not a victory, but a celebration . . . an end as well as a beginning . . . renewal as well as change." How does the device also organize the speech on a larger scale than that of the individual sentence?

2. Outline the topics covered by the speech. Does the order of the topics give the speech a "plot?" If you think so, tell how the plot serves the ending. If you think not, show how to change the order of topics without affecting the conclusion.

Suggestions for Writing

1. Where and how do you think Kennedy would change his speech, were he to take office today? Write an essay in which you address this issue and include a few paragraphs of the new speech as examples.

2. Write an essay analyzing the style of the speech in order to show how it is or is not an essay particularly suited to oral presentation.

The Surge to Democracy

Richard Falk

Written just before the peaceful revolutions of 1989 in Eastern Europe, this essay by Richard Falk foresees some of the forces that contributed to the success of these revolutions. Yet at the time of this book's publication, Falk seems to have misjudged some of the other issues involved in his topic. As a result, his essay is a useful example of both the possibilities and the dangers of political prediction.

In contrast to the preceding inaugural address by President Kennedy, Falk believes that the threats to democracy come not from other governments, but from the nature of government itself. Falk is a professor of international law at Princeton University, and the author of numerous books and articles on the problem of justice and order in governments. This essay was originally published in The Center Magazine.

An exciting contemporary political development is the eruption of various movements for democracy in socialist countries, in Third World countries, and in advanced industrial countries. This may seem to be an obvious element of the international picture today, but it was not occurring twenty years ago.

In the mid-1960s, there was the anticipation of the militarization of the world—at least of the Third World. In Eastern European countries, there was no political space for oppositional activity, and efforts to confront the state militarily were failing. In the advanced industrial countries, there was political passivity and no real prospect of reinvigorating the democratic process.

Today, however, peoples of diverse cultural and political environments are aspiring to achieve political space and to assert popular sovereignty. The modern state can employ a large secret police force, extend its military into the society, and try to dominate thought processes, but it cannot suppress this aspiration for popular sovereignty. That aspiration speaks to the character of politics itself and to the resilience of the human spirit.

Throughout our own history, the state has been challenged by citizens and coalitions convinced that particular state policies were wrong. Henry Thoreau conscientiously objected to our war with Mexico and the institutions of slavery by refusing to pay a poll tax, for which he spent a night in jail. The South tried to secede from the Union to preserve its prevailing lifestyle. In each case, a particular state policy was experienced as *substantively* unacceptable and not challengeable by the *procedures* at the disposal of the citizenry, that is, through elections, persuasion, and judicial access.

What are the new democratizing practices? In Eastern Europe, militant social movements for democracy and human rights now realize that it is self-destructive to confront the state militarily, that violence will not necessarily help their struggle for democratization.

There is the idea that capturing control over the state may not be a desirable goal, which is partly learned from the fact that when Marxism gained state power, it did not embody its vision in a new social order. The idea is that not everything that matters is at the center of the political system. The practices of how one lives life within the society—in terms of persons being trustful and honest in carrying out their work and human relations—are extraordinary challenges to the authoritarian state that relies on lying, distrust, and the undermining of personal integrity.

There is also a new understanding of the democratization process, specifically, that democratizing practices should occur at every level of social interaction, including how men and women relate to each other and how family life is organized and expressed, because that shapes our understanding of power and authority in a way that is ultimately the foundation for political life.

In *Letters from Prison,* Adam Michnik—one of the leaders of Solidarity—writes:

"The value of your participation cannot be gauged in terms of your chances of victory but rather by the value of your idea. In other words, you score a victory, not when you win power, but when you remain faithful to yourself. . . .

"We need people who do not lie publicly, whom we can trust, who reject compromise with the system of government that has been imposed on this nation—yet who do not ask for rash actions, call for terrorism, or organize urban or rural guerrillas. In other words, the classic dilemma can be described as grass-roots activity versus collaboration, not just as grass-roots activity versus insurrection."

Modern states—even the most democratic—have induced an ethos of passivity. People in general have become subjects rather than citizens. Their participation in the political process is merely a ritual. However, new social movements—such as the environmental movement, the women's movement, the antinuclear movement—are expressing political values and forms that cannot be expressed through conventional vehicles, namely, our two major political parties.

The development of and the reliance on nuclear weapons as instruments of security condition the character of democracy. Behind that conditioning is a familiar example from an introductory zoology course: When a frog is immersed in scalding water, it jumps to safety; when it is immersed in warm water that is gradually heated, it is ultimately scalded to death. In the nuclear age we have been scalded to death. We have accepted, as normal, certain political developments that have gradually encroached upon the democratic process of translating popular sovereignty into effective government.

From the beginning of democratic thought, wartime conditions have included the suspension of many of the features of democracy. A society prepared for nuclear war is a society perpetually poised on the brink of war. It is mobilized for war as a normal condition, and it can never be demobilized. The resulting national security doctrine has to be sustained by an inflated hostility toward one's adversary, because if a society wants to stay prepared for war, it must have somebody to fight. Everybody agrees we should prevent a nuclear war, but not everybody agrees on how that can be done.

A four-star commanding general of the Strategic Air Command—who, besides the president, is probably the most important person in the United States—has said that during the Cuban missile crisis he wished the Soviet Union had attacked Florida, because that would have given us the pretext for wiping the Russians off the face of the earth. He said that would have united our country. In other words, in his view, the United States had to find a nuclear war in order to become united.

The most important policy issue of our government is the invisible part of the governing process dealing with nuclear national security. The national security mystique serves as a pretext for the government keeping all kinds of things secret, not so much from the so-called enemy, as from the American people. Secrecy is needed in a democracy because the government wants to pursue a dual policy: It wants to do certain things that conform with the civic virtue of our society, but it also wants to do other things that are contrary to the civic virtue. Covert operations thus enable the government to do things under the name of realism that could not otherwise be justified in terms of its own creed. And because revelations of those things undermine the legitimacy of the governing process, the government has to keep them secret from the people.

Our government's nuclear national security consensus has so preempted the political consciousness of our society that our visible political process cannot openly challenge it. Our elections and political parties have to operate within the boundaries of that consensus. Those who raise even the slightest question about it lose their political credibility, as did George McGovern, Eugene McCarthy, Fred Harris, and others. This nuclear national security consensus greatly inhibits the mainstream politics of our society.

Our political discourse also has to operate within the boundaries of that consensus. Those who raise fundamental questions that people within the consensus do not have time to think about are not permitted to join the political debate. Samuel Huntington once said that the anti-Vietnam war movement was an expression of "democratic distemper." Managing political life in the nuclear age now means constraining expression and participation in that political life.

The United States and the Soviet Union have worked out the tacit rules of the geopolitical game: neither will directly intervene in the other's spheres of influence; both may intervene in the internal struggles of Third World countries. Some say those interventions risk escalating regional conflicts into a nuclear war. The political leadership in the United States, and, to some degree, in the Soviet Union, say their interventions in Third World struggles do not involve such a risk.

Those interventions greatly inhibit the political possibilities for self-determination in Third World societies. The United States validates its intervention in Nicaragua, for example, by saying that Nicaragua threatens our national security and that we are there to promote democracy. But if democracy means the assertion of popular sovereignty, then U.S. support for the *contras* is the frustration of democracy, and the Reagan Doctrine is antidemocratic.

In sum, we are witnessing an enormous upsurge of democratic and democratizing energy throughout the world today. At the same time, powerful bureaucratic, technological, and geopolitical forces are making it extraordinarily difficult for these movements to attain and maintain democracy.

Themes, Issues, and Ideas

1. When Falk considers the status of the democratic process in modern states, he comes to the conclusion that "people in general have become subjects rather than citizens." Based on Falk's description of a democratic state, what do you think is the crucial difference between a subject and a citizen? How would you characterize yourself in this regard?

2. Why, according to Falk, is secrecy necessary in a democracy? How does the policy of maintaining secrecy on some issues also serve to undermine the democratic process?

3. Citing the loss of political credibility in reference to George McGovern and Eugene McCarthy, among others, Falk says, "This nuclear national security consensus greatly inhibits the mainstream politics of our society." What might Falk reply to the objection that such a consensus *defines* mainstream politics?

Writing Suggestions and Techniques

1. Compare Falk's opening paragraph to his concluding one. What issue does not appear in both places? When, where, how, and why is *that* issue introduced?

2. In his first paragraph, democracy is compared to an "eruption." What other metaphors are used to describe democracy? What do they have in common? What is the general effect of this stylistic consistency?

Suggestions for Writing

1. Falk says, "Modern states—even the most democratic—have induced an ethos of passivity." Write an essay in which you support, oppose, or modify this contention.

2. Speaking of nuclear security, Falk says, "From the beginning of democratic thought, wartime conditions have included the suspension of many of the features of democracy." Do you agree with this thinking? Write an essay supporting or challenging the idea that democracy must sometimes sacrifice democratic ideals to preserve itself.

The United States and Latin America

Carlos Fuentes

Carlos Fuentes is famous both as a diplomat and as a writer of novels, including The Campaign *(1991),* Christopher Unborn *(1989), and* The Old Gringo *(1985), which was made into a motion picture. That book is about a real American writer, Ambrose Bierce, who ended his life in Mexico. Fuentes himself is a Mexican who spent a large part of his early life in the United States. He grew up in a family of diplomats, and has been the Mexican ambassador to France. The result of these cultural interconnections is a unique insight into the relations of Latin America and the United States. As he says in the following essay, he, like his father, has a "personal frontier" with the United States. The essay was first written as a speech delivered to the Center for the Study of Democratic Institutions and was published in* The Center *magazine.*

As a writer concerned with social and political issues, I would like to speak about three aspects of the relations between the United States and Latin America: the cultural, the political, and the economic.

One of my earliest memories is of looking at a photograph of my father, who was then working in the Mexican foreign service. He was straddling the frontier between the United States and Mexico, with one foot in Nogales, Arizona, and the other in Sonora, Mexico. That image became a part of my imagination and the way I look at relations between the two Americas. That frontier is not only the geographical border between the United States and all of Latin America, which begins with Mexico, it is the frontier between two cultures: the Nordic, Anglo-Protestant culture of North America and the Southern-Mediterranean, Anglo-Iberian culture of Latin America.

For the people of North America to truly understand the political phenomena of Latin America, they must first understand its cultural identity. Our mixed and varied cultural tradition comes from theocratic Indian empires, Spanish royal absolutism, the Holy Inquisition, the Counter-Reformation, the Council of Trent, and the worlds of Miguel de Cervantes and Santa Theresa. It is quite important that the people of North America understand the tradition of both the counter-conquest, which responded to conquests by Spain and Portugal, and the philosophy behind the Spanish royal absolutism, in which the political thinking of Latin America has deep roots.

Latin Americans are a compendium of scholasticism and Utopia. We are descendants of Saint Thomas Aquinas and Saint Thomas More. We believe in the common good and a teleology whereby unity and obtaining certain ends are sometimes more important than the pluralism that is needed to obtain them. These ends are granted from above or, when they are not, through authoritarian concession. At other times, they are wrested from below by violent revolution.

But another way to obtain those ends has come from the French Enlightenment, the American Revolution, and our own Wars of Independence during the 1800s and 1820s: democracy. Democracy in Latin America is fragile. It must come from a Latin American reality, not in spite of it. Our cultural tradition resembles the cultural tradition of North America—in both there have been civil wars, revolutions, and injustices—but our democracy cannot be a North American democracy: it must be a Mexican, Nicaraguan, Chilean, and Argentinean democracy.

We of the Americas should have a pact of cultural understanding. Achieving such a pact will, of course, take a long time. It will require that men and women of good will meet in universities, boardrooms, and institutions like the Center for the Study of Democratic Institutions. Until we achieve a pact of cultural understanding, some of us are trying to work out legal and diplomatic agreements to deal with the paramount fact of United States–Latin American coexistence: the enormous power of the United States and the obviously weak power of Latin America. The question is, can legal and diplomatic instruments be created that will curtail the power of the United States within limits acceptable to both parties?

Can the contentious issues that arise between the two be resolved? In the case of Central America today, I believe they can be resolved by diplomatic and legal means. One such means is the Contadora process, which is being offered by the governments of Panama, Colombia, Venezuela, and Mexico. The Contadora process addresses the security concerns of the United States and the countries of Latin America, and both would be severely affected by a generalized war in Central America.

When Latin America and the United States have cooperated—notably during the Franklin Roosevelt administration—they were able to achieve their goals together. However, when the United States acts alone—either by proxy, direct intervention, or applying pressure on weaker nations in the Western Hemisphere—it obtains Pyrrhic victories. But it is the people of both the United States and Latin America who will, in the end, have to pay an enormous price for those victories.

In spite of vast inequities, mixed priorities, and an intense lack of justice and equilibrium, Latin America has managed to develop substantially since the First World War. Today, the economic crisis in Latin America threatens that development. Economic activity, as well as economic justice, has declined. Productivity has decreased enormously. In the first half of 1986, Latin America produced 9 percent less per capita than the previous year. Per-capita income has fallen 15 percent in the last three years. Export and import levels have also fallen, while unemployment, inflation, and prices are up.

These economic hardships are tearing at the fragile social fabric of Latin America. If the economic problems are not solved, the unpoliticized subproletariats in the cities of Latin America might very well bring on violent situations. These people are perfect fodder for messianic demagogues who profit from the union of violence and religion.

Where will the money come from to make the enormous interest payments on Latin America's debt? Mexican President Miguel de la Madrid has said that we must do what we did in the past: grow and depend on our internal savings. For years, Latin America had been growing at the rate of 5, 6, and 7 percent based on its internal savings, incurring very little foreign debt. Brazilian President José Sarney has said that Brazil's debt will not be paid with the hunger of the Brazilian people.

It is admirable that the fragile young democracies of Latin America have not yet experienced political upheavals in the face of their enormous economic and social problems. The worst thing that could happen to the nations of Latin America as they cope with their problems would be an international conflict in their region.

Latin America is struggling to find its place in the world. It is undergoing social, political, and cultural transformations. At the same time, the United States is losing its hegemony in the world. The United States must adapt to that loss as well as accept a Latin America that is transforming.

Every man and woman in Latin America has a personal frontier with the United States. Before the end of this century, I believe that every man and woman in the United States will have a personal frontier with Latin America.

Themes, Issues, and Ideas

1. Fuentes begins by describing a picture of his father personally and physically acting as a medium of connection between Mexico and the United States. What other forms of interaction between the countries are mentioned in the essay?

2. What does Fuentes point to in the varied cultural background of Latin America that causes it to differ from the United States? What in that background causes it to resemble the United States?

3. Fuentes argues that we must first reach cultural understanding before we can reach legal and diplomatic understanding. What reasoning does he offer to support this claim?

Writing Strategies and Techniques

1. Speaking of direct and indirect United States unilateral intervention in Latin America, Fuentes says that the United States obtains "Pyrrhic victories." (Look this term up, if you do not already know it.) How does such a victory affect interaction differently from the first metaphor of the "personal frontier?"

2. At the end of his essay, Fuentes calls the democracies of Latin America "young" and says that "Latin America is struggling to find its place in the world." Yet civilization in Latin America is considerably older than that of North America, and Latin American Wars of Independence followed closely on the American Revolution. How does Fuentes justify the metaphors in his conclusion?

Suggestions for Writing

1. Fuentes speaks of three aspects of the relations between the United States and Latin America: the cultural, the political, and the economic. Write an essay stating which aspect seems most threatened

in the immediate future and which seems to offer the most promise of improvement. Be sure to support your claims with arguments and evidence.

2. What should our policy toward Latin America be? Write an essay expressing your own views and organize it like Fuentes's essay.

An Elephant in the Backyard

Flora Lewis

The world the United States will have to deal with in the twenty-first century is a large one, and heir to all the brutal legacies of the twentieth century. One of the most pressing issues, therefore, has been the effort to unify the European nations in a stable way, something that political leaders have been unable to do throughout 500 years and two world wars. In the way of this, says Flora Lewis, is Germany—currently one of the world's great economic powers, and still on the rise. Will Germany's own internal dissention leave its bloody mark on world peace in the next century, or will the global economy many Americans envision come into being smoothly?

Lewis was the foreign affairs columnist for the New York Times *from 1970 to 1992. An astute observer of Europe, she now lives in Paris. Her book* Europe: A Tapestry of Nations *was published in 1987.*

The most important difference now dividing Germans from their allies and neighbors is that while most everyone else talks of projection of a great new German strength from the center of the continent, the Germans feel suddenly weak and uncertain. No one foresaw the emotional, psychological and political problems that unification would bring, let alone the staggering economic and social difficulties that are still only beginning to be understood.

But just as the Berlin Wall blocked the view from the present to some distant horizon so long as it stood, so now does the aftermath of its demolition. There remains a kind of lace curtain where the Iron Curtain stood, separating an "us" and a "them," the genteel and the distressed. People look through it and resent or disdain what they see. From the other side, the "Wessies" look smug, arrogant, righteous, colonizing, greedy; and "Ossies" look incompetent, whiny, demand-

201

ing, lacking initiative and civic spirit. What to do about it is the great preoccupation of German leaders and opinion-makers, so heavy and urgent a concern that they find it hard to see why others cavil at German power. The more they advance with the totally unexpected task that was only an abstract hope for so long, the more they discover they must do and the more the target date for successful conclusion recedes. At this point they feel overwhelmed, not rambunctious; burdened, not burdensome.

Former Chancellor Helmut Schmidt, once called "Schmidt the Lip" for his indulgence in tart, unadorned recrimination when he thought it applicable, spoke of "a rather foul mood" in his speech on the second anniversary of unification. He placed much of the blame on the federal government, for its reckless encouragement of impossible expectations, for the "destructive revaluation" of the east mark at parity with the west's Deutsche-mark, for the "unholy property arrangements" providing for restitution in a way that blocks enterprise and investment, for imposition of too many complicated west German procedures that the eastern bureaucracy can't apply, and for borrowing rather than taxing to pay the huge bills. But above all he blamed Bonn for failing to tell "the full truth" and therefore failing to evoke the "solidarity" for which "sacrifice" could be justified.

"I am quite confident that we will be able to solve our problems and challenges," he said, offering a long list of proposals. But in the meantime, people in the west must understand that they will have to continue supporting the east until "well after the year 2000," and people in the east must develop "citizens initiatives" that are feasible, such as organizing day-care centers and providing sports fields and youth clubs, instead of waiting for the state to do everything, as in the past.

People in both east and west are "disappointed and bitter because of the general lack of leadership and the indecisiveness," he said. "As we enter the third year of unification, we cannot but acknowledge the existence of much moral decay. Let us therefore jointly defend with all our forces human decency in Germany."

These are the dominant concerns, aggravated by the continued shocking outbreaks of xenophobic violence by "skins"—now the German word for skinheads—on the neo-Nazi right and the "autonomous" left. Many, including President Richard von Weizsäcker, are moved to recall the Nazi-communist street brawls that helped to destroy the Weimar republic. Today's Germany isn't Weimar, but even the hint of its shadow is too horrible to disregard.

The problem of "asylum-seekers," some 500,000 this year, provoked by the opening of the eastern borders and Germany's both archaic and generous laws, is not necessarily the cause of these incidents but it is an excuse that comforts ultra-nationalists and opponents of democracy. (The notable absentees from the mammoth Berlin demonstration against the attacks on foreigners, where "left skins" pelted President von Weizsäcker, were the Bavarian CSU leaders, the local sister party of Chancellor Helmut Kohl's CDU. Bavarian prime minister Max Streible said he refused to take part "in a funeral march for a helpless democracy" and when he was praised by the tiny neo-Nazi Republican party, he said he didn't care who approved his comments. It isn't only thugs and easterners who spread the stench.

The antidotes Germans discuss are essentially the three recommended by Schmidt: a more vigorous, determined rejection of violence as word as well as deed; a more coherent, candid approach to the social and economic problems of unity; and Europe.

In the Adenauer days, Europe was enthusiastically welcomed as the essential cure for the German historical infirmity, the comforting frame in which Germany could emerge from pariah status and hold up its head on good terms with neighbors. The establishment still sees Europe as the necessary context for German self-reliance, the way to make sure its position as the weighty center doesn't inevitably lead weaker and insecure neighbors to form antagonistic encircling coalitions.

This was an important element in creating the Treaty of Maastricht—probably prematurely and certainly in slapdash ineptitude, which has had a lot to do with opposition in many Community states. Reunification and opening of Eastern Europe brought Mr. Kohl and French president Francois Mitterrand to decide they must hurry up to cement European union—monetary and if possible political and security—before centrifugal forces and especially the new imbalance of a big Germany undermined the process. They felt an injection of strong political will was needed for the race against time so filled with uncertainties. Mr. Kohl's only reservation was that the plan didn't go far enough in assuring a democratic base for a stronger European center, by reinforcing the European Parliament, but he compromised on that.

Neither of the leaders, and scarcely any other but Britain's, felt the necessity to prepare their people for a qualitative leap to shared sovereignty. They took Europhoria, the European momentum, for granted. But it faded on them, as the euphoria at the end of German and European partition faded in the face of harsh realities. *Heimat* became more of an issue than it had been anywhere in western Europe, except for Britain, since the Treaty of Rome was signed in 1957.

Heimat simply happens to be a German word, but *la patrie, la patria* will do as well. Doubts, based more on the sudden demand for change than on the idea of more integration, took hold everywhere. Denmark voted against the Treaty by a whisper, France barely endorsed it. Even in Holland, where there will not be a referendum, usually ardent pro-Europeans wondered aloud whether their Dutch ways might be uncomfortably subject to Italian or Greek preconceptions of society.

The preponderance of Germany was used crudely by opposite camps in the Maastricht arguments. Opponents of the Treaty said it would guarantee German dominance and German control. Advocates said it was the one way to constrain Germany and make sure its partners' voices would be heard. The issue wasn't really Germany but the deeper, emotional pull of traditional sovereignty as the guardian of national identities. The erosion of sovereignty had always been at the heart of the Community idea, but the evolution of the idea had come gradually, people got used to it a little at a time. Suddenly, many stopped to ask how far they really wanted to go, and how fast.

Each country clung to its own special symbol. For Germany, that turned out to be a Deutsche-mark, the incarnation of revival after disaster, the solid foundation of all the other good things that had come about in two generations. German opinion remains strongly pro-European, but there is uneasiness about letting unreliable, often profligate foreigners loose with decisions that can determine the value of German money. Mr. Kohl had to promise the *Bundestag* that it could vote again before a single currency and a single central bank take effect, though that is not provided in Maastricht—which precommits states that are economically eligible. This is not a matter of homeland; but a cautionary fear in a country proud of its economy and worried because it has so much to lose. It is in other countries that Union is seen as a challenge to identity.

The institutions and rules of the original six-member Common Market were based on the participation of three more-or-less equal middle-sized countries and three small ones, with voting weighted to make sure no two of the larger ones could gang up on all the others. Ways were found more or less to maintain the balance as the Community expanded to twelve. But now Germany is about one-and-a-half times more populous than France, Italy or Britain and a good deal sturdier economically. France considered its nuclear power as an equalizer in the core Franco-German partnership, and that had a lot to do with the persistent if quixotic French demand for a European defense policy, independent of the U.S. The collapse of the Soviet Union reduces even the supposition of the importance of the *force de frappe,* though it leaves French defense policy in its traditional contradiction—eager to cut reliance on the U.S. but just as eager to make sure the U.S. still helps to constrain Germany. Germany has become the elephant in the barnyard.

This is a geo-political fact existing whether or not there is a Community. But the Community itself faces an urgent need to readapt in view of enlargement. Early inclusion of Sweden, Austria, Finland, and probably Norway is seen as all the more desirable to find a new balance, but the old rules of decision probably can't be stretched to work with so many. Eventually, Central Europe and some of the new states in the Balkans and the east will have to be included. Commission president Jacques Delors talks of revamping institutions so they can accommodate up to 35 members. Germany's role in such a society is hard to foresee. The European idea is to make the rules in such a way that German preeminence will not mean dominance. These are questions yet to be answered, but many Europeanists feel the attempt must be made quickly, while the Germans still feel bewildered and preoccupied with domestic challenge.

The Germans can't really be blamed for being a good deal more present in the travails of Central Europe and the east than are their partners. They are more acutely aware of the dangers to western Europe if the eastern experiment with democracy and the free market blows up, and they would like France, Britain and the others to participate more in helping the new democracies, as would Poland, the Czechs and Slovaks, Hungary and the others, who don't want to rely so much on Germany. But all western governments are weak now and tend to look inward, which is not good for Europe. It will probably take more energetic U.S. leadership than recently practiced to provoke the kind of cooperative action needed, with NATO as a useful vehicle on security issues.

As a start, Poland, the Czechs and Hungary should be given a security involvement, not full membership but enough more than current consultative status to provide psychological and political assurance. Storms are brewing around Hungary that can make the Yugoslav wars seem only a tocsin. The weight of Germany on the east depends more on what others do or don't do than it does on geography or ambition.

The Community and NATO remain the necessary organizing poles to shape the new Europe in the world if there is not to be a dangerous relapse into 19th century rival nationalisms, hostile coalitions and the illusion that a balance of power keeps the peace. It isn't just the question of a European Germany or a German Europe, because that would break down again. It is of a European Germany or a

Europe that festers with dangers for itself and every part of the world involved with it.

Max Kohnstamm, a Dutchman who was an enthusiastic collaborator of Jean Monnet from the start of the Europe enterprise, told me recently, "I do not fear Germany now, they understand. But in 20 years? Will the next generation remember the lessons?" Monnet's central theme was that building institutions was the only way to keep the lessons of history learned. How right he was.

Themes, Issues, and Ideas

1. What, according to Lewis, is the biggest impediment to European unity as concerns Germany?

2. Why, other than out of general curiosity, should American readers be interested in European politics?

3. What domestic problems does the Germany-Europe conflict remind you of? What solutions has the American government come up with? How might Europe adopt such approaches?

Writing Strategies and Techniques

1. Why does Lewis use the expression "an elephant in the backyard" to describe Germany? What does the metaphor suggest?

2. What does Lewis mean by "centrifugal forces" which might undermine European unity? Describe the physical metaphor Lewis conjures up.

Suggestions for Writing

1. Write a scenario, without going too much into specifics, in which all the problems Lewis describes are peacefully ironed out.

2. Now write a scenario in which the problems Lewis describes lead to World War III.

Economic Time Zones: Fast vs. Slow

Alvin and Heidi Toffler

Many of the predictions that have been made about the twenty-first century involve time: specifically, the speeding-up of information via faxes, satellites, computer networking, and other technologies. But when some nations are so much faster than others, what effect will that discrepancy have on the coming global economy? That is the question asked, or rather answered, by Alvin and Heidi Toffler in this essay.

Alvin and Heidi Toffler are among the most prominent futurists in the world, and have been since the publication of Future Shock *in 1969. Their books* The Third Wave *and* Powershift *have had great influence on thinking about the next century, and in this essay they suggest that some predictions about a twenty-first–century "global village" may have been misfounded.*

In the next century, the great danger for humanity will not be the conflict between East and West, or even between North and South. It will be the decoupling of the fast world from the slow world.

As time itself has become a critical factor of production, the wealth gap has grown rapidly between societies whose accelerative economies are driven by knowledge and advanced technology and those societies whose economies are mired in traditional agriculture or bureaucratic smokestack industry.

Economic processes in *third wave* knowledge-driven societies are accelerating, while those in *first wave* agricultural societies and *second wave* industrial societies are lagging or stagnating. This gap in relative speed is widening.

As Ryszard Kapuscinksi has written, "By the beginning of the next century, there may be completely different worlds on the same planet. Unlike the vision we all held thirty years ago, the world is not converging, but spreading apart like the galaxies."

And time itself is a key force driving us apart. Because of the new information technologies, the old adage, "Time is money," is now obsolete. In the new accelerated system of wealth creation, it is being superseded by a new hidden law of economics in which time is no longer just money. Now each unit of saved time is actually worth more money than the last unit. The faster economic processes work, the more wealth is created in the same period with the same or even fewer resources.

The bar code on a pack of cigarettes, the computer in the Federal Express truck, the scanner at the supermarket checkout counter, robots with remote sensors on the assembly line, the electronic transfer of capital—all presage a twenty-first-century economy that will operate at nearly real-time, or instantaneous speeds.

The feedback loop between producer and consumer is nearly immediate. Thus, overnight, mail companies can locate your packages by computer anywhere at any time. Fickle fashion trends can be changed many times a year while keeping inventories low. For example, Haggar Apparel of Dallas is now able to restock its twenty-five hundred retail customers with slacks every three days instead of every seven weeks, as it once did.

This new system of wealth creation consists of an expanding global network of markets, banks, production centers, and laboratories in instant communication with one another, constantly exchanging huge flows of data and knowledge.

To be decoupled from this fast economy is to be excluded from the future.

If the poorer regions of the planet, from the third world to the post-communist East, continue to build economies based on cheap labor, raw materials, or clunky smokestack production, the future will pass them by.

Indeed, because of the acceleration of production, cheap labor is becoming expensive. Ford Motor Company recently brought a truck manufacturing plant back from Brazil to the United States because, despite the low labor costs, it took six months to manufacture a truck in Brazil compared to only forty-five days in the United States.

Similarly, a children's sleepwear designer based in Pennsylvania recently decided against manufacturing clothes in China because, despite paying the world's lowest wages, the Chinese ability to meet delivery deadlines is unreliable. The designer delivers hundreds of thousands of units of clothing to JC Penny, K-Mart and Sears, but if delivery is late by even one day the retailers refuse to accept the shipment. That is because one week small children want bunnies on their pajamas, and the next week they want bears. Consumer tastes, on which volume sales depend, change too rapidly to rely on China's slow and unreliable production.

But it is not only fashion that changes swiftly. So do high-technology products, from microchips to laser tools. As the new system of wealth creation spreads, labor costs shrink dramatically. In some advanced industries today, labor costs represent only 10 percent of the total cost of production. Far greater savings can be found through better technology, faster information flows, and streamlined organization than by squeezing workers. Low-wage muscle is no longer much of a competitive advantage in the emerging world economy.

The slow tempo of decision making in such places as China and the Soviet Union is also a reason for the collapse of many joint ventures. The endless negotiations and glacial pace of the bureaucratic chain of economic command kill deals regularly between fast and slow partners.

The slow world's raw materials are also devalued by accelerated production, which relies more on inputs of scientific innovation, knowledge, and organization than energy or other natural resources.

An example: In the future, superconductivity will radically reduce the need for energy by reducing losses during transmission. The experience of Japan's high-speed economy has already made this point clearly: In 1984 Japan consumed only 60 percent of the raw material required for the same volume of industrial output in 1973.

If catatonic agrarian societies and stagnant smokestack societies are to avoid becoming marginalized spectators of the future, perpetuating their misery, they will have to revolutionize their concepts of development.

Any slow country that wants to participate in tomorrow's global economy must make it a priority to couple electronically to the fast world. That not only means telephones but also computers, fax machines, satellites, fiber-optic communication systems, and other electronic networks. At least part of the population—the cities, the elites, and the manufacturing sector—must be linked electronically to the outside world.

Though this partial approach may be the most viable development strategy, and thus the one most likely to be followed, it raises another specter. In slow places like China or Africa, which are so weighed down by their agrarian masses, the global decoupling of fast and slow may be reproduced internally. While advanced sectors in Shanghai or Cairo may become coupled to the world economy, billions of peasants might remain technologically and politically decoupled in their own country.

But the problems of the slow world can never be completely decoupled from the well-being of the fast world. New links must be forged to avoid global conflict between those inside and those outside the accelerated economy.

The maldistribution of telecommunications in today's world is even more dramatic than the maldistribution of food. Of the 600 million telephones in the world, 450 million of them are located in nine countries. The lopsided distribution of computers, data bases, technical publications and research expenditures tells us more about the future potential of nations than all the gross national product figures ground out by economists.

The next century can be a promising one for all—but only if we see to it that the slow world is plugged into the fast one, closing the informational and electronic gap.

Themes, Issues, and Ideas

1. What, according to the authors, are the relative speeds of first, second, and third wave societies? What might be a conflict between two of these societies?

2. Are the Tofflers in favor of third world nations developing into societies like our own? What might be the advantages and disadvantages (to America) of such development?

3. If what the Tofflers say is true, why is the adage "time is money" obsolete?

Writing Strategies and Techniques

1. How would you describe the Tofflers' writing style? What effect does it have on a reader? What effect do you think is intended?

2. Why do the Tofflers choose the phrase "plugged into" in the last paragraph?

Suggestions for Writing

1. Write a science fiction story set in a world dominated by the "time gap."

2. Write an essay considering the time gap here in America.

Japan

Playing by Different Rules

James Fallows

James Fallows is what used to be called "an old Asia hand." As a reporter who has lived in the East for many years, he writes about Asian matters with more authority than most journalists can bring to this very important area that American foreign policy is facing as the twentieth century draws to its close.

Fallows was born in 1949 in Philadelphia and spent his undergraduate years at Harvard. He was a Rhodes Scholar at Oxford University before entering journalism as a free-lance magazine writer. This essay was published in The Atlantic *magazine, for which Fallows is an editor and frequent contributor.*

Something is peculiar about the way we discuss "trade wars." When America and Japan really were at war, each country was trying to blow the other up. Now the threat from Japan is—what? That its companies will devise more appealing products than our companies can, and will then offer them to us at a lower price. Where's the aggression or hostile intent? What makes this anything like Pearl Harbor?

Economists, of course, have comebacks to such questions. Maybe the Japanese are offering cut-rate goods today purely in hopes of squeezing out the competition and collecting big monopoly profits later on. Maybe we'll be forced into a kind of peonage if Japan comes to control all the high-grade, sophisticated manufacturing and we're left to sell soybeans and rent out our big-league ballplayers for service with the Hiroshima Carp.

Still, according to all the basic logic of our economic system, we shouldn't worry about trade wars, any more than we worry about being offered a gift. If another country will sell us goods for less than it costs us to make them, why should we complain? It doesn't really matter whether the supplying country is more efficient or is merely willing to "dump," selling the goods at a loss. In either case, foreign trade leaves us with the steel girders or the color TVs we might have made ourselves, *plus* the cash we've saved by buying for less. If the Japanese want to exploit themselves and sell below their true cost, that's their problem—all they're doing is raising our standard of living at the expense of theirs. If the Koreans are willing to work for low wages, we should be happy to buy their shoes for $8 instead of $48 and use the $40 for something else. The extra wealth for America— the $40 we get besides the pair of shoes—will presumably give us leeway to invest in newer, more productive industries, or simply to make up the lost incomes of people who used to produce shoes.

So goes the theory of free trade, as I learned it in my economics courses and as it's explained in America whenever someone wants to prove that protectionism is bad. I was steeped in the theory when I arrived in Japan, early last year. I still think it's the right answer to most of what's wrong with the world's economy. But I no longer think that it tells us much about dealing with Japan.

It's hard to make the objections to free trade with Japan sound as neat and elegant as the original theory itself. The objections center on this point: Free trade assumes certain things about human behavior that may not be correct when applied to the Japanese. This is not because the Japanese are a separate species, as they sometimes contend, but because their society's definition of the good life is different from Adam Smith's.

The Adam Smith, free-trade view of life rests on three pillars:

1.   Economic problems are always solved by *more* trade, not less. When goods flow from low-cost production sites to markets in higher-cost areas, everyone is better off. The more smoothly they flow, the greater the all-around benefit, since each part of the world is doing what it can do best.

2.   The desirability of more trade rests, in turn, on the assumption that the world is full of "economic men," who go through life making rational cost-benefit decisions. Their appetites and preferences may differ—if wages go up, some people will work more, because the payoff is greater, and others will work less, because they can earn what they need in a shorter time. But everyone will respond to market signals to get the best deal for himself. As a result, everyone will *naturally* act in a way that promotes international trade. Everyone wants a bargain; the best bargains are by definition available from the world's lowest-cost producers; freer trade will select the most effi-

cient producers and make more goods available at a lower overall cost.

3. This picture of economic man, in its turn, rests on an even deeper assumption about what life, or at least the commercial part of it, is for. Efficient production is good because it leads to lower prices, and lower prices are good because they let people have "more": more food, more clothes, more leisure, more variety, more of everything money can buy. And in providing more, the capitalist free-trade system offers its only justification for itself. Competitive capitalism is crueler than other economic systems—the bankruptcies, the unemployment. But in return it offers people more material wealth and a higher standard of living than any other system has done. For at least the past century America and most other developed nations have willingly accepted this bargain. No pain, no gain. By the logic of the market, competition is always good, because it offers people more, and a free world trading system is best, because it offers people most.

As long as all the participants are after the same thing— "more"—then the world trading system should work fine. Markets will clear. Like magnetism, sexual attraction, and other powerful interactions, free trade starts with two parties that have symmetrical goals and motivations, and it takes them toward a predictable result.

But suppose one participant doesn't have the same goals as the others. Then the results won't be what was expected—in an electromagnet, at a freshman mixer, or in the world trading system. Suppose, to stick to economics, that one country isn't really interested in buying products from anywhere else, because it is not powerfully motivated by lower prices, *because having more is not its principal goal.* Then free trade's solution to all problems—everyone should buy more from everyone else—won't necessarily make sense.

This, I've come to think, is the basic story of Japan and the United States—really, of Japan and the rest of the world. Japan is not mainly interested in a higher standard of living for its people; America is. Given those different starting points, free trade will almost inevitably lead to chronic trade surpluses for Japan, chronic deficits for the United States. That outcome is not necessarily bad in itself, but it forces us to make a choice that few politicians have yet offered to us. Which really bothers us more: the chronic "failures" in trade with Japan, or the violence we'd have to do to free trade to correct them?

Let me clarify what I'm *not* trying to say. To argue that Japan tends toward surplus does not mean that its industries, managers, and workers are the "best" in the world. Some of them may be; even so, free-trade theory assumes that trade accounts would still balance out. If Japan really were better at manufacturing than any other country, its exports would keep rising and so (because of supply-demand forces on the currency exchange) would the value of the yen. Goods from the rest of the world would become cheaper; its people, wanting "more," would recognize and seize their bargains. Equilibrium would be restored. This is essentially what happened to America in the generation after the Second World War. Our industries were world-beaters; our dollars grew strong, and we spent those dollars—and spent and spent. But the chronic trade imbalance reflects something more than Japanese manufacturing skill.

I also don't mean to say that the United States bears no responsibility for its trade and budget deficits. We're more responsible for the size of the deficits than anyone else is. The U.S. trade deficit was about $150 billion last year, or more than five times larger than the normal rate in the late 1970s. It could never have gotten so large so fast if the federal budget deficit had not been booming at the same time. (To summarize a long but now standard explanation: Japan and Germany *had* to run big trade surpluses with the United States in the 1980s, to earn the dollars they then lent us to cover our budget deficit.) Moreover, eliminating all identifiable trade barriers in Japan would, in the short run, eliminate only part of the United States–Japan trade deficit, since so many "imports" are really Japanese-made components for American products and subcontracts for American firms.

Finally, I would never deny that American business, American culture, American habits—let's face it, Americans—are to blame for many of our export failings. Our children don't learn enough about math or science, our smartest people end up planning hostile corporate takeovers or designing attack submarines, we don't naturally think of export markets, but our managers and unions do naturally think of getting all they can out of a company in the shortest possible time. Lee Iacocca tried to make himself the symbol of America's industrial rebirth, but by paying himself $20 million in a year when Chrysler's earnings declined, he has become as grim a symbol as Ivan Boesky of what the Japanese think is killing us.

This cultural-doom analysis is very familiar, and it can be overdone. Do U.S. companies think of the U.S. market first? That may say less about our parochialism than about the size of our market—a lot of Taiwanese companies think of America first too. Still, the charge that we've become culturally unfit is true enough to make us reexamine our schools, our management ethics, and ultimately our values. Unless we start correcting our own failings, we're in no position to hector the Japanese.

But even if America solved its cultural problems, even if our students joyfully tackled extra homework and employees strove always to enhance the honor of the firm, I suspect that Japan would still be involved in trade wars against us and others. The deficits would be smaller, but the tensions would still be there. The reason is that the free-trade solution—everyone buying more from everyone else—runs counter to a deeper value in Japanese life: the noncapitalist desire to preserve every Japanese person's place in the Japanese productive system. In the United States and in most of the world that Adam Smith described, people suffer indignities as *producers*—through layoffs, job changes, shifts into new businesses—in order to improve the welfare of the society's *consumers*. In Japan it's the other way around. The Japanese consumer's interest comes last—and therefore so does the motivation for buying from overseas.

Of course, the Japanese market is not as self-contained as Albania's, or as obviously tariff-bound as Taiwan's or South Korea's. One of the first things American visitors to Japan see, as they stumble bleary-eyed through Narita Airport, is the sign on every luggage cart reading IMPORT NOW!, conveniently in English. American brand names—McDonald's, Kentucky Fried Chicken, (Tokyo) Disneyland—are ubiquitous in Japan. Kenichi Ohmae, the author of *Beyond National Borders,* and the managing director of McKinsey & Company in Japan, has pointed out time and again that American-*owned* companies sell about as much to Japan as Japanese-owned companies do to the United States. (The difference, of course, is that most of the "American" products are made in Japan, in Japanese-American joint ventures, thereby protecting the Japanese producer's interests.) Japanese trade officials have a standard anyone-can-succeed-in-Japan presentation for foreign visitors, usually starring Mister Donut, Schick razors, and BMW cars. Its moral is, you can sell as long as you make a truly high-quality product (strike one against America) and strive earnestly to meet local tastes (strikes two and three, we're out).

Technically, the trade officials are right. With enough work, almost anything could be sold in Japan, even American rice or Korean cars. The difference is the natural tendency of the system. The United States, putting the consumer's interest first, naturally buys up whatever offers the best value, unless some lobby or cartel stands in the way. Japan, putting the (Japanese) producer's interest first, naturally resists importing anything but raw materials. Selling to America is like rolling a ball downhill. Selling to Japan is like fighting against guerrillas, or bailing against a siphon, or betting against the house. You can win, but the odds are not on your side.

None of the illustrations of this point is conclusive in itself, but together they suggest a deviation from the logic of capitalism and free trade. Capitalist societies are supposed to respond to price, so as to get "more." Japan does not.

Food is the classic illustration. Japan imports about half its calories, but if it cared mainly about price, it would import much more food. By refusing to import rice and blocking many other imports, Japan protects its farmers (and avoids antagonizing the gangsters in the beef industry) but penalizes every consumer in the country, through grotesquely inflated prices for food and land. Food may seem an exceptional case: It's an emotional issue; every major country protects its farmers to some degree; most Japanese still have a sentimental tie to the soil. What makes it so intriguing is that there's almost no complaint from the victims of the policy. Last spring a coalition of Japanese consumer groups protested food policy—but what concerned them was the suggestion that Japan should import more cheap food. They recommended that Japan's superexpensive rice should "never" be exposed to foreign competition.

The retail network is another famous example. A hundred years ago the United States had a retail system much like Japan's today: fragmented, diverse, family-owned, and inefficient. America doesn't have many Mom-and-Pop stores anymore (except for immigrant-run groceries), because they've been bulldozed under by Sears, Safeway, K mart, and other large-scale, low-cost operations. The Mom-and-Pops put up a political fight in the 1920s and 1930s and tried to outlaw the chain stores. But, as Thomas McCraw and Patricia O'Brien wrote recently in *America versus Japan,* they were snubbed by courts, legislatures, and even voters in referenda. Chain stores offered lower prices; therefore they were good. Japan has followed just the opposite course. In the past fifteen years government directives have made it harder to open discount stores, supermarkets, or other low-cost outlets that would improve the consumer's standard of living but would threaten the tiny greengrocer down the block.

Right-thinking Americans know that monopolies and cartels are bad, because they hurt the consumer. Japan *likes* cartels and some monopolies, because they strengthen Japanese producers against foreign competition. Japanese steelmakers, in the 1960s and 1970s, and semiconductor makers, in the 1970s and 1980s, have invested more heavily in advanced production equipment than any of them would have dared to on its own. It would be cheaper, in the short term, to keep using the old machines, which is what many American companies have done. The Japanese companies could take this "risk" because of their cartel-based faith that the famous Ministry of

International Trade and Industry, MITI, would divide up the work fairly whenever the market went slack.

Japanese taxpayers would save money if they bought military aircraft direct from American producers. Although our own military budget may make this hard to believe, it is cheaper to buy the next F-15 off the production line than to set up a production line of your own. Nonetheless, the F-15s that the Air Self-Defense Force flies are made in Japan, under American license. Japan is scheduled to introduce a new fighter plane late in this decade. Buying an existing American model would be cheaper—that is, would hold down Japanese taxes, would give Japanese consumers "more." But unless the trade-war pressure from America becomes too intense, Japan seems almost sure to build up its own fighter, at up to twice the cost of an imported plane.

One last, humble illustration is soda ash. This is an important chemical used for making glass, other chemicals, and detergents. Japanese soda-ash producers use petroleum-fired boilers that even in the cheap-oil days seemed to be burning money. American-made soda ash is cheaper. The American trade association that has been trying to sell it in Japan claims that it could be offered for significantly less than the made-in-Japan price. For years the association made no headway whatsoever. Then, in 1983, Japan's Fair Trade Commission found that Japanese companies were colluding to keep the Americans out. American suppliers quickly expanded their share of the market from 1 to 15 percent, but then got very little more. The yen has gone up, dollar prices have plummeted, but the market share has barely budged. An executive of Asahi Glass, a major purchaser, recently announced that he'd never leave his high-cost Japanese supplier—they'd been friends in school. "This isn't exactly collusion," an American diplomat told me. "It's simply a refusal to act on price."

Early this year the Organization for Economic Cooperation and Development, in Paris, offered an intriguing analysis of what the cumulative refusals to act on price meant for Japan. For 1986 as a whole, the average yen-dollar exchange rate was 169 to 1. At that rate Japan's per capita income was just below America's, and at the rates prevailing early this year, when the dollar plunged into the 140s, Japan was clearly the "richest" major country in the world. But the OECD went on to adjust incomes in each country for purchasing power and then recalculate the rate. In terms that matter to consumers, the "real" exchange rate was 223 to 1.

This is the single most illuminating statistic to come out of Japan. (Or maybe one of the two most illuminating. The other, which needs to be repeated as often as possible, is that at current market rates Japan's land all together is "worth" more than America's, even though the United States is twenty-five times as large.) It is important because of what it says about the repression of consumer interests in Japan. The gap between the official and "real" exchange rates—between something in the 140s to the 160s and 223—is the wealth that Japan has denied its own consumers in order to preserve its market share. To put it another way, the gap means that products from the rest of the world are available to the Japanese at astonishing bargain rates. For 140 yen a Japanese consumer can buy a dollar and use it to buy clothes, food, or machinery that would cost him more than 200 yen to buy at home. If Japan wanted to, it could even buy its way out of its domestic-housing problem. It can't import land, but by importing more food it could free up precious flatland now used for farming and let the Japanese move out of the "rabbit hutches."

The world would seem to be Japan's bargain basement, but Japan is not interested. What makes Japan unusual is not that it sells so much to other countries—West Germany's exports make up 34 percent of its gross national product, while Japan's make up 13 percent—but that it buys so little. West Germany imports the equivalent of 30 percent of its GNP, Japan about 10 percent—mainly raw materials it can't produce for itself. If the yen rises high enough, Japan will finally be priced out of its export surplus. But if it were a society of economic men, it would have begun buying its way out of the surplus long before now.

Understanding why Japan behaves this way would be a life's work. One theory, popular among the Japanese, holds that the trade surplus reflects the people's inborn frugality, moderation, and unsurpassed productive skill. Perhaps it reflects the bias of the political system toward paternalistic decisions, made by small elites sheltered from life as the ordinary consumer knows it. Japan is an impeccably free society but in practice not a very democratic one. The most important political decisions are always made by committees, oligarchies, bureaucracies, party-leadership councils. In an article called "The Japan Problem," published in *Foreign Affairs* late last year, the Dutch journalist Karel van Wolferen, who has lived in Japan for twenty-five years, argued that power in Japan was dispersed among a number of semi-autonomous baronies, each of which promoted its own interests and laughed off any attempt to change course. Prime Minister Nakasone, viewing the nation's predicament as a whole, might understand that Japan needed to start spending more on itself. But, van Wolferen said, all the component parts of the system—the huge industrial companies, the labor unions, MITI, the farmers—were programmed to build market share, cut profit when necessary, resist foreign penetration, and export, export, export. Early last year the Japanese government rolled the drums for the Maekawa report, an ambitious proposal to increase imports, improve living standards, shorten the work week to five days, and generally make Japan a nation of economic men. By the end of the year, according to a survey conducted by the Ministry of Labor, the number of firms with a five-day week appeared to have gone *down*. (On the other hand, in the wake of the Maekawa report the average Japanese worker was skipping out of the office at day's end a minute and fifteen seconds earlier.) The rest of the world may think Japan is rich, but its people seem to regard the *endaka*—"strong-yen"—crisis as the occasion for yet another round of belt-tightening. From September of 1985 to December of 1986 the yen's value against the dollar rose by almost 52 percent. But Toyota, Nissan, and Honda were so determined to hold on to market share that they swallowed most of the currency change and raised their dollar prices by only 15 percent.

There are other theories. For example, maybe the Japanese, with their rapidly aging population, are trying to sock their profits away in American investments even though it means short-term sacrifice. Someday they'll have to start importing, but before then they can build a big endowment of overseas investments that will help pay their big, looming pension bill. Or maybe the Japanese truly reject the "creative destruction" theory of capitalism, since they mourn the destructive part (lost jobs and markets) much more than they welcome the creativity (higher standard of living). In the two years of *endaka* the Japanese press has harped endlessly on the misery of "small and medium size enterprises," which are being squeezed out of their traditional export markets. Last summer I visited a few of these companies, including a knife factory in Seki. In a tin-roofed, junk-filled shed in the mountains I saw Japanese retirees grinding butcher knives by hand on antique grind wheels. An old man and an old woman were hand-gluing the red plastic sides onto "Swiss" army knives. The plant manager, his eyes practically brimming with tears, was sure I'd share his sorrow about his tragic loss of market share. And yes, it was too bad for him. But by any normal standard this factory should have moved out of Japan fifteen years ago, to Taiwan or India. Much more impressive installations in the United States have been destroyed by Japanese competition. The parallel does not seem to have occurred to anyone in Japan.

Preserving the existing order—continuing to buy soda ash from your school chum—seems more important to Japan than anything else. The two kinds of foreign purchases that have boomed in Japan—

tourism, and investment in foreign real estate—are different from other imports in that they pose no competition to anyone in Japan. The *Nihon Keizai Shimbun,* a distinguished paper comparable to *The Wall Street Journal,* ran an editorial last spring about low consumption levels, and pointed out that letting in more foreign labor would lower the cost of many services. But such a change would be too disruptive, the paper concluded. "Perhaps the high cost of living is the price we pay for social peace and harmony." When they tire of lending money to Americans, or buying real estate, or going on tours, the Japanese have very little to do with their money since they're so reluctant to import. Shares of stock are one thing they can buy, and prices on the Japanese stock market have been speculated up to stupendous levels. Nippon Telephone traded early this year with a price-to-earnings ratio of 250, and the Tokyo Stock Exchange as a whole had a P/E ratio of 56, about three times higher than that of the New York Stock Exchange. Memberships in Japanese golf clubs are traded on an official exchange; a place in the most prestigious club recently went for 400 million yen, or about $2.7 million. A headline in *The Wall Street Journal* early this year said, "Japan: So Much Yen, So Little Else."

No one can say that it's "wrong" for Japan to be a mercantilist society, piling up its trade profits rather than spending them. No one can say whether Japan will always behave the way it does now. Its biggest companies are rushing to set up factories overseas; unemployment is rising; profits are plunging; the strong yen is having its effect. (If Japan had been more consumer-oriented and willing to "act on price," a gentler shift in exchange rates might have increased domestic spending.) Just before the economic summit in Venice, Japan announced a $40 billion public-works program to boost consumption. It's conceivable that ten years from now warnings about Japan's chronic surplus will look as premature as warnings about the "petro-dollar" glut do now. But unless *endaka* or *kokusaika* ("internationalization") changes Japan's basic nature, "free trade" will almost certainly mean something like what it's meant for the past few years: big surpluses for Japan, big deficits everywhere else, a big flow of profits out from Japan to buy companies, buildings, Treasury bonds (but not manufactured products), overseas. That near certainty gives us our choice: Do we want to end the deficits or do we want to honor free trade? We can't do both.

Life as chronic debtors (which is to say, as free traders) might not be so bad. It would accomplish de facto what we could never manage officially: the merger of Japan and the United States. Our two economies are complementary (they make and save, we borrow and buy) and so are our natural resources, human talents, and even our foreign policies. The more deeply the Japanese become enmeshed in our society—owning much of the debt, the real estate, the market share—the more of a stake they will have in its well-being. Everyone in the United States feels bad about foreigners "taking over" American buildings and companies, but is anyone really hurt? When Japanese investors reopen old American factories, they bring new technology and create new jobs. When they buy real estate, they pay money to the (usually American) owners. Japanese investment has helped push the American stock market to its speculative highs, and has buoyed the real-estate market in New York, Honolulu, Washington, and Los Angeles. Some Americans resent the rising prices, but others enjoy the profits.

Permanent debtor status could also have its drawbacks. America would have less dependence of action, since it would have to keep foreign investors calm and confident. Putting the United States on a leash might be better for the world, but we would never choose this course ourselves. As our interest burden mounts, we'll have to slide down to a lower standard of living, consuming less and repaying more. (The Japanese are already underconsuming, of course, but they have never done otherwise.) And sometimes debt gets out of control, leading to inflation, panic, collapse.

If consumer welfare remains our goal, the United States would do best to stick to the free-trade route, despite the "deindustrialization" and debt. Restricting trade always means higher prices. We can resolve to work harder, teach our children more math, become more "competitive," all the while recognizing that Japan will never love our exports as much as we do theirs. But if we decide that continued debt is too dangerous, we'll have to go beyond "competitiveness." We'll need to change the rules.

This does not mean making Lee Iacocca speeches about the perfidious Japanese. They're simply doing what comes naturally to them. American politicians have been quoted in Japan as warning that trade sanctions would be the "equivalent of the A-bomb" or "really winning the war." The Japanese are too smart to let themselves be caught saying that a new car or computer chip of theirs will be the "equivalent of the Bataan Death March." In an editorial last spring *The New York Times* urged America to "badger them relentlessly for more access to their markets. . . ." What's the point of badgering them at all? Threats not backed up by action annoy the Japanese, make America look weak and nervous, and leave the bothersome trade patterns unchanged.

Instead of yelling and badgering, we should decide precisely what bothers us about the trade balance and then act calmly, without noise or threats, to change the rules where we think we must. Are we mainly worried about the overall trade balance? The Gephardt amendment, which would require sanctions against nations with chronic export surpluses, enjoys almost no respectable support, but it would force Japan to moderate its mercantilist behavior. Do we think there's too much foreign investment? We can limit it, as Japan has. Japan makes it hard for foreign companies to move in and set up wholly owned subsidiaries. Foreign investment in the United States would seem to help us, by bringing new technology and jobs. But if we feel that it's a threat, let's not yell at the Japanese; let's imitate them, with a change of investment rules.

Do we worry that Matsushita and Nissan will keep all the high-grade manufacturing work back in Osaka and Zama, leaving American workers to bolt parts together from a kit? The rising yen will put pressure on the Japanese to shift whole operations overseas; but if we're concerned, let's pass local-content laws.

Do we seethe about all the areas where American firms are competitive but are being frozen out of Japan? Let's not give speeches urging a more open attitude: when Japanese society does open up, it will be for its own reasons. Let's simply deny it markets reciprocally. For years American shipping firms complained about Japanese rules on "high cube containers"—the large metal boxes that are hauled across the country as truck trailers, loaded on ships, and unloaded in another port. Japan claimed that American containers were too big and dangerous; they had to be unloaded and their contents repacked in Japanese containers on arrival. The speeches and complaints went on; the Japanese stuck to their guns. But last year the U.S. Federal Maritime Commission started investigating the effect of Japanese restrictions, with a thinly veiled threat to restrict Japanese shipments to the United States in retaliation. Japan modified its rules, but after American shippers said the changes made no practical difference, the commission pursued its investigation. Recently the Japanese issued further-relaxed guidelines.

Stated that way, the story may seem to have a bully-boy moral, which is not my point. It's juvenile and dangerous to think that if we just get tough with the Japanese (or Russians), we can make them back down. The point is that in this case, without speeches, our government changed the rules; without rancor, the Japanese adapted. The more typical pattern is for our politicians to yell at the Japanese, without changing the rules. We've yelled because we're uneasy about the deficits, but we haven't done anything, because it would hurt us as consumers and impinge on free trade.

Let's be clear about it: Changing the trade imbalance *will* hurt us as consumers, because consumers' interests always suffer from any restriction on trade. Nonetheless, even the United States, consumer heaven, has restricted trade when free trade threatened other values. Child labor would make household help affordable again; totally unlimited immigration would probably take three dollars off the bill for a standard restaurant meal. Product-safety laws make everything cost more. Yet in all these cases our laws recognize that not even Americans live by the "standard of living" alone.

We may feel the same way about trade: that stable communities, predictable jobs, freedom from foreign interference, matter more than the best value for our money. If so, we can change the laws, mandating a different trade balance—and a lower standard of living. The Japanese have made a choice for their society, and we should make one for ours. That's better than thinking that we can talk the Japanese into behaving more like us, or relying on "free trade" to reach equilibrium again.

Themes, Issues, and Ideas

1. What does Fallows say are the different "rules" of production and consumption that the United States and Japan "play by?"

2. According to Fallows, how are "trade wars" different from real wars? Why does he say this difference is important to the nature of United States responses to Japan?

3. Toward the end of his essay Fallows says, "Permanent debtor status would also have its drawbacks." What are these drawbacks and what does Fallows suggest might be done about them?

Writing Strategies and Techniques

1. How does Fallows use the "game" metaphor to describe international trade? How does the metaphor implicitly define words like *fair* and *failure* in a different way than a metaphor of "war" would?

2. Toward the end of his essay Fallows uses an example of a small U.S. success involving shipping containers. What means does he employ to make it seem that this example is not unique and could be generalized by a proper U.S. policy?

Suggestions for Writing

1. "Preserving the existing order—continuing to buy soda ash from your school chum—seems more important to Japan than anything else." Write an essay analyzing the ways in which Fallows does or does not earn the right to assert this conclusion through the examples and arguments he provides.

2. Fallows suggests some possibilities for American action at the end of his essay. What are your views? Write an essay in which you outline a plan for our economic relations with Japan.

MAKING CONNECTIONS

1. President Kennedy's inaugural speech proposed a course of action for the United States in its influence on the world. Compare his speech to the selections by Richard Falk and Carlos Fuentes. Write an essay describing which proposals in Kennedy's speech have been achieved and which have not.

2. Flora Lewis discusses the problems the new Germany is facing in some detail. Richard Falk, on the other hand, takes a sort of bird's-eye view, looking at Europe from a global perspective. Which approach is more useful? Which is more interesting?

3. James Fallows says we should try to understand and accommodate ourselves to Japanese culture in order to deal with our relative weakness in trade with Japan. Suppose someone suggested that Latin American countries should strive to understand and accommodate themselves to the United States' position of strength. Write an essay in which you either imagine or describe Carlos Fuentes's reply, or make your own reply to Fallows.

4. Compare the way the Tofflers talk about the future with one of the other authors in this chapter. What are the differences, and how do they affect your own viewpoint? Who seems more authoritative? Who more persuasive? Why?

5. Using the material in this chapter as a source for topics and information, write the inaugural speech that you would like to hear delivered by the president of the United States in the year 2001.

CHAPTER SIX

American Life and Popular Culture

Style and Substance in the Shape of Things to Come

THE PAST AS PROLOGUE

A Eulogy for the Twentieth Century

Tom Wolfe

In his essay Tom Wolfe says that the particularly American contribution to the many innovations of the twentieth century was made in the area of "manners and mores," especially during the 1960s. Whether or not Wolfe is right in his assessment of the facts, he had good cause to know them, since it was in the 1960s that he and others began the kind of cultural reporting that quickly became known as the "New Journalism."

Wolfe was born in Richmond, Virginia, in 1931 and was educated at Washington and Lee University and at Yale University, where he took a Ph.D. in American Studies. He went on to work as a journalist, most notably for the New York Herald Tribune. *With books like* The Kandy-Kolored Tangerine-Flake Streamline Baby *(1965) and* The Electric Kool-Aid Acid Test *(1968), he began paying attention to popular culture and American lifestyle in a new way, and has kept a keen eye on the American scene ever since. He added to this collection most recently with his novel on the boom years of Wall Street in the 1980s,* The Bonfire of the Vanities.

In 1968, in San Francisco, I came across a curious foot-note to the psychedelic movement. At the Haight-Ashbury Free Clinic there were doctors who were treating diseases no living doctor had ever encountered before, diseases that had disappeared so long ago they had never even picked up Latin names, diseases such as the mange, the grunge, the itch, the twitch, the thrush, the scroff, the rot. And how was it that they had now returned? It had to do with the fact that thousands of young men and women had migrated to San Francisco to live communally in what I think history will record as one of the most extraordinary religious experiments of all time.

The hippies, as they became known, sought nothing less than to sweep aside all codes and restraints of the past and start out from zero. At one point Ken Kesey organized a pilgrimage to Stonehenge with the idea of returning to Anglo-Saxon civilization's point zero, which he figured was Stonehenge, and heading out all over again to do it better. Among the codes and restraints that people in the communes swept aside—quite purposely—were those that said you shouldn't use other people's toothbrushes or sleep on other people's mattresses without changing the sheets or, as was more likely, without using any sheets at all or that you and five other people shouldn't drink from the same bottle of Shasta or take tokes from the same cigarette. And now, in 1968, they were relearning the laws of hygiene . . . by getting the mange, the grunge, the itch, the twitch, the thrush, the scroff, the rot.

This process, namely the relearning—following a Promethean and unprecedented start from zero—seems to me to be the leitmotif of our current interlude, here in the dying years of the twentieth century.

Start from zero was the slogan of the Bauhaus School. The story of how the Bauhaus, a tiny artists' movement in Germany in the 1920s, swept aside the architectural styles of the past and created the glass-box face of the modern American city is a familiar one, and I won't retell it. But I should mention the soaring spiritual exuberance with which the movement began, the passionate conviction of the Bauhaus's leader, Walter Gropius, that by starting from zero in architecture and design man could free himself from the dead hand of the past. By the late 1970s, however, architects themselves were beginning to complain of the dead hand of the Bauhaus: the flat roofs, which leaked from rain and collapsed from snow, the tiny bare beige office cubicles, which made workers feel like component parts, the glass walls, which let in too much heat, too much cold, too much glare, and no air at all. The relearning is now under way in earnest.

The architects are busy rummaging about in what the artist Richard Merkin calls the Big Closet. Inside the Big Closet, in promiscuous heaps, are the abandoned styles of the past. The current favorite rediscoveries: Classical, Secession, and Moderne (Art Deco). Relearning on the wing, the architects are off on a binge of eclecticism comparable to the Victorian period's a century ago.

In politics the twentieth century's great start from zero was one-party socialism, also known as communism or Marxism-Leninism. Given that system's bad reputation in the West today (even among the French intelligentsia), it is instructive to read John Reed's *Ten Days That Shook the World*—before turning to Solzhenitsyn's *Gulag Archipelago*. The old strike hall poster of a Promethean worker in a blue shirt breaking his chains across his mighty chest was in truth the vision of ultimate human freedom the movement believed in at the outset. For intellectuals in the West the painful dawn began with the publication of the *Gulag Archipelago* in 1973. Solzhenitsyn insisted that the villain behind the Soviet concentration-camp network was not Stalin or Lenin (who invented the term concentration camp) or even Marxism. It was instead the Soviets' peculiarly twentieth-century notion that they could sweep aside not only the old social order but also its religious ethic, which had been millennia in the making ("common decency," Orwell called it) and reinvent morality . . . here . . . now . . . "at the point of a gun," in the famous phrase of the Maoists. Today the relearning has reached the point where even ruling circles in the Soviet Union and China have begun to wonder how best to convert communism into something other than, in Susan Sontag's phrase, *successful fascism*.

The great American contribution to the twentieth century's start from zero was in the area of manners and mores, especially in what was rather primly called "the sexual revolution." In every hamlet, even in the erstwhile Bible Belt, may be found the village brothel, no longer hidden in a house of blue lights or red lights or behind a green door but openly advertised by the side of the road with a thousand-watt back-lit plastic sign: Totally All-Nude Girl Sauna Massage and Marathon Encounter Sessions InSide. Up until two years ago pornographic movie theaters were as ubiquitous as the 7-Eleven, including outdoor drive-ins with screens six, seven, eight stories high, the better to beam all the moistened folds and glistening nodes and stiffened giblets to a panting American countryside. Two years ago the pornographic theater began to be replaced by the pornographic videocassette, which could be brought into any home. Up on the shelf in the den, next to the set of *The Encyclopaedia Britannica* and the great books, one now finds the cassettes: *Shanks Akimbo, That Thing with the Cup.* My favorite moment in Jessica Hahn's triumphal tour of medialand this fall came when a 10-year-old girl, a student at a private school, wearing a buttercup blouse, a cardigan sweater, and her school uniform skirt, approached her outside a television studio with a stack of *Playboy* magazines featuring the famous Hahn nude form and asked her to autograph them. With the school's blessing, she intended to take the signed copies back to the campus and hold a public auction. The proceeds would go to the poor.

But in the sexual revolution, too, the painful dawn has already arrived, and the relearning is imminent. All may be summed up in a single term, requiring no amplification: AIDS.

The Great Relearning—if anything so prosaic as remedial education can be called great—should be thought of not as the end of the twentieth century but the prelude to the twenty-first. There is no law of history that says a new century must start ten or twenty years beforehand, but two times in a row it has worked out that way. The nineteenth century began with the American and French revolutions of the late eighteenth. The twentieth century began with the formulation of Marxism, Freudianism, and Modernism in the late nineteenth. And now the twenty-first begins with the Great Relearning.

The twenty-first century, I predict, will confound the twentieth century notion of the Future as something exciting, novel, unexpected, or radiant; as Progress, to use an old word. It is already clear that the large cities, thanks to the Relearning, will not even look new. Quite the opposite; the cities of 2007 will look more like the cities of 1927 than the cities of 1987. The twenty-first century will have a retrograde look and a retrograde mental atmosphere. People of the next century, snug in their neo-Georgian apartment complexes, will gaze back with a ghastly awe upon our time. They will regard the twentieth as the century in which wars became so enormous they were known as World Wars, the century in which technology leapt forward so rapidly man developed the capacity to destroy the planet itself— but also the capacity to escape to the stars on spaceships if it blew. But above all they will look back upon the twentieth as the century in which their forebears had the amazing confidence, the Promethean *hubris,* to defy the gods and try to push man's power and freedom to limitless, godlike extremes. They will look back in awe . . . without the slightest temptation to emulate the daring of those who swept aside all rules and tried to start from zero. Instead, they will sink ever deeper into their neo-Louis bergères, content to live in what will be known as the Somnolent Century or the Twentieth Century's Hangover.

Themes, Issues, and Ideas

1. What cultural examples from the twentieth-century does Wolfe give of what he calls "starting from zero?" Can you think of others?

2. What does Wolfe mean by "the Great Relearning?" Why does he assign it to the twenty-first century rather than to the end of the twentieth century?

3. How, according to Wolfe, will twenty-first-century reality differ from what the twentieth century imagined it would be?

Writing Strategies and Techniques

1. Wolfe's second sentence of his first paragraph and the last sentence of his second paragraph end with the same list of words. What effect does the repetition create?

2. Wolfe refers twice to Prometheus. How does Prometheus serve as a symbol in Wolfe's argument? (If you do not know the figure, look him up.)

Suggestions for Writing

1. Wolfe calls his essay a "eulogy." Given his many criticisms of the period, do you think his title is an appropriate one? Write an essay in which you argue whether or not Wolfe's essay deserves its title.

2. Wolfe argues that "the twenty-first century will have a retrograde look and a retrograde mental atmosphere." Write an essay in which you (1) summarize Wolfe's arguments in support of this claim, and (2) attack, defend, or modify his contention with arguments and evidence of your own.

Ice-T: Is the Issue Social Responsibility or Free Speech?

Michael Kinsley/Barbara Ehrenreich

> *Michael Kinsley is one of the most visible of political commentators. As the editor of the* New Republic, *he is one of the principal voices behind what is in many ways the leading moderate journal in America, and he regularly represents the left on CNN's* Crossfire.
>
> *Barbara Ehrenreich is an accomplished essayist and social critic whose writings in* Time, Mother Jones, *and other magazines, along with her numerous books and appearances, place her in the cultural vanguard to the left of Kinsley.*
>
> *Both Kinsley and Ehrenreich were invited by* Time *magazine to discuss the ramifications of Ice-T's controversial rap song* Cop Killer.

Michael Kinsley:

How did the company that publishes this magazine come to produce a record glorifying the murder of police?

> I got my 12-gauge sawed off
> I got my headlights turned off
> I'm 'bout to bust some shots off
> I'm 'bout to dust some cops off . . .
> Die, Die, Die Pig, Die!

So go the lyrics to *Cop Killer* by the rapper Ice-T on the album *Body Count*. The album is released by Warner Bros. Records, part of the Time Warner media and entertainment conglomerate.

In a *Wall Street Journal* op-ed piece laying out the company's position, Time Warner Co-CEO Gerald Levin makes two defenses. First, Ice-T's *Cop Killer* is misunderstood. "It doesn't incite or glorify violence . . . It's his fictionalized attempt to get inside a character's head . . . *Cop Killer* is no more a call for gunning down the police than *Frankie and Johnny* is a summons for jilted lovers to shoot one another." Instead of "finding ways to silence the messenger," we should be "heeding the anguished cry contained in his message."

This defense is self-contradictory. *Frankie and Johnny* does not pretend to have a political "message" that must be "heeded." If *Cop Killer* has a message, it is that the murder of policemen is a justified response to police brutality. And not in self-defense, but in premeditated acts of revenge against random cops. ("I know your family's grievin'—f___ 'em.")

Killing policemen is a good thing—that is the plain meaning of the words, and no "larger understanding" of black culture, the rage of the streets or anything else can explain it away. This is not Ella Fitzgerald telling a story in song. As in much of today's popular music, the line between performer and performance is purposely blurred. These are political sermonettes clearly intended to endorse the sentiments being expressed. Tracy Morrow (Ice-T) himself has said, "I scared the police, and they need to be scared." That seems clear.

The company's second defense of *Cop Killer* is the classic one of free expression: "We stand for creative freedom. We believe that the worth of what an artist or journalist has to say does not depend on preapproval from a government official or a corporate censor."

Of course Ice-T has the right to say whatever he wants. But that doesn't require any company to provide him an outlet. And it doesn't relieve a company of responsibility for the messages it chooses to promote. Judgment is not "censorship." Many an "anguished cry" goes unrecorded. This one was recorded, and promoted, because a successful artist under contract wanted to record it. Nothing wrong with making money, but a company cannot take the money and run from the responsibility.

The founder of *Time,* Henry Luce, would snort at the notion that his company should provide a value-free forum for the exchange of ideas. In Luce's system, editors were supposed to make value judgments and promote the truth as they saw it. *Time* has moved far from its old Lucean rigidity—far enough to allow for dissenting essays like this one. That evolution is a good thing, as long as it's not a handy excuse for abandoning all standards.

No commercial enterprise need agree with every word that appears under its corporate imprimatur. If Time Warner now intends to be "a global force for encouraging the confrontation of ideas," that's swell. But a policy of allowing diverse viewpoints is not a moral free pass. Pro and con on national health care is one thing; pro and con on killing policemen is another.

A bit of sympathy is in order for Time Warner. It is indeed a "global force" with media tentacles around the world. If it imposes rigorous standards and values from the top, it gets accused of corporate censorship. If it doesn't, it gets accused of moral irresponsibility. A dilemma. But someone should have thought of that before deciding to become a global force.

And another genuine dilemma. Whatever the actual merits of *Cop Killer,* if Time Warner withdraws the album now the company will be perceived as giving in to outside pressure. That is a disastrous precedent for a global conglomerate.

The Time-Warner merger of 1989 was supposed to produce corporate "synergy": the whole was supposed to be more than the sum of the parts. The *Cop Killer* controversy is an example of negative synergy. People get mad at *Cop Killer* and start boycotting the movie *Batman Returns.* A reviewer praises *Cop Killer* ("Tracy Marrow's poetry takes a switchblade and deftly slices life's jugular," etc.), and *Time* is accused of corruption instead of mere foolishness. Senior Time Warner executives find themselves under attack for—and defending—products of their company they neither honestly care for nor really understand, and doubtless weren't even aware of before controversy hit.

Anyway, it's absurd to discuss *Cop Killer* as part of the "confrontation of ideas"—or even as an authentic anguished cry of rage from the ghetto. *Cop Killer* is a cynical commercial concoction, designed to titillate its audience with imagery of violence. It merely exploits the authentic anguish of the inner city for further titillation. Tracy Marrow is in business for a buck, just like Time Warner. *Cop Killer* is an excellent joke on the white establishment, of which the company's anguished apologia ("Why can't we hear what rap is trying to tell us?") is the punch line.

Barbara Ehrenreich:

Ice-T's song *Cop Killer* is as bad as they come. This is black anger—raw, rude and cruel—and one reason the song's so shocking is that in postliberal America, black anger is virtually taboo. You won't find it on TV, not on the *McLaughlin Group* or *Crossfire,* and certainly not in the placid features of Arsenio Hall or Bernard Shaw. It's been beaten back into the outlaw subcultures of rap and rock, where, precisely because it is taboo, it sells. And the nastier it is, the faster it moves off the shelves. As Ice-T asks in another song on the same album, "Goddamn what a brotha gotta do/To get a message through/To the red, white and blue?"

But there's a gross overreaction going on, building to a veritable paroxysm of white denial. A national boycott has been called, not just of the song or Ice-T, but of all Time Warner products. The President himself has denounced Time Warner as "wrong" and Ice-T as "sick." Ollie North's Freedom Alliance has started a petition drive aimed at bringing Time-Warner executives to trial for "sedition and anarchy."

Much of this is posturing and requires no more courage than it takes to stand up in a VFW hall and condemn communism or crack. Yes, *Cop Killer* is irresponsible and vile. But Ice-T is as right about some things as he is righteous about the rest. And ultimately, he's not even dangerous—least of all to the white power structure his songs condemn.

The "danger" implicit in all the uproar is of empty-headed, suggestible black kids, crouching by their boom boxes, waiting for the word. But what Ice-T's fans know and his detractors obviously don't is that *Cop Killer* is just one more entry in pop music's long history of macho hyperbole and violent boast. Flip to the classic-rock station, and you might catch the Rolling Stones announcing "the time is right of violent revoloo-shun!" from their 1968 hit *Street Fighting Man.* And where were the defenders of our law-enforcement officers when a white British group, the Clash, taunted its fans with the lyrics: "When they kick open your front door/How you gonna come/With your hands on your head/Or on the trigger of your gun?"

"Die, Die, Die Pig" is strong speech, but the Constitution protects strong speech, and it's doing so this year more aggressively than ever. The Supreme Court has just downgraded cross burnings to the level of bonfires and ruled that it's no crime to throw around verbal grenades like "nigger" and "kike." Where are the defenders of decorum and social stability when prime-time demagogues like Howard Stern deride African Americans as "spear chuckers?"

More to the point, young African Americans are not so native and suggestible that they have to depend on a compact disc for their sociology lessons. To paraphrase another song from another era, you don't need a rap song to tell which way the wind is blowing. Black youths know that the police are likely to see them through a filter of stereotypes as miscreants and potential "cop killers." They are aware that a black youth is seven times as likely to be charged with a felony as a white youth who has committed the same offense, and is much more likely to be imprisoned.

They know, too, that in a shameful number of cases, it is the police themselves who indulge in "anarchy" and violence. The U.S.

Justice Department has received 47,000 complaints of police brutality in the past six years, and Amnesty International has just issued a report on police brutality in Los Angeles, documenting 40 cases of "torture or cruel, inhuman or degrading treatment."

Menacing as it sounds, the fantasy in *Cop Killer* is the fantasy of the powerless and beaten down—the black man who's been hassled once too often ("A pig stopped me for nothin'!"), spread-eagled against a police car, pushed around. It's not a "responsible" fantasy (fantasies seldom are). It's not even a very creative one. In fact, the sad thing about *Cop Killer* is that it falls for the cheapest, most conventional image of rebellion that our culture offers: the lone gunman spraying fire from his AK-47. This is not "sedition"; it's the familiar, all-American, Hollywood-style pornography of violence.

Which is why Ice-T is right to say he's no more dangerous than George Bush's pal Arnold Schwarzenegger, who wasted an army of cops in *Terminator 2*. Images of extraordinary cruelty and violence are marketed every day, many of far less artistic merit than *Cop Killer*. This is our free market of ideas and images, and it shouldn't be any less free for a black man than for other purveyors of "irresponsible" sentiments, from David Duke to Andrew Dice Clay.

Just, please, don't dignify Ice-T's contribution with the word sedition. The past masters of sedition—men like George Washington, Toussaint-Louverture, Fidel Castro or Mao Zedong, all of whom led and won armed insurrections—would be unimpressed by *Cop Killer* and probably saddened. They would shake their heads and mutter words like "infantile" and "adventurism." They might point out that the cops are hardly a noble target, being, for the most part, honest working stiffs who've got stuck with the job of patrolling ghettos ravaged by economic decline and official neglect.

There is a difference, the true seditionist would argue, between a revolution and a gesture of macho defiance. Gestures are cheap. They feel good, they blow off some rage. But revolutions, violent or otherwise, are made by people who have learned how to count very slowly to ten.

Themes, Issues, and Ideas

1. Kinsley and Ehrenreich both address the issue of free speech. How do they differ on its application to *Cop Killer?* Do you find Kinsley's or Ehrenreich's perspective more convincing? Explain why.

2. Kinsley writes knowingly about mass media and big business. Do you find his authority pertinent to the discussion of *Cop Killer?*

What seems to be Ehrenreich's field of expertise? Compare it to Kinsley's.

3. Ehrenreich brings up the names of "past masters of sedition," such as George Washington, Fidel Castro, and Mao Zedong. Do you agree with her labeling of these figures? Do you agree with her judgment of Ice-T?

Writing Strategies and Techniques

1. Compare Kinsley's closing paragraph with Ehrenreich's. Which fits in better with the rest of each writer's essay? Which is more persuasive?

2. Kinsley maintains that Time Warner must accept responsibility for the records it produces, and brings *Time* magazine into his argument. Ehrenreich brings Kinsley in, implicitly, by mentioning *Crossfire,* a television show he is featured on. How do these strategies advance their arguments?

Suggestions for Writing

1. Write two short essays imitating Kinsley and Ehrenreich on opposite sides of an issue. If you want, imitate them as they might be if they switched positions on *Cop Killer.*

2. *Cop Killer* is now over two years old. Rewrite this argument, updating the subject. Do not use rap music as a topic.

Big Brother Is You, Watching

Mark Crispin Miller

Mark Crispin Miller is the author of Boxed In: The
Culture of Television, *as well as numerous essays on American popular culture and social history. He teaches film
studies at Johns Hopkins University, and is currently at
work on a book about the Gulf War. In the essay from which
this selection is taken, Miller compares the world of George
Orwell's* 1984 *to our own. In Orwell's novel, the superstate
of Oceania is ruled by the tyrannical Inner Party, as symbolized by Big Brother: The slogan "Big Brother Is Watching You" appears everywhere, and the Thought Police are
ever-alert for signs of discontent or nonconformity. Is this
so in our time? asks Miller, and his answer may surprise
you.*

Television's formal erasure of distinctness comple-
ments—or perhaps has actually fostered—a derisive personal style
that inhibits all personality, a knowingness that now pervades all TV
genres and the culture which those genres have homogenized. The
corrosive irony emanating from the Oceanic elite has been universal-
ized by television, whose characters—both real and fictional—relentlessly inflict it on each other and themselves, defining a negative ideal
of hip inertia which no living human being is able to approach too
closely. For example, in situation comedies or "sitcoms"—TV's definitive creation—the "comedy" almost always consists of a weak,
compulsive jeering that immediately wipes out any divergence from
the indefinite collective standard. The characters vie at self-contain-
ment, reacting to every simulation of intensity, every bright idea,
every mechanical enthusiasm with the same deflating look of jaded
incredulity. In such an atmosphere, those already closest to the
ground run the least risk of being felled by the general ridicule, and
so those characters most adept at enforcing the proper emptiness

239

are also the puniest and most passive: blasé wives and girlfriends, and—especially—blasé children, who, like Parsons' daughter, prove their own orthodoxy by subverting their subverted parents.

Nearly all of TV's characters—on sitcoms and in "dramas," on talk shows and children's programs—participate in this reflexive sneering, and such contemptuous passivity reflects directly on the viewer who watches it with precisely the same attitude. TV seems to flatter the inert skepticism of its own audience, assuring them that they can do no better than to stay right where they are, rolling their eyes in feeble disbelief. And yet such apparent flattery of our viewpoint is in fact a recurrent warning not to rise above this slack, derisive gaping. At first, it seems that it is only those eccentric others whom TV belittles. Each time some deadpan tot on a sitcom responds to his frantic mom with a disgusted sigh, or whenever the polished anchorman punctuates his footage of "extremists" with a look that speaks his well-groomed disapproval, or each time Johnny Carson comments on some "unusual" behavior with a wry sidelong glance into our living rooms, we are being flattered with a gesture of inclusion, the wink that tells us, "*We* are in the know." And yet we are the ones belittled by each subtle televisual gaze, which offers not a welcome but an ultimatum—that we had better see the joke or else turn into it.

If we see the joke, however, we are nothing like those Oceanic viewers "shouting with laughter" at the sight of their own devastation. All televisual smirking is based on, and reinforces, the assumption that we who smirk together are enlightened past the point of nullity, having evolved far beyond whatever datedness we might be jeering, whether the fanatic's ardor, the prude's inhibitions, the hick's unfashionable pants, or the snob's obsession with prestige. Thus TV's relentless comedy at first seems utterly progressive, if largely idiotic, since its butts are always the most reactionary of its characters—militarists, bigots, sexists, martinets. However, it is not to champion our freedom that TV makes fun of these ostensible oppressors. On the contrary: Through its derision, TV promotes only *itself,* disvaluing not Injustice or Intolerance but the impulse to resist TV.

Despite the butt's broad illiberality, what makes him appear ridiculous in TV's eyes is not his antidemocratic bias but his vestigial individuality, his persistence as a self sturdy and autonomous enough to sense that there is something missing from the televisual world, and to hunger for it, although ostracized for this desire by the sarcastic mob that watches and surrounds him. Like Winston Smith, the butt yearns for and exemplifies the past that brought about the present, and which the present now discredits through obsessive mockery. Whether arrogantly giving orders, compulsively tidying up, or longing for the good old days when men were men, the butt reenacts the type of personality—marked by rigidity and self-denial—that at first facilitated the extension of high capitalism but that soon threatened to impede its further growth. And it is just such endless growth that is the real point and object of TV's comedy, which puts down those hard selves in order to exalt the nothingness that laughs at them. Whereas the butt, enabled by his discrete selfhood, pursues desires that TV cannot gratify, we are induced, by the sight of his continual humiliation, to become as porous, cool, and acquiescent as he is solid, tense, and dissident, so that we might want nothing other than what TV sells us. This is what it means to see the joke. The viewer's enlightened laughter at those uptight others is finally the expression of his own Oceanic dissolution, as, within his distracted consciousness, there reverberates TV's sole imperative, which once obeyed makes the self seem a mere comical encumbrance—the imperative of total consumption.

Guided by its images even while he thinks that he sees through them, the TV viewer learns only to consume. That inert, ironic watchfulness which TV reinforces in its audience is itself conducive to consumption. As we watch, struggling inwardly to avoid resembling anyone who might stand out as pre- or non- or antitelevisual, we are already trying to live up, or down, to the same standard of acceptability that that TV's ads and shows define collectively: the standard that requires the desperate use of all those goods and services that TV proffers, including breath mints, mouthwash, dandruff shampoos, hair conditioners, blow-dryers, hair removers, eye drops, deodorant soaps and sticks and sprays, hair dyes, skin creams, lip balms, diet colas, diet plans, local frozen dinners, bathroom bowl cleaners, floor wax, car wax, furniture polish, fabric softeners, room deodorizers, and more, and more. Out of this flood of commodities, it is promised, we will each arise as sleek, quick, compact, and efficient as a brand-new Toyota; and in our effort at such self-renewal, moreover, we are enjoined not just to sweeten every orifice and burnish every surface, but to evacuate our psyches. While selling its explicit products, TV also advertises incidentally an ideal of emotional self-management, which dictates that we purge ourselves of all "bad feelings" through continual confession and by affecting the same stilted geniality evinced by most of TV's characters (the butts excluded). The unconscious must never be allowed to interfere with productivity, and so the viewer is warned repeatedly to atone for his every psychic eruption, like Parsons after his arrest for talking treason in his sleep: " 'Thoughtcrime is a dreadful thing, old man,' he said sententiously. 'It's insidious . . . There I was, working away, trying to do my bit—never knew I had any bad stuff in my mind at all.' "

Thus, even as its programs push the jargon of "honesty" and "tolerance," forever counseling you to "be yourself," TV shames you ruthlessly for every symptom of residual mortality, urging you to turn yourself into a standard object wholly inoffensive, useful, and adulterated, a product of and for all other products. However, this transformation is impossible. There is no such purity available to human beings, whose bodies will sweat and whose instincts will rage—however expertly we work to shut them off. Even Winston Smith, as broken as he is at the conclusion, is still impelled by his desires, which the Party could not extinguish after all, since it depends on their distorted energy. For all its chilling finality, in other words, the novel's closing sentence is merely another of the Party's lies. What O'Brien cannot achieve through torture, we cannot attain through our campaigns of self-maintenance—no matter how many miles we jog, or how devotedly, if skeptically, we watch TV.

Like the Party, whose unstated rules no person can follow rigidly enough, TV demands that its extruded viewers struggle to embody an ideal too cool and imprecise for human emulation. And like Winston Smith, we are the victims of Enlightenment in its late phase, although it is the logic of consumption, not the deliberate machinations of some cabal, that has impoverished our world in the name of its enrichment. As the creatures of this logic, we have become our own overseers. While Winston Smith is forced to watch himself in literal self-defense, trying to keep his individuality a hard-won secret, we have been forced to watch ourselves lest we develop selves too hard and secretive for the open market. In America, there is no need for an objective apparatus of surveillance (which is not to say that none exists), because, guided by TV, we watch ourselves as if already televised, checking ourselves both inwardly and outwardly for any sign of untidiness or gloom, moment by moment as guarded and self-conscious as Winston Smith under the scrutiny of the Thought Police: "The smallest thing could give you away. A nervous tic, an unconscious look of anxiety, a habit of muttering to yourself—anything that carried with it the suggestion of abnormality, of having something to hide." Although this description refers to the objective peril of life in Oceania, it also captures the anxiety of life under the scrutiny of television. Of course, all televisual performers must abide by the same grim advice or end up canceled; but TV's nervous viewers also feel themselves thus watched, fearing the same absolute exclusion if they should ever show some sign of resisting the tremendous pressure."

Television further intensifies our apprehension that we are being watched by continually assuring us that it already understands our innermost fears, our private problems, and that it even knows enough about our most intimate moments to reproduce them for us. The joy of birth is brought to us by Citicorp, the tender concern of one friend for another is presented by AT&T, the pleasures of the hearth are depicted for us by McDonald's. And on any talk show or newscast, there might suddenly appear the competent psychologist, who will deftly translate any widespread discontent into his own antiseptic terms, thereby representing it as something well-known to him, and therefore harmless. As we watch TV, we come to imagine that Winston Smith eventually discovers: "There was no physical act, no word spoken aloud, that they had not noticed, no train of thought that they had not been able to infer."

Television is not the cause of our habitual self-scrutiny, however, but has only set the standard for it, a relationship with a complicated history. It is through our efforts to maintain ourselves as the objects of our anxious self-spectatorship that we consummate the process of American Enlightenment, whose project throughout this century has been the complete and permanent reduction of our populace into the collective instrument of absolute production. This project has arisen not through corporate conspiracy but as the logical fulfillment, openly and even optimistically pursued, of the imperative of unlimited economic growth. Thus compelled, the enlightened captains of production have employed the principles, and often the exponents, of modern social science, in order to create a perfect work force whose members, whether laboring on products or consuming them, would function inexhaustibly and on command, like well-tuned robots.

As the material for this ideal, Americans have been closely watched for decades: in the factory, then in the office, by efficiency experts and industrial psychologists; in the supermarkets, then throughout the shopping malls, by motivational researchers no less cunningly than by the store detectives; in the schools, and then at home, and then in bed, by an immense, diverse, yet ultimately unified bureaucracy of social workers, education specialists, and "mental health professionals" of every kind. The psychic and social mutations necessarily induced by this multiform intrusion have accomplished what its first engineers had hoped for, but in a form, and at a cost, which they could never have foreseen: Americans—restless, disconnected, and insatiable—are mere consumers, having by now internal-ized the diffuse apparatus of surveillance built all around them, while still depending heavily on its external forms—TV, psychologistic "counseling," "self-help" manuals, the "human potential" regimens, and other self-perpetuating therapies administered to keep us on the job.

And so the project of industrial Enlightenment has only forced us back toward the same helpless natural state that Enlightenment had once meant to abolish. Both in America and in Oceania, the telescreens infantilize their captive audience. In *Nineteen Eighty-Four* and in 1984, the world has been made too bright and cold by the same system that forever promises the protective warmth of mother love, leaving each viewer yearning to have his growing needs fulfilled by the very force that aggravates them. So it is, first of all, with Orwell's famished hero. The figure who had slipped quickly into Victory Mansions, "his chin nuzzled into his breast," had tried unknowingly to transcend the Oceanic violence by mothering himself, but then ends up so broken by that violence that he adopts its symbol as his mother: "O cruel, needless misunderstanding!" he exults inwardly before the image of Big Brother's face. "O stubborn, self-willed exile from the loving breast!" And, as it is with Winston Smith in his perverted ardor, so it is with every vaguely hungry TV viewer, who longs to be included by the medium that has excluded everyone, and who expects its products to fulfill him in a way that they have made impossible.

What is most disconcerting, then, about the ending of *Nineteen Eighty-Four* is not that Winston Smith has now been made entirely unlike us. In too many ways, the ex-hero of this brilliant, dismal book anticipates those TV viewers who are incapable of reading it: "In these days he could never fix his mind on any one subject for more than a few moments at a time." At this moment, Winston Smith is, for the first time in his life, not under surveillance. The motto, "Big Brother Is Watching You," is now untrue as a threat, as it has always been untrue as an assurance. And the reason why he is no longer watched is that the Oceanic gaze need no longer see through Winston Smith, because he is no longer "Winston Smith," but "a swirl of gritty dust," as primitive and transparent as the Party.

As this Smith slumps in the empty Chestnut Tree, credulously gaping, his ruined mind expertly jolted by the telescreen's managers, he signifies the terminal fulfillment of O'Brien's master plan, which expresses the intentions not only of Orwell's fictitious Party, but of the corporate entity that, through TV, contains our consciousness today: "We shall squeeze you empty, and then we shall fill you with ourselves." The Party has now done for Winston Smith what all our advertisers want to do for us, and with our general approval—answer all material needs, in exchange for the self that might try to gratify them independently, and that might have other subtler needs as well. As a consumer, in other words, Orwell's ex-hero really has it made. "There was no need to give orders" to the waiters in the Chestnut Tree. "They knew his habits." Furthermore, he "always had plenty of money nowadays." In short, the Party has paid him for his erasure with the assurance, "We do it *all* for you." And so this grotesque before-and-after narrative ends satirically as all ads end in earnest, with the object's blithe endorsement of the very product that has helped to keep him miserable: "But it was all right, everything was all right, the struggle was finished. He had won the victory over himself. He loved Big Brother."

It is a horrifying moment; but if we do no more than wince and then forget about it, we ignore our own involvement in the horror and thus complacently betray the hope that once inspired this vision. Surely Orwell would have us face the facts. Like Winston Smith, and like O'Brien and the others, we have been estranged from our desire by Enlightenment, which finally reduces all of its proponents to the blind spectators of their own annihilation. Unlike that Oceanic audience, however, the TV viewer does not gaze up at the screen with angry scorn or piety, but—perfectly enlightened—looks down on its images with a nervous sneer which cannot threaten them and which only keeps the viewer himself from standing up. As you watch, there is no Big Brother out there watching you—not because there isn't a Big Brother, but because Big Brother is you, watching.

Themes, Issues, and Ideas

1. Is the "reflexive sneering" Miller describes typical of TV? Give five examples from television of what you think Miller means, and five examples that attempt to refute Miller's view.

2. What might be an example of a self "too hard and secretive for the open market?" Of a "butt?" Of TV "continually assuring us that it already understands our innermost fears, our private problems?"

3. In what way is the Party's boast, "We will squeeze you empty, and then we shall fill you with ourselves" true of today's society, in Miller's view? Give examples.

Writing Strategies and Techniques

1. Miller uses many quotations in his essay, both from *1984* and from TV. What are the effect of these quotations on the essay? Do you find them disruptive? Convincing? Why does Miller use them so often?

2. Does Miller impress you as someone familiar with popular culture, or as a professor in an ivory tower? Why?

Suggestions for Writing

1. Mark Miller has a very unusual view of television. Write an essay in which you describe three or four different ways of looking at TV. Explain which approach is closest to your own, and why.

2. Write a defense of television that takes TV as seriously as this attack does.

On "Junk Food for the Soul"

In Defense of Rock and Roll

Frank Zappa

Allan Bloom's The Closing of the American Mind *(1987) attacked rock and-roll music, among many other things, as a "junk food for the soul," and claimed that it was poisoning American lives now and through the foreseeable future. Famous rock artist Frank Zappa was born in 1940 and made his reputation in the 1960s as a performer with the rock group* The Mothers of Invention. *Over the years he has made many social observations and, among other things, brought the language of Valley Girls to national attention through his daughter, Moon Unit Zappa. He has also defended rock music against the attacks of Tipper Gore and the Parents Music Resource Center, which seeks greater parental control over lyrics. Most recently Zappa has billed himself as a consultant in commercial relations with the U.S.S.R. and has been a guest host on* Financial Network News. *Zappa published this attack of Bloom's critique in* New Progressive Quarterly.

The Nature of Music

Music is the soul's primitive and primary speech . . . without articulate speech or reason. It is not only not reasonable, it is hostile to reason. . . . Civilization . . . is the taming or domestication of the soul's raw passions. . . . Rock music has one appeal only, a barbaric appeal, to sexual desire—not love, not eros, but sexual desire undeveloped and untutored . . .   —A. Bloom

This is a puff pastry version of the belief that music is the work of the Devil: that the nasty ol' Devil plays his fiddle and people dance around and we don't want to see them twitching like that. In fact, if one wants to be a real artist in the United States today and comment on our culture, one would be very far off the track if one did something delicate or sublime. This is not a noble, delicate, sublime country. This is a mess run by criminals. Performers who are doing the crude, vulgar, repulsive things Bloom doesn't enjoy are only commenting on that fact.

In general, anti-rock propositions began when rock n' roll began, and most of these were racially motivated. In the fifties, petitions were circulated which said, "Don't allow your children to buy Negro records." The petitions referred to the "raw unbridled passion" of screaming people with dark skin who were going to drive our children wild. Some things never go out of fashion in certain ideological camps. They are like tenets of the faith.

Music's real effect on people is a new field of science called psychoacoustics—the way an organism deals with wiggling air molecules. Our ears decode the wiggling air molecules, and that gives us the information of a particular musical sound. Our brain says, "This is music, this is a structure," and we deal with it based on certain tools we have acquired.

I personally make music because I want to ask a question, and I want to get an answer. If that question and answer amuse me, then statistically, there are a certain number of other people out there who have the same amusement factor. If I present my work to them, they will be amused by it, and we will all have a good time.

I need to be amused because I get bored easily and being amused entertains me. If I could be easily amused, like many people who like beer and football, I would never do anything because everything that would be beautiful for my life would already be provided by American television.

But beer and television bore me, so what am I going to do? I am going to be alive for X number of years. I have to do something with my time besides sleep and eat. So, I devise little things to amuse myself. If I can amuse somebody else, great. And if I can amuse somebody else and earn a living while doing it, that is a true miracle in the twentieth century!

Music and the Dark Forces of the Soul

To Plato and Nietzsche, the history of music is a series of attempts to give form and beauty to the dark, chaotic, premonitory forces in the soul—to make them serve a higher purpose, an ideal, to give man's duties a fullness.
                                                                —A. Bloom

This is a man who has fallen for rock's fabricated image of itself. This is the worst kind of ivory tower intellectualism. Anybody who talks about dark forces is right on the fringe of mumbo jumbo. Dark forces? What is this, another product from Lucasfilm? The passions! When was the last time you saw an American exhibit any form of passion other than the desire to shoot a guy on the freeway? Those are the forces of evil as far as I am concerned.

If there are dark forces hovering in the vicinity of the music business, they are mercantile forces. We meet the darkness when we meet the orchestra committees, when we get in touch with funding organizations, when we deal with people who give grants and when we get into the world of commerce that greets us when we arrive with our piece of art. Whether it's a rock n' roll record or a symphony, it's the same machinery lurking out there.

The reason a person writes a piece of music has got nothing to do with dark forces. I certainly don't have dark forces lurking around me when I'm writing. If someone is going to write a piece of music, in fact they are preoccupied with the boring labor and very hard work involved. That's what's really going on.

What Makes Music Classical

Rock music.... has risen to its current heights in the education of the young on the ashes of classical music, and in an atmosphere in which there is no intellectual resistance to attempts to tap the rawest passions.... Cultivation of the soul uses the passions and satisfies them while sublimating them and giving them an artistic unity.... Bach's religious intentions and Beethoven's revolutionary and humane ones are clear enough examples.   —A. Bloom

This is such nonsense. All the people recognized as great classical composers are recognized at this point for two reasons:

One, during the time these composers were alive and writing they had patrons who liked what they did and who therefore paid them money or gave them a place to live so that the composers could stay alive by writing dots on pieces of paper. If any of the compositions these men wrote had not been pleasing to a church, a duke, or a king, they would have been out of work and their music would not have survived.

There is a book called *Grove's Dictionary of Music and Musicians,* with thousands of names in it. You have never heard of most of the people in that book, nor have you heard their music. That doesn't mean they wrote awful music, it means they didn't have hits.

So basically, the people who are recognized as the geniuses of classical music had hits. And the person who determined whether or not it was a hit was a king, a duke, or the church or whoever paid the bill. The desire to get a sandwich or something to drink had a lot to do with it. And the content of what they wrote was to a degree determined by the musical predilections of the guy who was paying the bill.

Today, we have a similar situation in rock n' roll. We have kings, dukes, and popes: the A&R guy who spots a group or screens the tape when it comes in; the business affairs guy who writes the contract; the radio station programers who choose what records get air play.

The other reason the classical greats survived is their works are played over and over again by orchestras. The reasons they are played over and over again are: (1) all the musicians in the orchestra know how to play them because they learned them in the conservatory; (2) the orchestra management programs these pieces because the musicians already know them and therefore it costs less to rehearse them; (3) the composers are dead so the orchestras pay no royalties for the use of the music.

Today, survivability is based on the number of specimens in the market place—the sheer numbers of plastic objects. Many other compositions from this era will vanish, but Michael Jackson's *Thriller* album will survive because there are 30 million odd pieces of plastic out there. No matter what we may think of the content, a future generation may pick up that piece of plastic and say, "Oh, they were like this."

I suppose somewhere in the future there will be other men like Bloom certifying that the very narrow spectrum of rock n' roll which survives composes the great works of the later half of the twentieth century.

The Difference Between Classical Music and Rock n' Roll

Rock music provides premature ecstasy and, in this respect, is like the drugs with which it is allied. . . . These are the three great lyrical themes: sex, hate and a smarmy, hypocritical version of brotherly love. . . . Nothing noble, sublime, profound, delicate, tasteful or even decent can find a place in such tableaux.   —A. Bloom

Again, Bloom is not looking at what is really going on here. The ugliness in this society is not a product of unrefined art, but of unrefined commerce, wild superstition, and religious fanaticism.

The real difference between the classics and rock n' roll is mostly a matter of form. In order to say we have written a symphony, the design we put on a piece of paper has to conform to certain specifications. We have an exposition that lasts a certain amount of time, then modulation, development, and recapitulation. It's like a box, like an egg carton. We must fill all the little spaces in the egg carton with the right forms. If we do, we can call it a symphony because it conforms to the spaces in that box.

Compare that creative process to rock n' roll. If we want to have an AM hit record, we have another egg carton to fill. We have an intro, a couple of verses, a bridge, another verse, and then a fade out. All of which requires a "hook." That's a very rigid form. If we wander away from that form, our song's not going to go on the radio because it doesn't sound like it fits into their format.

Now, whether the person writing the song graduated from a conservatory or whether they came out of a garage, they know that in order to finish a piece they have to do certain things to make it fit into a certain form. In the classical period the sonata or a concerto or symphony had to be that certain size and shape or else the king was not going to like it. One could die. These were literally matters of life and death, but not in the way Bloom defines them.

The Rock Business

The family spiritual void has left the field open to rock music. . . . The result is nothing less than parents' loss of control over their children's moral education at a time when no one else is seriously concerned with it. This has been achieved by an alliance between the strange young males who have the gift of divining the mob's emergent wishes—our versions of Thrasymachus, Socrates' rhetorical adversary—and the record-company executives, the new robber barons, who mine gold out of rock.   —A. Bloom

There is some truth to that, but how did we get to this point and what do we do about it?

We got here because teenagers are the most sought-after consumers. The whole idea of merchandising the prepubescent masturbational fantasy is not necessarily the work of the songwriter or the singer, but the work of the merchandiser who has elevated rock n' roll to the commercial enterprise it is.

In the beginning, rock n' roll was young kids singing to other kids about their girlfriends. That's all there was. The guys who made those records came from Manual Arts High School. They went into a recording studio, were given some wine, $25, and a bunch of records when their song came out as a single—which made them heroes at school. That was their career, not, "Well, we're not going to sing until we get a $125 thousand advance."

Today, rock n' roll is about getting a contract with a major company, and pretty much doing what the company tells you to do. The company promotes the image of rock n' roll as being wild and fun when in fact it's just a dismal business.

Record companies have people who claim to be experts on what the public really wants to hear. And they inflict their taste on the people who actually make the music. To be a big success, you need a really big company behind you because really big companies can make really big distribution deals.

Even people who are waiting to go into the business know it's a business. They spend a great deal of time planning what they will look like and getting a good publicity photo before they walk in the door with their tape. And the record companies tend to take the attitude that it doesn't make too much difference what the tape sounds like as long as the artists look right, because they can always hire a producer who will fix up the sound and make it the way they want it—so long as the people wear the right clothes and have the right hair.

Retaining Classical Music

Classical music is dead among the young. . . . Rock music is as unquestioned and unproblematic as the air the students breathe, and very few have any acquaintance at all with classical music. . . . Classical music is now a special taste, like Greek language or pre-Columbian archeology, not a common culture of reciprocal communication and psychological shorthand.   —A. Bloom

On this point, Bloom and I can agree, but how can a child be blamed for consuming only that which is presented to him? Most kids have never been in contact with anything other than this highly merchandised stuff.

When I testified in front of the Senate, I pointed out that if they don't like the idea of young people buying certain kinds of music, why don't they stick a few dollars back into the school system to have music appreciation? There are kids today who have never heard a string quartet; they have never heard a symphony orchestra. I argued that the money for music appreciation courses, in terms of social good and other benefits such as improved behavior or uplifting the spirit, is far less than the cost of another set of uniforms for the football team. But I frankly don't see people waving banners in the streets saying more music appreciation in schools.

When I was in school, we could go into a room and they had records there. I could hear anything I wanted by going in there and putting on a record. I won't say I enjoyed everything that was played for me, but I was curious, and if I had never heard any of that music I wouldn't know about it.

Once we're out of school, the time we can spend doing that type of research is limited because most of us are out looking for a job flipping hamburgers in the great tradition of the Reagan economic miracle. When all is said and done, that's the real source of America's barren and arid lives.

Themes, Issues, and Ideas

1. In his first paragraph, Zappa says, "Performers who are doing the crude, vulgar, repulsive things Bloom doesn't enjoy are only commenting on that fact." In context, how does his argument for art as "commentary" work? What do you think about it? Do you think vulgar language is needed to discuss vulgarity, for example?

2. Zappa says that "the ugliness in this society is not a product of unrefined art, but of unrefined commerce, wild superstition, and religious fanaticism." Where and how in his essay does he support these counterexplanations?

3. Zappa uses the word "boring" several times. As a writer, does he ever seem bored in his essay? Locate some moments where you feel *some* mood, then characterize the mood created by his style and the ways that style creates the mood.

Writing Strategies and Techniques

1. What is the effect created by Zappa's attribution of quotations to "A. Bloom?" What other attributions would create different effects, for example, "Dr. Allan Bloom?"

2. Zappa seems to assume that some concepts are inherently ridiculous ("the nasty ol' Devil") and that some deserve more respect ("a new field of science called psychoacoustics"). Make a list of both kinds of concepts. What qualities seem to characterize each list?

Suggestions for Writing

1. Zappa arranges his remarks around a series of quotations from Bloom, which he then comments on. Write an essay in which you do the same for Zappa. Quote some of his remarks and attack, defend, or modify them.

2. Until the very end Zappa seems to move toward a greater degree of agreement with Bloom's assessments, though he continues to disagree with Bloom's causal explanations. How do you stand? Write an essay in which you position yourself with respect to either Frank Zappa or Allan Bloom on the article's common issues.

Into the Nineties and Beyond

The Coming Revolution in Film and TV

James Monaco

James Monaco is founder and president of Baseline, an information service for the entertainment industries, and the author of How to Read a Film (1977) and other books about the media. In an essay first published in American Film magazine, Monaco takes a quick look back before speculating that "film and TV in the nineties and beyond will have little if anything to do with the nineteenth-century technology that did serve us so well up until recently." The skycam, high density television, and laser technology are among the tools of the future, and Monaco hopes that these tools will lead to innovations as exciting as those that the older technology produced and is still producing. Looking at his children who, unlike himself, grew up with today's technologies, Monaco says, "I hope and believe there will be millions more like them in the nineties who will take their rightful place with the priests of sounds and images and experience the joy of creation as often as the dubious pleasure of consumption."

More than ten years ago, in November 1978, I finished writing a book called *American Film Now*. Using all the then-latest computer techniques, we brought it to publication in record time, joking that if we followed a normal leisurely book production schedule we'd have to change the title to *American Film a Little While Ago*.

That was then, this is now, and our impatience seems a little silly. Time ran faster then, now it shuffles and lurches. When a second

255

edition of the book was published in 1984, surprisingly little had to be revised.

That's a little sad for those of us who can remember what time was like in the sixties and before, when new things seemed to be happening every week on the film scene. It's not such a very great distance from *Animal House* (1978) to *Police Academy V* (1988). Or from *Kramer vs. Kramer* to *Fatal Attraction*. In 1978, the film magazines were full of articles about Coppola, Spielberg, and Lucas, and in 1988, they're still good copy, and no young director, to my knowledge, has risen up to challenge them, their ideas, or their way of filmmaking.

I keep remembering a line from Alain Tanner's *Le Milieu du Monde* (1974), which showed a certain prescience about the fifteen or twenty years to come: "We live in a time of normalization when change is permitted and nothing changes."

It's a poetic line that has stuck with me right through the seventies, when we kept waiting for things to happen, and the eighties, when we decided we had things to do other than wait. I don't dislike movies now, they're just "normalized": homogenized, industrialized, and with a lack of that sharp and heady generational, political tension that fired not just movies but most culture and politics until the day the music died, more than fifteen years ago.

In a curious way, the generation of the sixties succeeded all too well. Movies (and television) are overflowing now with the stuff lacking in films then. Issues? If he's paid attention to his movies-of-the-week, there isn't a kid over eight who doesn't know all about AIDS, the homeless, the bomb, the inexorable pollution of the environment, abortion, the destruction of the ozone, and sex of all sorts. Aesthetic innovation? After 30 minutes of MTV you'd probably want to declare a moratorium on yet a different angle, yet another cut. Politics? Well, come on now, you can't have everything.

A time of "normalization" is also a time of summation and synthesis. Don't blame the movies for the mesmerizing stasis of the last fifteen years. We're just at the top of the Hegelian roller coaster. And events move exceedingly slow. Try to extrapolate from the past fifteen years yet another future for *American Film Now,* and you're likely to turn in your video club card. The past is clearly the wrong place to look. We've spent quite enough time going back to the future.

While American filmmakers and TV people have been synthesizing and re-synthesizing the last fifty years of our film culture ever so slowly during the 1980s, new tools have been developing that provide at least the possibility for a bright and invigorating new future for the medium. The key here is that film and TV in the nineties and beyond will have little if anything to do with the nineteenth-century technology that did serve us so well up until recently.

Before we even begin to look at the tools we may be using in the nineties, let's remember that film has been, and still is, a very conservative and often introverted art. The technology is still rooted firmly in the nineteenth century, a mixture of mechanics and chemistry. The narrative structures were set in the 1940s for film (and 1950s for TV). The last significant technical innovation, widescreen, dates from the early fifties, thirty-five years ago. Forty years ago, the businessmen in charge of the front office turned their backs on TV, leaving an important new means of distribution in the twentieth century to the radio moguls; the radio people quickly fashioned TV in their own image.

Even the American "new wave" of fifteen or twenty years ago was then, and continues to be, imbued with a historic conservatism. Lucas and Spielberg are praised for recreating and playing homage to the genres of the past. Martin Scorsese rings changes on them and fights the quixotic battle against colorization. (How ironic that while Scorsese works hard to preserve the black-and-white films of the thirties and forties, the Eastman Color films of the seventies and eighties are deteriorating within months rather than years and may only be saved in something like the filmmakers' original vision if colorization and other electronic techniques are used to restore them.) Even Coppola, after the adventures of *The Godfather* and *Apocalypse Now,* has most recently contributed icons of the fifties and forties in *Peggy Sue Got Married* and *Tucker.*

So, let's face it—filmmakers don't like new stuff. And that's OK. We probably have enough great film accumulated over the last sixty or seventy years to keep us and our children busy for quite some time.

No, if innovation is to come, it's going to be on the TV or video front or, even more likely, from renegades entirely outside the Hollywood/New York orbit. In aesthetic terms, television has been notably more interesting than theatrical film for more than ten years now. I don't just mean MTV and the video revolution. Much more important, the writers and directors who congregated at MTM in the early eighties are responsible, with *Hill Street Blues, St. Elsewhere,* and *L.A. Law,* for the freshest narrative structures since Jean-Luc Godard rethought the medium in the sixties. Their peculiar blend of self-consciousness, wit, and intelligent pathos is a fine base to build on in the nineties as our entertainments become more direct, complex, and conversational.

Now, the tools.

For me, one of the more exciting technical innovations of recent years is Garrett Brown's Skycam, an exciting invention for its simplicity and practicality as well as its effect. Brown, who'd already left an impact on the industry with his Steadicam of the seventies, has almost singlehandedly (give Arriflex, the New Wave, and the Louma crane some credit) liberated the camera from the track-and-trucking rut in which it got stuck in the twenties.

The Skycam device hangs a camera from four cables suspended from posts at the four corners of the shooting area. The cables are raised, lowered and moved laterally by computer-driven winches controlled by the cameraman, who sits off-site watching the image on a monitor. The exhilaration you feel from watching a well-shot Skycam image is unique (outside of your own dreams, that is). Skycam brings a really new glamour to the image, and its potential has yet to be explored. After inventing the device and building the prototype, which was rushed to completion in an attempt to fulfill a contract with ABC for the 1984 Olympics, Brown moved on to other interests, licensing Skycam to a Philadelphia outfit named Skyworks Inc.

Neither Brown nor Skyworks were able to raise sufficient funds in the United States to go beyond the prototype. After renting Skycam I for several sporting events and films such as *Birdy, Slugger's Wife,* and *The Boy Who Could Fly,* Skyworks negotiated a licensing/production agreement with a Japanese company, Tamco Co. Ltd. The prototype was shipped to Japan in 1986. The production models, made in the United States, will be available in late 1989.

Another technology of the early eighties that won't have any real effect until the nineties is high-definition television (HDTV). First introduced in 1981 by CBS and NHK of Japan (using Sony, Matsushita and Ikegami equipment), HDTV has just now become a subject of interest at the Federal Communications Commission (FCC).

Although there are several competing standards, I've seen the Sony 1, 125-line HDTV image and I'm here to tell you that this is really something special. What Cinerama pretended to be, HDTV is. Although the resolution of the 1,125-line picture is more than twice the current American standard, the psychological effect is nothing less than breathtaking.

If you're severely nearsighted, take your glasses off. That's the American television standard today. Now put them on. That HDTV. If you're not nearsighted, perhaps you can gain a measure of the same effect by comparing the best color television image available today with the very earliest, shadowy, black-and-white studio shots in which one was lucky to make out the eyes, lips, and nose on a face. There were no grays, just black and white.

Even a short 15-minute demo travelogue tape seems to open up a new world on the screen. In a word: Detail now counts for more than atmosphere within the frame. You realize that the reason for the classic close-ups and two-shots during the last ninety years of film history is that that's all anyone could effectively show. There were landscapes, yes, but they were Turneresque impressions. Now you can see the trees as well as the forest. Indeed, you can see the leaves on the trees. The amount of visual information you apprehend raises the level of the experience by several magnitudes.

In the sixties, director Richard Lester played with little side jokes that decorated the fringes of a shot. With HDTV, those subsidiary interest focuses are there whether you want them to be or not. The whole idea of the image has to be rethought. Think about it for awhile: Until now, we could only sequence images. Now, the 1960s experiments with multiple images become practical. It's the difference between an intimate supperclub performance and grand opera.

Until I'd actually seen an HDTV image, I figured, well, it's as good as 35 mm. No, it's markedly better. It's even better than the best 70mm projections I've seen, in no small part because HDTV has a higher frame rate than film, creating less flicker and better motion portrayal. Perhaps Douglas Trumball's Showscan approaches the image quality of HDTV, but HDTV has a significant advantage: It's homey, close, and controllable. You don't have to sit in front of a giant screen somewhere in a techie temple.

Perhaps the bottom line is that HDTV now, for the first time, fully allows the small screen to compete with the large in terms of image quality. The balance of economic power long ago shifted from film to television. And now, for the nineties, the balance of artistic power shifts to moviemakers whose main area of expertise is tape rather than film.

From now on, we'll focus evermore intently on the electronic image. Old-fashioned filmmakers who use the mechanical/chemical process that was popular in the twentieth century will be revered as quaint throwbacks to another time. But TV is finally to be where the action is.

One of the main reasons HDTV hasn't moved more quickly during the last few years is that it didn't have to. The Skycam is a lovely example of a tool invented by a professional for professionals because there was a need. There's no "need" for HDTV.

But when laser technology was developed in the 1960s, no one could have foretold that its main market would be in record players. And when nameless engineers first attached a television screen to a commercial computer in the sixties, how could they have known that the technology they borrowed just to display rows of crude capital letters faster would come full circle within thirty years? But that's just what is about to happen.

HDTV may be a technology of the future, but you may be surprised to learn that hundreds of thousands of us already work all day long with this superior technology in high-resolution computer monitors.

As computers, film, video, music, and even print begin to merge, input devices will prove most exciting in their implications. Up until now, you've pretty much had to take what the sound-and-image-makers dish out. That's sometimes a very pleasant experience, but it's passive. As laser disc pioneer Bob Stein says, "Broadcast television is a really dangerous medium." With luck, the age of broadcast is behind us and the age of "narrowcast" and "intercast" and "selfcast" before us.

In fact, no matter what the FCC decides about standards, HDTV is likely to appear on our computer screens before it appears on NBC. Right now, with off-the-shelf technology, you can set up a Macintosh with its standard color monitor and a few auxiliary boards, which will allow you to watch a couple of movies in windows on the screen while reading text, listening to music on the MIDI interface and maybe faxing to a friend. This'll set you back about as much as a high-end projection TV and it's a hell of a lot more fun to look at. It's not HDTV yet, but it is computer TV.

When Apple cofounder Steven Jobs designed his monolithic black magnesium box for his new computer company, NeXT, he thought to license the complete works of Shakespeare from Oxford University Press. They come free on the 256-megabyte optical disk. Perhaps five years from now, when the next NeXT makes its appearance, Jobs will throw in the complete works of Hitchcock, too—or, better yet, Jean-Luc Godard, since this fusion that awaits us reminds me of nothing so much as the movies that last great filmmaker made before the revolution.

Yeah, I know all this techno-flaunting can be tiring at times. Yes, it all sounds like the 1939 World's Fair: "In the future, kiddo, we'll all be commuting on our Skycams and our clothes will be HDTV images!" But as the micro people say, "Give a kid a hammer and everything's a nail." And we've no guarantee at all that in the future grown-ups will wield these new hammers with wit, passion, and intelligence. For all I know the next generation of imagemakers will be much like the present: kids who love the tools, love the things they make with the tools, but don't know what to do with the things they make with the tools. Great at sex but don't know how to make love.

Yet, as Eric Rohmer once reminded us, it's always best to take Pascal's gamble: Bet on the existence of God (even if it's technology); you've got nothing to lose.

Our family just bought a new remote-control TV. (There was a room in the house that somehow didn't have one.) Watching my kids experiment with the remote control, scanning station after station, first I thought: How different the world is for them, how saturated they are with images and sounds. They've consumed more in their first eight or ten years of life than I had in my first twenty. I took their restless scanning to mean they were bored with the variety available and sated with the richness of the images.

Then they went into the other room and, as they so often do, turned on the Macintosh and began to write and type and paint and draw and, yes, play games.

Then I realized it wasn't boredom and satiety I'd witnessed; it was mastery and confidence. And they've been lucky enough to experience the keyboard and the mouse, the microphone and the camera—the input as well as the output. I hope and believe there will be millions more like them in the nineties who will take their rightful place with the priests of sounds and images and experience the joy of creation as often as the dubious pleasure of consumption.

Themes, Issues, and Ideas

1. Early in his essay, Monaco says, "In a curious way, the generation of the sixties succeeded all too well." What does he mean by this paradox, and what evidence does he bring to illustrate it?

2. Monaco believes that new technologies fuel new artistic revolutions. What is his reasoning, and what evidence does he bring to support the idea?

3. Much of the article is spent on the subject of HDTV. Why is this topic so important to Monaco, and what distinguishes its importance from that of the other technologies he describes?

Writing Strategies and Techniques

1. Monaco begins and ends his essay with a personal anecdote. Where else does he insert a personal note? How well do you think he moves between the roles of objective and personal reporting?

2. How would you characterize Monaco's relationship with his audience, created by his style? How, for example, do his many contractions work in this regard? Does he ever address his audience directly?

Suggestions for Writing

1. What do you think of Monaco's claim that, due to the age we live in, movies are in a state of "mesmerizing stasis?" Write an essay exploring your sense of the level of innovation in films you've seen lately.

2. Monaco claims that his children's actions display not boredom with technology, but confidence in its use. Write an essay describing your own experiences with some of the technologies (for example, computers and remote-control TV) Monaco mentions. Begin by describing your first memories of technologies you choose.

MAKING CONNECTIONS

1. Tom Wolfe sees the next century differently than do most other authors in this chapter. He says, "The twenty-first century, I predict, will confound the twentieth-century notion of the Future as something exciting, novel, unexpected, or radiant; as Progress, to use an old word." Write an essay comparing and contrasting Wolfe with the other authors on the issue of the future.

2. Michael Kinsley and Barbara Ehrenreich both make valid arguments about Ice-T's lyrics. Will their arguments about free speech and social responsibility still be as valid in the world that James Monaco describes?

3. Mark Crispin Miller makes the most radical critique of popular culture in this chapter. Do you find such a critique provocative? Compare Miller, as a social critic, with two of the other writers in this chapter.

4. Tom Wolfe, who begins this chapter, claims that ideas create cultural innovations. James Monaco, on the other hand, follows Marshall McLuhan in saying that technology informs culture, not the other way around. Write an essay considering both sides of the question, both in regard to these essays and to your own impressions. Make sure to back up your statements with evidence and argument.

5. After finishing the other essays in this chapter, do you think they confound or bear out Tom Wolfe's remarks about America in the twentieth century? What are some cultural phenomena that you think should have been included in this chapter, and how might they have supported or undermined Wolfe's argument?

CHAPTER SEVEN

Mortality and the Human Spirit

Struggles of Belief and Doubt

THE
PAST AS
PROLOGUE

A Defence of Skeletons

G. K. Chesterton

G. K. Chesterton (1874–1936) was one of the most prolific and original writers of the modern era. Although he began writing in an age that treasured progress and scientific enlightenment above all things, Chesterton took an opposite stance, standing up for old Europe, Christianity, and the medieval mind, and trying to persuade others to revere as he did "the teeming vitality of the dead." Although primarily a journalist, Chesterton wrote extensively in other genres, including literary criticism, biography, social policy, moral theology and apologetics, poetry, drama, detective stories (Father Brown was his most famous creation), novels, and children's books. He died in 1936, having seen his worst predictions for the modern world (world war, fascism, hopelessness, and worse) begin to come true, but having borne it all with his characteristic good humor.

In "A Defence of Skeletons," Chesterton turns his feverish attention to a typical image of death: the human skeleton. In this reading, he manages to encapsulate his own view of the universe into the space of a very few pages.

The importance of the human skeleton is very great, and the horror with which it is commonly regarded is somewhat mysterious. Without claiming for the human skeleton a wholly conventional beauty, we may assert that he is certainly not uglier than a bull-dog, whose popularity never wanes, and that he has a vastly more cheerful and ingratiating expression. But just as man is mysteriously ashamed of the skeletons of the trees in winter, so he is mysteriously ashamed of the skeleton of himself in death. It is a singular thing altogether, this horror of the architecture of things. One would think it would be most unwise in a man to be afraid of a skeleton, since Nature has set curious and quite insuperable obstacles to his running away from it.

One ground exists for this terror: a strange idea has infected humanity that the skeleton is typical of death. A man might as well say that a factory chimney was typical of bankruptcy. The factory may be left naked after ruin, the skeleton may be left naked after bodily dissolution; but both of them have had a lively and workmanlike life of their own, all the pulleys creaking, all the wheels turning, in the House of Livelihood as in the House of Life. There is no reason why this creature (new, as I fancy, to art), the living skeleton, should not become the essential symbol of life.

The truth is that man's horror of the skeleton is not horror of death at all. It is man's eccentric glory that he has not, generally speaking, any objection to being dead, but has a very serious objection to being undignified. And the fundamental matter which troubles him in the skeleton is the reminder that the ground-plan of his appearance is shamelessly grotesque. I do not know why he should object to this. He contentedly takes his place in a world that does not pretend to be genteel—a laughing, working, jeering world. He sees millions of animals carrying, with quite a dandified levity, the most monstrous shapes and appendages, the most preposterous horns, wings, and legs, when they are necessary to utility. He sees the good temper of the frog, the unaccountable happiness of the hippopotamus. He sees a whole universe which is ridiculous, from the animalcule, with a head too big for its body, up to the comet, with a tail too big for its head. But when it comes to the delightful oddity of his own inside, his sense of humour rather abruptly deserts him.

In the Middle Ages and in the Renaissance (which was, in certain times and respects, a much gloomier period) this idea of the skeleton had a vast influence in freezing the pride out of all earthly pomps and the fragrance out of all fleeting pleasures. But it was not, surely, the mere dread of death that did this, for these were ages in which men went to meet death singing; it was the idea of the degradation of man in the grinning ugliness of his structure that withered the juvenile insolence of beauty and pride. And in this it almost assuredly did more good than harm. There is nothing so cold or so pitiless as youth, and youth in aristocratic stations and ages tended to impeccable dignity, an endless summer of success which needed to be very sharply reminded of the scorn of the stars. It was well that such flamboyant prigs should be convinced that one practical joke, at least, would bowl them over, that they would fall into one grinning man-trap, and not rise again. That the whole structure of their existence was as wholesomely ridiculous as that of a pig or a parrot they could not be expected to realize; that birth was humorous, coming of age humorous, drinking and fighting humorous, they were far too young and solemn to know. But at least they were taught that death was humorous.

There is a peculiar idea abroad that the value and fascination of what we call Nature lie in her beauty. But the fact that Nature is beautiful in the sense that a dado or a Liberty curtain is beautiful, is only one of her charms, and almost an accidental one. The highest and most valuable quality in Nature is not her beauty, but her generous and defiant ugliness. A hundred instances might be taken. The croak-ing noise of the rooks is, in itself, as hideous as the whole hell of sounds in a London railway tunnel. Yet it uplifts us like a trumpet with its coarse kindliness and honesty, and the lover in 'Maud' could actually persuade himself that this abominable noise resembled his lady-love's name. Has the poet, for whom Nature means only roses and lilies, ever heard a pig grunting? It is a noise that does a man good—a strong, snorting, imprisoned noise, breaking its way out of unfathomable dungeons through every possible outlet and organ. It might be the voice of the earth itself, snoring in its mighty sleep. This is the deepest, the oldest, the most wholesome and religious sense of the value of Nature—the value which comes from her immense baby-ishness. She is as top-heavy, as grotesque, as solemn and as happy as a child. The mood does come when we see all her shapes like shapes that a baby scrawls upon a slate—simple, rudimentary, a million years older and stronger than the whole disease that is called Art. The objects of earth and heaven seem to combine into a nursery tale, and our relation to things seems for a moment so simple that a dancing lunatic would be needed to do justice to its lucidity and levity. The tree above my head is flapping like some gigantic bird standing on one leg; the moon is like the eye of a cyclops. And, however much my face clouds with sombre vanity, or vulgar vengeance, or con-temptible contempt, the bones of my skull beneath it are laughing for ever.

Themes, Issues, and Ideas

1. What does Chesterton suggest is the primary value of skeletons?

2. Why do such things as skeletons and the grunts of pigs represent, to Chesterton, "the deepest, the oldest, the most wholesome and religious sense of the value of Nature?"

3. What is Chesterton assuming when he writes of the universe as humorous, top-heavy, etc.? Is such poetic language reconcilable with serious issues?

Writing Strategies and Techniques

1. How would you describe the voice that this essay is written in? Is it one you would be inclined to admire or respect? Is it an attractive voice? A convincing one? Explain your answer.

2. G. K. Chesterton was famous for certain rhetorical techniques, such as the alliteration in the last sentence. Find another writing strategy Chesterton uses.

Suggestions for Writing

1. Pretend you are G. K. Chesterton and write an editorial on a current topic that might appear in tomorrow's paper.

2. Write a response, in Chesterton's voice, to Camille Paglia's essay (see Chapter 2).

Apocalypse Now?

Bill Lawren

The word millennium *means "thousand years," and we are about to complete not the first but the second thousand years since the birth of Christ. Visions of the planet earth's last days were once before focused on the completion of a millennium, as Bill Lawren reports in this essay. Lawren compares the expressions of hope and fear manifested a thousand years ago to those we're beginning to see today, which will surely continue to increase in intensity as this century draws to a close. Does "millenarianism" work merely as an "anxiety feedback loop," to be laid to rest by its own media overkill? This question is only one of many that you will no doubt read in other essays and articles as the year 2000 approaches.*

Lawren has worked as a free-lance essayist and magazine writer. He is the author of a book, The General and the Bomb, *that deals with the development of the most popular secular candidate for the production of the apocalypse.*

The end of the world is coming—again: 989 years ago, as the odometer of Western history approached its first millennium, the whole of Europe was seized by a paroxysm of preapocalyptic shivers. People rushed to embrace an endless succession of self-proclaimed prophets, even fought pitched battles over the saintly relics that were seen as paid admissions to the Second Coming. So great was the millenarian fervor, according to legend, that on the stroke of midnight on Jan. 1, 1000, the population of an entire country—Iceland—converted en masse to Christianity, apparently as a spiritual prophylactic against the coming apocalypse.

Now it's our turn. Just as Europe went collectively berserk in preparation for the first millennium, there are signs of what one observer calls "an avalanche of nuttiness" in anticipation of the second. *The* best-selling book since the 1970s (over 25 million copies to date), *The Late, Great Planet Earth,* by Hal Lindsey, prophesies a full-blown last-days scenario from the Book of Revelation, replete with nuclear wars, China attacking Israel, and the Second Coming.

Other end-of-the-world scenarios abound: The Rev. Jerry Falwell sees Western society unraveling under the onslaught of the devil's trinity—communists, feminists, and homosexuals. The Rev. Tim LaHaye, a Falwell disciple whom one writer calls the populist philosopher of the right-wing evangelical movement, imagines a chaotic Second Coming featuring a worldwide epidemic of plane, bus, and train wrecks. "Who can imagine," he told reporter Frances Fitzgerald, "the chaos on the freeways when automobile drivers are snatched out of their cars?" And psychic Ruth Montgomery foresees a cosmic ecodisaster in which the North and South poles suddenly change places, turning the surface of the planet inside out and in general wreaking havoc on real estate values.

Apocalyptic visions are, of course, the stock in trade of right-wing preachers and popular psychics, but during the Reagan era, fundamentalist imaginings of disaster did begin to seep into the culture at large. Ronald Reagan himself, in one of his nationally televised debates with Walter Mondale, spoke of having "philosophical discussions" with people who believed that "the biblical prophecies of Armageddon" were "coming together" in our time. Reagan was responding to a question about nuclear weapons and, according to Spencer Weart, author of *Nuclear Fear: A History of Images,* he was at the time only one of "5 to 10 million Americans . . . who believed that there was a good chance that the Armageddon of the Bible was imminent in nuclear form."

Millennial Madness

Add to that the numbers of people who are suffering anxiety attacks over AIDS, global warming, ozone depletion, and the proliferation of chemical weapons, and you have a disturbingly large population susceptible to millennial madness.

Even supposedly sober observers are taking positions in the millenarian parade. Novelist, poet, and science writer Brad Leithauser, whose new novel *Hence* is set around the year 2000, is convinced the second millennium is going to bring a "psychological shift" that will "literally redefine what it means to be a human being."

Leithauser takes the more pessimistic meteorologists at their word and thinks that global weather patterns will undergo random, even chaotic, changes produced by the dreaded greenhouse effect. In his novel, Leithauser envisions religious leaders seizing on the resultant perturbations—flooded cities, soaring cancer rates, and what have you—and taking them "as a sign that the end is nigh." Leading right-wing televangelists will preach blood purges and practice sacrificial rites on prime-time TV.

At the same time, Leithauser thinks, a combination of high-speed living and runaway technology will serve further to alienate people from themselves. "Machines that can do anything will become cheap and move into your house," Leithauser predicts, and invasive media will bring an inescapable barrage of stimuli. In this atmosphere of "ever-shortening collective memory," books will become passé. Indeed, any form of reflective solitude will become "quietly sinful," says a character in Leithauser's novel, and seeking it out will require "almost an act of social defiance."

Economic pundit Ravi Batra, who predicted a worldwide financial collapse in his book *The Great Depression of 1990,* is equally convinced that by the dawn of the second millennium people will have undergone a thorough spiritual and economic transformation. "Unbridled prosperity and unchecked expression of greed cannot go on forever," he warns. Soon, the fiduciary voices of the rich will superheat the global economy to the point of explosion and collapse, in the wake of which "society will border on chaos. There will be a polarization of society into two classes—the haves and the have-nots—and there will be a lot of crime and street demonstrations" as the angry have-nots clamor for food, shelter, and social justice.

But Batra, unlike Leithauser, sees the coming bimillennial breakdown as cathartic, a sort of purge by fire on the way to a better world. From the ashes of economic and social collapse, he says, will rise a "higher consciousness"—a climate in which pornography, selfishness, and extreme concentration of wealth are reviled and society becomes "more concerned with the handicapped and the underdog." On the job, he foresees "far more democratic large factories, where employees not only sit on boards of directors but actually run companies." Meanwhile, discipline will capture the home-and-family front, with "children obeying their parents more, and more family stability, fewer divorces."

A Utopian Society

Although Batra does not consider himself a New Age prophet, his quasi-utopian scenario and notions of "higher consciousness" sound remarkably like the prognostications of the New Agers. Ken Carey, author of *Starseed Transmissions* and a number of other New Age handbooks, envisions the year 2000 A.D. as a sort of psychic watershed. Beyond it, he believes, lies "a realizable utopian society, a society characterized by compassion and by the understanding that we're all in this together." The coming of the second millennium, Carey thinks, will bring "a real sense of a new beginning." He foresees a postmillennial world in which people and nations "open their hearts in love, and solve their problems creatively, through communication and dialogue rather than conflict."

All in all, Carey thinks the turning of the calendar is challenging humanity "to look at some alternate ways of being. We realize that we need to come up with something new, and that's created a tremendous openness both in leadership around the world and in individual lives. It has created a condition on earth for which we have no historical precedent."

Others see precedent staring them squarely in the face. To Carl Raschke, director of the Institute for the Humanities at the University of Denver, the upsurge in millenarian thinking represents "a replaying of the apocalyptic fervor of the 1960s," not the year 1000. "The old millenarianism," he says, "could be understood only in the framework of traditional Christian belief. The new millenarian consciousness is basically political and secular. The longing for a world beyond has pretty much subsided—we're not necessarily expecting the end of the world in a literal sense, but a total transformation of this world."

The dissolution of the Christian context does put something of a crimp in the importance of the second millennium—especially for those who never set their calendars that way in the first place. Says Oren Lyons, a Native American leader who is faithkeeper of the Turtle clan of the Onondaga Nation and a professor of American studies at the University of Buffalo: "We appreciate that the turning of the year 2000 represents some sort of continuum from the perspective of our white brothers, but to us it's just another day."

And there are others equally unimpressed by the millenarian fervor. Michael Murphy, cofounder of the Esalen Institute in San Francisco and Big Sur, for one. "Out here in California," Murphy says, "people seem to have a real hunger for apocalypse, and they find something to attach it to—the Kohoutek comet, the Big Earthquake— every couple of years. So the year 2000 is just one of a number of events that can get people thinking about the end of the world."

Deep Into the Universe

For Murphy, the larger impact on millenarian consciousness will come with the operation of giant space telescopes and sophisticated supercolliders. Those tools, which will enable us to peer farther out and farther into our universe than ever before, "are going to provide some surprises. By themselves," Murphy says, "they're going to extend our outsight and our insight so radically that it will profoundly affect our thinking. So there's a lot in the works," he concludes, "that's going to make the decades ahead very exciting, but it's not just the year 2000 that's going to do it."

While Lyons and Murphy find talk of millenarian consciousness unimportant or at least benign, a few observers see in it the potential for something more ominous. Raschke sees the possibility of a surge in world terrorism, a modern version of the Viking raids of the first millennium. He also sees a potential danger in "the New Age talk about purification—the idea that people who aren't in tune with the cosmos and so get in the way of the coming New Age will have to be purified." To him, "This sounds a bit like the anti-Semitic pogroms of the Middle Ages."

James Oberg, a Houston-based science writer and founding member of the Committee for the Scientific Investigation into Claims of the Paranormal, is even more concerned. He worries principally about those purveyors of millenarian notions who "get a sense of intellectual and emotional power in being a member of a small group that knows the future."

Among this group, he believes, the approach of the year 2000 will bring "a synergistic climb toward panic" that will produce social effects that are both "substantial" and "potentially dangerous." "At some point," Oberg says, "we'll begin to see that these are not just innocent diversions. These people will make bad and harmful decisions about their future lives—going off to join survivalist shelters, stopping the educational process, refusing medical care—because of these apocalyptic beliefs."

End-of-the-world prophecies tend to generate an "anxiety feedback loop" in the public at large, Oberg thinks, and he would like to see television and radio cut that loop by treating such prophecies skeptically and rationally—not just as "a funny story to end the six o'clock news." Oberg is now amassing files of apocalyptic predictions so this committee can publicize their failure when the second millennium turns and we all find the world still intact.

What is it about the human psyche or the perennial human condition that creates, as one observer has put it, an "appetite for apocalypse?"

British historian Norman Cohn, author of *The Pursuit of the Millennium,* believes that appetite often comes from fear. In Cohn's view, the poor man's traditional hope for a better tomorrow gives way in times of crisis—to be replaced by another impulse entirely. When historical conditions create "mass disorientation and anxiety," he writes, "traditional beliefs about a future golden age . . . serve as vehicles for social aspirations and animosities. . . . The usual desire of the poor to improve the material conditions of their lives becomes transfused with fantasies of a world reborn into innocence through a final, apocalyptic massacre."

Or perhaps Frank Kermode has it right when he says, in his book *The Sense of an Ending,* that all human beings are born and die "in the middest," in the middle of history. So we must make up stories, "fictive concords," that "give meanings to lives" and "humanize the common death" in the infinite perspective of time past and time to come.

In any case, the coming of the second millennium almost certainly will inspire an ever-growing variety of gloom-or-glory prophecies.

Of course, it could well be that, given the power of the media not only to spread the news but to anticipate it, by the time 2000 actually rolls around we will, in Brad Leithauser's words, "all be bored to tears." In that case, it'll be time to start cooking up apocalyptic scenarios for the next Big One.

Themes, Issues, and Ideas

1. Early in the essay, Lawren calls a belief in the end of the world "millennial madness." Yet he points to many current fears that have scientific credentials—nuclear disaster, ozone depletion, and global warming, among others. On what bases does he distinguish real threats from imaginary ones throughout the essay? Give some examples.

2. Lawren quotes James Oberg as saying that some believers in a coming apocalypse "get a sense of intellectual and emotional power in being a member of a small group that knows the future." Given that the future is supposed to be a *disaster,* how does this psychology work? Can you understand and explain it? What thoughts and emotions would be engendered in you, were you to know the inevitable date of your own death?

3. Lawren quotes novelist Brad Leithauser as saying that, due to media hype, by the time the year 2000 actually arrives we will "all be bored to tears." Do you think so? What thought have you already given to the millennium? Do you expect to spend more time thinking about it as it approaches?

Writing Strategies and Techniques

1. Lawren seems to maintain a cheerful view of a gloomy subject. What writing techniques does he use to maintain his attitude in his presentation?

2. Lawren uses both a scientific and a religious vocabulary. Examine three or four paragraphs that follow each other, and describe the ways in which Lawren moves between the two vocabularies and how this movement serves to affect the reader.

Suggestions for Writing

1. This essay first appeared in the magazine *Psychology Today,* a publication that approaches psychology as a science. Do you find any evidence of style, content, or general approach that would have led you to suspect the initial audience of this essay? Write an analysis of the author's relation to his audience as expressed in his style.

2. Lawren describes the views of both believers and skeptics on the evidence for the apocalypse. Write an essay analyzing and exemplifying the different ways in which each side approaches the concept of "evidence." Be sure to bring evidence of your own to support your analysis.

Facing Up to Global Repentance

Rosemary Ruether

Most opinions about the future of our world have centered around questions of food, energy, politics, and other practical matters. But as Rosemary Ruether points out, without a transcendent faith, we cannot hope to make changes important enough to save our world. In Chapter 10, Al Gore, in his essay, "Ecology: the New Sacred Agenda" will put it into more secular terms; here, in an essay taken from Christianity and Crisis, *Ruether looks on a troubled future from a distinctly Christian perspective.*

*Ruether is the author of over two dozen books, includ-*ing A Democratic Catholic Church *(1992) and* New Woman, New Earth: Sexist Ideologies and Human Libera tion *(1975).*

The World Watch Institute reports that humanity has 40 years in which to make major changes if we are not to face extreme global disasters in the second quarter of the 21st century (*State of the World*, 1990). That statement is not extremist, but truthful, and the details add up to a daunting picture of the future. I am convinced that it will take a powerful faith—faith in God rather than only in ourselves and our own powers—to face this future, and to struggle for a more just and peaceful world.

Here is a sketch of the truths we must acknowledge.

- **We are facing the end of the petroleum age.** At present rates of consumption, without allowing for any expansion of use, accessible sources of petroleum will run out about 2030. If instead of moving toward conservation and alternative energy, the U.S. continues to make petroleum the centerpiece of our energy supply, the Gulf War will have been only the beginning of expensive high-tech wars fought to control oil, wars that will have a heavy cost for the whole world, and finally for ourselves.

277

- *The earth's ability do produce food is declining.* The doubling of the world's grain harvest as a result of petroleum-based fertilizers, pesticides, and mechanization during the Green Revolution hit its limits in the 1980s, and its adverse effects began to take their toll. In many areas food-producing capacity is declining due to drought and desertification, acid rain, and soil salination.

  Meanwhile, some 24 billion tons of topsoil are being lost each year from the world's croplands, and the U.S. continues to push agricultural methods that exaggerate these trends. The emphasis on the Western meat diet also means that a large percentage of the world's grain harvest is used to feed animals, rather than human beings.

- *The 1980s saw a shift from greater equalization of resources between rich and poor people to greater gaps.* Around the world, 90 to 99 percent of the wealth is concentrated in the hands of the top 10 percent of the population, particularly the top 1 percent, while a larger percentage of the population falls into dire poverty. The middle classes struggle to keep even.

  At the same time, the lion's share of each country's wealth, particularly in the last decade, has been used on armaments. In 1972, $197 billion was spent on armaments worldwide. In 1987 this figure had expanded five-fold to over $1000 billion (one trillion), some 5.5 percent of the aggregate global economic product.

- *The world's population is rapidly exploding.* In 1930 world population was two billion people. By 1975 it had doubled to four billion. By the year 2000 it may well reach six billion. Yet during the 1980s, the U.S., under pressure from conservative religious and social groups, cut funding for research and promotion of family planning worldwide. The issue here is a stark choice between voluntary population control, preferably before conception, and millions of infants and children dying in the first years of life. At present some 15 million children under the age of one die each year due to famine and disease.

Imagine Life Anew

Can we face this almost apocalyptic scenario, or will we run away from it, seeking either to deny its possibility or else (if we can) wall ourselves into dwindling enclaves of privilege, while the rest of the world goes under?

The people of my generation, those born in the 1930s, stand responsible before the generation born in the 1970s, who must carry the burden of the world we have made. Whether we see ourselves as culpable or simply as actors in a drama we did not foresee or control, reality remains the same. We need ways of expressing our sorrow and working through our grief. We also need to be able to find the grace to stand up together and begin to imagine healing and new possibilities.

This is very much a matter of faith, of spirituality and soul-healing. New technologies and organizational strategies are crucial, but without a new vision, our technologies and organizations will only recycle toxicity, rather than generate renewed life.

Let us begin to imagine life—not as hoarding power by rendering our competitors powerless, not as feasting by starving children, not as going faster and faster in a system that is eating up its own foundations. No, let us cleave to a vision of life that is reciprocal and compassionate in the fullest sense: feeling the joys and wounds of others as one's own.

What does this mean? It means pulling our bomber pilots out of the sky and forcing them and us to stand before the people of Baghdad as they pick up the pieces of their lives. It means feeling the bombs that ripped through their flesh as tearing into our spirit as well. Loving your neighbor as yourself means acknowledging that we are all children of one earth, created by the same God, sustained by the same sun and earth under the same sky. Finally we cannot live through making others die. We cannot prosper by impoverishing others. This may appear to work for awhile, but in the end it is an illusion.

We need a profound global *metanoia*, a repentance that makes our interconnectedness a felt knowledge of our hearts and minds. I suspect that this must start by reaching out across those divides that we have raised the highest. Only a year ago that meant Americans and Russians reaching across the divide created by the Cold War.

Today, it also means reaching out to the Arab and Islamic worlds, which have been retooled as the new Satans. And to the poor of every land, the real casualties of every war. And finally, in our race to annihilate enemies, we meet ourselves coming around the corner, weapons in hand, and we recognize in our own face both aggressor and victim.

Earth-healing

How do we begin to withdraw our projections of light and darkness, God and Satan, and recognize the mixture of both in each of us? How do we begin to think the earth-healing "we," of Americans and Russians, Anglos and Arabs, Israelis and Palestinians, white and black, East and West, North and South? How can we begin to understand a God who did not choose us against them, but created one universe in which all our manynesses converge and interconnect in one covenant of grace and hope?

With the world of life we can begin to reshape our ways of driving engines to produce, transport, cook, and heat, by drawing on renewable sources of energy. We can begin to relearn the ancient wisdoms of renewing the earth, even as we draw from it our daily bread. We can begin to imagine communities of livable proportions, and more just interdependencies.

The technological and organizational tools for such transformations can stimulate and delight the best creative abilities of this generation and the generations to come. Challenges aplenty exist for the next 40 years. What is wanting is not the skills, but the heart; a heart rooted in compassion, justice, and mercy, rather than envy and enmity. In the words of the ancient biblical author, "I set before you two ways, life and death. Choose life."

Themes, Issues, and Ideas

1. What does Ruether say is most important to saving the world?

2. According to Ruether, our plans for the future too often involve either stark denial or a crafty plan that walls us in. Based on today's newspaper, do you believe this is true?

3. A question Ruether might be asked is "Why bring God into it?" How do you think she might answer? How has she anticipated this question?

Writing Strategies and Techniques

1. Ruether's essay falls into two parts, a factual one and a homiletic one. Why do you think this is so? Why are the two parts in their particular order?

2. Who does Ruether mean by "our?" What is the effect on her essay of such broad terms as "our," "spirit," "global," and "faith?" As a reader, how do you respond to such terms?

Suggestions for Writing

1. Write an essay criticizing such a plan for the future as the one Ruether proposes.

2. Write a critique of the moral approach to practical matters.

Our Lost Heritage: New Facts on How God Became a Man

Riane Eisler

Throughout the twentieth century, modern feminist scholarship has continued to question basic tenets of our civilization. As the twenty-first century approaches, one of the most fundamental of all beliefs has come under the spotlight: the identity of the creator of the universe. Although all serious Christian, Jewish, and Islamic doctrines consider God to transcend human limitations such as gender, representations of God have traditionally been male. In "Our Lost Heritage: New Facts on How God Became a Man," Riane Eisler looks at the history of this idea, and the extent to which it has affected society.

Riane Eisler (b. 1931) is a leading feminist writer and codirector of the Center for Partnership Studies. She is also the author of such books as Dissolutions: No Fault Divorce, Marriage, and the Future of Women, *and* The Chalice and the Blade: Our History, Our Future.

In the nineteenth century, archeological excavations began to confirm what scholars of myth had long maintained—that goddess worship preceded the worship of God. After reluctantly accepting what no longer could be ignored, religious historians proposed a number of explanations for why there had been this strange switch in divine gender. A long-standing favorite has been the so-called Big Discovery theory. This is the idea that, when men finally became aware that women did not bring forth children by themselves—in other words, when they discovered that it involved their sperm, their paternity—this inflamed them with such a new-found sense of importance that they not only enslaved women but also toppled the goddess.

Today, new archeological findings—particularly post–World War II excavations—are providing far more believable answers to this long-debated puzzle. For largely due to more scientific archeological methods, including infinitely more accurate archeological dating methods such as radiocarbon and dendrochronology,[1] there has been a veritable archeological revolution.

As James Mellaart of the London University Institute of Archeology writes, we now know that there were in fact many cradles of civilization, all of them thousands of years older than Sumer, where civilization was long said to have begun about five thousand years ago.[2] But the most fascinating discovery about these original cultural sites is that they were structured along very different lines from what we have been taught is the divinely, or naturally, ordained human order.

One of these ancient cradles of civilization is Catal Huyuk, the largest Neolithic site yet found. Located in the Anatolian plain of what is now Turkey, Catal Huyuk goes back approximately eight thousand years to about 6500 B.C.E.—three thousand years before Sumer. As Mellaart reports, this ancient civilization "is remarkable for its wall-paintings and plaster reliefs, its sculpture in stone and clay . . . , its advanced technology in the crafts of weaving, woodwork, metallurgy . . . , its advanced religion . . . , its advanced practices in agriculture and stockbreeding, and . . . a flourishing trade. . . ."[3]

But undoubtedly the most remarkable thing about Catal Huyuk and other original sites for civilization is that they were *not* warlike, hierarchic, and male-dominated societies like ours. As Mellaart writes, over the many centuries of its existence, there were in Catal Huyuk no signs of violence or deliberate destruction, "no evidence for any sack or massacre." Moreover, while there was evidence of some social inequality, "this is never a glaring one." And most significantly—in the sharpest possible contrast to our type of social organization—"the position of women was obviously an important one . . . with a fertility cult in which a goddess was the principal deity."[4]

Now it is hardly possible to believe that in this kind of society, where, besides all their other advances, people clearly understood the principles of stockbreeding, they would not have also had to under-

---

[1]Radiocarbon dating is a method of establishing the age of prehistoric artifacts by measuring the radioactivity of carbon; dendrochronology is a dating procedure based on counting the growth rings of trees.

[2]J. Mellaart, *The Neolithic of the Near East* (New York: Charles Scribner's Sons, 1975). [Au.]

[3]J. Mellaart, *Catal Huyuk* (New York: McGraw-Hill, 1967), p. 11. [Au.]

[4]Ibid., pp. 69, 225, 553. [Au.]

stand that procreation involves the male. So the Big Discovery theory is not only founded on the fallacious assumption that men are naturally brutes, who were only deterred from forcefully enslaving women by fear of the female's "magical" powers of procreation; the Big Discovery theory is also founded on assumptions about what happened in prehistory that are no longer tenable in light of the *really* big discoveries we are now making about our lost human heritage—about societies that, while not ideal, were clearly more harmonious than ours.

But if the replacement of a Divine Mother with a Divine Father was not due to men's discovery of paternity, how did it come to pass that all our present world religions either have no female deity or generally present them as "consorts" or subservient wives of male gods?

To try to answer that question, let us look more carefully at the new archeological findings.

Logic would lead one to expect what ancient myths have long indicated and archeology has since confirmed: that since life issues from woman, not man, the first anthropomorphic deity was female rather than male. But logical or not, this position was hardly that of the first excavators of Paleolithic caves, some of whom were monks, such as the well-known Abbé Henri Breuil. They consistently refused to see in the many finds of twenty-five-thousand-year-old stylized female sculptures what they clearly were: representations of a female divinity, a Great Mother. Instead, the large-breasted, wide-hipped, bountiful, and often obviously pregnant women these men christened "Venus figurines" were described either as sex objects (products of men's erotic fantasies) or deformed, ugly women.[5] Moreover, in order to conform to their model of history as the story of "man the hunter" and "man the warrior," they refused to see what was actually in the famous cave paintings. As Alexander Marshack has now established, not only did they insist that stylized painting of tree branches and plants were weapons, they sometimes described these pictures as backward arrows or harpoons, chronically missing their mark![6] They also, as Andre Leroi-Gourhan noted in his major study of the Paleolithic, insisted on interpreting the already quite advanced art of the period as an expression of hunting magic, a view borrowed from

[5]See, for example, E. O. James, *The Cult of the Mother Goddess* (London: Thames and Hudson, 1959), and M. Gimbutas, "The Image of Woman in Prehistoric Art," *Quarterly Review of Archeology,* December 1981. [Au.]

[6]A. Marshack, *The Roots of Civilization* (New York: McGraw-Hill, 1972). [Au.]

extremely primitive contemporary societies like the Australian aborigines.[7]

Although Leroi-Gourhan's interpretation of the objects and paintings found in Paleolithic caves is in sexually stereotyped terms, he stresses that the art of the Paleolithic was first and foremost religious art, concerned with the mysteries of life, death, and regeneration.[8] And it is again this concern that is expressed in the rich art of the Neolithic, which, as Mellaart points out, not only shows a remarkable continuity with the Paleolithic,[9] but clearly foreshadows the great goddess of later Bronze Age civilizations in her various forms of Isis, Nut, and Maat in Egypt, Ishtar, Lillith, or Astarte in the Middle East, the sun-goddess Arinna of Anatolia, as well as such later goddesses as Demeter, Artemis, and Kore in Greece, Atargatis, Ceres, and Cybele in Rome, and even Sophia or Wisdom of the Christian Middle Ages, the Shekinah of Hebrew Kabalistic tradition, and, of course, the Virgin Mary or Holy Mother of the Catholic Church about whom we read in the Bible.[10]

This same prehistoric and historic continuity is stressed by UCLA archeologist Marija Gimbutas, whose monumental work, *The Goddesses and Gods of Old Europe,* brings to life yet another Neolithic civilization: the indigenous civilization that sprang up in the Balkans and Greece long, long before the rise of Indo-European Greece.[11] Once again, the archeological findings in what Gimbutas termed the civilizations of Old Europe not only demolish the old "truism" of the "warlike Neolithic" but also illuminate our true past, again showing that here, too, the original direction of human civilization was in some ways far more civilized than ours, with pre-Indo-Europeans living in far greater harmony with one another and the natural environment.

Moreover, excavations in Old Europe, like those unearthed in other parts of the ancient world, show that what brought about the onset of male dominance both in heaven and on earth was not some sudden male discovery. What ushered it in was the onslaught of barbarian hordes from the arid steppes and deserts on the fringe areas of

[7]A. Leroi-Gourhan, *Prehistoire de l'Art Occidental* (Paris: Edition D'Art Lucien Mazenod, 1971). [Au.]

[8]Ibid. [Au.]

[9]J. Mellaart, *Catal Huyuk,* p. 11. [Au.]

[10]See, for example, R. Eisler, *The Chalice and the Blade: Our History, Our Future* (New York: Harper and Row, 1987); M. Stone, *When God Was a Woman* (New York: Harvest, 1976); E. Neumann, *The Great Mother* (Princeton, NJ: Princeton University Press, 1955). [Au.]

[11]M. Gimbutas, *The Goddesses and Gods of Old Europe* (Berkeley, CA: University of California Press, 1982). [Au.]

our globe. It was wave after wave of these pastoral invaders who destroyed the civilizations of the first settled agrarian societies. And it was they who brought with them the gods—and men—of war that made so much of later or recorded history the bloodbath we are now taught was the *totality* of human history.

In Old Europe, as Gimbutas painstakingly documents, there were three major invasionary waves, as the Indo-European peoples she calls the Kurgans wiped out or "Kurganized" the European populations. "The Old European and Kurgan cultures were the antithesis of one another," writes Gimbutas. She continues:

> The Old Europeans were sedentary horticulturalists prone to live in large well-planned townships. The absence of fortifications and weapons attests the peaceful coexistence of this egalitarian civilization that was probably matrilinear and matrilocal. . . . The Old European belief system focused on the agricultural cycle of birth, death, and regeneration, embodied in the feminine principle, a Mother Creatrix. The Kurgan ideology, as known from comparative Indo-European mythology, exalted virile, heroic warrior gods of the shining and thunderous sky. Weapons are nonexistent in Old European imagery; whereas the dagger and battle-axe are dominant symbols of the Kurgans, who, like all historically known Indo-Europeans, glorified the lethal power of the sharp blade.[12]

So while we are still commonly taught that it was to Indo-European invaders—such as the Aechaean warriors, celebrated by Homer, who eventually sacked Troy—that we owe our Western heritage, we now know that they in fact did not bring us civilization. Rather, they destroyed, degraded, and brutalized a civilization already highly advanced along wholly different lines. And, just as the factuality of how these truly savage peoples demoted both women and goddesses to the subservient status of consort or wife has now been established, the fact [that] they brought in warfare with them is also confirmed.

Once again, as when Heinrich Schliemann defied the archeological establishment and proved that the city of Troy was not Homeric fantasy but prehistoric fact, new archeological findings verify ancient legends and myths. For instance, the Greek poet Hesiod, who wrote about the same time as Homer, tells us of a "golden race," who lived in "peaceful ease" in a time when "the fruitful earth poured forth her

[12]M. Gimbutas, "The First Wave of Eurasian Steppe Pastoralists in Copper Age Europe," *Journal of Indo-European Studies*, 1977, p. 281. [Au.]

fruits." And he laments how they were eventually replaced by "a race of bronze" who "ate not grain" (in other words, were not farmers) and instead specialized in warfare ("the all-lamented sinful works of Ares were their chief care").[13]

Perhaps one of the most fascinating legends of ancient times is, of course, that of the lost civilization of Atlantis. And here again, as with the once only legendary city of Troy, archeological findings illuminate our true past. For what new findings suggest is what the eminent Greek scholar Spyridon Martinatos already suspected in 1939: that the legend of a great civilization which sank into the Atlantic is actually the garbled folk memory of the Minoan civilization of Crete and surrounding Mediterranean islands, portions of which did indeed disappear into the sea after unprecedented volcanic eruptions sometime after 1500 B.C.E.[14]

First discovered at the turn of this century, the once unknown Bronze Age civilization of ancient Crete has now been far more extensively excavated. As Nicolas Platon, former superintendent of antiquities in Crete and director of the Acropolis Museum, who excavated the island for over thirty years, writes, Minoan civilization was "an astonishing achievement." It reflected "a highly sophisticated art and way of life," indeed producing some of the most beautiful art the world has ever seen. Also in this remarkable society—the only place where the worship of the goddess and the influence of women in the public sphere survived into historic times, where "the whole of life was pervaded by an ardent faith in the goddess Nature, the source of all creation and harmony"—there was still "a love of peace, a horror of tyranny, and a respect for the law."[15]

And once again, it was not men's discovery of their biological role in paternity that led to the toppling of the goddess. It was another, final Indo-European invasion: the onslaught of the Dorians, who, with their weapons of iron, as Hesiod writes, brought death and destruction in their wake.[16]

So the revolution in norms that literally stood reality on its head—that established this seemingly fundamental and sacrosanct idea that we are the creations of a Divine Father, who all by Himself brought forth all forms of life—was in fact a relatively late event in

---

[13]Hesiod, quoted in J. M. Robinson, *An Introduction to Early Greek Philosophy* (Boston: Houghton Mifflin, 1968), pp. 12–14. [Au.]

[14]S. Martinatos, "The Volcanic Destruction of Minoan Crete," *Antiquity,* 1939, 13:425–439. [Au.]

[15]N. Platon, *Crete* (Geneva: Nagel, 1966), pp. 48, 148. [Au.]

[16]Hesiod, see note 13. [Au.]

the history of human culture. Moreover, this drastic change in direction of cultural evolution, which set us on the social course that in our nuclear age threatens to destroy all life, was certainly not predetermined or, by any stretch of the imagination, inevitable. Rather than being some mystical mystery, it was the substitution of a force-based model of social organization for one in which both the female and male halves of humanity viewed the supreme power in the universe not as the "masculine" power to destroy but rather as the "feminine" power to give and nurture life.

Another popular old idea about this change was that it was the replacement of matriarchy with patriarchy. But my research of many years shows that matriarchy is simply the flip side of the coin to the *dominator* model of society, based upon the dominance of men over women that we call patriarchy. The real alternative to patriarchy, already foreshadowed by the original direction of human civilization, is what I have called the *partnership* model of social relations.[17] Based upon the full and equal partnership between the female and male halves of our species, this model was already well established a long time ago, before, as the Bible has it, a male god decreed that woman be subservient to man.

The new knowledge about our true human heritage is still meeting enormous resistance, with traditional "experts" from both the religious and academic establishments crying heresy. But it is a knowledge that, in the long run, cannot be suppressed.

It is a knowledge that demolishes many old misconceptions about our past. It also raises many fascinating new questions. Is the real meaning of the legend of our fall from paradise that, rather than having transgressed in some horrible way, Eve should have obeyed the advice of the serpent (long associated with the oracular or prophetic powers of the goddess) and *continued* to eat from the tree of knowledge? Did the custom of sacrificing the first-born child develop after the destruction of this earlier world—as the Bible has it, after our expulsion from the Garden of Eden—when women had been turned into mere male-controlled technologies of reproduction, as insurance of a sort that conception had not occurred before the bride was handed over to her husband?

[17]See, for example, R. Eisler, *The Chalice and the Blade;* R. Eisler "Violence and Male-Dominance: The Ticking Time Bomb," *Humanities in Society,* Winter–Spring 1984, 7:1/2:3–18; R. Eisler and D. Loye, "The 'Failure' of Liberalism: A Reassessment of Ideology from a New Feminine-Masculine Perspective," *Political Psychology,* 1983, 4:2:375–391; R. Eisler, "Beyond Feminism: The Gylan Future," *Alternative Futures,* Spring–Summer 1981, 4:2/3:122–134. [Au.]

We may never have complete answers to such questions, since archeology only provides some of the data and ancient writings, such as the Old Testament, were rewritten so many times, each time to more firmly establish, and sanctify, male control.[18] But what we do have is far more critical in this time when the old patriarchal system is leading us ever closer to global holocaust. This is the knowledge that it was not always this way: there are viable alternatives that may not only offer us survival but also a far, far better world.

Themes, Issues, and Ideas

1. Would you describe Eisler's theory as feminist? Why or why not? How do ideas about gender work here?

2. What are the religious implications of Eisler's theory?

3. Eisler describes the earliest Mother Creatrix–worshipping societies as being peaceful and agrarian, but soon corrupted and overthrown by warrior tribes. What evidence does she offer for this view? What evidence does she offer for her views about prehistoric religion?

Writing Strategies and Techniques

1. What does Eisler's approach to writing seem to be? Which writer in this book does she most remind you of? Why?

2. Where in her essay does Eisler suddenly shift styles, and why? Is it an effective transition?

Suggestions for Writing

1. Using a variety of academic sources, write a description of one of the prehistoric societies Eisler discusses.

2. Write an essay outlining how a return to female-creation myths could enrich the world.

---

[18]Ibid. [Au.]

The Never-ending Fight

Isaac Asimov

Isaac Asimov, scientist and science fiction writer, was one of the most prolific writers in the history of the printed word, the author of over 300 books. In an essay originally published in The Humanist *magazine, Asimov's view of the future state of the human spirit is frankly at odds with some of the attitudes found in the previous essays in this chapter. Asimov claims to speak for reason and the scientific pursuit of truth, which he sees not only as the proudest achievement of the modern age but also as, in the words of his title,* The Never-ending Fight. *Asimov, however, does not underrate what he sees as the powers of unreason. He modestly concludes: "If we're still here a century from now, we'll know we're winning."*

Isaac Asimov was born in Russia in 1920. His family came to New York when he was young and he was educated at Columbia University, taking B.A., M.A., and Ph.D. degrees in chemistry. When this essay was published, Asimov was president of the American Humanist Association. He died in 1992, at the age of 72.

I was interviewed on television recently and, in answering the questions, I found myself expressing my contempt for the various superstitious beliefs that plague humanity.

The interviewer asked, "But since, by your own admission, most people believe this sort of thing and find solace or comfort in it, why do you want to deprive them of it?"

I answered as best I could in the brief time available to me before the camera. But I can do it better now with more space at my disposal. This, in essence, is what I said.

There are two reasons. In the first place, I have the call to do so, the call to point out the uselessness of superstition. Everyone is perfectly ready to believe theists when they say they have the call to preach their version of the word of God and to accord them a kind of humble respect for having such a noble mission. Why, then, should I

290 MORTALITY AND THE HUMAN SPIRIT

be scorned because I have the call to preach my version of the word of reason?

I have my own notion of what it means to be rational and to look at the universe clearly. Unlike theists, I threaten no one with hellfire if they refuse to agree with every word I say; nor do I attempt to bribe them with tales of eternal bliss if only they accept my every syllable. Rather, I preach a universe in which there is neither threat nor bribe but merely something one strives to understand merely for the sake of understanding.

Unlike theists, I do not claim to have a pipeline to something supernatural. I do not claim to have absolute truth and an eternal answer to every problem past, present, or future. Rather, I offer the fallible human mind doing the best it can to improve its view somewhat from generation to generation.

And what I ask is merely that I be given a chance to express this rather modest and humble attitude without let or hindrance.

Secondly, it is no defense of superstition and pseudoscience to say that it brings solace and comfort to people and that therefore we "elitists" should not claim to know better and to take it away from the less sophisticated.

If solace and comfort are how we judge the worth of something, then consider that tobacco brings solace and comfort to smokers; alcohol brings it to drinkers; drugs of all kinds bring it to addicts; the fall of cards and the run of horses bring it to gamblers; cruelty and violence bring it to sociopaths. Judge by solace and comfort only and there is no behavior we ought to interfere with.

To be sure, it is easy to see that all these things bring harm to their practitioners, but can it not be argued that if some people get pleasure out of a practice that does harm to them it is nevertheless their body, their choice, their health, and their life to do with as they wish? Who are we to be the "big brother" who attempts to dictate our notion of a superior way of life to others against their will?

There is indeed something to this if it is *only* the practitioner's body and health and life that is involved and no one else's. But what of the smoker whose effluvium damages the lungs of nonsmokers forced to breathe his or her reek? What of the drinker who drives and kills? What of the addict who lures others into addiction? What of the sociopath who directly harms others as his or her path to joy?

By and large, then, society demands that these harmful physical practices be controlled insofar as it can be done humanely.

But, in that case, why should we not be at least as deeply concerned with the pernicious effects of superstition? Those who believe in magical methods of preventing or curing disease often do not turn to rational methods till it is too late. Those who believe that disasters are the work of inscrutable supernatural forces do not search for rational ways of preventing them or ameliorating their effects. Those who believe that humanity is under the beneficent control of supernatural forces that will see us through all our problems if we only "have faith" do not seek natural solutions to those problems.

We live in times when overpopulation, pollution, the greenhouse effect, the thinning of the ozone layer, the deterioration of the environment, the destruction of the forests and of wildlife, and the dangers of multiplying nuclear armaments all threaten us with the destruction of civilization and the radical reduction in the very viability of Earth. If our only answer to all this is a superstitious reliance on something outside ourselves as a solution to all those problems, we are making that destruction certain.

Yes, we will have our solace and comfort till the moment of the destruction, and we might console ourselves with the thoughts that we will all meet in a better world than this one and that indeed the Bible predicts the destruction of this world. But how many really believe that, even among those who say they do?

I notice little in the way of great joy at the death of friends and loved ones, little triumph in their having passed on to heavenly glory sooner than they might otherwise have done so. When an earthquake kills two thousand people at a blow, we do not rejoice that the innocent among them are now in heaven, but we raise powerful hosannahs if even *one* child is rescued alive from the ruins and is condemned to wait another sixty years, perhaps, before experiencing bliss.

I notice that all the people who are absolutely convinced that the United States is under the special protection of a powerful deity ("In God We Trust" it says on all our coins) are not at all certain that that deity is capable of protecting us unaided and insist that we have armed forces that are second to none. I myself feel safer if our defenses are strong, but I do not expect any supernatural force to help out. Why do the Falwells and the other television preachers feel the need?

And, as a matter of fact, average people living average lives, however much they may "believe" in God and in whatever religion they have been brought up to believe, act as though the world is in the grip of evil forces that must be held off in silly ways.

How many countless millions of people, even in "sophisticated" Western societies, place their faith not in God but in rabbits' feet, in horseshoes, in four-leaf clovers, in Saint Christopher medals, or in lucky pieces of an infinite number of shapes and forms? How many are terrified of black cats crossing their path, of ladders being walked under, of mirrors being broken, of aces of spades being turned up?

How many countless millions who explain that they are sure that God holds the key to the future and loves us all nevertheless feel much better consulting fortune-tellers, tea-leaf readers, crystal-ball gazers, and (especially if in high political office) astrologers, who apparently know the future just as well as God does and can give advice on what to do and not do that God (out of selfishness?) withholds?

Let us consider a small example of how the universe looks to the superstitious. August 8, 1988, is written "8/8/88" in brief form. The concatenation of eights looks somehow significant. It is based, of course, on the numbering of the days, months, and years according to a strictly human-arranged system that has no cosmic significance whatsoever. Nevertheless, uncounted people played the number 888 in lotteries on that day in the belief that the random fall of whatever system is used to choose the number is influenced by this strictly human convention. They lost, of course, for I'm told 888 turned up not on 8/8/88 but on the *next* day. Consequently, nothing was said. However, there was a one-in-one-thousand chance that 888 would indeed have appeared on 8/8/88, and, if it had, how many millions would have hailed it as "proof" of the truth of numerology?

Let us consider a large example of how the universe looks to the superstitious. Every once in a while, some region suffers a drought. In the summer of 1988, the United States suffered the worst drought in over fifty years. Presumably God has a divine plan for humanity, which seems inscrutable to us because our knowledge is finite and his is infinite and even a bad drought is for our long-term good. There may even be people who believe this and say this and are thankful there is a drought that may ruin them, because they know that it is all part of a marvelous plan for their long-term good. I suspect they are in the minority, though, for the more usual practice is to pray for rain—that is, to beg God over and over to abandon his plan, whatever it was, and do something for the short-term advantage of those praying. And if the rains do come, that proves the efficacy of prayer—and no one says that it rather proves the irresolution of God and his readiness to abandon his plan. And you know, if he was so ready to abandon his plan, he might just as well not have sent the drought in the first place. (You might argue that God's plan was to keep the drought going till humanity turned humbly to him and begged and begged and begged, so that he could demonstrate his power, but I've always thought that to be a rather petty interpretation of the ways of a supposedly infinitely beneficent deity.)

And, of course, there are many superstitions that have nothing to do with the dominant religion of the Western world. All sorts of peculiar beliefs arise about the Bermuda Triangle, about pyramid power, about flying saucers, about transmigration of souls, and all of them instantly attract the enthusiastic beliefs of millions.

The magazine *Science News* once questioned a number of scientific authorities on the Velikovskian theory of astronomical hopscotch that defies all the most elementary notions of celestial mechanics. All the authorities questioned gave reasoned refutations of this or that. I did not. I simply said, "There is no idea, however ridiculous on the very face of it, that some people won't instantly hug to their breasts and be ready to die for." Some issues later, the Velikovskians had their chance to reply, and every last one of them attacked my statement and left all the others alone. I had, quite obviously, struck a nerve.

Well, then, what do I expect of the next century? Assuming that we avoid destruction from the dogged adherence of humanity to superstition and its rejection of rationality, will we at least make a little progress in our cause?

I'm sorry. I don't think so. In addressing the humanists of 2089 (and I am sure there will be humanists in the world of 2089, if there should indeed be a world of 2089), I would have to say this.

Despite all the further advance of technology, despite the fact that we have computerized the world, despite the fact that robots are doing the menial work of humanity and that human beings are freed to work creatively at human tasks, despite the fact that we have expanded to the moon and beyond and are rapidly penetrating the solar system generally, and despite the fact that we understand the universe far better than we used to a century ago, the vast majority of human beings still take solace and comfort in their various superstitions and still follow any pied piper who fills their ears with notes of nonsense while filling his or her own pockets with money. And we are still in the minority and still struggling to convince people that, if, indeed, there were a god, he would in the end reject anyone who failed to make use of that one truly godlike gift.

But if that is so, and if we are engaged in a never-ending fight with no victory in sight, why continue?

Because we must. Because we have the call. Because it is nobler to fight for rationality without winning than to give up in the face of continued defeats. Because whatever true progress humanity makes is through the rationality of the occasional individual and because any one individual we may win for the cause may do more for humanity than a hundred thousand who hug their superstitions to their breast.

Themes, Issues, and Ideas

1. How does Asimov handle the objection that he and people like him are "elitists?" As a college student, have your views ever been objected to on this basis? How did you, or would you, respond? In what ways is Asimov's whole essay a kind of response?

2. Asimov raises a question at the end of his essay: "If we are engaged in a never-ending fight with no victory in sight, why continue?" How does he answer his own question? What do you think of the answer? Does the beginning of his essay convince you that he believes in his conclusion? Why, or why not?

3. Imagine a debate between a believer in the New Age and Isaac Asimov on the subject of the healing power of crystals. On what general matters might they agree—the need for evidence, for example? In what ways might they disagree on the same issues? For example, would they give the same weight to personal testimony?

Writing Strategies and Techniques

1. In what ways do the metaphors of "threat" and "bribe," as applied to his opponents, serve Asimov's argument at the beginning of his essay? What metaphors does he use to define his own manner of argumentation? How do they serve his purpose?

2. Asimov says, "I notice little in the way of great joy at the death of friends and loved ones, little triumph in their having passed on to heavenly glory sooner than they might otherwise have done so." How does Asimov's irony work? What point does it make for his argument? Rewrite the point in a way that does not use irony, but retains roughly the same meaning. What, if anything, has been lost by the change in tone?

Suggestions for Writing

1. In his last paragraph, Asimov expresses his ultimate reasons for the position he takes using terms that include "call" and "nobler." Surely these terms are not among those employed in scientific proof. Citing and analyzing particular examples, write an essay in which you describe the nonscientific aspects of Asimov's argument in favor of science.

2.   Suppose someone told Isaac Asimov, "You blame preachers for threatening their hearers with hellfire and bribing them with promises of heaven, but you implicitly threaten your audience with universal annihilation through the nuclear power invented by science and bribe the audience with thoughts of further scientifically produced material comforts, in order to make your audience worship your ideas of 'rationality.' " Write an essay in which you either come to Asimov's defense, or continue the attack. Be sure to use specific examples and reasoned arguments.

The Code of the Universe

James A. Haught

The essays in this chapter have ranged in subject from religion to science, and almost all of the writers included have used religion *and* science *as a pair of words with opposed meanings. Yet investigative reporter James Haught—winner of thirteen national awards for articles and editorials—finds that science offers him a religious sense of mystery, awe, and a key to understanding. Haught breaks down the usual dichotomy of the physical and the spiritual and suggests that phenomena like electrons and quarks, galaxies and black holes, electromagnetic radiation, DNA and cells, gravity, molecular bonds, the speed of light, and the power in the nucleus all contain a gospel more profound than any written by humans.*

Haught was born in West Virginia in 1932, where he has spent almost his entire life. He has long worked for the Charleston Gazette *in Charleston, West Virginia. This essay was originally published in* The Humanist *magazine.*

Did you know that Albert Einstein, although Jewish, went through a brief childhood phase of devout Christianity? In an autobiographical sketch written at age sixty-seven, he described his short-lived faith, planted in him by daily indoctrination at a Catholic school to which his parents had sent him:

> Thus I came—despite the fact that I was the son of entirely irreligious (Jewish) parents—to a deep religiosity, which, however, found an abrupt ending at the age of twelve. Through the reading of popular scientific books I soon reached the conviction that much in the stories of the Bible could not be true. The consequence was a positively fanatic freethinking coupled with the impression that youth is intentionally being deceived by the state through lies; it was a crushing impression.

Suspicion against every kind of authority grew out of this experience, a skeptical attitude toward the convictions which were alive in any specific social environment—an attitude which has never left me, even though later on, because of a better insight into the causal concessions, it lost some of its original poignancy.

It is quite clear to me that the religious paradise of youth, which was thus lost, was a first attempt to free myself from the chains of the "merely personal," from an existence which is dominated by wishes, hopes, and primitive feelings. Out yonder there was this huge world, which exists independently of us human beings and which stands before us like a great, eternal riddle, at least partially accessible to our inspection and thinking. The contemplation of this world beckoned like a liberation. . . .

The road to this paradise was not as comfortable and alluring as the road to the religious paradise, but it has proved itself as trustworthy, and I have never regretted having chosen it.

Commenting on Einstein's reminiscence, physicist Heinz Pagels wrote:

What this passage reveals is a conversion from personal religion to the "cosmic religion" of science, an experience which changed him for the rest of his life. Einstein saw that the universe is governed by laws that can be known by us but that are independent of our thoughts and feelings.

The existence of this cosmic code—the laws of material reality as confirmed by experience—is the bedrock faith that moves the natural scientist. The scientist sees in that code the eternal structure of reality, not as imposed by man or tradition but as written into the very substance of the universe. This recognition of the nature of the universe can come as a profound and moving experience to the young mind.

Looking into the soul of the universe isn't just for world-class physicists. It can happen to anyone who ponders the awesome discoveries of science, from quarks to quasars.

When I was a farmboy in Wetzel County, West Virginia, my grandfather taught me the orbits of Earth and the moon, and I thought it was utterly amazing that these colossal balls weighing quintillions of tons were whirling and circling and rolling forever in open space—and that we live on one of them.

When I studied chemistry in high school and learned the combining valences of atoms, I thought it was utterly amazing that this hidden code governs virtually all matter—Earth and the moon, our bodies, trees, water, air. How could atoms lock together into substances because of gaps in their outer layers of electrons—electrons eternally streaking at nearly the speed of light?

Why do the mysterious electrical parts of atoms whirl forever, like the planets and stars?

Why do electrically neutral atoms seize onto each other, just because their outer electron layers lack the magic number of eight?

Why do they turn into remarkably different things as they combine? Hydrogen gas and oxygen gas are nothing like water, yet they constitute it. Some carbon atoms lock in tetrahedrons to become diamonds; others lock in layers of six-sided carbon rings to become graphite pencil lead.

Why do atoms link into carbon-based molecules that link into amino acids that link into proteins that link into living cells as complex as whole cities—and why does all this link into a thinking, feeling, loving, fearing, aging, dying human?

How can a combination of amino acids write a symphony or join the Republican party or commit stock fraud or feel patriotism for a section of Earth likewise composed of molecules?

The old "planetary" model of the atom was envisioned like a solar system—orbits around a nucleus. This raised a far-out theory that our solar system might be an atom in some stupefyingly larger universe and that our atoms might be tiny solar systems with people living on some of the particles. I first encountered this idea in a *Captain Marvel* comic book. The great astronomer Harlow Shapley once gave a talk at West Virginia State College. I hung around afterward and asked him, "What's the name of the theory that atoms might be solar systems?" He looked at me and said, "The name of it is damn nonsense." I later learned that it's called the subatomic universe theory—but Shapley's name probably is better.

During this period, when I was muddling over the boggling impossibilities that science revealed, I started reading books on Einstein and relativity and found that *his* scientific truth was even more astonishing. What our common sense tells us is real *can't* be real if space shrinks to nonexistence or time runs slower and stops under some conditions.

I hatched mental experiments that short-circuited my brain. For example, Einstein says the speed of light is the great constant of the universe—nothing can go faster. He also says all speeds are relative between moving objects. Well, if you strike a match, photons of visible light fly out in all directions. If one photon is going west at the speed of light and another is going east at the speed of light, how fast are they separating from each other?

It gets even worse when you read quantum physics. The more I studied, the more I developed an eerie sense that the world we think we inhabit and all existing things are some sort of fiction.

For example, take steel. It can be a one-hundred-foot bridge girder or it can be the coil of a bass piano string, a long wire spiraled into a hard spring. All the curves of that spring are composed of iron atoms locked rigidly to each other in a strong crystal lattice that is nearly unbreakable.

And yet, those atoms are an illusion of emptiness. They are a void of unknowable electrical charges. They are virtually a vacuum. They are as empty as the solar system. If you look at the night sky and see how remote the planets are, that's how remote the parts of an atom are from each other.

If an atom were the size of a fourteen-story building, the nucleus would be a grain of salt in the middle of the seventh floor, too tiny to be seen. Therefore, heavy, rigid steel doesn't exist the way we think it does. It's 99.999999 percent vacuum—as empty as the night sky.

Sometimes I picture atoms as soap bubbles: empty but bumping against each other and sticking together. The buzzing outer electrons are negative, and they repel the negative electron clouds of adjoining atoms; this holds the atoms apart and gives them an illusion of solidity. Yet, they are bound to each other by valence bonds and hydrogen bonds and Van der Waals bonds and other electrical links.

Atom emptiness is the key to white dwarfs, pulsars, and black holes.

At the end of their life cycles, stars explode. Then, what's left of them collapses, and gravity pulls the collapsing material into incredible density. If the residue is small, compressed electrons in the seething stellar plasma of crushed atoms push back fiercely and resist further collapse. This produces a white dwarf that is nearly impossible to comprehend.

The material of a white dwarf weighs around ten tons per thimbleful. How could something the size of a thimble be so heavy that one hundred strong men couldn't lift it? It might crush a house. A large crane would be required to pick it up.

But that's just the first step in removing the empty space inside atoms. A teenage genius, Subrahmanyan Chandrasekhar, computed that, if a collapsing star has 1.4 times the mass of our sun, its gravity would be too great to be stopped by the resistance of the electrons. He didn't know it, but he was predicting pulsars, or neutron stars, which later were discovered. Their enormous gravity squeezes the electrons into the nucleus of each atom, where they merge with protons to form a solid mass of neutrons. This material weighs about 10 million tons per cubic centimeter.

A cubic centimeter is the size of a bouillon cube. Can you imagine a bouillon cube weighing more than the World Trade Center? But that's what matter is when the empty space is removed between the nucleus and the electrons of atoms.

If 10 million tons of actual substance is the size of a bouillon cube, how much real material is in a 180-pound man or a 120-pound woman? Not as much as a dust speck. Not enough to see with a microscope. Our five-foot or six-foot bodies, like all material things, are an illusion made of vacuum and whirling electrical charges.

It gets worse. Even the packed neutrons in a pulsar are not basic material. They, too, are empty and compressible. If the remains of a collapsing star are 3.2 times larger than our sun, the gravity is too strong to be checked at the pulsar level. The collapse continues until it passes the point of no return—the Schwarzchild radius—and becomes a black hole, the ultimate pit of gravity, where everything is compressed to *nothing*.

If planet Earth were squeezed to its Schwarzchild radius, *it would be the size of a pearl*. Can anyone imagine the matter of the entire Earth being reduced to fingernail size—but retaining all its weight—and continuing to shrink beyond that point?

This isn't Captain Marvel comics. Pulsars are real. So are black holes, the astrophysicists say. If they are actuality, then what is our everyday world?

The nonreality of matter is just one of many enigmas that science reveals. Consider these:

- As we lie in bed, we are flying 67,000 miles an hour around the sun and 600,000 miles an hour around the Milky Way galaxy.

- When we see the North Star, we are looking back in time to the medieval era, because the light we see began traveling 680 years ago.

- Every second, the visible universe expands by a volume as large as the Milky Way.

- Peaceful atoms of rock, lying still for centuries, have a power in their nuclei that is beyond comprehension: Only as much matter as a *dime* was transformed into the energy that destroyed Hiroshima and killed 140,000 people.

- The smallness of atoms likewise is beyond grasping: A cubic inch of air contains 300 *billion billion* molecules, all moving at 1,000 miles an hour and hitting each other 5 billion times a second.

- Although atoms are generally indestructible, their electrons keep coming loose to produce lightning and the other electricity of the world.

- The light we see, the *sun warmth* we feel, the radio and television signals we receive, the X-rays we use—all of these come from electrons. Electromagnetic radiation is emitted by excited electrons oscillating or dropping to lower layers in atoms.

- All life on Earth comes from a tiny electric current: When sunlight hits chlorophyll molecules, excited outer electrons jump through a mosaic of molecules, and this energy drives plant processes.

- As for the DNA that conveys our genetic code, there is six feet of it inside each cell of our bodies. The body has more than 10 trillion cells, so every person contains *several billion miles* of DNA.

These are profoundly important topics, yet, when I try to discuss science with my chums in the news business or music circles or political groups, they look at me as if I'm babbling in the Unknown Tongue. They are highly educated people who know multitudes of facts, but they shrug at what I think are the most crucial facts of all.

If religion and philosophy are an attempt to comprehend the universe and the meaning of life, then science is the best portal. Every time I learn another rule of subatomic forces or cell behavior or galactic motion, I get an eerie sense of glimpsing the mysterious code underlying our existence. Physicists often apply the word *God* to this order, but they don't mean *God* in the church sense.

In a world of supernatural religions, mystical religions, guilt-based religions, violent religions, money-collecting religions, social club religions, and cult religions, grasping the code of the universe is the most religious experience I know.

Themes, Issues, and Ideas

1. Why do you think Haught begins his essay with an account of Einstein's early religious experience? Haught later reports his own wonder stimulated by *Captain Marvel* comics. Would that anecdote have made an equally effective beginning? Explain your answer.

2. Haught apparently takes his title from a passage he quotes by Heinz Pagels on the laws of material reality: "The scientist sees in that code the eternal structure of reality, not as imposed by man or tradition but as written into the very substance of the universe." What do Haught and Pagels find attractive about the concept of a "code?" What does that metaphor imply about the nature of the

universe that the metaphor of "natural laws" does not? How do Haught, Pagels, and Einstein compare in this regard with the New Age believers Christopher Lasch and Jake Page describe earlier in this book?

3. Haught reports his own early belief in a theory that our solar system might be an atom in a larger universe, along with a scientist's response to that theory. Why do you think this experience did not disillusion Haught in his general tendency to speculate and wonder? What does the anecdote add to the essay? Would you feel differently were it not included?

Writing Strategies and Techniques

1. Is there any "plot" to the many examples of scientific phenomena that Haught includes? What connects the examples he uses and keeps them from being merely a random list?

2. Haught is a reporter. Do you notice any journalistic techniques employed in his essay? How, if at all, does he modify his style for an educated rather than a general audience? Point to particular examples.

Suggestions for Writing

1. In the beginning of his essay, Haught quotes Albert Einstein as saying that his early religiosity was an attempt to free himself from "the chains of the 'merely personal.' " How might the personal be seen as an imprisonment of the spirit? Write an essay comparing and contrasting science and religion as ways to transcend the self.

2. Write an essay comparing, in both style and content, this essay and Jonathan Edwards's "Sinners in the Hands of an Angry God."

MAKING CONNECTIONS

1. Write an essay comparing and contrasting G. K. Chesterton and Isaac Asimov. How are their styles different? How are their approaches different? Are both men addressing the same issues?

2. What might Asimov make of Rosemary Ruether's piece? What would Chesterton make of Riane Eisler's? If you were to make debate teams of these authors, who would be on which team, and why?

3. Isaac Asimov lists some of the problems mentioned by Bill Lawren in his essay, among them, overpopulation, the greenhouse effect, the thinning of the ozone layer, and the general deterioration of the environment. Write an essay comparing the content and manner of Asimov's response to those who believe that the end of the world is at hand.

4. Different styles appear in these essays: humor in Chesterton; profundity in Asimov; scientific solemnity in Eisler. What other styles do you find in these selections? Which styles do you think work best for the topic of mortality? Which writer's style advances the writer's thought best?

5. Where does G. K. Chesterton's view of the world fit in with James Haught's? What does the answer to this question tell you about both writers?

CHAPTER
EIGHT

Science, Technology, and Human Life

Some Issues of Modern Medicine

THE PAST AS PROLOGUE

1933 Medicine

Lewis Thomas

When Lewis Thomas (b. 1913) began the medical training described in his essay, medicine consisted largely of diagnosing a disease and predicting its probable course. By the time he finished medical school, however, science had created a technology that allowed medicine to cure *diseases—a technology taken for granted today. Thomas himself played a part in some of the astounding triumphs of medicine since then. He has been a medical doctor, a research biologist, and a prolific writer on medicine both for technical and general audiences. Among his many books,* The Lives of a Cell *won the National Book Award in 1975. This essay is a chapter in* The Youngest Science: Notes of a Medicine Watcher *(1983).*

I was admitted to medical school under circumstances that would have been impossible today. There was not a lot of competition; not more than thirty of my four hundred classmates, most of these the sons of doctors, planned on medicine. There was no special curriculum; elementary physics and two courses in chemistry were the only fixed requirements; the term "premedical" had not yet been invented. My academic record at Princeton was middling fair; I had entered college at fifteen, having been a bright enough high-school student, but then I turned into a moult of dullness and laziness, average or below average in the courses requiring real work. It was not until my senior year, when I ventured a course in advanced biology under Professor Swingle, who had just discovered a hormone of the adrenal cortex, that I became a reasonably alert scholar, but by that time my grade averages had me solidly fixed in the dead center, the "gentlemen's third," of the class. Today, I would have been turned down by every place, except perhaps one of the proprietary medical schools in the Caribbean.

I got into Harvard, the hardest, by luck and also, I suspect, by pull. Hans Zinsser, the professor of bacteriology, had interned with my father at Roosevelt and had admired my mother, and when I went to Boston to be interviewed in the winter of 1933, I was instructed by the dean's secretary to go have a talk with Dr. Zinsser. It was the briefest of interviews, but satisfactory from my point of view. Zinsser looked at me carefully, as at a specimen, then informed me that my father and mother were good friends of his, and if I wanted to come to Harvard he would try to help, but because of them, not me; he was entirely good-natured, but clear on this point. It was favoritism, but not all that personal, I was to understand.

My medical education was, in principle, much like that of my father. The details had changed a lot since his time, especially in the fields of medical science relating to disease mechanisms; physiology and biochemistry had become far more complex and also more illuminating; microbiology and immunology had already, by the early 1930s, transformed our understanding of the causation of the major infectious diseases. But the *purpose* of the curriculum was, if anything, even more conservative than thirty years earlier. It was to teach the recognition of disease entities, their classification, their signs, symptoms, and laboratory manifestations, and how to make an accurate diagnosis. The treatment of disease was the most minor part of the curriculum, almost left out altogether. There was, to be sure, a course in pharmacology in the second year, mostly concerned with the mode of action of a handful of everyday drugs: aspirin, morphine, various cathartics, bromides, barbiturates, digitalis, a few others. Vitamin B was coming into fashion as a treatment for delirium tremens, later given up. We were provided with a thin pocket-size book called *Useful Drugs,* one hundred pages or so, and we carried this around in our white coats when we entered the teaching wards and clinics in the third year, but I cannot recall any of our instructors ever referring to this volume. Nor do I remember much talk about treating disease at any time in the four years of medical school except by the surgeons, and most of their discussions dealt with the management of injuries, the drainage or removal of infected organs and tissues, and, to a very limited extent, the excision of cancers.

The medicine we were trained to practice was, essentially, Osler's medicine. Our task for the future was to be diagnosis and explanation. Explanation was the real business of medicine. What the ill patient and his family wanted most was to know the name of the illness, and then, if possible, what had caused it, and finally, most important of all, how it was likely to turn out.

The successes possible in diagnosis and prognosis were regarded as the triumph of medical science, and so they were. It had taken long decades of careful, painstaking observation of many patients; the publication of countless papers describing the detailed aspects of one clinical syndrome after another; more science, in the correlation of the clinical features of disease with the gross and microscopic abnormalities, contributed by several generations of pathologists. By the 1930s we thought we knew as much as could ever be known about the dominant clinical problems of the time: syphilis, tuberculosis, lobar pneumonia, typhoid, rheumatic fever, erysipelas, poliomyelitis. Most of the known varieties of cancer had been meticulously classified, and estimates of the duration of life could be made with some accuracy. The electrocardiogram had arrived, adding to the fair precision already possible in the diagnosis of heart disease. Neurology possessed methods for the localization of disease processes anywhere in the nervous system. When we had learned all that, we were ready for our M.D. degrees, and it was expected that we would find out about the actual day-to-day management of illness during our internship and residency years.

During the third and fourth years of school we also began to learn something that worried us all, although it was not much talked about. On the wards of the great Boston teaching hospitals—the Peter Bent Brigham, the Massachusetts General, the Boston City Hospital, and Beth Israel—it gradually dawned on us that we didn't know much that was really useful, that we could do nothing to change the course of the great majority of the diseases we were so busy analyzing, that medicine, for all its facade as a learned profession, was in real life a profoundly ignorant occupation.

Some of this we were actually taught by our clinical professors, much more we learned from each other in late-night discussions. When I am asked, as happens occasionally, which member of the Harvard faculty had the greatest influence on my education in medicine, I no longer grope for a name on that distinguished roster. What I remember now, from this distance, is the influence of my classmates. We taught each other; we may even have set careers for each other without realizing at the time that so fundamental an educational process was even going on. I am not so troubled as I used to be by the need to reform the medical school curriculum. What worries me these days is that the curriculum, whatever its sequential arrangement, has become so crowded with lectures and seminars, with such masses of data to be learned, that the students may not be having enough time to instruct each other in what may lie ahead.

The most important period for discovering what medicine would be like was a three-month ward clerkship in internal medicine that was a required part of the fourth year of medical school. I applied for the clerkship at the Beth Israel Hospital, partly because of the reputation of Professor Hermann Blumgart and partly because several of my best friends were also going there. Ward rounds with Dr. Blumgart were an intellectual pleasure, also good for the soul. I became considerably less anxious about the scale of medical ignorance as we followed him from bed to bed around the open circular wards of the B.I. I've seen his match only three or four times since then. He was a tall, thin, quick-moving man, with a look of high intelligence, austerity, and warmth all at the same time. He had the special gift of perceiving, almost instantaneously, while still approaching the bedside of a new patient, whether the problem was a serious one or not. He seemed to do this by something like intuition; at times when there were no particular reasons for alarm that could be sensed by others in the retinue, Blumgart would become extremely alert and attentive, requiring the resident to present every last detail of the history, and then moving closer to the bedside, asking his own questions of the patient, finally performing his physical examination. To watch a master of physical diagnosis in the execution of a complete physical examination is something of an aesthetic experience, rather like observing a great ballet dancer or a concert cellist. Blumgart did all this swiftly, then asked a few more questions, then drew us away to the corridor outside the ward for his discussion, and then his diagnosis, sometimes a death sentence. Then back to the bedside for a brief private talk with the patient, inaudible to the rest of us, obviously reassuring to the patient, and on to the next bed. So far as I know, from that three months of close contact with Blumgart for three hours every morning, he was never wrong, not once. But I can recall only three or four patients for whom the diagnosis resulted in the possibility of doing something to change the course of the illness, and each of these involved calling in the surgeons to do the something—removal of a thyroid nodule, a gallbladder, an adrenal tumor. For the majority, the disease had to be left to run its own course, for better or worse.

There were other masters of medicine, each as unique in his way as Blumgart, surrounded every day by interns and medical students on the wards of the other Boston hospitals.

The Boston City Hospital, the city's largest, committed to the care of indigent Bostonians, was divided into five separate clinical services, two staffed by Harvard Medical School (officially designated as the Second and Fourth services), two by Tufts, and one by Boston University. The most spectacular chiefs on the Harvard faculty were aggregated on the City Hospital wards, drawn there in the 1920s by the creation of the Thorndike Memorial Laboratories, a separate research institute on the hospital grounds, directly attached by a series of ramps and tunnels to the buildings containing the teaching wards. The Thorndike was founded by Dr. Francis Weld Peabody, still remembered in Boston as perhaps the best of Harvard physicians. Peabody was convinced that the study of human disease should not be conducted solely by bedside observations, as had been largely the case for the research done by physicians up to that time, nor by pure bench research in the university laboratories; he believed that the installation of a fully equipped research institute, containing laboratories for investigations of any promising line of inquiry, directly in communication with the hospital wards, offered the best opportunity for moving the field forward.

Peabody was also responsible for the initial staffing of the Thorndike. By the time I arrived, in 1937, the array of talent was formidable: George Minot (who had already received his Nobel prize for the discovery of liver extract as a cure for pernicious anemia), William Castle (who discovered the underlying deficiency in pernicious anemia), Chester Keefer, Soma Weiss, Maxwell Finland, John Dingle, Eugene Stead—each of them running a laboratory, teaching on the wards, and providing research training for young doctors who came for two- or three-year fellowship stints from teaching hospitals across the country. The Thorndike was a marvelous experiment, a model for what were to become the major departments of medicine in other medical schools, matched at the time only by the hospital of the Rockefeller Institute in New York.

Max Finland built and then ran the infectious disease service. He and his associates had done most of the definitive work on antipneumococcal sera in the treatment of lobar pneumonia, testing each new preparation of rabbit antiserum as it arrived from the Lederle Laboratories. Later, Finland's laboratories were to become a national center for the clinical evaluation of penicillin, streptomycin, chloromycetin, and all the other antibiotics which followed during the 1950s and 1960s. As early as 1937, medicine was changing into a technology based on genuine science. The signs of change were there, hard to see because of the overwhelming numbers of patients for whom we could do nothing but stand by, but unmistakably there all the same. Syphilis could be treated in its early stages, and eventually cured, by Paul

Ehrlich's arsphenamine; the treatment took a long time, many months, sometimes several years. If arsphenamine was started in the late stages of the disease, when the greatest damage was under way—in the central nervous system and the major arteries—the results were rarely satisfactory—but in the earliest stages, the chancre and then the rash of secondary syphilis, the spirochete could be killed off and the Wassermann reaction reversed. The treatment was difficult and hazardous, the side effects of the arsenical drugs were appalling, sometimes fatal (I cannot imagine such a therapy being introduced and accepted by any of today's FDA or other regulatory agencies), but it did work in many cases, and it carried a powerful message for the future: It was possible to destroy an invading microorganism, intimately embedded within the cells and tissues, without destroying the cells themselves. Chemotherapy for infectious disease in general lay somewhere ahead, and we should have known this.

Immunology was beginning to become an applied science. Thanks to the basic research launched twenty years earlier by Avery, Heidelberger, and Goebbel, it was known that pneumococci possessed specific carbohydrates in their capsules which gave rise to highly specific antibodies. By the mid-1930s, rabbit antipneumococcal sera were available for the treatment of the commonest forms of lobar pneumonia. The sera were difficult and expensive to prepare, and sometimes caused overwhelming anaphylactic reactions in patients already moribund from their infection, but they produced outright cures in many patients. Pernicious anemia, a uniformly fatal disease, was spectacularly reversed by liver extract (much later found to be due to the presence of vitamin B_{12} in the extracts). Diabetes mellitus could be treated—at least to the extent of reducing the elevated blood sugar and correcting the acidosis that otherwise led to diabetic coma and death—by the insulin preparation isolated by Banting and Best. Pellagra, a common cause of death among the impoverished rural populations in the South, had become curable with Goldberger's discovery of the vitamin B complex and the subsequent identification of nicotinic acid. Diphtheria could be prevented by immunization against the toxin of diphtheria bacilli and, when it occurred, treated more or less effectively with diphtheria antitoxin.

All these things were known at the time of my internship at the Boston City Hospital, but they seemed small advances indeed. The major diseases, which filled the wards to overflowing during the long winter months, were infections for which there was no treatment at all.

The two great hazards to life were tuberculosis and tertiary syphilis. These were feared by everyone, in the same way that cancer is feared today. There was nothing to be done for tuberculosis except to wait it out, hoping that the body's own defense mechanisms would eventually hold the tubercle bacillus in check. Some patients were helped by collapsing the affected lung (by injecting air into the pleural space, or by removing the ribs overlying the lung), and any number of fads were introduced for therapy—mountain resorts, fresh air, sunshine, nutritious diets—but for most patients tuberculosis simply ran its own long debilitating course despite all efforts. Tertiary syphilis was even worse. The wards of insane asylums were filled with psychotic patients permanently incapacitated by this disease—"general paresis of the insane"; some benefit was claimed for fever therapy; but there were few real cures. Rheumatic fever, the commonest cause of fatal heart disease in children, was shown by Coburn to be the result of infection by hemolytic streptococci; aspirin, the only treatment available, relieved the painful arthritis in this disease but had no effect on the heart lesions. For most of the infectious diseases on the wards of the Boston City Hospital in 1937, there was nothing to be done beyond bed rest and good nursing care.

Then came the explosive news of sulfanilamide, and the start of the real revolution in medicine.

I remember the astonishment when the first cases of pneumococcal and streptococcal septicemia were treated in Boston in 1937. The phenomenon was almost beyond belief. Here were moribund patients, who would surely have died without treatment, improving in their appearance within a matter of hours of being given the medicine and feeling entirely well within the next day or so.

The professionals most deeply affected by these extraordinary events were, I think, the interns. The older physicians were equally surprised, but took the news in stride. For an intern, it was the opening of a whole new world. We had been raised to be ready for one kind of profession, and we sensed that the profession itself had changed at the moment of our entry. We knew that other molecular variations of sulfanilamide were on their way from industry, and we heard about the possibility of penicillin and other antibiotics; we became convinced, overnight, that nothing lay beyond reach for the future. Medicine was off and running.

Themes, Issues, and Ideas

1. Thomas writes, "The treatment of disease was the most minor part of the curriculum, almost left out altogether." Why was this the case? What did his medical study mainly consist of in college?

2. By 1937, "the signs of change were there," writes Thomas. What were those signs and what did they portend?

3. Thomas distinguishes between the responses of the interns and those of the older physicians to the new discoveries in medicine. What does he imply were the reasons for this difference? Do any additional reasons suggest themselves to you? Explain.

Writing Strategies and Techniques

1. Thomas ends his essay with the metaphor of a race: "Medicine was off and running." What other sources of metaphor does Thomas employ? Pick some examples and explain how they contribute to his writing.

2. This essay is on science and medicine, but it is written for a generally educated audience. How does Thomas try to avoid technical language in his explanations? Point to some examples and show how they work to make technical content understandable to the nontechnical reader.

Suggestions for Writing

1. Thomas praises his teacher Dr. Blumgart for his brilliant abilities in diagnosis and prediction, and for his manner with his patients. Write an essay analyzing the manner of Lewis Thomas's strengths in exposition. How does he maintain the relationship he creates with his audience?

2. Pick a subject that you have studied (mathematics or art, for example) and write an essay on the history of your training. Include a sketch of at least one instructor who influenced you for better or for worse.

Body Doubles

Jeffrey Kluger

Giving a patient "medicine" implies introducing foreign chemicals into the human body in order to cure it from the "outside," as it were. But that implication may change by the millennium. Among the most promising advances of modern science and medical technology is what might be called an "inside approach"—an attempt to help the body's own natural defense mechanisms cure what ails it. The cure involves the manipulation of proteins. Some of these manipulations, along with their often miraculous results and still more miraculous promises, are explored by Jeffrey Kluger in this essay, first published in Omni *magazine.*

It was late afternoon in 1985, and Wolfgang Sadee was becoming impatient. For close to a week now the tall, graying scientist had been in and out of his University of California laboratory, squinting into a microscope at a handful of cells and waiting for them to grow. Not much of a trick for most cells, but these were nerve cells: They can't regenerate themselves. That's why people with damaged spinal cords usually have damaged spinal cords for the rest of their lives.

"During the gestation period our nerves grow with no trouble at all, " Sadee explains in a heavy German accent. "But once we've developed, that process stops. Our bodies seem to lose whatever guidance system allows nerves to grow."

Sadee was watching this particular group of cells because of a hunch he had. A year earlier, a group of researchers had discovered a complicated protein that they called nerve growth factor (NGF). Sadee and other researchers suspected that NGF acted as the guidance system for the growth of gestating nerve cells *and* that it might also help to regulate fully developed ones.

After six days of patient—and painstaking—work, he got his answer. "I looked into the microscope and was astounded," he says. "The nerve cells were suddenly sprouting all sorts of interconnections among themselves. They were growing, weaving together. Somehow, just a few molecules of NGF had electrically excited them, making them do all sorts of things they ordinarily wouldn't do. This protein is remarkable stuff"—as it turns out, the stuff medical dreams are made of.

Sadee suspects the protein will be instrumental in helping to heal injured spinal cords and to treat Alzheimer's disease and certain childhood cancers. But NGF is only one of a battery of proteins whose secret powers are being revealed in a new branch of medical science that may change forever the landscape of disease.

This new science involves nothing more glamorous than proteins—or more specifically, the manipulation of proteins. But its potential rivals that of the Salk vaccine and the Jarvik-7 put together. With simple tinkering, proteins may have the capacity to control cancer, heart disease, diabetes, and AIDS; speed wound healing and bone setting; treat kidney disorders; ease the pain of childbirth; and lead to a safe, reliable contraceptive. Within a decade, maybe two, nearly half of all existing therapies or drug treatments could be thrown on the medical ash heap, replaced by the results of protein manipulation.

The premise behind the new science is simple. There are two basic molecules of life: nucleic acids and proteins. "Nucleic acids are our raw materials," says cell biologist Frances Brodsky, a colleague of Sadee's at the University of California at San Francisco (UCSF). "They have one important job: to build proteins. And proteins are nothing less than the functional molecules of our bodies."

Hormones are proteins; antibodies are proteins; neurotransmitters and other brain chemicals are proteins. Cells, tissues, and organs are all made of proteins. It's proteins' omnipresence that is central to their potential: Learn to alter one protein to change the course of one malady and you can apply the techniques to a host of our problems. That's the theory, anyway, and it seems to be paying off.

Scientists learned long ago that some proteins are rather simple—necklaces of a couple dozen amino acids linked end to end in a specific order. Other proteins are impossibly long, tangled affairs, composed of hundreds, even thousands, of amino acids. Each is built by the body with exquisite precision: Not one more acid than is needed is in each chain, and not a single link is out of order.

Through nature has been assembling proteins since life began on Earth, it wasn't until the 1970s that scientists made their first tentative efforts to whip up some of the stuff on their own. The investigators discovered that at least for simple proteins like insulin, the manufacturing job could be relatively easy: Simply hang one amino acid from a thin rod made of organic resin, then chemically attach another and another and another, until a strand of the desired composition and length is achieved. "It's like an electric train set," says clinical pharmacologist Ferid Murad, acting chair of Stanford University's department of medicine. "You just keep adding the right amino acids until you've got the protein you want."

For more complicated proteins—anything longer than 30 amino acids or so—the task is different. Here, living cells must be recruited to assist in the manufacturing process. Scientists first snip a little RNA (a specific type of nucleic acid) from a sample of the protein they want to mass-produce: then, using this as a sort of cellular instruction manual, they assemble the appropriate enzymes to synthesize a single gene from that protein. The new gene is inserted into the nucleus of living bacterium, usually the simple *E. coli,* in part because it is easy to grow and too fragile to live outside the lab should some bacteria escape. From this point on, the process is automatic.

"The bacterium is stupid," explains Stanford endocrinologist Ron Rosenfeld, one of the major pioneers in protein research. "It accepts the new gene as its own. When the gene instructs the *E. coli* to start creating the protein, the *E. coli* complies. In effect, the bacteria become a little factory for whatever we want to make." The *E. coli* are then stored in vats, where they obediently and endlessly churn out whatever they've been told. Later the vats are opened, the bacteria are killed, and the protein is purified.

It was this technique, known as recombinant DNA, that first inspired a new group of researchers to study proteins. Sadee himself, trained at institutes in Zurich and Berlin, came to the United States in 1971 intending to study drug chemistry and metabolism. But the potential of protein research was too seductive. "I realized that protein manipulation might one day be an accomplishment every bit as significant as the discovery of DNA," he says in his UCSF office. "Once the structure of these substances is completely understood, medicine will have succeeded in cracking the second genetic code."

Opiate Boosters

So promising is the field that Sadee is having trouble deciding where to focus his attention. At the moment he's concentrating on creating new types of pain relievers and anesthetics. Though the body produces its own opiates, Western scientists have rarely paid much attention to them. Instead they have relied on synthetic anesthetics that work on the body like a chemical clubbing, easing pain not by relaxing the central nervous system but by doping and dosing it.

Sadee believes the natural opiates can do a better job and with fewer side effects.

"The first step," he explains, "is to study natural opiates like endorphins to understand how they work. Then we can try to mimic them synthetically."

If all goes well, researchers will one day be able to change the amino acid sequence of a particular endorphin or other opiate to tailor it to perform a specific task or to serve the needs of specific patients.

Such mutated molecules are known as muteins. Short, manually built muteins are easy enough to assemble: Simply change the order of the amino acids when they're being chemically strung together and the resulting protein will perform differently. But longer, more complicated recombinantly-built muteins are a bit trickier, requiring scientists to craft an entirely new gene that, when inserted into the *E. coli* nucleus, will instruct it to produce an entirely new protein. Tough as this process may be, Sadee believes the medical benefits will be worth the scientists' sweat. "Every place we look in the body," he says, "another healing protein appears." Researchers have found a protein called relaxin that seems, appropriately enough, to relax the uterus during childbirth. There are others that work as growth factors to help bones heal. Another, called erythropoietin, affects bone marrow stem cells and could be used to treat anemia. "There's no limit to these substances," Sadee says, "and the faster we learn to use them, the more people we'll be able to help."

The Versatile Monoclonal

Cell biologist Frances Brodsky wasn't wooed into the study of proteins as Sadee was. She is a first- generation researcher whose work with monoclonal antibodies has spurred her confidence in the importance of protein manipulation.

Antibodies are immune-system killer cells that prowl the human body looking for disease, including malignancies, flushing out affected cells and annihilating them on the spot. These search-and-destroy proteins are produced naturally in the spleen and every day protect the body from disease. But often antibodies are too inefficient to destroy fast-growing cancer cells, and disease takes hold.

At the beginning of the decade investigators began to develop procedures to enhance antibodies' effectiveness. The ideas was to use outside help in the form of artificially produced antibodies. "We take a single spleen cell and immortalize it, cloning it and growing it outside the body," explains Brodsky. Then researchers arm the anti-bodies with a toxic chemical that is deadly to cancer cells. Once the altered cells, called monoclonal antibodies, are introduced into the body, they need no assistance from the immune system to kill the cancer cells. "This magic-bullet approach to cancer therapy is still in the experimental stage," says Brodsky, "but initial results look promising."

But monoclonals could do more than treat cancer. Indeed, Brodsky sees practically no limit to their versatility. "Monoclonals are vehicles that could carry material to any part of the body," she says. "It's possible that you could use them to carry genetic material into a cell and reverse genetic defects."

In Brodsky's and others' scientific scenarios, a patient with a congenital disease like, say, diabetes wouldn't simply be treated for the illness but would be genetically retooled with new, healthy DNA coding for proper processing of sugar. "We're learning to mimic viruses," she says, "which do their work in exactly the same way: entering cells and bringing their own genetic material along."

At the Biological Therapy Institute in Franklin, Tennessee, still another spin has been put on monoclonal technology. There resident doctors tailor antibodies for each patient. Rather than just building a single monoclonal missile to carry the same genetic payload in all patients, the scientists are developing antibodies that are slightly different for every recipient.

"The first thing we do," explains Institute oncologist Robert Oldham, "is take a biopsy of the tumor and look to see if we have antibodies already on the shelf that will stick to it. If we do, we make up a cocktail of those antibodies and treat the patient with it. If we don't, we start making up new antibodies, trying to find the ones that will work best on that patient's malignant cells."

Oldham's program is expensive: Patients pay $35,000. And the Institute offers no guarantees. "The fee is for our research," Oldham says. "It's a 'best effort' kind of thing: The patients are not purchasing a product."

But guaranteed expense and unguaranteed results aren't the only drawbacks to Oldham's program. Of even greater concern is the effect that such personalized treatments could have on the development of more mainstream cancer therapies. Where, many ask, will science get research volunteers when more and more cancer patients are disappearing into private institutes hoping—and paying—for their own custom-made cures?

"That's a bugaboo ethical question," answers Institute president Louis Berneman. "Historically, dramatic breakthroughs in managing diseases are not seen through experiments and control groups but through actual long-term treatment programs like ours. Besides, no patients are accepted into the institute's program unless they have already failed or are likely to fail standard therapies."

AIDS

The hunt for a recombinant vaccine to immunize people against the AIDS virus has spawned some of the most important protein work. At American drug companies like Genentech, Cetus, and Chiron, scientists are exploring an approach in which a protein mimicking the cell wall of the AIDS virus could be synthesized recombinantly and then injected into the bloodstream. Essentially a viral skin without the guts, the cellular shell would represent just enough of the virus to cause the immune system to produce antibodies against the disease but *not* enough to cause actual sickness. "All vaccines work essentially this way," explains Rosenfeld.

Elsewhere, other even more imaginative techniques are being tried. At the Pierre and Marie Curie Institute in Paris, researcher Daniel Zagury is experimenting with a sort of piggyback vaccine in which bits of the AIDS virus are inserted into smallpox vaccine and then introduced into the body. Since the smallpox virus is alive—though stripped of its disease-causing properties—it behaves far more aggressively than a simple cell wall. Rather than passively drifting through the bloodstream, it actively invades the body's cells. The smallpox vaccine could thus serve as a cellular vehicle to deliver the AIDS vaccine quickly and more efficiently. Zagury has already inoculated a dozen volunteers and—significantly—himself with the hybrid vaccine. Preliminary blood studies indicate that the experimental cells do indeed cause the immune system to produce antibodies to the AIDS virus.

The next step will be to discover whether these antibodies actually protect against the disease. But that, of course, is a knotty business. In order to verify his theories, Zagury and his group of volunteers will have to expose themselves to the AIDS virus, a step they have been understandably reluctant to take. For this reason, all the volunteers are from Zaire, a country where AIDS is raging through the population almost unchecked. The grim reality of infection rates indicates that when Zagury's subjects return home, at least one of them is likely to come in contact with the virus naturally. Only when this happens can the effectiveness of the vaccine be determined.

Interleukin-2

Dick Howser had a headache. And it wasn't a night he could *afford* a headache. In a few minutes ABC Television would switch on its cameras, and a worldwide audience would settle back to watch baseball's 1986 All-Star game. As manager of the Kansas City Royals, the World Series champions, Howser was given the honor of leading the American League team that night. It was another plum, another perk, in what had been a year of triumph. It should have been a night to treasure. But he had this headache.

Actually, Howser had been hurting for days, and he was beginning to worry. After the game—which his American Leaguers won three to two—he finally agreed to fly home for a checkup.

Howser's doctor didn't like what he heard: the persistent pulse of the pain, its location, its duration. Worse, the patient seemed confused, disoriented, fuzzy. The doctor asked Howser some routine questions: Did he recognize the baseball executive—and close friend—standing next to him? Well, no. Did his team win or lose yesterday? Uh, they won. What was the score? The All-Star manager had no idea.

Tests revealed that Howser had a glioblastoma, a vicious form of malignant brain tumor striking only half a dozen out of every 100,000 people. He would immediately undergo surgery and begin therapy. Even so, there was a very good chance he could die within a few months.

But for close to a year, Dick Howser managed to hold the disease at bay. Howser's doctor, Skip Jacques of the Huntington Medical Research Institutes in Pasadena, California, refused to claim a cure or even predict a lengthy remission. He boasted of only one thing: For a time, Dick Howser beat the odds, and he beat them courtesy of interleukin-2.

Hundreds of amino acids long, interleukin-2 is made naturally by the lymph glands and is responsible for helping T cells—major components of the immune system—grow and divide. The more numerous and aggressive T cells are, the better chance they have of combating bodily invaders, including cancers. Scientists have long known that if interleukin-2 could be harnessed therapeutically, it could go a long way in battling malignancies.

The technique Jacques and other doctors use is relatively simple: A few of a patient's T cells are withdrawn from the body, isolated in dishes, and mixed with interleukin-2 that has been derived from animals or manufactured recombinantly.

"Mixing interleukin-2 with T cells is a little like giving a mean drunk a drink," Jacques says. "It makes them much fiercer." And much more numerous. When the doctors return and open their dishes, they've got a teeming population of excited T cells. Reintroduced into the patient's body, the cells hunt down a malignancy and attack it. Indeed, like bloodhounds, they may sometimes be exposed to the scent of their quarry before the chase begins: While the T cells are still being grown in the lab, doctors often drop in a few of the patient's cancer cells to sensitize the hunters to the prey.

Interleukin-2 is now being used experimentally to treat all manner of cancers, from body-wide systemic diseases like leukemia to localized tumors like Howser's. As similar as the chemistry of the different treatments is, the mechanics vary. Leukemia can be treated with a simple interleukin-2 injection; cancers like Howser's demand a more complicated treatment. The patient's harvested T cells are mixed into a plasma goo made up of a calcium, nutrients, and a little extra interleukin-2—"to keep the cells nice and vicious," Jacques says. Rolled into a ball to approximate the size of the now-absent tumor, the plasma is inserted into the hole left in the brain. "A brain tumor is a little like a tennis ball in a bowl of Jell-O," says Jacques. "You can take the ball out, but you can't be sure how much fuzz was left behind. And it's the fuzz we're going after."

Some patients may need just one treatment; others, several. Howser received two in his last nine months. Even the most optimistic study shows that interleukin-2 was effective in just 31 percent of malignancies. In the case of diseases like Howser's, however, in which survival rates are less than 2 percent, interleukin-2's success rate looks good.

Good enough, in fact, to get people like Jacques thinking about the future. "I hate to sound like a homeopath," he says, "but this treatment is a natural treatment. One day we may even see people taking preventive doses of interleukin-2 just to keep their immune systems up. This could lead practically anywhere."

But interleukin-2 has some serious side effects, including liver damage, fluid retention, kidney damage, and psychological problems such as hallucinations and severe mood disturbances. One of the goals of protein research is to develop methods for removing the side-effect-producing elements in interleukin-2 while retaining its therapeutic properties.

Despite the considerable problems to be overcome, Jacques is convinced that immunotherapies like monoclonal antibodies and interleukin-2 represent the future of cancer care. "The new treatments have gotten us off the constant merry-go-round of chemotherapy," he explains. "Chemo gets the cancer cell count down, but too often, it doesn't get that last cell. In theory, the immune system should be able to do that. We're just helping it along."

Human Growth Hormone

More than a decade ago, as an intern in pediatric endocrinology, Ron Rosenfeld first met an eleven-year-old patient named Dennis Palmer (not his real name). Dennis was suffering from a serious case of childhood growth deficiency and had been brought to Rosenfeld for treatment. For the next eleven years Rosenfeld met with his patient almost weekly, administering carefully controlled doses of a newly discovered protein known as human growth hormone (hGH). Extracted from the pituitary glands of human cadavers, hGH was expensive and in limited supply, but in patients like Dennis, it seemed to do the trick. Over the course of eleven years the boy grew steadily taller until, by age twenty-two, he had finally moved in the range of normal height for his age.

But in 1984 Dennis began having trouble. When he showed up for one of his weekly treatments, Rosenfeld noticed that his gait had become awkward, his step wobbly. Within a few weeks his speech became labored and slurred. Over time, dementia set in. Stripped of motor and speech skills, the patient lost all touch with his surroundings. By 1985 Dennis Palmer was dead, a victim of an extraordinarily rare illness known as Creutzfeldt-Jakob disease.

What worried Rosenfeld most was that Creutzfeldt-Jakob bore a striking resemblance to an obscure disease known as kuru, which appears almost exclusively among primitive New Guinea tribesmen. Western doctors who had treated kuru victims suspected that the disease was caused by a tribal funeral custom in which portions of the brain of the deceased were eaten by mourners; when the brain tissue was ingested, so was a naturally occurring, disease-causing chemical known as prion. Was it possible that prion was also present in brain-derived hGH? The answer turned out to be yes. Within a few months three other patients receiving the growth hormone had died of Creutzfeldt-Jakob. The Food and Drug Administration (FDA) pulled hGH from the shelves, a move that left thousands of growth-hormone-deficient children without any treatment at all. The only alternative was to develop a safe synthetic form of hGH. Genentech Incorporated, a bioengineering firm in California, had been working on a synthetic hGH substitute for several years. "But by 1985," explains

Rosenfeld, who had been casually involved with Genentech's work, "it became obvious that the work had to be completed fast and that the FDA had to grant its approval of the stuff."

In the fall of that year the FDA did just that, licensing prion-free hGH for therapeutic use. For Rosenfeld the moment was more than a breakthrough. "The kind of patient we see most often in pediatric endocrinology is the child with growth deficiency," he says. "What were we supposed to do in 1985? Stop treating them? With recombinant technology we suddenly had the capability to synthesize unlimited amounts of safe hGH and to do so faster and cheaper. At the moment, about twenty thousand people worldwide are receiving the medication."

To be sure, even lab-created hGH is pricey. The hormone sells for up to $35 per milligram; a year's treatment can run between $5,000 and $25,000, and some children must be on medication for 5, 10, or even 15 years. Rosenfeld concedes that this raises some ethical questions. "Who should pay for the treatment? Will we get into a situation where only the affluent will be allowed to grow? Worse, for those who *can* afford hGH, the question arises as to how short is too short? Will parents start giving the hormone to normal-size children in order to make them taller?"

Despite such concerns, Rosenfeld remains one of the more vocal partisans of protein tinkering. Like Sadee, he is old enough to remember the time before science knew what to do with proteins, and, like Sadee, he sees the field's potential. "Basically, the apparatus is now in place to synthesize any protein at all. What's more, we're not limited simply to copying the proteins that already exist in nature. If we wanted, we could make a super growth hormone. We could learn to make cancer-fighting proteins like interferon or a substance known as tumor necrosis factor, which shrinks malignant growths. We could manufacture vaccines against all manner of illnesses: meningitis, encephalitis, influenza, and malaria."

The field is wide open. At the Syntex Drug Company in Palo Alto, California, scientists are working on a recombinant synthesis of a hormone known as inhibin, which is capable of adjusting the fertility functions of the pituitary gland and providing safe birth control in both males and females. In other labs, studies are taking place that could synthesize vaccines for Epstein-Barr virus and foot-and-mouth disease. Elsewhere, protein researchers are working on recombinant cures for malaria.

Indeed, even the soberest scientists agree that there is nothing that the new research couldn't someday treat or cure. We don't just contain protein, the thinking goes, we *are* protein. And once you know how to handle the clay, you can make the sculpture come out any way you want.

Of course, such power carries its share of responsibilities—both ethical and scientific. Some skeptics worry that in the process of developing a new vaccine, scientists may accidentally create a new virus. It's certainly possible, and protein researchers are well aware of the dangers. Nevertheless, these scientists are also aware of the other side of the moral coin. If they can learn to make proteins that will cure or prevent a disease, isn't there an obligation to do so?

For Wolfgang Sadee and the other architects of protein structure, the answer is a resounding yes. They also have the pleasure of working in a field where there's no need to exaggerate the possibilities. "It is the responsibility of scientists not to generate optimism and hope where there is none," says Sadee. "But in the case of proteins, there is much of both."

Themes, Issues, and Ideas

1. In general, what advantages does protein manipulation offer over more conventional therapies? Why is so much expected from this field in the near future?

2. The discussion of interleukin-2 ends with a list of serious side effects caused by this treatment. The discussion of human growth hormone (hGH) also contains information about hazards. What are the possible dangers in each treatment, and what are the possible benefits? Which treatment strikes you as the safer bet, and why?

3. What does Louis Berneman of the Biological Therapy Institute call "a bugaboo ethical question?" Do you agree with him? What other ethical questions does the essay raise? How are they related? How do they differ?

Writing Strategies and Techniques

1. One way to make an unfamiliar topic more familiar to an audience is to employ similes or metaphors in which the unfamiliar is likened to the familiar. In Kluger's essay, for example, one doctor compares a brain tumor to a tennis ball in a bowl of Jell-O. Find other examples and show how they are effective.

2. Kluger links each of his medical topics to a story that includes a prominent figure and minor characters. How else do these stories resemble one another? How do they differ?

Suggestions for Writing

1. In his next-to-last paragraph, Kluger writes, "Of course, such power carries its share of responsibilities—both ethical and scientific." Write an essay in which you argue what those responsibilities are or should be on the basis of this article and other readings.

2. Kluger's subject includes some of the latest, most complex scientific areas, yet he tries to write for a generally educated audience. Write an essay in which you analyze the ways in which Kluger attempts to make topics understandable and interesting to his intended audience.

The Gene Dream

Natalie Angier

Scientists are now attempting to map the complete human genetic code, a goal whose achievement will revolutionize science and will have enormous effects on scientific ethics. Those involved in the Human Genome Initiative use some of the same biological techniques described by Jeffrey Kluger in the preceding essay, but they attack similar problems on a vastly more ambitious scale. Unlocking the human gene code may be science's greatest dream—or nightmare—in the twenty-first century.

In this essay, which first appeared in American Health *magazine, science writer Natalie Angier focuses on health as a point of view that organizes her exploration of a problem whose implications extend well beyond medicine. Angier, a free-lance writer based in New York City and author of* Natural Obsession: The Search for the Oncogene *(1988), draws on her expert knowledge of this essay's subject.*

At first glance, the Petersons* of Utah seem like a dream family, the kind you see only on television. They're devout, traditional and very, very loving. Bob Peterson works at a hospital near home to support the family while he finishes up a master's program in electrical engineering. Diane, who studied home economics at Brigham Young University, is a full-time wife and mother. And her time is certainly full: The Petersons have five sons and two daughters, ranging in age from two to thirteen. (As Mormons, the parents don't practice birth control.)

The children are towheaded, saucer-eyed, and subject to infectious fits of laughter. During the summer months, the backyard pool is as cheerily deafening as the local Y. Says Diane, "Our kids really like just spending time together."

Yet for all the intimacy and joy, the Petersons' story is threaded with tragedy. One of the daughters has cerebral palsy, a nerve- and

*Not their real name.

muscle-cell disorder. The malady isn't fatal, but the girl walks with great difficulty, and she's slightly retarded. Three of the other children suffer from cystic fibrosis, a devastating genetic disease in which the lungs become clogged with mucus, the pancreas fails, malnutrition sets in, and breathing becomes ever more labored. Thus far, their children's symptoms have been relatively mild, but Bob and Diane know the awful truth: Although a person with cystic fibrosis may live to be twenty or even thirty, the disease is inevitably fatal.

"Right now, the kids don't act sick," says Bob. "They go on thinking, 'I have a normal life,'" But, he admits softly, "We know it won't last forever. If they do get bad, then we won't have a choice. We'll have to put them in a hospital."

The Petersons realize their children's ailments aren't likely to be cured in the immediate future, but they're battling back the best way possible. Bob, Diane, and their seven children, as well as the three surviving grandparents, have all donated blood samples to biologist Ray White and his team at the University of Utah in Salt Lake City. Scientists are combing through the DNA in the blood, checking for the distinctive chemical patterns present only in cystic fibrosis patients.

Their work is part of a vast biomedical venture recently launched by the government to understand all the genes that either cause us harm or keep us healthy. It's medicine's grandest dream: By comprehending the genome—the complete set of genetic information that makes us who we are—in minute detail, scientists hope an answer to answer the most enigmatic puzzles of human nature. The effort is so immense in its scale and goals that some have called it biology's equivalent of the Apollo moonshot, or the atom bomb's Manhattan project.

In fact, it's the most ambitious scientific project ever under taken; it will cost a whopping $3 billion and take at least fifteen years to complete. By the time researchers are through, they will have deciphered the complete genome. They'll have drawn up a detailed genetic "map," with the size, position, and role of all 100,000 human genes clearly marked. And they'll have figured out each gene's particular sequence of chemical components, called nucleotides.

Though there are only four types of nucleotides, represented by the letters A, T, C, and G, spelling out all the combinations that make up our total genetic heritage will fill the equivalent of one million pages of text. "What we'll have," says Dr. Leroy Hood, a biologist at the California Institute of Technology in Pasadena, "is a fabulous 500-volume 'encyclopedia' of how to construct a human being." Nobel laureate Walter Gilbert goes so far as to describe the human genome as "the Holy Grail of biology."

Some scientists, however, think their colleagues are chasing a will-o'-the-wisp. Current genetic engineering techniques, say critics, are too embryonic to attempt anything as massive as sequencing the entire genome. Dr. Robert Weinberg of the Whitehead Institute in Cambridge, MA, calls the whole project "misguided" and doubts that scientists will gain major insights even if they can sequence it.

Still, researchers involved in the Human Genome Initiative insist the knowledge will revolutionize the fields of medicine, biology, health, psychology and sociology, and offer a bounty of applications. Using advanced recombinant DNA techniques, scientists will pluck out the genes that cause the 4,000 known hereditary diseases, including childhood brain cancer, familial colon cancer, manic depression, Huntington's disease—the neurological disorder that killed folk singer Woody Guthrie—and neurofibromatosis, or Elephant Man's disease. Beyond analyzing rare inherited disorders, researchers will glean fresh insights into the more common and complicated human plagues, such as heart disease, hypertension, Alzheimer's, schizophrenia, and lung and breast cancer. Those studies will enable scientists to develop new drugs to combat human disease.

But the Genome Initiative is not restricted to the study of sickness. As biologists decode the complete "text" of our genetic legacy, they'll be asking some profound questions: Are there genes for happiness, anger, the capacity to fall in love? Why are some people able to gorge themselves and still stay slim, while others have trouble losing weight no matter how hard they diet? What genetic advantages turn certain individuals into math prodigies, or Olympic athletes? "The information will be fundamental to us *forever,*" says Hood, "because that's what we are."

The most imaginative scientists foresee a day when a physician will be able to send a patient's DNA to a lab for scanning to detect any genetic mutations that might jeopardize the patient's health. Nobel laureate Paul Berg, a biochemistry professor at Stanford, paints a scenario in which we'll each have a genome "credit card" with all our genetic liabilities listed on it. We'll go to a doctor and insert the card into a machine. Instantly reading the medical record, the computer will help the doctor to put together a diagnosis, prognosis, and treatment course. Says Caltech's Hood, "It's going to be a brave new world."

Coping with that new world will demand some bravery of our own. Once our genetic heritage has been analyzed in painstaking detail, we'll have to make hard choices about who is entitled to that information, and how the knowledge should be used. This technology is proceeding at an incredible rate, and we have to be sure that it doesn't lead to a discrimination in jobs, health insurance or even basic rights, says Dr. Jonathan Beckwith, a geneticist at Harvard Medical School. "We don't want a rerun of eugenics, where certain people were assumed to be genetically inferior, or born criminals."

For better or worse, politicians are convinced that the knowledge is worth seeking. This year, Congress has earmarked almost $50 million for genome studies and, if current trends continue, by 1992 the government should be spending about $200 million annually. Opponents worry the price tag could leave other worthy biomedical projects in the lurch.

Even at that level of funding, the genome project could be beyond the resources of any single country. That's why research teams from Europe, Asia, North America, and New Zealand have joined to form the Human Genome Organization. Among other goals, the newly created consortium plans to distribute money for worthwhile projects worldwide. Meanwhile, the Paris-based Center for the Study of Human Polymorphism distributes cell samples to researchers and shares their findings through an international data bank.

In this country, Nobel laureate James Watson, the co-discoverer of the molecular structure of DNA, is in charge of human genome research at the National Institutes of Health. And Dr. Charles Cantor, a highly respected geneticist from New York's Columbia University, has accepted the top spot at the Department of Energy's Human Genome Center.

The Genetic Haystack

The Genome Initiative is sure to affect everybody. Doctors estimate that each of us carries an average of four to five severe genetic defects in our DNA. The majority of those mutations are silent: They don't affect you. However, if you were to marry someone who carries the same defect, you could have a child who inherits both bad genes and is stricken with the disease.

Most genetic flaws are so rare that your chances of encountering another silent carrier are slim—let alone marrying and conceiving a child with such a person. But some defects are widespread. For example, five out of one hundred harbor the mutant cystic fibrosis gene; seven out of one hundred blacks carry the trait for sickle cell anemia. Bob and Diane Peterson are both cystic fibrosis carriers—but they didn't realize their predicament until they gave birth to afflicted children.

For all the improvements of the last ten years, prenatal diagnosis techniques remain limited. Doctors can screen fetuses for evidence of about 220 genetic disorders, but most of the tests are so time-consuming and expensive they won't be done unless family history suggests the child may have a disease.

One reason it's difficult to screen for birth defects is that most genes are devilishly hard to find. The 50,000 to 100,000 genes packed into every cell of your body are arrayed on 23 pairs of tiny, sausage-shaped chromosomes, which means that each chromosome holds a higgledy-piggledy collection of up to 4,400 genes. Scientists cannot look under a microscope to see the individual genes for cystic fibrosis, Down's syndrome, or any other birth defect; instead, they must do elaborate chemical operations to distinguish one human gene from another. So daunting is the task of identifying individual genes that scientists have determined the chromosomal "address" of only about 2 percent of all human genes. "It's like finding a needle in a haystack," says Utah's Ray White.

Scientists must first chop up the twenty-three pairs of human chromosomes into identifiable pieces of genetic material and then study each fragment separately. To make the cuts, they use restriction enzymes—chemicals that break the bonds between particular sequences of nucleotides, the chemical components of genes.

Normally, restriction enzymes snip genetic material at predictable points, as precisely as a good seamstress cuts a swatch of fabric. But scientists have found that the enzymes also cut some fragments at unexpected places, yielding snippets that are longer than normal. It turns out that these variations are inherited, and many have been linked to certain genetic abnormalities. The fragments even serve as reference points for map-making efforts. The DNA segments produced by this technique are nicknamed "riff-lips," for restriction fragment length polymorphisms (RFLPs).

In the past three years, DNA sleuths have used the technique to isolate the genes for Duchenne's muscular dystrophy, one of the most common genetic diseases; a grizzly childhood eye cancer; and a hereditary white-blood-cell disease commonly called CGD. But the technique remains labor-intensive and in some ways old-fashioned. Armies of graduate students and postdoctoral fellows do the bulk of the work, using tedious, error-prone methods.

Scientists everywhere are racing to build superfast computers to sort through chromosome samples and analyze RFLP patterns. Until they're devised, researchers are learning to make do. At White's lab, for instance, researchers have jerry-rigged a device that automatically dispenses exceedingly small samples of DNA into rows of test tubes. "It can do in two days what used to take a researcher two weeks," says a technician.

The Hapgoods Become Immortal

Despite all the technology, the genome project remains deeply human—even folksy. That's because the people donating their blood and genes are from ordinary families who happen to have something extraordinary to offer. They're families like the Petersons, whose DNA may contain clues to cystic fibrosis.

Or they're families like the Hapgoods, whose greatest claim to fame may be the ability to live long and multiply. Brenda and Sam Hapgood,* a Mormon couple in their early fifties, are plump and boisterous, and love to be surrounded by people. That may explain why, although they have five girls, four boys, three sons-in-law, two daughters-in-law and five grandchildren, they wouldn't mind having a few more kids around. Says Brenda, "I almost wish I hadn't stopped at nine!"

The Hapgoods are one of forty Utah families helping White construct a so-called linkage map of human DNA. He's trying to find chemical markers in the genome that are "linked" with certain genes. The markers will serve as bright signposts, dividing the snarl of genes into identifiable neighborhoods—just as road signs allow a traveler to pin down his location. Finding those markers is a crucial first step toward identifying the genes themselves, and for providing researchers with a decent chart of the terrain.

That's where the Hapgoods come in. To detect those tiny patches in the DNA that stand out from the background of surrounding genetic material, White must be able to compare the genomes of many related people over several generations. Mormon families are large, and they don't tend to move around much, so it's easy for White to get blood samples from many generations of a given family.

"The researchers told us there are lots of big families around," says Brenda. "What made us special was that all the grandparents were still with us."

In 1984, Brenda, Sam, their parents, and nine children all donated blood to White's researchers. Lab technicians then used a special process to keep the blood cells alive and dividing forever—ensuring an infinite supply of Hapgood DNA for study. "Our linkage families are becoming more and more important as we go to the next stage of mapping," says Mark Leppert, one of White's colleagues. "Hundreds of researchers from all over will be using the information from their DNA."

---

*Not their real name.

"We're going to go down in medical history!" Brenda says excitedly. "But you know what I'm really worried about?" one son-in-law teases her. "They might decide to clone you!"

Another reason the Hapgoods were chosen for the linkage study is because, in contrast to the Petersons, they didn't seem to have any major hereditary diseases. White wanted his general-purpose map to be a chart of normal human DNA. Ironically, however, two years after the Hapgoods first donated blood, one of the daughters gave birth to a son with a serious genetic defect known as Menkes' disease, a copper deficiency.

The child is two years old but looks like a deformed six-month-old. He has one hundred or more seizures a day. Half his brain and most of his immune system have been destroyed. Cradled in his mother Carol's arms, he moans steadily and sadly. "This is as big as he'll get," says Carol. "He'll only live to be four at the very most."

Carol and Brenda hope that the genome project will someday bring relief for Menkes victims. "We originally volunteered for the study to help the scientists out, to help their research," says Brenda. "But now we see that it could be important for people like us."

The Big Payoff

"You don't need to have the whole project done before you start learning something," says Dr. Daniel Nathans, a Nobel laureate and professor of molecular biology and genetics at Johns Hopkins University in Baltimore. "There are things to be learned every step of the way." The first spin-offs are likely to be new tests for hereditary diseases. Within one to three years, biologists hope to have cheap and accurate probes to detect illnesses known to be caused by defects in a single gene, such as susceptibility to certain kinds of cancers.

Another inherited ailment that could quickly yield to genome research is manic depression, which is also thought to be caused by an error in any one of several genes. The psychiatric disorder afflicts 1 percent of the population—2.5 million people in the United States alone—yet it's often difficult to diagnose. With the gene isolated, experts will be better able to distinguish between the disease and other mood disorders, explains Dr. Helen Donis-Keller, a professor of genetics at Washington University in St. Louis.

Of even greater relevance to the public, the Genome Initiative will give investigators their first handle on widespread disorders such as cancer, high blood pressure, and heart disease. Researchers are reasonably certain that multiple DNA mutations share much of the blame for these adult plagues, but as yet they don't know which genes are involved. Only when biologists have an itemized map of the genome will they be able to detect complex DNA patterns that signal trouble in many genes simultaneously.

As the quest proceeds, surprises are sure to follow. "There are probably hundreds or thousands of important hormones yet to be isolated," says Dr. David Kingsbury, a molecular biologist at George Washington University. Among them, he believes, are novel proteins that help nerve cells grow, or *stop* growing. Such hormones could be made into new cancer drugs that target tumors while leaving the rest of the body unscathed.

"I have an intuitive feeling that this is going to open up all sorts of things we couldn't have anticipated," says Donis-Keller. "Even mundane things like obesity and baldness—imagine the implications of having new therapies for them!"

The human genome also holds keys to personality and the emotions. Department of Energy gene chief Charles Cantor says it's estimated that half of our 100,000 genes are believed to be active only in brain cells, indicating that much of our DNA evolved to orchestrate the subtle dance of thought, feeling, memory, and desire. "There are genes that are very important in determining our personality, how we think, how we act, what we feel," says Cantor. "I'd like to know how these genes work." Donis-Keller is also curious. "Is panic disorder inherited? Is autism?" she wonders. "These are controversial questions we can start to clarify."

Like the first Apollo rocket, the Human Genome Initiative has cleared the launch pad in a noisy flame of promise. Its crew is international, and so too will be the fruits of exploration. When the human genome is sequenced from tip to tail, the DNA of many people is likely to be represented—perhaps that of the Hapgoods and the Petersons, perhaps that of a Venezuelan peasant family. "It's going to be a genetic composite," predicts Yale professor of genetics Frank Ruddle. "The Indians will work on their genomes, the Russians on theirs, the Europeans on theirs. We'll pool the data and have one great patchwork quilt.

"I get a lot of pleasure out of thinking of this as a world project. No one single person will be immortalized by the research. But it will immortalize us all."

Themes, Issues, and Ideas

1. In speculating on the possible significance of the information acquired from the Genome Initiative, Dr. Donis-Keller says, "Even mundane things like obesity and baldness—imagine the implications of having new therapies for them!" List some of the implications you imagine, both positive and negative, of the ability to alter relatively minor imperfections in appearance or behavior.

2. What are the basic elements of the genetic "map?" According to researchers, how will a knowledge of the size, position, and role of these elements be useful?

3. As Angier suggests, the information contained in an individual's genome could be abused. In what ways might this happen?

Writing Strategies and Techniques

1. Does the essay's title strike you as an effective one? In what ways do you imagine Angier hopes it will affect her audience? What effect does the rhyme create?

2. Do the scientists quoted *sound* like the conventional idea of how you think a scientist should sound? Stylistically speaking, what do the speeches in Angier's sources have in common? Do you think the quotations add to the essay? Explain.

Suggestions for Writing

1. Angier stresses the usefulness and desirability of knowing your genetic profile. Can you think of a situation in which you might *not* want to know certain features? What attitude might be elicited by the knowledge of your genetic limitations? Write an essay giving your reasons for or against knowing your entire genetic makeup.

2. This essay focuses largely on health, but as Angier herself acknowledges, issues beyond health may also be involved. Write an essay speculating on the possible uses and abuses caused by greater knowledge of the human genetic code.

When Is a Mother Not a Mother?

Katha Pollitt

> *As some of the essays in this book suggest, ethics and law are not keeping up with medical technology. Dilemmas and disputes that would have been unimaginable only a generation ago are commonplace today, and the effects of genetic engineering and advanced eugenics in the future remain a mystery. In the present day, however, the problems we face are not insoluble. Katha Pollitt addresses one of them in "When Is a Mother Not a Mother?"*
>
> *Pollitt was born in 1949 and attended Radcliffe College. She became associate editor of* The Nation, *where this essay was first published, in 1991.*

To the small and curious class of English words that have double and contradictory meanings—"moot," for example, and "cleave"—the word "mother" can now be added. Within the space of a single dazzling week this fall, this hoary old noun was redefined so thoroughly, in such mutually exclusive ways, that what it means now depends on which edition of the newspaper you read.

On October 23 in Orange County, California, Superior Court Judge Richard Parslow decided that the rightful mother of Baby Boy Johnson was not Anna Johnson, the black "gestational surrogate" who, for $10,000, carried him and birthed him, but Crispina Calvert, the wombless Asian-born woman who provided the egg from which, after in vitro fertilization with her (white) husband's sperm and implantation in Ms. Johnson, the baby grew. Declining, he said, to play Solomon and put the baby in the "crazy-making" position of having "two mothers"—or to follow California law, which defines the mother as the woman who gives birth to the child—Judge Parslow ruled that genes make the mom, as they do the dad. Anna Johnson was merely a kind of foster mother, a "home," an "environment."

One wonders what Judge Parslow would make of a headline two days later. "Menopause Is Found No Bar to Pregnancy" announced *The New York Times,* reporting that doctors had succeeded in making six prematurely menopausal women pregnant by implanting them with donated eggs fertilized in vitro with their husband's sperm. By Judge Parslow's reasoning, of course, those women are merely foster mothers, homes and environments, but so far no one has suggested this, much less called for a re-evaluation of Johnson's claim in the light of new information about the value women place on pregnancy and childbirth and the persistent (if apparently erroneous) belief that the resultant babies belong to them.

To their credit, commentators have not regarded these developments with unalloyed rapture. Perhaps they learned something from the Baby M fracas [see Pollitt, "The Strange Case of Baby M," May 23, 1987]. In that dispute, you will remember, many intelligent people persuaded themselves that the baby's rightful mother was a woman who had *no* biological connection to it, and that its real mother, Mary Beth Whitehead, was a grasping madwoman because she did not think she was, as child psychologist Lee Salk put it, a "surrogate uterus." The New Jersey Supreme Court disagreed and, lo and behold, none of the confidently predicted dire consequences ensued. Women are not regarded as too emotional to make binding contracts, as some feminists feared, nor has motherhood been more deeply consigned to the realm of instinct and mystification. The child, now a toddler, has not been destroyed or corrupted by contact with her mother: Mary Beth Whitehead, the supposed Medea of the Meadowlands, turns out to be such a good mom, in fact that *New York Times* columnist Anna Quindlen, who observed one of the child's visits, felt moved to recant her earlier anti-Whitehead position. Indeed, the only consequences have been positive: The child knows both her parents; paid Baby M–style surrogacy has been outlawed in two states, the contracts declared unenforceable in three; Noel Keane, the infamous baby broker who boasted that he had made $300,000 in fees the year of the Baby M contract, has found another métier.

As our Eastern European friends are now reminding us, however, markets must be served. The New Jersey Supreme Court put a damper on Baby M–style contract motherhood—now commonly referred to as "traditional surrogacy," as though it came over with the Pilgrims—but it seems to have spurred science and commerce on to more ingenious devices. And so we have Baby Boy Johnson. Thanks to Baby M, we are a little sheepish, a little wiser. Ellen Goodman has called for the banning of gestational surrogacy for pay; like millions of other middle-aging moms, she wonders if being able to bear a child in one's 50s is really an unmitigated blessing. But we have not yet, as a society, begun to face the underlying ideas about class, race, children and, above all, women that the new maternities rely on.

Take class. By upholding the Johnson-Calvert contract, Judge Parslow opens the door to the sale of poor women's bodies to well-off couples. It is disingenuous to claim, as does Polly Craig of the Los Angeles Center for Surrogate Parenting, that $10,000 is not enough money to motivate a woman to sell her womb, and that gestational surrogates simply enjoy being pregnant, want to help others, or wish to atone for a past abortion. Why offer payment at all, if it serves no function? And why, if gestational surrogacy is such an occasion for pleasure, altruism and moral purification, don't prosperous women line up for it? The Calverts—she a nurse, he an insurance broker—presumably possess a wide female acquaintanceship in their own income bracket, none of whom felt friendship required of them that they turn over their bodies to the Calvertian zygote. Instead the couple approached Johnson, a sometime welfare recipient, single mother and low-paid worker at Crispina Calvert's hospital.

No, money is the motivator here. Ten thousand dollars may not seem like a lot to Craig and her clients, but it's a poor person's idea of major cash—as much as 25 percent of American women earn in a whole year of full-time employment. It's quite enough to becloud good judgment. "You wave $10,000 in front of someone's face," said Anna Johnson, "and they are going to jump for it." By "someone," Johnson meant women like herself, shuttling between welfare and dead-end jobs, single, already supporting a child, with a drawerful of bills and not much hope for the future.

In a particularly nasty wrinkle, gestational surrogacy invites the singling out of black women for exploitation. It's not just that blacks are disproportionately poor and desperate, more like to be single mothers and more likely to lack the resources to sue. It's that their visible lack of genetic connection with the baby will argue powerfully against them in court. (Indeed, about the Baby Boy Johnson case hovers the suggestion that the Calverts chose Johnson for precisely this reason.) Judge Parslow's comparison of Johnson to a foster mother is interesting in view of the fact that foster mothers who grow attached to their charges and try to keep them are regarded with much popular sympathy and sometimes even succeed. But it is safe to say that few American judges are going to take seriously the claims of a black woman to a nonblack child. Black women have, after all, always raised white children without acquiring any rights to them. Now they can breed them, too.

There are those who worry about the social implications of gestational surrogacy but who still think Judge Parslow made the right choice of homes for Baby Boy Johnson. Be that as it may, Anna

Johnson wasn't suing for custody but for visitation. She wanted to be a small part of the child's life, for him to know her and for her to know him. Why would that be so terrible? As Dr. Michelle Harrison, who testified for Johnson, wrote in *The Wall Street Journal,* Judge Parslow wasn't being asked to divide the child between three parents; the Calverts had in fact so divided him when they chose to produce a baby with Johnson's help. Recent court decisions (not to mention social customs like open adoption, blended families and gay and lesbian co-parenting) have tended to respect a widening circle of adult relationships with children. Every state, for instance, gives grandparents access to grandchildren in the case of a divorce, regardless of the wishes of the custodial parent. Stepparents and lesbian co-parents are demanding their day in court. In 1986 California state courts upheld the right of a sperm donor to sue for parental rights when the artificial insemination did not involve a doctor (the old turkey baster method). Why isn't *that* prospect too "crazy-making" for California? Or, for that matter, mandatory joint custody, an innovation that California pioneered? Given the increasing number of children living outside the classic nuclear-family arrangement, and the equanimity with which the courts divide them up between competing adults, it seems rather late in the day to get all stuffy about Anna Johnson.

The most important and distressing aspect of Judge Parslow's decision, however, is that it defines, or redefines, maternity in a way that is thoroughly degrading to women. By equating motherhood with fatherhood—that is, defining it solely as the contribution of genetic material—he has downgraded the mother's other contributions (carrying the fetus to term and giving birth) to services rather than integral components of parenthood. Under this legal definition, a normally pregnant women is now baby-sitting for a fetus that happens to be her own. "In a debate over nature vs. nurture, the winner is nature," read the *New York Times* pull-quote. But why define "nature" as DNA rather than as the physiological events of pregnancy and birth? There's nothing "natural" about egg donation, which involves the hormonal priming of an infertile woman, the extraction of an egg by delicate technology, fertilization in a dish with masturbated sperm and implantation of the zygote in another. And to call pregnancy and childbirth "nurture" seems a feeble way to describe the sharing of the body and the risking of health, well-being and even life itself that is required to bring another life into existence. Like "parenting," another fashionable buzzword, "nurture" is a bland social-sciency word that belittles a profound relationship and masks the role of women in gender-neutral language.

The picture of pregnancy as biological baby-sitting has many sources. It's as old as Aeschylus, who had Athena acquit Orestes of matricide in *The Eumenides* on the ground that mothers are merely "nurses" of men's seed, and as new as those ubiquitous photos of fetuses seeming to float in empty space. But its major proponents today are the anti-abortionists. In order to maximize the claims of the fetus to personhood, they must obscure the unique status of the pregnant woman: She is not making a person, because the fertilized egg already *is* a person; she's only caring for it, or housing it, or even (as one imaginative federal judge wrote), holding it captive. Ironically, the movement that claims to celebrate motherhood is led by its own logic to devalue the physical, emotional and social experience of pregnancy. If unwanted pregnancy is just an "inconvenience," how serious an occasion can a *wanted* pregnancy be? If mass adoption is the answer to 1.6 million annual abortions, how strong can the ties be between mother and newborn? When ethicists fret that professional women may resort to gestational surrogacy to avoid "putting their careers on hold," they betray more than antiquated views about the capacities of pregnant women to get out of bed in the morning. They reveal their own assumption that pregnancy is a trivial, empty experience with nothing positive about it except the end product, the genetically connected baby. They then compound the insult by attributing this view to a demonized fantasy of working women—cold, materialistic, selfish, corrupted by "male values"—that is, those held by the ethicists themselves. Is there any evidence that working women—even MBAs, even lawyers—see pregnancy this way? Who do the pundits think are mobbing infertility clinics and signing on for donated eggs? A couple needs two incomes just to pay the doctors.

Why is the primacy of genetics so attractive? At the moment, genetic determinism is having one of its periods of scientific fashion, fueling the fear that an adopted baby will never "really" be yours. At the same time, hardening class distinctions make the poor, who provide most adoptive babies, seem scary and doomed: What if junior took after his birth parents? It's not an accident that sperm donors and now egg donors are largely recruited among middle-class professionals—they're not just white, they're successful and smart—and that the commercial aspects of the transaction ($50 for sperm, $1,500 for an egg) are disguised by calling it a "donation." You can buy a womb because wombs don't really matter, but if the all-important DNA must come from a third party, it should come as a gift between equals.

The main reason for our love affair with genes, though, is that men have them. We can't get all the way back to Aeschylus, with man as seed sower and woman as flowerpot (although we acknowledge it in our language, when we call women "fertile" or "infertile," like farmland). Women, we now know, have seeds too. But we can discount the aspects of procreation that women, and only women, perform. As the sociologist Barbara Katz Rothman has noted, Judge Parslow's decision follows the general pattern of our society, in which women's experiences are recognized to the extent that they are identical with men's, and devalued or ignored to the extent that they are different. Thus, Mary Beth Whitehead won back her parental rights because the New Jersey Supreme Court acknowledged her *genetic* contribution: Baby M was half hers. And the postmenopausally pregnant, egg-donated women achieve parental rights by being married to their babies' fathers, not through their own contributions.

Of the two practices—actually a single practice with two social constructions—gestational surrogacy is clearly the more repellent, but to see its real meaning it must be looked at with egg donation as its flip side. Taken together they bring pregnancy into line with other domestic tasks traditionally performed by women—housework, child care, sex. Performed within marriage, for no pay, these activities are slathered with sentimentality and declared beyond price, the cornerstone of female self-worth, family happiness and civilization itself. That is the world inhabited by prosperous married women now able to undergo pregnancy thanks to egg donation. That the egg is not their own is a detail; what counts is that they are able to have a profound and transforming life experience, to bond prenatally with their baby and to reproduce the genes of their husband. But look what happens when the checkbook and the marriage certificate are in the other hand: Now the egg is the central concern, pregnancy and childbirth merely a chore, prenatal bonding a myth. Like all domestic labor performed for pay—housecleaning, baby-sitting, prostitution—childbearing in the marketplace becomes disreputable work performed by suspect, marginal people. The priceless task turns out to have a price after all: about $1.50 an hour.

What should happen now? Some suggest that new methods of parenthood require a new legal principle: pre-conception intent. Instead of socio-bio-ethical headaches—Who is the mother? Who is the father? What's best for the child? What's best for society?—we could have a simple rule of thumb: Let the seller beware. But at what cost to economic fairness, to principles of bodily integrity, to the nonmarketplace values that shape intimate life? Why not let the *buyer* beware? We cannot settle thorny questions by simply refusing to ask them.

A doctrine of pre-conception intent could, moreover, turn ordinary family law into fruit salad. Most pregnancies in the United States, after all, are not intended by either partner. They occur for dozens of reasons: birth-control failure, passion, ignorance, mixed messages, fear. The law wisely overlooks these sorry facts. Instead, it says Here is a child, here are the parents, next case. Do we really want to threaten a philosophy aimed, however clumsily, at protecting children from pauperism and abandonment? If pre-conception intent caught on with the general public, no single mother would be able to win child support; no single father could win parental rights. A woman's right to abortion could be conditioned on her pre-conception intent as evidenced, for example, by her use or neglect of birth control. In fact, in several states, laws have already been proposed that would restrict abortion to women who could prove contraceptive failure (a near impossibility, if you think about it, which is probably the point).

Perhaps the biggest problem with pre-conception intent, however, is that it ignores almost everything about the actual experience of becoming a parent of either sex. Planning to have a baby is not the same as being pregnant and giving birth, any more than putting on sexy underwear is like making love. The long months of pregnancy and the intense struggle of childbirth are part of forming a relationship with the child-to-be, part of the social and emotional task of parenthood. Not the only part, or even a necessary part—I am not suggesting that adoptive parents do not "really" become mothers and fathers. But is there a woman who feels exactly the same about the baby in the ninth month, or during delivery or immediately after, as she did when she threw away her diaphragm? When friends and relatives assure ambivalent parents-to-be not to worry, they'll feel differently about the baby when they feel it kick, or go through Lamaze together, or first hold their newborn in their arms, are they only talking through their hats? Whether or not there is a purely biological maternal instinct, more mothers, and more fathers, fall in love with their babies than ever thought they would. Indeed, if they did not, most babies would die of neglect in their cribs. How can we respect this emotional and psychological process—indeed, rely on it—and at the same time forbid it to the Mary Beth Whiteheads and the Anna Johnsons? I don't think we can.

Pre-conception intent would wreak havoc on everyone—men, women and children—and for what? To give couples like the Calverts a risk-free shot at a genetically connected baby. It makes more sense to assimilate surrogacy to already existing values and legal principles. In my view, doing so would make payment illegal and pre-birth contracts unenforceable. We don't let people sell their organs or work at slave wages; we don't hold new mothers to pre-delivery adoption arrangements; we don't permit the sale of children; we don't enforce contracts that violate human dignity and human rights. We respect the role of emotion and change and second thoughts in private life: We let people jilt their fiancées, and we let them divorce their spouses. True, we uphold prenuptial agreements (a mistake, in my opinion), but they're about property. If someone signed a premarital contract never to see his children again in the case of a divorce, what judge would uphold it? Those children weren't even conceived when that contract was signed, the judge would point out—and furthermore they have rights that cannot be waived by others, such as the right to contact with both parents after divorce. The children of surrogates—even nongenetic surrogates like Anna Johnson—have the right to know the woman though whose body and through whose efforts they came into the world. We don't need any more disposable relationships in the world of children. They have quite enough of those already.

In order to benefit a very small number of people—prosperous womb-infertile couples who shun adoption—paid surrogacy does a great deal of harm to the rest of us. It degrades women by devaluing pregnancy and childbirth; it degrades children by commercializing their creation; it degrades the poor by offering them a devil's bargain at bargain prices. It creates a whole new class of emotionally injured children rarely mentioned in the debate: the ones the surrogate has already given birth to, who see their mother give away a newborn, or fight not to.

It is hard for Americans to see why they shouldn't have what they want if they can pay for it. We would much rather talk about individual freedoms and property rights, rational self-interest and the supposed sanctity of contracts, than about the common good or human dignity, or the depths below which no person should be allowed to sink. But even we have to call it quits somewhere. As we decided 130 years ago, the buying and selling of people is a very good place to draw the line.

Themes, Issues, and Ideas

1.   Much of Pollitt's analysis hinges on the differing definitions of "motherhood." What are the various ones she mentions? Which seems most reasonable to you? Why?

2. Pollitt brings up slavery several times in the course of her argument. How far do you think the analogy between slavery and surrogate motherhood should go?

3. Pollitt's perspective is obviously a feminist one. Or is it? Give your opinion, and back it up with examples from the essay.

Writing Strategies and Techniques

1. "We cannot settle thorny questions by simply refusing to ask them," says Pollitt. How is this statement reflected in her style? What does that style accomplish for the reader?

2. Pollitt is very good at punctuating an argument with an effective, direct statement. How does this technique further her argument? Give examples.

Suggestions for Writing

1 Write an essay discussing another biomedical ethics issue from Katha Pollitt's point of view.

2. Is it fair to compare biomedical ethics with slavery? Write an essay that uses quotations from Pollitt's piece to support your opinion.

The Pushers in the Suites

Cynthia Cotts

Medical science may be progressing at lightning speed, but business ethics are not. The result, as Cynthia Cotts points out in her essay, can often be the twisting of new medical discoveries to suit corporate purposes. Through a complex web of factors, the drug Xanax, which was developed to treat panic disorders, is becoming itself something like a disease.

Cotts is a New York writer who covers drug issues in modern America. Her work has appeared in numerous magazines and newspapers.

Ever had a panic attack? If not, you will soon. The Upjohn Company is busy educating the public about panic disorder, and while the diagnosis is legitimate, Upjohn's interest is proprietary: It manufactures Xanax, the only drug approved for the treatment of panic.

Symptoms of a panic attack include rapid heartbeat, chest pain and dizziness. The typical patient is a women who, after several attacks in a shopping mall or in traffic, ends up too scared to go out at all. But lo and behold: Symptoms disappear if she starts taking Xanax.

Xanax (*a k a* alprazolam) belongs to the class of minor tranquilizers known as benzodiazepines. Compared with other classes of drugs used to treat panic, Xanax kicks in quicker and producers fewer unpleasant side effects. Patients like Xanax, and doctors share their gratification. But after several months, when the consensus is that patients should be weaned off the medication, they find out the bad news: They're addicted. (Hereafter, the term "dependent" will be used. The psychiatric establishment reserves "addiction" to describe the behavior associated with obtaining illegal drugs.)

Many panic patients need more than 4 milligrams of Xanax a day. On that dosage, they're sure to become so dependent that if they stop medication abruptly, they might have a seizure and die. Even if they taper off slowly, withdrawal symptoms often persist for weeks. Experts recommend a strict tapering regime that lasts months—but even then, panic symptoms may come back worse than ever.

Xanax isn't the only way to treat panic. The best doctors tailor treatment to the individual, often using first medication and then "cognitive/behavioral" therapy, designed to help the patient analyze her fears and then confront them. And while research suggests that psychotherapy has a lower rate of relapse than drug therapy, Upjohn thinks medication works best.

The story begins in 1981, when Xanax was introduced. By 1987 the palindromic upstart had replaced Valium as America's most prescribed tranquilizer. Soon afterward, clinical trials established Xanax as an effective treatment for panic disorder, and in 1990 the Food and Drug Administration approved Xanax for panic. In recent years Halcion and Xanax have accounted for almost half of Upjohn's earnings. But as Halcion came under siege in 1991 for the unpredictable responses it provoked (think of George Bush in Japan), Upjohn began to depend on Xanax. It raised the price of the drug by 10 percent last year, then again by 9 percent this past February. This year revenues from the panic pill are expected to reach well over $600 million.

To maintain profits, Upjohn needs cheerleaders like Jerilyn Ross, president of the Anxiety Disorders Association of America. Ross makes speeches encouraging panickers to seek treatment, and the earnest brunette recently appeared in a video news release paid for by Upjohn to push Xanax (VNRs are the TV equivalent of advertorials, promotional clips slickly produced to resemble the news [see Steven T. Taylor and Morton Mintz, "A Word From Your Friendly Drug Company," October 21, 1991]). Of course, Ross needs Upjohn as well. Upjohn has contributed to the A.D.A.A. every year since 1984, and last year it bankrolled an A.D.A.A. opinion poll about panic.

In 1989 Upjohn gave $1.5 million to the American Psychiatric Association, which used the "unrestricted" grant to produce educational videos about panic, anxiety, and depression. (Technically, unrestricted means "no strings attached.") "People don't understand mental illness, and there's a valid educational job to be done," says John Blamphin, the A.P.A.'s director of public affairs. "On the other hand, Upjohn has medications for anxiety disorder and panic. The more people know about the illnesses and get into treatment, the more likely their medications are going to be prescribed."

When asked about Upjohn's promotion of panic, company spokesman Godfrey Grant explained, "We're trying to do something that is in our interest, but it is also a legitimate project to make the public more aware" of a disabling illness.

At the A.P.A.'s annual meeting this past May in Washington, Upjohn's self-interest was symbolized by a black Xanax sign on a pole. The sign revolved high above the convention center floor, towering over exhibits for other over-hyped psychoactive drugs, such as Prozac and BuSpar. At the foot of the pole, Upjohn's Panic Interactive Learning Center seated eight at a time. Curious visitors could don headphones and touch their personal video screen to activate segments offering the medical overview, case histories or the physicians' perspective. Naturally, all the doctors urged medication for panic.

Upjohn wasn't just hawking at the A.P.A. convention; it also funded a three-hour symposium, "Panic Disorder: Consensus for the '90s." Speakers included Dr. James Ballenger of the Medical University of South Carolina, who declared that tranquilizer dependence is "probably the most controversial issue in psychiatry" today. In a recent interview Ballenger blamed the uproar on media hysteria, pointing out that the benefits of Xanax as a treatment for panic usually outweigh its risks. "Patients hear things that unnecessarily scare them," he intoned, "and they feel guilty about becoming dependent. But dependence is not a weakness. It's a physiological condition." Translation: Even though a patient who tries to kick Xanax cold turkey can expect insomnia, nausea and hallucination, she shouldn't think of herself as an *addict.*

Drug companies reach into deep pockets to fund their marketing campaigns—after all, drug manufacturing is the most profitable industry in the country. In 1990 the top ten pharmaceutical companies had a profit margin three times that of the average Fortune 500 company. Over the past decade drug prices have risen at almost triple the rate of inflation.

Despite its fabulous profits, the industry is now on the run. The F.D.A. has tightened standards for advertising and promotion, and the F.B.I. is targeting illicit distribution of pharmaceuticals. A handful in Congress have begun calling for regulatory controls.

In defense, the pill czars have been pouring money into marketing. By now their methods of directly pitching products are well known. At meetings sponsored by drug companies, doctors are wined, dined and dazzled by promoters of the host's drug du jour. Magazine ads like those for Rogaine make heady promises, then list the side effects in fine print. But the industry's most insidious activity is still a trade secret: marketing and lobbying disguised as public education.

Drug companies use "educational" campaigns to whip up consumer demand and to instill antiregulatory sentiment.

In addition to direct lobbying of lawmakers, drug companies channel their message through front groups that present themselves as "objective." The sleaziest kind of front group is the nonprofit, often no more than a tax exempt I.D. number, a ream of letterhead and a room in the office of a P.R. company. Invoking a distinguished membership, the group presents the "scientific" side of an issue to lawmakers and medical professionals—without disclosing that a drug company supplied both the medium and the message.

A less cynical type of front is the patient advocacy group. After taking money from the drug companies, advocates become their unwitting mouthpieces. For example, when representative Pete Stark began drafting a bill for prescription accountability last year, he received calls from such advocates as the Anxiety Disorders Association, the California Cancer Pain Initiative and the Oncology Nursing Society. They were concerned that Stark's legislation would stop patients from getting the drugs they needed—a misconception promoted by lobbyists. Not coincidentally, each group is dependent on pharmaceutical largesse.

Nine states already have a drug law known as triplicate prescription, or "trip scrip." Every time a doctor writes a prescription for narcotics, amphetamines or barbiturates, he or she has to file one copy with the state health agency. Variations exist: New York has added benzodiazepines—the class that includes Xanax—to its regulated pharmacopoeia. Under Oklahoma's electronic system, pharmacists report prescriptions just as they report charges on a credit card. Stark's proposal would take it one step further, requiring pharmacists nationwide to report all prescriptions.

One goal of trip scrip is to monitor the black market. Truckdrivers, for example, stay up with amphetamines, and crackheads come down with Xanax. In Washington, where Xanax is known on the street as "Double X," street use is growing and dangerous. The drug can be lethal when mixed with alcohol, and abusers often land in the emergency room.

In addition to tracking "scrip doctors," who knowingly prescribe to abusers, trip scrip identifies doctors with bad prescribing habits. According to recent estimates, careless doctors have put 2 million senior citizens in the United States at risk of becoming dependent on tranquilizers. No one knows how many of them are currently hooked.

New York's monitoring of "benzos" is widely viewed as a success. The program has cut prescriptions, reduced street sales and overdoses, and saved the state Medicaid program $37 million in two years. "Nobody is saying benzodiazepines are bad drugs," explains Arthur Levin, head of New York's Center for Medical Consumers and a champion of trip scrip. "They're drugs whose risks have been understated, and which are prescribed for longer than they should be."

Attempts to control legal drug abuse and dependence have long been opposed by the pharmaceutical industry, which rightly fears such regulation will cut into profits. Trip scrip is no exception. After feeling the pinch in New York, leading benzo manufacturers Upjohn and Hoffman-LaRoche joined forces to prevent the model from being copied elsewhere. The legerdemain in this one campaign shows just how sophisticated the industry's covert operations can be.

Early last year a faithful tribe of professionals were invited to a symposium called "Triplicate Prescription: Issues and Answers." The symposium was sponsored by the Medical Society of the State of New York and was funded in part by an "unrestricted grant" from Upjohn to the nonprofit arm of MSSNY.

On February 28, 1991, prominent doctors and patient advocates convened in a New York City hotel. They argued that New York's program had kept patients from getting their tranquilizers—and had stigmatized them to boot. One speaker, Dr. Michael Weintraub of the University of Rochester, explained how a study he performed "proves" that in New York doctors are prescribing inappropriate drugs to patients who need benzos. Weintraub's study, which Levin calls "junk," was partially underwritten by Hoffman-LaRoche.

The one-sidedness of the symposium left some participants confused. What about the advantages—the Medicaid savings, the drying up of the black market? "Maybe I was too naïve," one audience member recalls, "but I was looking for a spirited debate." (According to Michael Delaney of MSSNY, state health officials declined to attend.)

In February 1991 the society released a sixteen-page symposium report, "News of New York," that proclaimed the failure of trip scrip. The report parroted Upjohn's official objections to trip scrip: It doesn't cure drug abuse, it stops patients from getting medication, it's too expensive. Soon after publication, copies came into the hands of the Committee for Responsible Use of Psychiatric Medication, a nonprofit organization of medical professionals that is funded by Upjohn. The committee attached a cover letter to "News of New York" and commenced a mass mailing to medical professionals and lawmakers nationwide. Upjohn's name did not appear anywhere.

One lawmaker was curious about the committee's home office in New York: 114 Fifth Avenue, (212)886-3125. When he called, a recorded message invited him to press zero. A receptionist answered,

"G.T.F.H. Can I help you?" Gross Townsend Frank Hoffman—114 Fifth Avenue, (212) 886-3100—is a P.R. agency specializing in health care. Upjohn is one of its clients.

According to Upjohn spokeswoman Florence Steinberg, "The committee has sent out mailings on a variety of issues." She acknowledged that Gross Townsend "helped put together the materials" in the symposium package, but added, "The committee and MSSNY are totally separate."

Ultimately, the committee's mailing served Upjohn's political purposes: It helped prevent New York's experiment from spreading. Last year, when the California legislature met to consider monitoring benzos, a doctor in attendance brandished the report as proof that the New York model didn't work. The California lawmakers decided to leave benzos alone.

Further evidence of Upjohn's agenda can be found in a February 1991 interoffice memo written by senior marketing analyst Robert Martin. The subject was a Gallup poll questioning 200 New York physicians about the effects of trip scrip on their prescribing habits. Citing the high number of objections to the regulation, Martin concluded, "The Gallup survey has effectively identified several of the key issues that must be addressed at the 28 February meeting in New York."

Was the poll used to spin the symposium? Florence Steinberg said Upjohn commissioned the poll "to provide insight into public opinion. If the information was available [for the symposium], then it added more to the debate." At Upjohn, though, "information" is just sugarcoating. Don't swallow before you read the fine print.

Themes, Issues, and Ideas

1. According to Cotts, what are the means by which Xanax has been sold to the general public?

2. After reading Cotts's piece, what is your opinion of Upjohn's marketing techniques?

Writing Strategies and Techniques

1. Jerilyn Ross, according to Cotts, is an "earnest brunette" and a "cheerleader." Are such references fair or unfair? Why or why not?

2. Is "The Pushers in the Suites" a polemical essay, a piece of investigative reporting, or something else? Explain your answer.

Suggestions for Writing

1. Does Cotts seem to have a favorable impression of medical science? What can you say about the fairness of her attitude?

2. Write a letter to Cotts from a Xanax user.

The Frontier Within

J. Madeline Nash

Medical progress has raised a host of questions about the twenty-first century: What developments will genetic engineering bring? Will fetal tissue be used in medicine? Will AIDS and cancer ever be cured? But of all medical frontiers, neurology is the most mysterious. What is the brain? Is there a physical cause for every mental, moral, and spiritual state? What does a more advanced neuroscience bode for human life?

In the following reading, J. Madeline Nash looks at some of the possibilities being raised about the brain. This essay originally appeared in a special issue of Time *magazine in 1992 dealing with the future.*

Contemplate for a moment a tangle of seaweed tossed up on the shore. This is what a neuron looks like, surrounded by a thicket of tiny tendrils that serve as communications channels. Now multiply that neuron 100 billion times. Crammed into the skull of every human individual are as many neurons as there are stars in the Milky Way. Each one of these receives inputs from about 10,000 other neurons in the brain and sends messages to a thousand more. The combinatorial possibilities are staggering. The cerebral cortex alone boasts 1 million billion connections, a number so large, marvels neuroscientist Gerald Edelman in his recent book about the brain, *Bright Air, Brilliant Fire,* that "if you were to count them, one connection per second, you would finish counting some 32 million years after you began."

Assembled by nature and honed by evolution, the convoluted 3-lb. organ positioned between our ears represents a triumph of bioengineering, one that continues to elude comprehension and defy imitation. "The brain," declares molecular biologist James Watson, co-discoverer of the physical structure of DNA, "is the most complex thing we have yet discovered in our universe." The quest to understand the biology of intelligence is likely to occupy the minds of the world's best scientists for centuries to come. The task may prove more challenging than those alive today suppose, requiring perhaps new breakthroughs in physics and chemistry. Meanwhile, the knowledge spawned by this search promises to transform society. Here is what lies ahead:

Computers Will Emulate the Brain But Not Replace It

From the wheeled cart to the printing press, from the telephone to the airplane, inventions have enormously expanded the repertoire of human capabilities, and this trend will continue, even accelerate. In this century computers have provided instant access to awesome number-crunching power and a vast storehouse of information. In coming centuries they will augment and amplify human skills in far more astounding ways. Thus, while the brains will not undergo much in the way of biological evolution, humans, assisted by ever more powerful computers, will become capable of far greater intellectual feats. "We won't recognize any difference in brains themselves," emphasizes Maxwell Cowan, chief scientific officer of the Howard Hughes Medical Institute in Bethesda, Maryland. "But we will recognize enormous differences in what brains know and understand."

Intriguingly, the brain's expanding knowledge of itself has begun to suggest radical new approaches to computer design. Like the brain, the computers of the future will not execute tasks in serial lockstep but will be capable of doing a million things in parallel. The chips of which they are composed may well be silicon, but they will mimic biological systems in almost every other way. A tantalizing hint of what the future holds comes from a type of computer known as a neural network. Employing the time-tested tactic of trial and error, these assemblages of artificial neurons have already "learned" to recognize scribbled handwriting, deduce principles of grammar and even mimic the acoustic sensitivity of the barn owl. By cobbling several of these sensory systems together, scientists will certainly be able to create, say, a robot that combines a barn owl's hearing with the ability to track moving objects and issue an ear-piercing hoot. Home gardeners may well employ an artificial owl to chase away rabbits and deer, but they will hardly consider it an intellectual equal. "Let me put it this way," laughs Caltech physicist Carver Mead, a legendary designer of computer chips, "Two hundred years from now, I will not be having this conversation with a piece of silicon."

The Deaf Will Hear, the Blind See, the Lame Walk

By the end of the century, if not before, scientific insight into the perceptual centers of the human brain should vanquish these ancient afflictions. Already scientists have developed a cochlear implant that bypasses nonfunctioning hair cells in the ear and stimulates the nerve leading to the auditory cortex of the brain. Says Michael Merzenich, a neurophysiologist at the University of California, San Francisco: "We know that these inputs to the brain are distorted, yet the patients who have worn them for a while insist that what they hear sounds perfectly normal." What appears to occur, says Merzenich, is that the brain somehow manages to adjust its connections to make sense of the distortions it receives. This clear demonstration of the plasticity inherent in the adult brain lends hope that scientists of the future will succeed in performing other similar feats. One of these might well be the ability to equip artificial limbs with electronic "neurons" that can respond to signals relayed by the brain. These circuits might even include the equivalents of the axons and dendrites that link one neuron to another.

Almost certainly, scientists will master techniques for stimulating injured neurons to regenerate themselves. The brains and spinal columns of adult mammals do not possess this ability, at least not yet. A clue that this should be possible comes from frogs and salamanders, whose central nervous systems miraculously regrow following injury. Scientists have discovered several proteins that may eventually be deployed to rejuvenate broken spinal cords and damaged optic nerves. "I don't hold out too much hope for bionic man." says Michael Stryker, a colleague of Merzenich's who specializes in vision. "I think we will get there faster using biological techniques."

Genetic Engineering Will Extend to Mental Traits

Scientists are currently absorbed in tracking down genes believed to be responsible for such mental illnesses as manic depression and schizophrenia. Eventually, they can be expected to broaden their goals and seek out the genetic tool kit for building such intellectual traits as musical talent, mathematical genius and, above all, personality. Shyness, for instance, appears to have a genetic basis; assertiveness and hair-trigger anger probably do as well. Like it or not, predicts Dr. Lewis Judd, chairman of the psychiatry department at the University of California at San Diego, "We are going to find that the attitudes we take, the choices we make, are far more influenced by heredity than we ever thought."

For the next century or two, if not beyond, schemes for improving the brain through genetic tinkering are likely to be confounded by a combination of social taboos, legal restrictions and sheer biological ignorance. But when the genes that underlie personality and behavior are isolated and understood, society will reach a critical ethical divide. A Pandora's box of options that were not available in centuries past will suddenly pop wide open. Should would-be parents who learn a fetus has inherited a strong likelihood of developing a serious but treatable mental illness opt for an abortion? Should they choose gene therapy to replace the defective DNA in their newborn child's brain cells? And while they're contemplating all this, might they not consider conferring on their offspring desirable traits like intelligence?

Mind Reading Will Be More Than a Parlor Game

The machines that make images of the brain today are large, expensive contraptions that only major medical centers can afford. But just as computers have become ever smaller, cheaper and more powerful, so will the ultrafast successors to present-day positron-emission tomography and magnetic-resonance imaging scanners. Washington University neurologist Marcus Raichle predicts, in fact, that the "brain scopes" of the future will make a big splash at Disneyland and other theme parks. One can imagine lines of vacationers waiting to have their thoughts and emotions imaged in garish hues.

But these machines will also be put to serious purpose. Consider, for example, the tantalizing evidence that certain patterns of brain activity correlate with higher achievement levels. Competing educational strategies might someday be judged by whether they stimulate specific areas of the brain and how strongly. "Is phonics really the best way to teach reading?" muses Dr. Raichle. "Or is it just another silly idea? By looking at the brain, I think we'll discover the answer to that question." And to others as well. Many mothers-to-be have wondered whether playing music and reciting poetry can influence embryonic brain development in desirable ways. Someday they may be able to judge for themselves.

More important, tomorrow's brain scanners will be able to assess intellectual strengths and weaknesses in preschool children. A wide spectrum of mental weaknesses will become targets for early intervention. Dyslexia could be diagnosed in infancy, the time when brain plasticity is highest. Therapies could then be monitored by charting changes in neuronal firing patterns.

Brains Will Be Healthier, Happier

Prominent mainstays of the pharmacopoeia of the future will be compounds that prevent nerve cells from dying. Much of the devastation caused by stroke is believed to occur because the directly injured neurons release massive quantities of the neurotransmitter glutamate. Normally, tiny bursts of glutamate act as signals between one neuron and another, triggering the brief opening of minuscule channels that allow calcium to pass through the cell's protective membrane. Too much glutamate, however, causes the channels to remain open too long, permitting an abnormal, and lethal, influx of calcium. Soon drugs that mop up excess glutamate or block its action may make this sort of stroke-related brain damage as preventable as tissue damage from gangrene. Similar strategies should likewise succeed in protecting neurons from the ravages of Alzheimer's disease.

Needless to say, expanding knowledge of the brain's complex biochemistry and how it goes awry will bring about more effective treatments for depression and schizophrenia, panic attacks and obsessive compulsions, alcoholism and drug addiction. Along the way, scientists will gain profound insights into the biochemical signals that create the astounding range of human emotions. "Which peptides make you sad, which ones make you happy, and which ones make you feel just grand?" wonders Columbia University neuroscientist Eric Kandel. That knowledge could conceivably translate into an ability to fine-tune those states at will — through either pharmacology or sophisticated biofeedback techniques.

Certainly nothing in the past 100,000 years of cultural evolution can prepare future generations for the moment when science lays bare, as it most certainly will, the secrets of the human mind. "We will be rendered naked," predicts Tufts University philosophy professor Daniel Dennett, "in a way that we've never been naked before. The mind boggles at the varieties of voyeurism, eavesdropping, and intrusion that will become possible." Concepts like good and evil, free will and individual responsibility, will presumably survive the upheaval, but not before being shaken to their deepest foundations. Imagine, for a moment, that a psychiatrist could peer into the psyche of a serial killer. Could the doctor see what was wrong? If he could, would he know how to fix it?

The great adventure on which modern neuroscience has embarked will end up challenging our most cherished concepts of who we are. "In the end, we will even figure out how this tissue in our skulls produces the states of self-awareness we refer to as consciousness," ventures John Searle, a philosopher of science at the University of California, Berkeley. But just as understanding the Big Bang has not permitted humans to create new universes at will, understanding consciousness will probably not allow us to construct an artificial brain. Besides, says University of Iowa neurologist Dr. Antonio Damasio, "a brain is not likely to work without a body." At the very least, a disembodied brain would be extremely disoriented and terribly unhappy.

In the coming centuries, one imagines, the desire to create monstrous caricatures of ourselves will dissipate. At long last, we will reclaim the awe and wonder our predecessors reserved for machines and turn them back toward our biological selves. Like Narcissus, we will behold the image of our minds and lose ourselves in endless admiration.

Themes, Issues, and Ideas

1. Is it fair to say that Nash has an optimistic attitude toward the future? Are there any points in her piece when you sense that the future might not be so bright?

2. "Like Narcissus, we will behold the image of our minds and lose ourselves in endless admiration." Does this sound like a particularly healthy or appealing destiny?

3. According to Nash, "[c]oncepts like good and evil, free will, and individual responsibility will presumably survive the upheaval ... " Why? And what would a world be like without these things? Is such a world compatible with the rosy view of the future Nash describes?

Writing Strategies and Techniques

1. What do you think of the "experts" Nash quotes? Are they the best judges of the future and the consequences of neuroscience? Give your opinion of scientists as futurists.

2. What is the basic structure of Nash's piece? What moves it forward? How is Nash's tone partially achieved through this structure?

Suggestions for Writing

1. Write a medical history of the twenty-first century, based on the assumption that all of Nash's predictions came true.

2. Write a horror story that includes at least four of Nash's predictions.

MAKING CONNECTIONS

1. One constant throughout these essays has been the place of the doctor as chief medical practitioner. What do these essays suggest about the evolution of the profession?

2. Write a response to J. Madeline Nash's rosy view of science, using some of the perspectives gleaned from Katha Pollitt and Cynthia Cotts.

3. In their respective essays, Jeffrey Kluger and Natalie Angier address similar topics. Considering these topics, which author do you think writes best for a college student audience? Write an essay weighing the merits of both writers from a student's point of view.

4. It might be said that the medical profession of Lewis Thomas's youth was most concerned with understanding and predicting death, while modern advances have the luxury of being concerned with life. Yet, as some of the other authors here point out, medical tinkering with human life is not always such a blessing. Using the evidence and arguments available to you from the essays in this chapter, write an essay in which you argue for your point of view of the proper limits of medical intervention.

5. What are some future biomedical debates that might be in an anthology called *Readings for the 22nd Century?*

CHAPTER NINE

Science, Technology, and Human Living

Adapting to a Changing World

Liberty, Quality, Machinery

Aldous Huxley

Technology *is usually defined as "applied science, " or as the realization in practical terms of the power of the knowledge produced by scientific inquiry into the workings of the natural world. But what are the results of technology when it is applied to human life? And how will the ceaseless advances of technology enhance (or inhibit) human life in the future?*

These questions about technology and its role in the future have been frequently raised in modern times. Aldous Huxley (1894–1963), one of the twentieth century's most prominent novelists, prophets, and social critics, addressed the issue of technology throughout his career. A prolific writer, he is most widely known as the author of Brave New World *(1932), a science-fiction version of a deplorable future that became a famous symbol in itself like Thomas More's* Utopia *and George Orwell's* 1984. *In this essay, from his collection* Tomorrow and Tomorrow and Tomorrow *(1956), Huxley finds hope in the fact that the do-it-yourselfer—of all people—can escape the oppressiveness of technology.*

John Ruskin deplored the railway engine. It might be useful; but why, why did it have to *look* like a railway engine? Why couldn't it be dressed up as a fiery dragon, breathing flames as it rushed along, and flapping iron wings? Machines, Ruskin thought, and all their productions are intrinsically hideous. If we must have them, let it be with Gothic trimmings.

To William Morris, power-driven contraptions were odious, even in fancy dress, even when disguised as wiverns or basilisks. He objected to them on aesthetic grounds, and, as a sociologist, he loathed them. In the process of creating ugliness and multiplying monotony, machines had destroyed the old order and were turning the men and women who tended them into brutes and automata. Morris's ideal was the Middle Ages. Not, it goes without saying, the real Middle Ages, but an improved Victorian version of Merrie England—clean, kindly, and sensible, free from bad smells and religious dogmas, from bubonic plague and papal indulgences and periodic famines. A snug little world of healthy, virtuous craftsmen, craftswomen, and craftschildren, producing not for somebody else's profit but for their own use and for the greater glory of God, and having, in the process, a really wonderful time.

Today we like to think of applied science as a kind of domesticated djinn, indentured to the service of the no-longer-toiling masses. Half a century ago Tolstoy saw in applied science the greatest threat to liberty, the most powerful instrument of oppression in the hands of tyrants. "If the arrangement of society is bad (as is ours) and if a small number of people have power over the majority and oppress them, every victory over Nature will inevitably serve to increase that power and that oppression. This is what is actually happening." It was for this reason (among others) that Tolstoy advocated a return to handicraft production within village communities, which were to be, as nearly as possible, self-sufficient. His greatest disciple, Mahatma Gandhi, preached the same doctrine—and lived long enough to see the nation, whose independence he had won, adopt a policy of all-out industrialization.

It is easy enough to detect the flaws in these classical arguments against machinery and in favor of a return to handicraft production. All of them fail to take into account the most important single fact of modern history—the rapid, the almost explosive increase in human numbers. Within the combined life spans of Tolstoy and Gandhi the population of the planet was more than trebled. Let us consider a few of the aesthetic, psychological, and political consequences of this unprecedented event in human history.

By no means all the ugliness of which Ruskin and Morris complained was due to the substitution of machine production for handicrafts. Much of it was simply the result of there being, every year, more and more people. Beyond a certain point, human beings cannot multiply without producing an environment which, at the best, is predominantly dreary, soul-stultifying, and hideous, at the worst foul and squalid into the bargain. There have been beautiful cities of as many as two or three hundred thousand inhabitants. There has never been a beautiful city of a million or over. The old, unindustrialized parts of Cairo or Bombay are worse than fully industrialized London, or New York, or the Ruhr. Man cannot live satisfactorily by bricks and mortar alone. This would be true even if the bricks and mortar were put together in decent houses. In actual practice a little good architecture has always been surrounded, in the world's great capitals, by vast expanses of mean and dreary squalor. In the small cities of earlier centuries, filth and ugliness surrounded the splendid churches and palaces; but these slums were to be measured in acres, not in square miles. Small quantities of man-made squalor can be taken with impunity, particularly when associated with the woods and fields which surrounded the small city on every side, endowing it, as an urban unit, with a kind of over-all beauty of its own. This kind of over-all urban beauty has never existed in a great metropolis, most of which must always seem, by the mere fact that it goes on and on, unutterably dull, hideous and soul-destroying. What Ruskin and William Morris were really objecting to was the consequence, not of machinery, but of Victorian fertility combined with improved sanitation and cheap food from the New World. Families were large and, for the first time in history, most of their members survived infancy and grew up to produce large families of their own—and, in the process, to create hundreds of monster cities, tens of thousands of square miles of squalor and ugliness.

Thanks to the advanced technology of which Tolstoy and Gandhi so passionately disapproved, one-third, more or less, of the earth's twenty-five hundred million inhabitants enjoy unprecedented prosperity and longevity, and the remaining two-thirds contrive, however miserably, to remain alive, on the average, for thirty years or so. A return to handicraft production would entail the outright liquidation, within a few years, of at least a billion men, women, and children. Moreover, if, while returning to handicraft production, we were to maintain our present standards of cleanliness and public health, numbers would tend once more to increase, and within half a century the liquidated billion would be back again, and ripe for new famines and another liquidation. Where Nature kills the majority of human beings in childhood, the practice of contraception is suicidal. But where human beings understand the principles of sanitation and where, consequently, most of the members of large families survive to become parents in their turn, it is unrestricted fertility that threatens to destroy not merely happiness and liberty, but, as numbers outrun resources, life itself. Generalized death control imposes the duty of generalized birth control. Gandhi was aware of the population problem and hoped (he can hardly have believed) that it could be solved by the inculcation of sexual continence among young married couples. In actual fact it is unlikely to be solved until such time as the physiologists and pharmacologists can provide the Asiatic and African masses with a contraceptive pill that can be swallowed, every few weeks, like an aspirin tablet. Within a generation of the discovery of such a pill, world population may be stabilized—somewhere, let us hope, on this side of five thousand millions. After which it may be possible to raise the standard of Far Eastern, Middle Eastern, Near Eastern, African, and Caribbean living to levels somewhat less subhuman than those now prevailing—a feat which will require all man's good will, all his best intelligence and (far from a return to handicraft production) a yet more advanced technology.

But the fact that man cannot now survive without advanced technology does not mean that Tolstoy was entirely wrong. Every victory over Nature does unquestionably strengthen the position of the ruling minority. Modern oligarchs are incomparably better equipped than were their predecessors. Thanks to fingerprinting, punched cards, and IBM machines, they know practically everything about practically everyone. Thanks to radios, planes, automobiles, and the whole huge armory of modern weapons, they can apply force wherever it is called for, almost instantaneously. Thanks to the media of mass communication, they can browbeat, persuade, hypnotize, tell lies, and suppress truth on a national, even a global scale. Thanks to hidden microphones and the arts of wire tapping, their spies are omnipresent. Thanks to their control of production and distribution, they can reward the faithful with jobs and sustenance, punish malcontents with unemployment and starvation. Reading the history, for example, of the French Revolution and Napoleon's dictatorship, one is constantly amazed at the easy-going ineptitude of earlier governmental procedures. Until very recent times such liberties as existed were assured, not by constitutional guarantees, but by the backwardness of technology and the blessed inefficiency of the ruling minority.

In the West our hard-won guarantees of personal liberty have not, so far, been offset by the political consequences of advancing technology. Applied science has put more power into the hands of the ruling few; but the many have been protected by law and, to make assurance doubly sure, have created (in the form of trade unions, cooperatives, political machines, and lobbies) great systems of power to counterbalance the power systems of the industrialists, government officials, and soldiers, who own or can command the resources of modern technology. Where, as in Russia or in Nazi Germany, the masses have not been protected by law and have been unable to create or maintain their own defensive power systems, Tolstoy's predictions have been fulfilled to the letter. Every victory over Nature has been at the same time a victory of the few over the many. And all the while the machinery of mass production is growing larger, more elaborate, increasingly expensive. In consequence its possession is coming to be confined more and more exclusively to the wielders of financial power and the wielders of political power—to big business, in a word, and big government. Never was there a greater need for the old Eternal Vigilance than exists today.

But here let us note a development entirely unforeseen by Ruskin and Morris, by Tolstoy, Gandhi, and most even of the more recent philosophers and sociologists who have viewed with alarm man's increasing dependence on the machine as producer of necessities and luxuries, the dispenser of entertainment and distractions, the fabricator of synthetic works of art, of tin or plastic surrogates for the immemorial products of manual skill. While big machines have been growing spectacularly bigger, new races of dwarf machines have quietly come into existence and, at least in America, are now proliferating like rabbits. These little machines are for private individuals, not for the great organizations directed by the wielders of financial and political power. They are produced by big business; but their purpose, paradoxically enough, is to restore to the individual consumer some, at least, of that independence of big business which was his in that not-too-distant past, when there was no big business to depend on. Small power tools, in conjunction with new gadgets of every variety, new synthetic raw materials, new paints and putties, new solders and adhesives, have called into existence (and at the same time have been called into existence by) a new breed of artisans. These new artisans pass their working hours in a factory that turns out mass-produced goods, in an office that arranges for their distribution, in a store that sells them, a truck or train that delivers them to their destination. But in their spare time—and a forty-hour week leaves a good deal of spare time—they become craftsmen, using the tools and materials supplied by the mass producers, but working for themselves, either for the sheer fun of it, or because they cannot afford to pay someone else to do the job, or else (deriving pleasure from what they are forced to do by economic necessity) for both reasons at once.

The "do-it-yourself" movement has its comic aspects. But then so does almost everything else in this strange vale of tears and guffaws, which is the scene of our earthly pilgrimages. The important fact is not that amateur plumbing is a fruitful subject for the cartoonist, but that something is actually being done to solve, at least partially, some of the problems created by a technology rapidly advancing, in industry after industry, toward complete automation. Millions of persons have grown tired of being merely spectators or listeners, and have decided to fill their leisure with some kind of constructive activity. Most of this activity is utilitarian in character; but there are also many cases in which these new handicraft workers of the machine age supplement their utilitarian hobbies with the practice of one of the fine arts. There is a countless host, not only of amateur plumbers, but also of amateur sculptors, painters, ceramists. Never before has there been so general an interest in art (you can buy books on Picasso and Modigliani at the five-and-ten), and never before have there been so many wielders of paintbrushes and modelers of clay. Are we then (in spite of all that Ruskin and Morris and their followers said about machinery) on the threshhold of a new Golden Age of creative achievement? I wonder. . . .

Art is not one thing, but many. Metaphysically speaking, it is a device for making sense of the chaos of experience, for imposing order, meaning, and a measure of permanence on the incomprehensible flux of our perpetual perishing. The nature of the order imposed, of the significance discovered and expressed, depends upon the native endowments and the social heredity of the person who does the imposing, discovering, and expressing. And this brings us to art as communication, art as the means whereby exceptionally gifted individuals convey to others their reactions to events, their insights into the nature of man and the universe, their visions of ideal order. All of us have such visions and insights; but whereas ours are commonplace, *theirs* are unique and enlightening. Art-as-communication is pretty pointless, unless the things communicated are worth communicating. But even in cases where they are not worth communicating, art is still valuable—if not to the persons who look at it, at least to those who produce it. For art is also a method of self-discovery and self-expression; an untier of knots, an unscrambler of confusions; a safety valve for blowing off emotional steam; a cathartic (the medical metaphor is as old as Aristotle) for purging the system of the products of the ego's constant auto-intoxication. Art-as-therapy is good for everybody—for

children and the aged, for imbeciles and alcoholics, for neurotic ado-
lescents and tired businessmen, for prime ministers on weekends and
monarchs on the sly (Queen Victoria, for example, took drawing lessons from Edward Lear, the author of *The Book of Nonsense*). Art-as-
therapy is even good for great artists.

> To me alone there came a thought of grief;
> A timely utterance gave that thought relief,
> And I again am strong.

Besides being a masterpiece of art-as-communication, Wordsworth's
great Ode was also a (to him) most salutary dose of art-as-therapy.
Involving, as they do, the highest manual skill, sculpture, painting,
and ceramics are more effective as therapy than is poetry, at any rate
Western poetry. In China writing is a branch of painting—or perhaps
it would be truer to say that painting is a branch of the fine art of
writing. In the West the writing even of the noblest poem is a purely
mechanical act and so can never afford psychological relief comparable to that which we obtain from an art involving manual skill.

The spread of amateur housebuilding, of amateur painting and
sculpture, will soothe many tempers and prevent the onset of a host
of neuroses, but it will not add appreciably to the sum of architectural,
pictorial, and plastic masterpieces. At every period of history the
number of good artists has been very small, the number of bad and
indifferent artists very great. Because immense numbers of people
now practice art as therapy, it does not follow that there will be any
noticeable increase in the output of masterpieces. Because I feel better for having expressed my feelings in a daub, it does not follow that
you will feel better for looking at my daub. On the contrary, you may
feel considerably worse. So let us practice art-as-therapy, but never
exhibit the stuff as though it were art-as-communication.

We should not even expect to see an increase in the amount of
good craftsmanship. In the past good craftsmanship has been contingent on two factors—intense and prolonged specialization in a single
field, and ignorance of every style but that which happens to be
locally dominant. Before the invention of foolproof machines nobody
became an acknowledged master of his craft without going through a
long apprenticeship. Moreover, the Jack-of-All-Trades was, prover-
bially and almost by definition, the master of none. If you wanted to
have your house thatched, you went to the thatcher; if you needed a
table, you applied to the joiner. And so on. Specialization in the crafts
and arts goes back to remotest antiquity. Archaeologists assure us that
the great paleolithic cave paintings were executed, in all probability,

by teams of traveling artists, whose native skill had been increased by constant practice. As for flint arrowheads, these were manufactured in places where the raw material was plentiful and distributed to consumers over enormous areas.

Our new artisans, with their power tools and amazingly diversified raw materials, are essentially Jacks-of-All-Trades, and their work consequently is never likely to exhibit the kind of excellence which distinguishes the work of highly trained specialists in a single craft. Moreover, the older craftsmen took for granted the style in which they had been brought up and reproduced the old models with only the slightest modification. When they departed from the traditional style, their work was apt to be eccentric or even downright bad. Today we know too much to be willing to follow any single style. Scholarship and photography have placed the whole of human culture within our reach. The modern amateur craftsman or amateur artist finds himself solicited by a thousand different and incompatible models. Shall he imitate Phidias or the Melanesians? Miró or van Eyck? Being under no cultural compulsion to adopt any particular line, he selects, combines, and blends. The result, in terms of art-as-significant-communication, is either negligible or monstrous, either an insipid hash or the most horrifying kind of raspberry, sardine, and chocolate sundae. Never mind! As a piece of occupational therapy, as a guarantee against boredom and an antidote to television and the other forms of passive entertainment, the thing is altogether admirable.

Themes, Issues, and Ideas

1. What does technology have to do with what Huxley calls "the most important single fact of modern history—the rapid, the almost explosive increase in human numbers?" According to Huxley, what has been the cause of these numbers and what are their potential results?

2. With what reasoning does Huxley support this contention: "Every victory over Nature does unquestionably strengthen the position of the ruling minority?" Do you agree? Why, or why not?

3. What, according to Huxley, is the reason for technology's failure in the West to tyrannize its inhabitants?

Writing Strategies and Techniques

1. After discussing the "do-it-yourself" movement, Huxley ends his paragraph with ellipsis marks (. . .). What is the effect of this technique?

2. By the end of a paragraph that begins with a discussion of metaphysics, Huxley has cited Aristotle, Queen Victoria, and Edward Lear as examples. What is the effect of the mixture in this list of intellectual status? Does Huxley use this same device elsewhere?

Suggestions for Writing

1. Huxley says that art gives meaning to the chaos of experience and can act as an antidote to combat technology's potential evils. Do you agree with him? Write an essay in which you attack, support, or modify Huxley's views about the relations between art and technology.

2. Huxley claims that liberty was formerly ensured "not by constitutional guarantees, but by the backwardness of technology and the blessed inefficiency of the ruling minority." Write an essay analyzing the ways in which Huxley tries to show that advanced technology is a danger to human liberty.

Old News Is Good News

Bill Moyers

Bill Moyers is the host of a long-running interview series on public television. Over the past ten years, Moyers has interviewed leading thinkers, politicians, writers, and scholars in America. A conscientious critic of the press in this essay, he writes about the danger of mixing "hard news" and entertainment. As a journalist and producer as well as an interviewer, Moyers has seen many changes in American mass media, and it is these changes he addresses here.

This piece was originally published in New Perspec tives Quarterly.

Mine is the reporter's perspective—one small fish in that vast ocean we call the media. I want to put in a word for the craft, for reporting, the old-fashioned kind.

When I began working for *Harper's* in 1970, I thought I understood what the word "news" meant, where information stopped and entertainment began; what newspapers did that was different from television. Since then, we have witnessed a media explosion, the effect of which is like standing at ground zero seconds after the explosion of the atomic bomb. Walter Lippmann told us that journalism is a picture of reality people can act upon. What we see today is a society acting upon reality refracted a thousand different ways.

Where is America's mind today? It's in the organs, for one thing. Now folks can turn on a series called *Real Sex* and watch a home striptease class; its premier was HBO's highest-rated documentary for the year. Or they can flip over to NBC News and get *I Witness Video*. There they can see a policeman's murder recorded in his cruiser's camcorder, watch it replayed and relived in interviews, complete with ominous music. Or they can see the video of a pregnant woman plunging from a blazing building's window, can see it several times, at least once in slow motion. Yeats was right: "We have fed the heart of our fantasies, and the heart's grown brutal from the fare."

I wonder if *Real Sex* and *I Witness Video* take us deeper into reality or insanity? How does a reporter tell the difference anymore in world where Oliver Stone can be praised for his "journalistic instincts" when he has Lyndon Johnson tell a cabal of generals and admirals: "Get me elected and I'll get you your war."

Rolling Stone dubs all this the "New News." Straight news—the Old News by *Rolling Stone's* definition—is "pooped, confused, and broke." In its place a new culture of information is evolving—"a heady concoction, part Hollywood film and TV, part pop music and pop art, mixed with popular culture and celebrity magazines, tabloid telecasts, cable and home video." Increasingly, says the magazine, the New News is seizing the function of mainstream journalism, sparking conversation and setting the country's social and political agenda. So it is that we first learn from Bruce Springsteen that the jobs aren't coming back. So it is that inner-city parents who don't subscribe to daily newspapers are taking their children to see the movie *Juice* to educate them about the consequences of street violence; that young people think Bart Simpson's analysis of America more trenchant than many newspaper columnists; that we learn just how violent, brutal and desperate society is, not from the establishment press, but from Spike Lee, Public Enemy, the Geto Boys and Guns N' Roses.

I don't want to seem a moralist. The public often knows what's new before we professionals do. But there's a problem. In this vast pounding ocean of media, newspapers are in danger of extinction. I don't mean that they're going to disappear altogether—but I do feel that we are in danger of losing the central role the great newspapers have historically played in the functioning of our political system.

Once newspapers drew people to the public square. They provided a culture of community conversation. The purpose of news was not just to represent and inform, "but to signal, tell a story and activate inquiry." When the press abandons that function, it no longer stimulates what the American philosopher John Dewey termed "the vital habits" of democracy—"the ability to follow an argument, grasp the point of view of another, expand the boundaries of understanding, debate the alternative purposes that might be pursued."

I know times have changed, and so must the newspapers. I know that while it's harder these days to be a reporter, it's also harder to be a publisher, caught between *Sesame Street* and Wall Street—between the entertainment imperatives that are nurtured in the cradle and survival economics that can send a good paper to the grave.

Taken together, these assumptions and developments foreshadow the catastrophe of social and political paralysis. But what's truly astonishing about this civic disease is that it exists in America just as a series of powerful democratic movements have been toppling autocratic regimes elsewhere in the world. While people around the globe are clamoring for self-government, millions of Americans are feeling as if they have been locked out of their homes and are unable to regain their rightful place in the operation of democracy. On the other hand, those same millions want to believe that it is still in their power to change America.

The Center for Citizen Politics at the University of Minnesota reports that beneath America's troubled view of politics "is a public that cares very deeply about public life. This concern is a strong foundation for building healthy democratic practices and new traditions of public participation in politics."

People want to know what is happening to them, and what they can do about it. Listening to America, you realize that millions of people are not apathetic; they want to signify; and they will respond to a press that stimulates community without pandering to it; that inspires people to embrace their responsibilities without lecturing or hectoring them; and that engages their better natures without sugar-coating ugly realities or patronizing their foibles.

I sense we're approaching Gettysburg, the moment of truth, the decisive ground for this cultural war—for publishers especially. Americans say they no longer trust journalists to tell them the truth about their world. Young people have difficulty finding anything of relevance to their lives in the daily newspaper. Non-tabloid newspapers are viewed as increasingly elitist, self-important, and corrupt on the one hand; on the other, they are increasingly lumped together with the tabloids as readers perceive the increasing desperation with which papers are now trying to reach "down-market" in order to replace the young readers who are not replacing their elders.

Meanwhile, a study by the Kettering Foundation confirms that our political institutions are fast losing their legitimacy; that increasing numbers of Americans believe they are being dislodged from their rightful place in democracy by politicians, powerful lobbyists and the media—three groups they see as an autonomous political class impervious to the long-term interests of the country and manipulating the democratic discourse so that people are treated only as consumers to be entertained rather than citizens to be engaged.

Themes, Issues, and Ideas

1. Moyers quotes a number of experts—philosophers, scientists, etc.—in his essay. Do you find these authorities convincing? Does Moyers himself come across, or qualify, as an "expert?"

2. "I wonder," Moyers writes, "if *Real Sex* and *I Witness Video* take us deeper into reality or insanity?" Is this a fair question? Why or why not? Compare shows like the ones Moyers mentions to public broadcasting shows like Moyers's own.

Writing Strategies and Techniques

1. The author of this essay takes a very cautious, modest tone throughout. What effect does this have on the reader? How does he create this tone? Give examples.

2. "I don't want to seem a moralist," says Moyers. Why not? *Is* Moyers a moralist?

Suggestions for Writing

1. Write an essay refuting Bill Moyers, copying his style as closely as possible.

2. Write a transcript of a Bill Moyers interview show on which you discuss television with Moyers. Or, write a transcript in which Bart Simpson is the interview guest.

The Politics of Culture

Jan Wenner

Jan Wenner is the founder and editor of Rolling Stone, *the first major countercultural magazine of the 1960s to go mainstream. As the editor of* Rolling Stone, *Wenner has had a guiding influence on American mass culture for twenty-five years. Culture is not just a sidelight, Wenner maintains; "hard news" gets late what "culture news" gets early. Since his magazine was directly attacked by Bill Moyers in his essay "Old News is Good News," Wenner was invited by* New Perspectives Quarterly *to respond.*

Around the world and in our own country, the battles being waged have more to do with culture than with politics. Mainstream media in the U.S. ignored cultural news throughout the 1960s and '70s, yet it has been the cultural events of those years—changing sexual and family values, growing cynicism and alienation among the young, ethnic and cultural tensions, etc. that have come to define the political values of the '90s in the U.S.

The so-called "entertainment media" have been following these changes all along. In fact, *Rolling Stone* was founded on the premise that cultural news was important political news. We saw early on that cultural, artistic and, ultimately, political styles all take shape in the popular-culture cauldron.

People can debate high-brow versus low-brow culture, or rail against the entertainment media's frivolity. But the fact remains that though rap and riots, sexual roles and family values are finally being covered in the traditional press, all these issues were explored much earlier, in much greater depth and with more feeling in the entertainment media.

The mainstream press is now having to play catch-up, and it's going to be an uphill battle because it has for so long misinformed the public by misreading what's really on people's minds. Worse, they have repeated the most fallacious remarks by politicians about what's really at stake in this country, without examining those remarks—which, by the way, is the role the great newspapers *used* to play so well.

In a way, the traditional press is coming full circle. After years and years of missing the story and losing its readership, this political season—particularly *The New York Times* and *Newsweek*—have really focused on the issues. They have gone into great depth on economic issues and they are no longer allowing politicians to make statements that are merely repeated and left unchallenged.

Television coverage, on the other hand, continues to be abysmal. With regard to the Democratic and Republican conventions this summer, the television anchors and reporters simply stood in the way of what TV does best, which is to present the news unfiltered. During both conventions, talking heads focused on the technicalities of speeches and how they were delivered rather than what was said. A very limited number of people actually had anything valuable to add to the political proceedings. Certainly no one needed a pompous Dan Rather telling them what was going on. These "personalities" need to get out of the way and let Americans see and judge the political process for themselves.

De-massifying the Media

No one should lament the fact that a decentralization and defusion of news has taken place. Such a change does not mean that we will now depend on *Us Magazine* to tell us about economic issues, or Bart Simpson to enlighten us about foreign affairs. It's not an either/or proposition. Pure political reporting is extremely important and cannot be replaced. But I daresay that these days Bart Simpson is more attuned to the American people's cynicism about the values and priorities of this country than any number of other programs that are on the air.

As news outlets have decentralized—through cable and alternative press publications—there has also been an integration of cultural and political news. It seems that the mainstream media have finally realized that they cannot understand the workings of this country unless they understand the politics of culture. This integration of cultural and political news—the trend so many journalistic purists lament—is a welcome change, as far as I'm concerned. Such admixing—think of *Murphy Brown,* Ice T, or Oliver Stone's *JFK* on the "entertainment" side—has given access to those whose voices and perspectives were rarely heard in the traditional press but whose critiques of American values and priorities are shared by millions of people. Whether the issue is police brutality, single-parenthood or government coverups, it has often been the "entertainment media" that has pushed the debate onto America's political agenda.

Themes, Issues, and Ideas

1. Wenner makes the case that hard news that does not recognize popular culture is narrow and behind the times. Do you agree? How might the "politics of culture" work with regard to an issue currently in the press?

2. Wenner defends Bart Simpson, calling him "more attuned" than many other TV characters to American moods. What is the advantage of being so attuned? How might traditional journalism benefit from such knowledge?

Writing Strategies and Techniques

1. Compare Jan Wenner's style to Bill Moyers's. Which is more convincing? Why? Give examples.

2. Wenner uses the words "culture" and "cultural" often in his essay. Just what do these words mean as Wenner uses them? Compare a dictionary definition of these terms to the way Wenner and other writers use them. What are the advantages and disadvantages of a term as broad and flexible as "culture?"

Suggestions for Writing

1. Write an essay examining a piece of popular culture such as a TV show, a recording, or a magazine such as *Rolling Stone;* then write a news story from five years in the future describing its political effects.

2. Write an essay comparing Jan Wenner's view of popular culture with Mark Crispin Miller's. Use Bart Simpson as an example.

Imperial English: The Language of Science?

Anne Eisenberg

As writers such as Amy Tan in "Mother Tongue" have pointed out, language is bound to be one of the main cultural issues of the twenty-first century. In "Imperial English: The Language of Science," Anne Eisenberg points out that even when a language such as English does become the standard, the same forces that brought it into universal use may also make it obsolete.

This essay was originally printed in Scientific American. *Anne Eisenberg is a professor at Polytechnic University in Brooklyn, New York "where,"* Scientific American *added, "a very popular Japanese language course was recently begun."*

Werner Heisenberg learned Latin, Greek and French when he was a gymnasium student in Munich. Later, when he worked in Copenhagen, he tackled English and Danish, using mealtimes as his language lab: English conversation during breakfast; Danish read aloud from the newspaper by his landlady afterward.

This is not the kind of anecdote we associate with today's science majors in the U.S., that resolutely monolingual lot. Science students here are rarely to be found in a school language lab, much less a spontaneous one, and when they do speak another language, it is usually because of family background, not classroom instruction. Then they graduate, attend a conference with colleagues from other countries and discover the international hallmark of U.S. science: linguistic incompetence.

We are the people who can no longer be bothered to learn another language. To be sure, we really haven't had to since the 1960's, for in the years since World War II English has gradually become the lingua franca of science. Today it is the universal currency of international publications as well as of meetings. Those of us who need to keep up with, say, *Angewandte Chemie* need not worry about mastering German; we can leave it to the journal's staff, whose English is no doubt immaculate, to provide us with a convenient international edition published, of course, in English.

It wasn't always this way. For 200 years before World War II, most scientific work was reported in German, French or English, in that order of importance. People who wanted to keep up with a specialization had to learn the dominant language of the field. For example, scientists who wished to understand quantum mechanics in the 1920's had to learn German. Sir Nevill Mott comments, "Apart from Dirac, I don't think anyone in Cambridge understood [quantum mechanics] very well; there were no lectures on it, and so the only thing to do was to learn German and read the original papers, particularly those of Schrödinger and Born's *Wellenmechanik der Stossvorgänge* ['Wave Mechanics of Collision Processes']."

German, French and English were the customary languages of meetings, too. At Niels Bohr's institute in Copenhagen, for example, John A. Wheeler recalls that most seminars were held in German, occasionally in English. Bohr, who spoke English and German with equal ease, fluctuated between them, adding Danish as a counterpoint. No one had to learn French, though, for Bohr's knowledge of it was limited. "I have it from an eyewitness," Abraham Pais writes, "that he once greeted the French ambassador to Denmark with a cordial *aujourd'hui*."

After World War II, the linguistic balance of power shifted. The U.S. economy boomed, and science grew rapidly as vast federal expenditures, often fueled by the cold war, poured into research and development. U.S. scientists flocked to conferences, bringing their language with them; U.S. scientific publications burgeoned, and their huge readerships made them highly desirable to scientists throughout the world who realized English was a medium through which they could be widely read and cited.

With technical dominance came the beginning of linguistic dominance, first in Europe, then globally. Only the French and the Soviets put up a spirited resistance. At one international conference when de Gaulle was still in power, for instance, a member of the French contingent began reporting in French and then, sensing that many of the important U.S. scientists in the audience did not understand him, switched to English. Then he watched as all of his French colleagues rose as a group and exited. The Soviets, too, did what they

could to fight the English monopoly, providing expensive simultane-
ous technical translations and bilingual commentaries or even resorting to French as the lesser evil—anything to avoid the language of the
enemy.

Today in the former U.S.S.R., linguistic opposition has dissolved with the union. Even the French, who fiercely cherish their
language, have accepted the practicality of English for publishing the
proceedings of international meetings: the 12th Colloquium on High
Resolution Molecular Spectroscopy was held last year in Dijon, but
the only speech in French during the five days of the meeting was the
mayor's welcoming address.

The rest of the world's scientists, too, have fallen in step. English was already in place in India, Nigeria and many other countries
where it had been left behind by the British, to be widely adopted as
a practical second language that united diverse populations. The Japanese readily inserted the language of the victor into their children's
school programs; Korean and Chinese scientists were delighted to
take up membership in the English-speaking club.

English is indeed the new Latin. It has become a successor to the
scholarly language once so powerful that Christian Huygens delayed
publishing *Traité de la Lumière* for 12 years in hopes of translating it
into Latin so as "to obtain greater attention to the thing." And there is
a second way that English may parallel Latin. Latin outlived the
Roman Empire, surviving long after the government that spread it
through the world had vanished. So may the international use of
English outlast U.S. scientific dominion. The ascent of English, after
all, had little to do with any inherent linguistic virtues. True, English
has an unusually rich vocabulary; instead of resisting new terms, we
welcome them, particularly in science and technology—*les anglicis-
mes* have conquered the world. But it was scientific leadership, not a
flexible lexicon, that sparked the diffusion of English. Many now say
this leadership is faltering. Consider, for instance, last year's top
holders of new U.S. patents: Toshiba, Mitsubishi and Hitachi.

This year, although English continues to reign, small changes
are in the wind. For example, more than 860 Japanese language programs are running in U.S. schools, and there is even an occasional
undergraduate science department promoting German. Who knows,
the students enrolling in these foreign language classes might even
learn a bit more about English, or, to put it in Geothe's words, *Wer
fremde Sprachen nicht kennt, weiss nichts von seiner eigenen.*

Themes, Issues, and Ideas

1. What reasons, in their order of importance, does Eisenberg give for the ascendancy of English?

2. Are there any other examples you can think of of politics affecting language? How might German and Japanese rivalry with the United States affect our use of everyday English?

3. What is Eisenberg's point in ending her essay with an untranslated quotation from German?

Writing Strategies and Techniques

1. How would you characterize Eisenberg's attitude in this essay? How does she create this tone?

2. Why does Eisenberg begin with a story about Werner Heisenberg?

Suggestions for Writing

1. Write an essay comparing English to another once-powerful force. Compare the reasons for the decline of both.

2. Pick one of the reasons Eisenberg gives for the success of English in scientific writing, and apply it to some other field, such as movies or television.

Is Progress Obsolete?

Christopher Lasch

Christopher Lasch is one of the most provocative and insightful of American cultural historians. Throughout his career, he has angered both the left and the right with his critiques of American society, most notably in The Culture of Narcissism *(1979) and* The True and Only Heaven *(1991). Lasch is a professor of history at the University of Rochester.*

In this essay, written for a special issue of Time *magazine on the coming century, Lasch argues that progress, the pride of American society for so long, has finally run up against the wall.*

Progress and democracy, we assume, go hand in hand. Progress means abundance; more labor-saving machines, more comforts, more choices. It means a rich life for everyone, not for the privileged classes alone. Or so we used to believe, until recent events began to suggest that progress may have limits after all.

Compared with the rest of the world, industrial nations enjoy a lavish standard of living. The affluence generated by industrialism looks even more impressive when compared with living standards that prevailed throughout most of the millennium now drawing to a close. Goods that would once have been considered luxuries have become staples of everyday consumption. Medicine has reduced infant mortality and conquered many of the diseases that formerly struck down people in their prime. A vast increase in life expectancy dramatizes the contrast between our world and that of our ancestors in the distant past.

To be sure, we pay a price for progress. Constant change gives rise to widespread nervousness and anxiety. In solving old problems, we often create new ones in their place. Improvements in life expectancy make possible an aging population that puts a growing strain on the health-care system. Private cars give us unprecedented mobility but swell the volume of traffic to the point of gridlock. In the course of enjoying the delights of consumption, we generate so much garbage that we are running out of places to dump it.

Yet none of this destroys our faith in progress. The benefits, we think, outweigh the costs. As long as the question of progress is posed in this way, the question answers itself. The price may be high, but few would seriously choose not to pay it. Progress is an offer we have been unable to refuse.

The real question today is whether progress has built-in limits. Environmentalists argue that the earth will not support indefinite economic expansion along the old lines. Reports of global warming, damage to the ozone layer and long-term atmospheric shifts caused by deforestation raise further doubts about unlimited growth. Even though much of this evidence remains controversial, it has already transformed the debate about progress. For the first time we find ourselves asking not whether endless progress is desirable but whether it is even possible, as we have known it in the past.

The global distribution of wealth raises the same question in a more urgent form. If we consider the effect of extending Western patterns of consumption to the rest of the world, the potential impact on the earth is truly staggering. Imagine the populations of India and China equipped with two cars to a family, air conditioning in private homes and appliances galore, participating fully in a consumer economy that already makes heavy demands on the world's environment even when it is confined to a mere fraction of the world's population. It is obvious that the wasteful, heedless life now enjoyed by the West cannot be made available to everyone without stretching the energy resources of the earth, as well as its adaptive capacity, beyond the breaking point.

The idea of progress loses all meaning if progress no longer implies the democratization of affluence. It was the prospect of universal abundance that made progress a morally compelling ideology in the past. According to the old way of thinking, the productive forces unleashed by industrialism generated a steadily rising level of demand. Even humble men and women could now see the possibility of bettering their condition. The desire for a full life, formerly restricted to the rich, would spread to the masses. The expansion of desire—the motor of progress—would assure the expansion of the economic machinery necessary to satisfy it. Economic development would thus continue indefinitely in a self-generating upward spiral, without any foreseeable end or limit.

But affluence for all now appears unlikely, even in the distant future. The emergence of a global economy, far from eliminating poverty, has widened the gap between rich and poor nations. The revolution of rising expectations may not be self-generating, as we had thought. It may even be reversible. Famine and plague have returned to large parts of the world. Poverty is spilling over into the developed nations from the Third World. Desperate migrants pour into our cities, swelling the vast army of the homeless, unemployed, illiterate, drug-ridden, derelict and effectively disenfranchised. Their presence strains existing resources to the limit. Medical and educational facilities, law-enforcement agencies and the supply of available jobs—not to mention the supply of racial and ethnic goodwill, never abundant to begin with—all appear inadequate to the enormous task of assimilating what is essentially a surplus population.

The well-being of democracy, a political system that implies equality as well as liberty, hangs in the balance. A continually rising standard of living for the rich, it is clear, means a falling standard of living for everyone else. Forcible redistribution of income on a massive scale is an equally unattractive alternative. The best hope of reducing the gap between rich and poor lies in the gradual emergence of a new consensus, a common understanding about the material prerequisites of a good life. Hard questions will have to be asked. Just how much do we need to live comfortably? How much is enough?

Such questions implicitly challenge the notion of progress, which is usually taken to mean there is no such thing as enough. The prospect of a world in which people voluntarily agree to set limits on their acquisitive appetite bears little resemblance to what is conventionally understood as progress. But then neither does the prospect of a world in which unparalleled affluence coexists with frightful depths of misery and squalor.

Themes, Issues, and Ideas

1. Is it true, as Lasch says, that "none of [our problems] destroys our faith in progress?" Give examples both supporting and refuting this statement.

2. The dynamic Lasch explains in the paragraph beginning "The idea of progress . . ." is somewhat complex. Give an example that might demonstrate it.

3. "How much is enough?" Lasch asks. What is your answer to this question? Using Lasch's test, could the earth support "enough" for everyone in China and India?

Writing Strategies and Techniques

1. Lasch's style of writing, here as elsewhere, is objective and forceful, like that of a wise judge. Does this style appeal to you? Does it tend to persuade you?

2. Lasch, like all the authors in this book, makes certain assumptions about the world and about his reader. Identify five of each type of assertion.

Suggestions for Writing

1. Write an essay in which you apply Lasch's thesis to progress in your hometown.

2. Write an essay defending the idea of progress that specifically addresses Lasch's argument.

MAKING CONNECTIONS

1. In "Old News Is Good News," Bill Moyers talks about the dangers of too much public information. Describe how even trivial and distracting information can be easily dangerous.

2. Compare Jan Wenner's idea of popular culture in "The Politics of Culture" to Mark Crispin Miller's "Big Brother is You, Watching" (Chapter 6). What does each writer think is the source of popular culture? Write an essay explaining each writer's assumptions about the nature and dynamics of American mass culture.

3. The fears and the hopes brought about by technology are two of the themes that run through the essays in this chapter. Describe the relationship between the two, and, using information from as many readings as you wish, write an essay stating and supporting your opinions on what we have to expect from technology now and in the near future.

4. Anne Eisenberg describes how science developed an international language—English. Based on the other readings in this chapter, describe what an international language of the future might be. What kind of "language" do you mean?

5. What in Aldous Huxley's argument would Christopher Lasch most agree with?

CHAPTER
TEN

Science, Technology, and the Human Environment

You and the Earth of Tomorrow

THE PAST AS PROLOGUE

Silent Spring

A Fable for Our Time

Rachel Carson

Rachel Carson (1907–1964) studied at the Johns Hopkins University and the Marine Biological Laboratory at Woods Hole, Massachusetts. Her books about the natural world Under the Sea Wind *(1951) and* The Sea Around Us *(1954) were enormous bestsellers, and as a nature writer she is remembered as a pioneer.*

It is her book Silent Spring *(1962) for which she is best remembered.* Silent Spring, *from which this excerpt is taken, first sounded the alarm about the damaging effects of chemical pesticides and fertilizers. President John F. Kennedy took notice of the book and ordered a federal investigation whose aftereffects are still being felt today. As an environmental advocate and as a woman, Rachel Carson was a model who will be followed far into the twenty-first century.*

There was once a town in the heart of America where all life seemed to live in harmony with its surroundings. The town lay in the midst of a checkerboard of prosperous farms, with fields of grain and hillsides of orchards where, in spring, white clouds of bloom drifted above the green fields. In autumn, oak and maple and birch set up a blaze of color that flamed and flickered across a backdrop of pines. Then foxes barked in the hills and deer silently crossed the fields, half hidden in the mists of the tall mornings.

Along the roads, laurel, viburnum and alder, great ferns and wildflowers delighted the traveler's eyes through much of the year. Even in winter the roadsides were places of beauty, where countless birds came to feed on the berries and on the seed heads of the dried weeds rising above the snow. The countryside was, in fact, famous for the abundance and variety of its bird life, and when the flood of migrants was pouring through in spring and fall people traveled from great distances to observe them. Others came to fish the streams, which flowed clear and cold out of the hills and contained shady pools where trout lay. So it had been from the days many years ago when the first settlers raised their houses, sank their wells, and built their barns.

Then a strange blight crept over the area and everything began to change. Some evil spell had settled on the community: mysterious maladies swept the flocks of chickens; the cattle and sheep sickened and died. Everywhere was a shadow of death. The farmers spoke of much illness among their families. In the town the doctors had become more and more puzzled by new kinds of sickness appearing among their patients. There had been several sudden and unexplained deaths, not only among adults but even among children, who would be stricken suddenly while at play and die within a few hours.

There was a strange stillness. The birds, for example—where had they gone? Many people spoke of them, puzzled and disturbed. The feeding stations in the backyards were deserted. The few birds seen anywhere were moribund; they trembled violently and could not fly. It was a spring without voices. On the mornings that had once throbbed with the dawn chorus of robins, catbirds, doves, jays, wrens, and scores of other bird voices there was now no sound; only silence lay over the fields and woods and marsh.

On the farms the hens brooded, but no chicks hatched. The farmers complained that they were unable to raise any pigs—the litters were small and the young survived only a few days. The apple trees were coming into bloom but no bees droned among the blossoms, so there was no pollination and there would be no fruit.

The roadsides, once so attractive, were now lined with browned and withered vegetation as though swept by fire. These, too, were silent, deserted by all living things. Even the streams were now lifeless. Anglers no longer visited them, for all the fish had died.

In the gutters under the eaves and between the shingles of the roofs, a white granular powder still showed a few patches; some weeks before it had fallen like snow upon the roofs and the lawns, the fields and streams.

No witchcraft, no enemy action had silenced the rebirth of new life in this stricken world. The people had done it themselves.

This town does not actually exist, but it might easily have a thousand counterparts in American or elsewhere in the world. I know of no community that has experienced all the misfortunes I describe. Yet every one of these disasters has actually happened somewhere, and many real communities have already suffered a substantial number of them. A grim specter has crept upon us almost unnoticed, and this imagined tragedy may easily become a stark reality we all shall know.

Themes, Issues, and Ideas

1. Does Carson's image of environmental devastation seem characteristic of her time? Why or why not?

2. What are some of the gifts of nature to the town? Which are most important among these? Why?

3. What other scenes of lifelessness and desolation does Carson's fable remind you of?

Writing Strategies and Techniques

1. Why is this essay called "a fable?" How is it like or unlike other fables?

2. When Carson speaks about "evil spells" and "strange blights" she is not using the language of science. What language is she using? Why?

Suggestions for Writing

1. Write a fable, similar to Carson's, but about a city.

2. Write an essay considering nature as you have experienced it. How has it been threatened? What changes have you seen that seemed mysterious at the time?

Ecology: The New Sacred Agenda

Al Gore

Al Gore has long been an advocate on environmental issues, first as a senator from Tennessee, and currently in his position as Vice President of the United States. His 1992 book Earth in the Balance *was a bestseller nationwide, and helped many thousands of Americans understand the environmental issues that Gore has felt most needed addressing.*

The reading below was taken from an issue of New Perspectives Quarterly *in which Gore, then a senator, established a moral footing for his environmental crusade. Here, Gore goes beyond statistics and puts forth the idea of environmental responsibility as the last gasp of faith by a secular, consumption-based society. Whether or not Gore's position changes with his new job is something any reader of the following essay will certainly want to pursue.*

I fear that we are on a downslope toward a future catastrophic event that will dim history. At a gut level, people throughout the world realize that the environment is the issue of our time. In the not too distant future, there will be a new "sacred agenda" in international affairs: policies that enable the rescue of the global environment. I agree with the Spring 1989 issue of *NPQ* that this task will one day join, and then perhaps supplant, efforts to prevent the world's incineration through nuclear war as the principal test of statecraft.

When we consider the relationship of the human species to the planet Earth, not much change is visible in a single year, in a single nation. Yet, if we look at the entire pattern of that relationship from the emergence of the species until today, a distinctive contrast in very recent times clearly conveys the danger to which we must respond. It took ten thousand human lifetimes for the population to reach two billion. Now, in the course of a single human lifetime the world population is rocketing from two billion toward ten billion, and is already halfway there.

Startling graphs showing the loss of forest land, topsoil, stratospheric ozone, and species all follow the same pattern of sudden, unprecedented acceleration in the latter half of the 20th century. And yet, so far, the pattern of our politics remains remarkably unchanged. To date, we have tolerated self-destructive behavior and environmental vandalism on a global scale.

Even with top-level political focus, the pervasive nature of all the activities that cumulatively create the greenhouse effect make the global solutions almost unimaginably difficult. Therefore, our first task is to expand the circumference of what is imaginable. It is not now imaginable, for example, to radically reduce CO_2 emissions. Even if all other elements of the problem are solved, a major threat is still posed by emissions of carbon dioxide, the exhaling breath of the industrial culture upon which our civilization rests. Yet, emissions must be curbed. We can make that task imaginable by building our confidence with successful assaults on more easily achievable targets, like elimination of CFCs and reversing the practice of deforesting the earth.

The cross-cut between the imperatives of growth and the imperatives of environmental management represents a supreme test for modern industrial civilization. Can we devise dynamic new strategies that will accommodate economic growth within a stabilized environmental framework?

The effort to solve the global environmental problem will be complicated not only by blind assertions that more and more environmental manipulation and more and more resource extraction are essential for economic growth. It will also be complicated by the emergence of simplistic demands that development, or technology itself, must be stopped. This is a crisis of confidence that must be addressed.

There is no assurance that a balance can be struck. Nevertheless, the effort must be made. And because of the urgency, scope and even the improbability of complete success in such an endeavor, I will borrow from military terminology: To deal with the global environment, we will need the environmental equivalent of the Strategic Defense Initiative—a Strategic Environment Initiative. Even opponents of SDI, of which I am one, recognize that this effort has been remarkably successful in drawing together previously disconnected government programs, in stimulating development of new technologies, and in forcing a new wave of intense analysis of subjects previously thought to have been exhausted.

I have likened our newfound awareness of ozone depletion and the greenhouse effect to the Kristallnacht which forewarned the holocaust. The logic of this analogy can be extended, as *NPQ* editor Nathan Gardels did in his foreword to the Spring 1989 issue on the ecology, to include Hannah Arendt's memorable notion of "the banality of evil" which emerged from her reflections on Hitler's lieutenants at the Eichmann trial.

My own religious faith teaches me that we are given dominion over the earth, but that we are also required to be good stewards. If, during our lifetimes, we witness the destruction of half the living species God put on this earth, we will have failed in our responsibility as stewards. Are those actions, because of their result, "evil?" The answer depends upon our knowledge of their consequences. The individual actions that collectively produce the world's environmental crisis are indeed banal when they are looked at one by one—the cutting of a tree, the air conditioning of a car. The willingness to trace the line of responsibility from individual action to collective effect is a challenge that we as a civilization have not yet learned to master.

"Evil" and "good" are terms not frequently used by politicians. And, yes, we know from historical experience the dangers of mixing public policy and religion. but, in my own view, while we must avoid zealotry, this ecological crisis cannot be met without reference to spiritual values.

In truth, as a civilization, we don't have much faith left. The idea that we can totally abandon any but the secular values comes perilously close to saying that nothing has worth unless it can be consumed in our lifetimes.

The word "faith" need not be defined in conventional religious terms. Whether or not an individual has faith in life after death, they must have faith that life on earth continues after their death. If we are so far gone as a civilization that such a belief system cannot be put together, then nothing can save this species.

Ultimately, I believe that the ecological solution will be found in a new faith in the future of life on earth after our own, a faith in the future that sacrifices in the present, a new moral courage to choose higher values in the conduct of human affairs, and a new reverence for absolute principles that can serve as guiding stars by which to map the future course of our species.

Themes, Issues, and Ideas

1. What, according to Gore, are our best reasons for preserving the environment?

2. Gore states that, "as a civilization we don't have much faith left." Do you agree with this statement? Can you provide some evidence for both sides of the question?

3. At the end of his essay, Gore calls for a "new reverence for absolute principles that can serve as guiding stars . . ." What might some of those principles be?

Writing Strategies and Techniques

1. The Vice President has often been criticized for the stilted, wooden character of his speeches. Based on this essay, would you say that is a fair assessment? Give examples from the reading to support your view.

2. In what ways is the style of this essay much like the positions that it advocates?

Suggestions for Writing

1. Write an essay in which you describe your feelings toward subsequent generations, possibly in the form of a letter to your grandchildren.

2. "The idea that we can totally abandon any but the most secular values comes perilously close to saying that nothing has worth unless it can be consumed in our lifetimes." Write an essay affirming or denying this statement of Gore's, using examples from your own experience as well as from this and other reading selections.

In the Jungle

Annie Dillard

As the South American rain forests continue to disappear, they become an ever-more precious resource for industrialized peoples like ourselves. At least Annie Dillard, in visiting the Napo River in the Ecuadorian jungle, found it so. To Dillard, the rain forest is not so much a corner of the world, but a part of the world's real self. In this selection from her book Teaching a Stone to Talk *(1988), Dillard describes a place so remote that it seems to be at the center of everything.*

Dillard first sprang to prominence as a nature writer in 1974, when her first book, Pilgrim at Tinker Creek, *won that year's Pulitzer prize. Her most recent books include* The Writing Life *(1991) and* An American Childhood *(1987).*

Like any out-of-the-way place, the Napo River in the Ecuadorian jungle seems real enough when you are there, even central. Out of the way of *what*? I was sitting on a stump at the edge of a bankside palm-thatch village, in the middle of the night, on the headwaters of the Amazon. Out of the way of human life, tenderness, or the glance of heaven?

A nightjar in deep-leaved shadow called three long notes, and hushed. The men with me talked softly in clumps: three North Americans, four Ecuadorians who were showing us the jungle. We were holding cool drinks and idly watching a hand-sized tarantula seize moths that came to the lone bulb on the generator shed beside us.

It was February, the middle of summer. Green fireflies spattered lights across the air and illumined for seconds, now here, now there, the pale trunks of enormous, solitary trees. Beneath us the brown Napo River was rising, in all silence; it coiled up the sandy bank and tangled its foam *in* vines that trailed from the forest and roots that ᵒped the shore.

Each breath of night smelled sweet, more moistened and sweet ₐny kitchen, or garden, or cradle. Each star in Orion seemed to tremble and stir with my breath. All at once, in the thatch house across the clearing behind us, one of the village's Jesuit priests began playing an alto recorder, playing a wordless song, lyric, in a minor key, that twined over the village clearing, that caught in the big trees' canopies, muted our talk on the bankside, and wandered over the river, dissolving downstream.

This will do, I thought. This will do, for a weekend, or a season, or a home.

Later that night I loosed my hair from its braids and combed it smooth—not for myself, but so the village girls could play with it in the morning.

We had disembarked at the village that afternoon, and I had slumped on some shaded steps, wishing I knew some Spanish or some Quechua so I could speak with the ring of little girls who were alternately staring at me and smiling at their toes. I spoke anyway, and fooled with my hair, which they were obviously dying to get their hands on, and laughed, and soon they were all braiding my hair, all five of them, all fifty fingers, all my hair, even my bangs. And then they took it apart and did it again, laughing, and teaching me Spanish nouns, and meeting my eyes and each other's with open delight, while their small brothers in blue jeans climbed down from the trees and began kicking a volleyball with one of the North American men.

Now, as I combed my hair in the little tent, another of the men, a free-lance writer from Manhattan, was talking quietly. He was telling us the tale of his life, describing his work in Hollywood, his apartment in Manhattan, his house in Paris. . . . "It makes me wonder," he said, "what I'm doing in a tent under a tree in the village of Pompeya, on the Napo River, in the jungle of Ecuador." After a pause he added, "It makes me wonder why I'm going *back*."

The point of going somewhere like the Napo River in Ecuador is not to see the most spectacular anything. It is simply to see what is there. We are here on the planet only once, and might as well get a feel for the place. We might as well get a feel for the fringes and hollows in which life is lived, for the Amazon basin, which covers half a continent, and for the life that—there, like anywhere else—is always and necessarily lived in detail: on the tributaries, in the riverside villages, sucking this particular white-fleshed guava in this particular pattern of shade.

What is there is interesting. The Napo River itself is wide (I mean wider than the Mississippi at Davenport) and brown, opaqu and smeared with floating foam and logs and branches from the jungle. White egrets hunch on shoreline deadfalls and parrots in flocks dart in and out of the light. Under the water in the river, unseen, are anacondas—which are reputed to take a few village toddlers every year—and water boas, stingrays, crocodiles, manatees, and sweet-meated fish.

Low water bares gray strips of sandbar on which the natives build tiny palm-thatch shelters, arched, the size of pup tents, for overnight fishing trips. You see these extraordinarily clean people (who bathe twice a day in the river, and whose straight black hair is always freshly washed) paddling down the river in dugout canoes, hugging the banks.

Some of the Indians of this region, earlier in the century, used to sleep naked in hammocks. The nights are cold. Gordon MacCreach, an American explorer in these Amazon tributaries, reported that he was startled to hear the Indians get up at three in the morning. He was even more startled, night after night, to hear them walk down the river slowly, half asleep, and bathe in the water. Only later did he learn what they were doing: they were getting warm. The cold woke them; they warmed their skins in the river, which was always ninety degrees; then they returned to their hammocks and slept through the rest of the night.

The riverbanks are low, and from the river you see an unbroken wall of dark forest in every direction, from the Andes to the Atlantic. You get a taste for looking at trees; trees hung with the swinging nests of yellow troupials, trees from which ant nests the size of grain sacks hang like black goiters, trees from which seven-colored tanagers flutter, coral trees, teak, balsa and breadfruit, enormous emergent silk-cotton trees, and the pale-barked *samona* palms.

When you are inside the jungle, away from the river, the trees vault out of sight. It is hard to remember to look up the long trunks and see the fans, strips, fronds, and sprays of glossy leaves. Inside the jungle you are more likely to notice the snarl of climbers and creepers round the trees' boles, the flowering bromeliads and epiphytes in every bough's crook, and the fantastic silk-cotton tree trunks thirty or forty feet across, trunks buttressed in flanges of wood whose curves can make three high walls of a room—a shady, loamy-aired room where you would gladly live, or die. Butterflies, iridescent blue, striped, or clear-winged, thread the jungle paths at eye level. And at your feet is a swath of ants bearing triangular bits of green leaf. The ants with their leaves look like a wide fleet of sailing dinghies—but they don't quit. In either direction they wobble over the jungle floor s far as the eye can see. I followed them off the path as far as I dared, and never saw an end to ants or to those luffing chips of green they bore.

Unseen in the jungle, but present, are tapirs, jaguars, many species of snake and lizard, ocelots, armadillos, marmosets, howler monkeys, toucans and macaws and a hundred other birds, deer, bats, peccaries, capybaras, agoutis, and sloths. Also present in this jungle, but variously distant, are Texaco derricks and pipelines, and some of the wildest Indians in the world, blowgun-using Indians, who killed missionaries in 1956 and ate them.

Long lakes shine in the jungle. We traveled one of these in dugout canoes, canoes with two inches of freeboard, canoes paddled with machete-hewn oars chopped from buttresses of silk-cotton trees, or poled in the shallows with peeled cane or bamboo. Our part-Indian guide had cleared the path to the lake the day before; when we walked the path we saw where he had impaled the lopped head of a boa, open-mouthed, on a pointed stick by the canoes, for decoration.

This lake was wonderful. Herons, egrets, and ibises plodded the sawgrass shores, kingfishers and cuckoos clattered from sunlight to shade, great turkeylike birds fussed in dead branches, and hawks lolled overhead. There was all the time in the world. A turtle slid into the water. The boy in the bow of my canoe slapped stones at birds with a simple sling, a rubber thong and a leather pad. He aimed brilliantly at moving targets, always, and always missed; the birds were out of range. He stuffed his sling back in his shirt. I looked around.

The lake and river waters were as opaque as rain-forest leaves; they are veils, blinds, painted screens. You see things only by their effects. I saw the shoreline water roil and the sawgrass heave above a thrashing *paichi*, an enormous black fish of these waters; one had been caught the previous week weighing 430 pounds. Piranha fish live in the lakes, and electric eels. I dangled my fingers in the water, figuring it would be worth it.

We would eat chicken that night in the village, and rice, yucca, onions, beets, and heaps of fruit. The sun would ring down, pulling darkness after it like a curtain. Twilight is short, and the unseen birds of twilight wistful, uncanny, catching the heart. The two nuns in their dazzling white habits—the beautiful-boned young nun and the warm-faced old—would glide to the open cane-and-thatch schoolrooms in darkness, and start the children singing. The children would sing in piping Spanish, high-pitched and pure; they would sing "Nearer My Got to Thee" in Quechua, very fast. (To reciprocate, we sang for them "Old MacDonald Had a Farm"; I thought they might recognize the animal sounds. Of course they thought we were out of our minds.) A the children became excited by their own singing, they left their log benches and swarmed around the nuns, hopping, smiling at us, everyone smiling, the nuns' faces bursting in their cowls, and the clear-voiced children still singing, and the palm-leafed roofing stirred.

The Napo River: it is not out of the way. It is *in* the way, catching sunlight the way a cup catches poured water; it is a bowl of sweet air, a basin of greenness, and of grace, and, it would seem, of peace.

Themes, Issues, and Ideas

1. Judging by this essay, where do you think Annie Dillard is from? What might this essay be like if she had stayed on the Napo River for a year?

2. "Out of the way of *what?*" asks Dillard. Make a list of ten things the Napo River is, and is not, out of the way of.

3. Compare Dillard's river to Carson's town. Which seems a better example of "harmony?" Explain why.

Writing Strategies and Techniques

1. How does Dillard combine physical detail and narrative exposition to describe the Napo River?

2. How would it affect Dillard's piece if: 1) the little girls had pulled her hair; 2) the little boy hit and killed the birds he was shooting at; and 3) Dillard's hand *had* been bitten by a piranha and become infected?

Suggestions for Writing

1. Write a parody of "In the Jungle" in which the situations described in Writing Strategies and Techniques, question 2, occur.

2. Write a parody of "In the Jungle" about a shopping mall or other local place.

Ages of Plenty

Arthur C. Clarke

Arthur C. Clarke was born in 1917. As a writer of science fiction and a speculator on scientific facts, he has spent a good part of the twentieth century looking ahead to the next one. His books were always popular, yet he achieved even greater fame with Stanley Kubrick's success- ful 1968 film 2001: A Space Odyssey. *Clarke's screenplay, based on his novel, was nominated for an Academy Award.*

In this essay taken from his book Profiles of the Fu- ture *(1985), Clarke examines the future of the human envi- ronment in its most basic elements: matter and energy. He begins by reminding us that Einstein has shown these two necessities of life to be interchangeable.*

The raw materials of civilization, as of life itself, are matter and energy, which we now know to be two sides of the same coin. For most of human history, and all of prehistory, only the most modest quantities of either were used by men. During the course of a year, one of our remote ancestors consumed about a quarter of a ton of food, half a ton of water and negligible quantities of hide, sticks, stones and clay. The energy he expended was that created by his own muscles, plus an occasional small contribution in the form of wood fires.

With the rise of technology, that simple picture has changed beyond recognition. The yearly consumption of the average American citizen is almost a ton of steel, seven tons of coal and hundreds of pounds of metals and chemicals whose very existence was unknown to science a century ago. Every year, over *twenty tons* of raw materials are dug from the earth to provide a modern man with the necessities— and luxuries—of life. No wonder that we hear warnings of critical shortages, and are told that within a few generations copper or lead may be added to the list of rare metals.

Most of us take little notice of these alarms, because we have heard them before—and nothing has happened. The unexpected dis- covery of huge oilfields on the sea beds has, for the time bein silenced the Cassandras of the petroleum industry, who have predicted that we would be running out of petrol by the end of this century. They were wrong this time—but in the slightly longer run, they will be right.

Whatever new reserves may be discovered, "fossil fuels" such as coal and oil can last only for a few more centuries; then they will be gone for ever. They will have served to launch man's technological culture into its trajectory, by providing easily available sources of energy, but they cannot sustain civilization over thousands of years. For this, we need something more permanent.

Today, there can be little doubt that the long-term (and perhaps the short-term) answer to the fuel problem is nuclear energy. The weapons already now stockpiled by the major powers could run all the machines on earth for decades if their energies could be used constructively. The warheads in the American arsenals alone are equivalent to thousands of millions of tons of oil or coal.

It is not likely that fission reactions (those involving such heavy elements as thorium, uranium, and plutonium) will play more than a temporary role in terrestrial affairs; one hopes not, for fission is the second dirtiest and most unpleasant method of releasing energy that man has ever discovered.* Some of the radio-isotopes from today's reactors will still be causing trouble and perhaps injuring unwary archaeologists, a thousand years from now.

But beyond fission lies fusion—the welding together of light atoms such as hydrogen and lithium. This is the reaction that drives the stars themselves; we have reproduced it on earth, but have not yet tamed it. When we have done so, our power problems will have been solved forever—and there will be no poisonous by-products, but only the clean ash of helium.

Controlled fusion is the supreme challenge of applied nuclear physics; some scientists believe it will be achieved in ten years, some in fifty. But almost all of them are sure that we will have some fusion power long before our oil and coal run out, and will be able to draw fuel in virtually unlimited quantities from the sea.

It may well be—indeed, at the moment it appears very likely— that fusion plants can be built only in very large sizes, so that no more than a handful would be required to run an entire country. That they can be made small and portable—so that they could be used to drive vehicles, for example—appears most improbable. Their main function

---

*The dirtiest is the coal-fueled power station. One can imagine the fury of the environmentalists ⌐ a nuclear-based society, if someone proposed the building of such a monstrosity. Jane Fonda ɔuld have done a superb job, starring in *The Carbon Syndrome*.

will be to produce large quantities of thermal and electrical energy, and we will still be faced with the problem of getting this energy to the millions of places where it is needed. Existing power systems can supply our houses—but what about our automobiles and aircraft, in the Post-Petroleum Age?

The desirable solution is some means of storing electricity which will be at least ten, and preferably a hundred, times more compact than the clumsy and messy batteries that have not improved fundamentally since the time of young Tom Edison. This urgent need has already been mentioned in connection with electric automobiles, but there are countless other requirements for portable energy. Perhaps the forced draught of space technology will lead us fairly quickly to a light-weight power-cell, holding as much energy per pound as petrol when we consider some of the other marvels of modern technology, it seems a modest enough demand.

A much more far-fetched idea is that we might be able to broadcast power from some central generating station, and pick it up anywhere on earth by means of a device like a radio receiver. On a limited scale, this is already possible, though only at great difficulty and expense.

Well-focused radio beams carrying up to 1,000 hp of continuous energy can now be produced and part of this energy could be intercepted by a large antenna system several miles away. Because of the inevitable spreading of the beam, however, most of its energy would be wasted, so the efficiency of the system would be very low. It would be like using a search-light, ten miles away, to illuminate a house; most of the light would splash over the surrounding landscape. In the case of a high-powered radio beam, the lost energy would not merely be wasteful—it would be quite dangerous, as the builders of long-range radars have already discovered.

Another fundamental objection to radio-power is that the transmitter would have to pump out the same amount of energy whether or not it was being used at the other end. In our present distribution systems, the central generating plant does not produce electricity until we call for it by switching on an appliance; there is "feedback" from consumer to generator. It would be extremely difficult, though not impossible, to arrange this with a radio power system.

Beamed radio power seems impracticable, therefore, except for very special applications; it might be useful between satellites and space vehicles if they were close together and not changing their relative positions. It would be quite hopeless, of course, for moving vehicles—the very case where it is most badly needed.

Broadcast power, if it is ever achieved, must depend upon some principle or technology at present unknown. Fortunately, it is something we must have—merely something that would be useful. If necessary, we will manage without it.

As pure speculation, we should mention the possibility that other power sources may exist in the space around us, and that we may one day be able to tap them. Several are already known, but they are all extremely feeble or suffer from fundamental limitations. The most powerful is the radiation field of the Sun—that is, sunlight—and we are already using this to operate our space vehicles. The output of the solar hydrogen reactor is gigantic—about 500,000,000,000,000,000,000,000 hp—but by the time it reaches Earth the flood of energy has been drastically diluted by distance. A rough and easily remembered figure is that the energy of sunlight at sea-level is about 1 hp per square yard; it varies widely, of course, with atmospheric conditions. So far we have been able to convert about one-tenth of this energy into electricity (at a cost of a few thousand dollars per horsepower for present-day solar cells!), so a 10 hp automobile would require about 1,000 square yards of collecting surface—even on a bright, sunny day. This is hardly a practicable proposition.

We cannot tap the flood of solar energy profitably unless we move much closer to the Sun; even on Mercury, we could produce only about 1 hp of electrical energy per square yard of collecting surface. One day it may be possible to set up light-traps very close to the Sun,* and beam the resultant energy to the points where it is required. If fusion power is not forthcoming, we will be forced to take some such drastic step as this. But spaceships had better avoid those power-beams; they would be very effective death-rays.

All the other known energy sources are millions of times weaker than sunlight. Cosmic rays, for example, carry about as much energy as starlight; it would be much more profitable to build a moonbeam-powered engine than one driven by cosmic radiation. This may seem a paradox, in view of the well-known fact that these rays are often of enormous energy and can inflict severe biological damage. But the high energy rays (actually, particles) are so few and far between that their *average* power is negligible. If it were otherwise, we should not be here.

The Earth's gravitational and magnetic fields are sometimes mentioned as potential sources of energy, but these have serious limitations. You cannot draw energy out of a gravitational field without letting some heavy object—already placed at a convenient altitude—fall through it. This, of course, is the basis of hydro-electric power,

---

* solar surface, there is 65,000 hp of energy to be picked up from every square yard!

which is an indirect way of using solar energy. The sun, evaporating water from the ocean, creates the mountain lakes whose gravitational energy we tap with our turbines.

Hydro-electric power can never provide more than a few percent of the total energy needed by the human race, even if (which heaven forbid) every waterfall on the planet were funneled into penstocks. All other ways of harnessing gravitational energy would involve the movement of matter on a very large scale: flattening mountains, for example. If we ever undertake such projects, it will be for quite other purposes than the generation of power, and the total operation will almost certainly leave us with a net energy loss. Before you can pull down a mountain, you have to break it to pieces.

The Earth's magnetic field is so extremely feeble (a toy magnet is thousands of times stronger) that it is not even worth considering. From time to time one hears optimistic talk of "magnetic propulsion" for space vehicles, but this is a project somewhat comparable to escaping from Earth via a ladder made of cobwebs. Terrestrial magnetic forces are just about as tough as gossamer.

Yet so much of the universe is indetectable to our senses, and so many of its energies have been discovered only during the last few moments of historic time, that it would be rash to discount the idea of still unknown cosmic forces. The concept of nuclear energy seemed nonsense only a lifetime ago, and even when it was proved to exist, most scientists denied that it could ever be tapped. There is considerable evidence that a flood of energy is sweeping through all the stars and planets in the form known as neutrino radiation which taxes all our powers of observation. So might Sir Isaac Newton, for all his genius, have failed to detect anything emerging from a radio antenna.

For terrestrial projects, it does not greatly matter whether or not the universe contains unknown and untapped energy sources. The heavy hydrogen in the seas can drive all our machines, heat all our cities, for as far ahead as we can imagine. If, as is perfectly possible, we are short of energy two generations from now, it will be through our own incompetence. We will be like Stone Age men freezing to death on top of a coal bed.

For most of our raw materials, as for our power sources, we have been living on capital. We have been exploiting the easily available resources—the high-grade ores, the rich lodes where natural forces have concentrated the metals and minerals we need. These processes took a billion years or more; in mere centuries, we have looted treasures stored up over aeons. When they are gone, our civilization cannc mark time for a few hundred million years until they are restored.

404 SCIENCE, TECHNOLOGY, AND THE HUMAN ENVIRONMENT

Once more, we will be forced to use our brains instead of our muscles. As Harrison Brown has pointed out in his book *The Challenge of Man's Future,* when all the ores are exhausted we can turn to ordinary rocks and clays. "One hundred tons of average igneous rock such as granite contains 8 tons of aluminum, 5 tons of iron, 1,200 pounds of titanium, 180 pounds of manganese, 70 pounds of chromium, 40 pounds of nickel, 30 pounds of vanadium, 20 pounds of copper, 10 pounds of tungsten, and 4 pounds of lead."

To extract these elements would require not only advanced chemical techniques, but very considerable amounts of energy. The rock would first have to be crushed, then treated by heat, electrolysis, and other means. However, as Harrison Brown also points out, a ton of granite contains enough uranium and thorium to provide energy equivalent to fifty tons of coal. All the energy we need for the processing is there in the rock itself.

Another almost limitless source of basic raw materials is the sea. A single cubic mile of sea-water contains, suspended or dissolved, about 150,000,000 tons of solid material. Most of this (120,000,000 tons) is common salt, but the remaining 30,000,000 tons contains almost all the elements in impressive quantities. The most abundant is magnesium (about 18,000,000 tons) and its large-scale extraction from the sea during the Second World War was a great, and highly significant, triumph of chemical engineering. It was not, however, the first element to be obtained from sea-water, for the extraction of bromine in commercial quantities started as early as 1924.

The difficulty with "mining" the sea is that the materials we wish to win from it are present in very low concentrations. That 18,000,000 tons of magnesium per cubic mile is an enormous figure (it would supply the world's needs, at the present rate, for several centuries), but it is dispersed in 4 *billion* tons of water. Regarded as an ore, therefore, sea-water contains only four parts of magnesium per million; on land, it is seldom profitable to work rocks containing less than one part in a hundred of the commoner metals. Many people have been hypnotised by the fact that a cubic mile of sea-water contains about twenty tons of gold, but they would probably find richer paydirt in their own back-gardens.

Nevertheless, the great developments in chemical processing that have taken place in recent years—especially as a result of the atomic energy programme, where it became necessary to extract very small amounts of isotopes from much larger quantities of other materials—suggest that we may be able to work the sea long before we exhaust the resources of the land. Once again, the problem is largely one of power—power for pumping, evaporation, electrolysis. Success may come as part of a combined operation; the efforts underway in many countries to obtain drinkable water from the sea will produce enriched brines as a by-product, and these may be the raw materials for the processing plants.

One can imagine, perhaps before the end of this century, huge general-purpose factories using cheap power from thermo-nuclear reactors to extract pure water, salt, magnesium, bromine, strontium, rubidium, copper, and many other metals from the sea. A notable exception from the list would be iron, which is far rarer in the oceans than under the continents.

If mining the sea appears an unlikely project, it is worth remembering that for more than seventy years we have been mining the atmosphere. One of the big, but now forgotten, worries of the nineteenth century was the coming shortage of nitrates for fertilizers; natural sources were running low, and it was essential to find some way of "fixing" the nitrogen in the air. The atmosphere contains some 4,000 million million tons of nitrogen, or more than a million tons for every person on Earth, so if it could be utilised directly there would never be any fear of further shortages.

This feat was achieved, by several methods, in the opening years of this century. One process involves the brute-force "burning" of ordinary air in a high-powered electric arc, for at very high temperatures the nitrogen and oxygen in the atmosphere will combine. This is an example of what can be done when cheap power is available (the Norwegians were able to pioneer the process, thanks to their early lead in hydroelectric generation) and it is perhaps a pointer for the future.

The really lavish use of concentrated energy sources for mining has hardly begun, but the Russians have been experimenting with high-frequency arcs and rocket jets to break up or drill rocks too tough to be worked in any other way. And ultimately, of course, there is the prospect of using nuclear explosions for large-scale mining, if the problems of radio-active contamination can be avoided.

When we consider that our deepest mines (now passing the 7,000-foot level) are mere pin-pricks on the surface of our 8,000-mile diameter planet, it is obviously absurd to talk about fundamental shortages of *any* element or mineral. Within five—certainly ten—miles of us lie all the raw materials we can ever use. We need not go after them ourselves; mining by human workers is, none too soon, disappearing from beneath the face of the earth. But machines can operate quite happily in temperatures of several hundred degrees and at pressures of scores of atmospheres, and this is just what the robot moles of the near future will be doing, miles beneath our feet.

Of course it is far too difficult, and too expensive, to work seams several miles down—with existing techniques. Very well: We will have to discover wholly new methods as the oil-drillers and the sulphur miners have already done. The projects will be forced upon us by sheer necessity as well as scientific curiosity.

Now let us widen our horizons somewhat. So far, we have been considering only *this* planet as a source of raw materials, but the Earth contains only about three-millionths of the total matter in the Solar System. It is true that more than 99.9 percent of that matter is in the Sun, where at first sight it would appear to be out of reach, but the planets, satellites, and asteroids contain between them the mass of 450 Earths. By far the greatest part of this is in Jupiter (318 times the mass of Earth) but Saturn, Uranus, and Neptune also make sizeable contributions. (95, 15, and 17 Earths, respectively.)

In view of the present astronomical cost of space-travel (very approximately $1,000 per pound of payload for even the simplest orbital missions) it may seem fantastic to suggest that we will ever be able to mine and ship megatons of raw materials across the Solar System. Even gold could hardly pay its way, and only diamonds would show a profit.

This view, however, is coloured by today's primitive state of the art, which depends upon hopelessly inefficient techniques. It is something of a shock to realize that, if we could use the energy really effectively, it would require only about ten pence worth of chemical fuel to lift a pound of payload completely clear of the Earth—and perhaps one or two pence to carry it from Moon to Earth. For a number of reasons, these figures represent unattainable ideals; but they do indicate how much room there is for improvement. Some studies of nuclear propulsion systems suggest that, even with techniques we can imagine today, space-flight need be no more expensive than jet transportation; as far as inanimate cargoes are concerned, it may be very much cheaper.

Consider first the Moon. Its mineral resources are enormous, and some of them may be unique. Because the Moon has no atmosphere, and has a rather weak gravitational field, it would be quite feasible to project material from its surface "down" to Earth by means of electrically powered catapults or launching tracks. No rocket fuel would be needed—only a few pence worth of electrical energy per pound of payload. (The capital cost of the launcher would, of course, be very great; but it could be used an indefinite number of times.)

It would thus be theoretically possible, as soon as large-scale industrial operations commence on the Moon, to ship back lunar products on a considerable scale, aboard robot freighters which could glide to assigned landing areas after they had dissipated their 25,000 mph re-entry speed in the upper atmosphere. The only rocket fuel used in the entire process would be negligible amounts for steering and altitude control; all the energy would be provided by the fixed power-plant of the Moon-based launcher.

Going still farther afield, we know that there are enormous quantities of metal (much of it the highest grade of nickel-iron) floating round the Solar System in the form of meteorites and asteroids. The largest asteroid, Ceres, has a diameter of 450 miles, and there may be thousands over a mile across. It is interesting to note that a single iron asteroid, 300 yards in diameter, would supply the world's present needs for a year.

What makes the asteroids particularly promising as a source of raw materials is their microscopic gravity. It needs practically no energy to escape from them; a man could jump off one of the smaller asteroids with ease. When nuclear propulsion systems have been perfected, it would be practical to nudge at least smaller asteroids out of their orbits and inject them into paths that would lead, after a year or so, to the vicinity of Earth. Here they might be parked in orbit until they were cut up into suitably sized pieces; alternatively, they might be allowed to fall directly to Earth.

This last operation would require almost no consumption of fuel, as the Earth's gravitational field would do all the work. It would, however, require extremely accurate and completely reliable guidance, for the consequences of error would be too terrible to contemplate. Even a very small asteroid could erase a city, and the impact of one containing a year's supply of iron would be equivalent to a 10,000 megaton explosion. It would make a hole at least ten times as large as a Meteor Crater—so perhaps we had better use the Moon, not the Earth, for a dumping-ground.

If we ever discover means of controlling or directing gravitational fields such astronomical engineering operations would become much more attractive. We might then be able to absorb the enormous energy of a descending asteroid and use it profitably, as today we use the energy of falling water. The energy would be an additional bonus, to be added to the value of the iron mountain we had gently lowered to Earth. Although this idea is the purest fantasy, no project which obeys the laws of the conservation of energy should be dismissed out of hand.

Lifting material from the giant planets is a very much less attractive proposition than mining the asteroids. The huge gravitational fields would make it difficult and expensive, even given unlimited amounts of thermo-nuclear power—and without this assumption there is no point in discussing the matter. In addition, the Jupiter-type worlds appear to consist almost entirely of valueless light elements such as hydrogen, helium, carbon, and nitrogen; any heavier elements will be locked up thousands of miles down inside their cores.

The same arguments apply, even more strongly, to the Sun. In this case, however, there is a factor which we may one day be able to use to our advantage. The material in the Sun is in the plasma state— that is, it is at such a high temperature that its atoms are all electrified or ionized. Plasmas conduct electricity far better than any metals, and their manipulation by magnetic fields is the basis of the important new science of magneto-hydrodynamics—usually, for obvious reasons, referred to as MHD. We are now using many MHD techniques in research and industry, to produce and contain gases at temperatures of millions of degrees, and we can observe similar processes in action on the Sun, where the magnetic fields around sunspots and flares are so intense that they hurl Earth-sized clouds of gas thousands of miles high in defiance of the solar gravity.

Tapping the Sun may sound like a fantastic conception, but we are already probing its atmosphere with our radio beams. Perhaps one day we may be able to release or trigger the titanic forces at work there, and selectively gather what we need of its incandescent substance. But before we attempt such Promethean exploits, we had better know exactly what we are doing.

Having, in imagination, raided the Solar System in the search for raw materials, let us come back to Earth and explore a completely different line of thought. It may never be really necessary to go beyond our own planet for anything we need—for the time will come when we can create any element, in any quantity, by nuclear transmutation.

Until the discovery of uranium fission in 1939, practical transmutation remained as much a dream as it had been in the days of the old alchemists. Since the first reactors started operating in 1942, substantial amounts (to be measured in tons) of the synthetic metal plutonium have been manufactured, and vast quantities of other elements have been created as often unwanted and embarrassingly radioactive by-products.

But plutonium, with its overwhelmingly important military application, is a very special case, and everyone is aware of the cost and complexity of the plants needed to manufacture it. Gold is cheap by comparison, and synthesizing common metals like lead or copper or iron seems about as probable as mining them from the Sun.

We must remember, however, that nuclear engineering is in roughly the same position as chemical engineering at the beginning of the nineteenth century, when the laws governing reactions between compounds were just beginning to be understood. We now synthesize, on the largest scale, drugs and plastics which yesterday's chemists could not even have produced in their laboratories. Within a few generations, we will surely be able to do the same thing with the elements.

Starting with the simplest element hydrogen (one electron revolving around one proton) or its isotope deuterium (one electron revolving round a nucleus of a proton plus a neutron) we can "fuse" atoms together to make heavier and heavier elements. This is the process operating in the Sun, as well as in the H-bomb; by various means, four atoms of hydrogen are combined to make one of helium, and in the reaction enormous quantities of energy are released. (In practice, the third element in the Periodic Table, lithium, is also employed.) The process is extremely difficult to start, and still harder to control—but it is only the very first step in what might be christened "nuclear chemistry."

At even higher pressures and temperatures than those produced in today's thermo-nuclear explosions or fusion devices, the helium atoms will themselves combine to form heavier elements; this is what happens in the cores of stars. At first, these reactions release additional energy, but when we reach elements as heavy as iron or nickel the balance shifts and extra energy has to be supplied to create them. This is a consequence of the fact that the heaviest elements tend to be unstable and break down more easily than they fuse together. Building up elements is rather like piling up a column of bricks; the structure is stable at first, but after a while it is liable to spontaneous collapse.

But there are other ways of starting reactions, besides heat and pressure. The chemists have known this for many years; they employ catalysts which speed up reactions or make them take place at far lower temperatures than they would otherwise do. Much of modern industrial chemistry is founded on catalysts (vide the "cat crackers" of the oil refineries) and the actual composition of these is often a closely guarded trade secret.

Are there nuclear, as well as chemical catalysts? Yes: In the Sun, carbon and nitrogen play this role. There may be many other nuclear catalysts, not necessarily elements. Among the legions of misnamed fundamental particles which now perplex the physicist—the mesons and positrons and neutrinos—there may be entities that can bring about fusion at temperatures and pressures that we can handle. Or there may be completely different ways of achieving nuclear synthesis, as unthinkable today as was the uranium reactor only thirty years ago.

The seas of this planet contain 100,000,000,000,000,000,000 tons of hydrogen and 20,000,000,000,000 tons of deuterium. Soon we will learn to use these simplest of all atoms to yield unlimited power. Later—perhaps very much later—we will take the next step, and pile our nuclear building blocks on top of each other to create any element we please. When that day comes, the fact that gold, for example, might turn out to be slightly cheaper than lead will be of no particular importance.

This survey should be enough to indicate—though not to prove—that there need never be any permanent shortage of raw materials. Yet Sir George Darwin's prediction that ours would be a Golden Age compared with the aeons of poverty to follow, may well be perfectly correct. In this inconceivably enormous universe, we can never run out of energy or matter. But we can all too easily run out of brains.

In the twenty years since the above words were written, there has been an enormous outpouring of books and studies (e.g., the Club of Rome reports) warning of impending shortages of energy and raw materials. Many of those warnings are fully justified; the conclusion drawn from them by some naive pessimists, that our technological civilization is doomed to collapse, is not.

Since this book is not concerned with *the* Future, but with the whole range of possible futures, such issues—matters of life and death though they are—lie beyond its scope. Nevertheless, it may seem irresponsible not to pay some attention to the world-as-it-probably-will-be, rather than as we would like it to be.

To repeat: In an *absolute* sense, there is no real shortage of energy or materials, though often they may not be available in the form—or at the price—that we would desire. What we are short of is time; there is a grave mismatch between our present needs, and our future capabilities.

At the risk of gross oversimplification, I am tempted to sum up our chief current dilemma in these words: The age of cheap energy is over. The age of free energy still lies fifty years ahead.

Themes, Issues, and Ideas

1. According to Clarke, what would be the optimal source of future energy? If that source proves impossible, what does he say might be an alternative source? Explain why these are the leading candidates.

Now that the Cold War is over, it appears that some Americans are searching for a new scapegoat to blame for the current chaos in the economy. Environmentalists have quickly become the new target of the right. Although it is dispiriting to be assailed as the destroyer of the American way of life, the backlash is not necessarily a reason to despair. More than anything, the ferocious antagonism now being directed toward environmentalists proves that the environmental movement has made major inroads into the public psyche.

Conservatives are now reacting to the environmental movement as if it were a formidable political opponent. While they may be overestimating the current power of the environmental community, there are encouraging signs that the movement is indeed being transformed into what right-wingers fear most: a broadly based political force capable of challenging the corporate status quo.

The Democratic Party, as well, has wisely recognized the emerging power of the environmental movement. Democratic presidential candidate Gov. Bill Clinton picked Sen. Al Gore (D-Tenn.) as his running mate precisely because Gore is an environmental champion and would appeal to the growing number of Americans who are concerned about the environment. Indeed, in his nomination acceptance speech, Gore forecast the potential power of the environmental movement when he said, "The environment will become the central organizing principle of the 21st century."

One can sense in many places across the country the rising energy of green politics—an emerging political philosophy that broadens the focus of environmentalism to include peace, community, justice technology, and animal rights issues. Despite the noisy clamoring of the environmental backlash, green politics is making itself felt in three slowly evolving trends, each of which seems to be setting the stage for a significant break from politics-as-usual in years to come.

First, the environmental movement is broadening to include other constituencies. Activists from beyond the typical white, middle-class constituency of environmentalism have begun to view a healthy environment as central to their own concerns and have begun to work closely with environmentalists.

Hundreds of African-Americans, Hispanics, Native Americans, and Asians assembled in Washington last fall for the first National People of Color Environmental Leadership Summit. Representing communities not traditionally active in environmental causes, delegates came to this meeting to organize against the environmental assaults experienced disproportionately by minority, poor, and working-class people—threats like toxic waste dumps, hazardous waste incinerators, lead poisoning, poor air quality, and lac of access to healthy food. Conference participants argued that the struggle for a healthy environment is part of the struggle for social justice and that only a healthy environment can provide the basis for a healthy and just economy.

Feminists are also broadening their politics to encompass the environment. Last fall, the Women's Foreign Policy Council, chaired by former U.S. Rep. Bella Abzug, sponsored the first World Women's Congress for a Just and Healthy Planet. More than 1,500 activist women from 83 countries attended this unprecedented conference to discuss the effect of environmental degradation on women and families worldwide.

Even labor leaders have begun to talk seriously about how they might align themselves with environmentalists while at the same time devising strategies to provide an economic safety net for workers who lose jobs as a result of environmental protection measures.

There is more good news. At the state and local level, Green parties are being organized, and hundreds of independent, green-oriented (although they seldom use this phrase to describe themselves) legislators across the country are becoming increasingly successful at passing environmental-protection legislation in their communities. For example, in 1990 alone, 140 recycling laws were passed by state legislatures.

This year, California became the second state, following Alaska, to officially recognize the Greens as a political party. More than 83,000 Californians registered with the Green Party, qualifying the party to have its candidates on the November 3 election ballot. The Green Party has also been working to gain official recognition in Arizona, Hawaii, Missouri, and Pennsylvania.

In many areas of the country where Green parties have not yet made inroads, scores of state and local legislators have been working with national progressive policy groups such as the Center for Policy Alternatives and Renew America, in Washington, D.C., and smaller, more localized groups, such as Local Solutions to Global Pollution in Berkeley, California, to develop environmental protection legislation and strategies for its passage in their communities.

A third hopeful development is occurring, of all places, on Capitol Hill. Green politics is quietly emerging as a distinct new political presence in the U.S. Congress. In researching *Voting Green,* we sifted through a couple of thousand pieces of proposed federal legislation (covering issues ranging from transportation to foreign policy to animal rights to agriculture) in search of evidence of green thinking about the problems America faces. To our surprise, we found nearly 300 bills proposed between January 1989 and June 1991 that fit our criteria. We tracked and graded all 535 members of Congress, marking on a "report card" whether they had supported each of these bills or not. Because much of this legislation is far-sighted and visionary, little of it has made it out of committee to the floor of the House or Senate for a vote. We therefore decided to track support for these innovative bills by noting which legislators were sponsoring and co-sponsoring the legislation.

We ended up with an intriguing finding: A small but solid group of U.S. legislators, a good 10 percent of the Congress, is proposing and supporting radical new solutions for America. Ten years ago, there was no trace of a "green contingent" in Congress, but now a discernible group can be identified. Foremost among these congressional greens is Al Gore, whose presence on the Democratic ticket this fall is another sign of growing interest in green politics.

The bills introduced and supported by these legislators prescribe nearly everything that environmentalists have advocated and fought for in areas ranging from agriculture to animal rights to foreign policy. Taken together, their bills provide a virtual "greenprint" for a new green society. They are the bridge between idealistic green visions and the complex realities of modern society.

These three new trends are still in their infancy, but they are the seeds of a national political movement. If these trends continue to flourish, they could produce a powerful new political force. At the core of these trends is a revolutionary concept: the idea of placing the environment at the center of pubic life and then planning economic, social, and other policies around it.

While the environmental movement has made considerable gains over the past two decades, especially in raising the public's consciousness, the movement as it is presently constituted is reaching the limit of what it can accomplish. Environmentalism as it is practiced in this country is too narrow, which has made it vulnerable to charges of elitism. The environmental movement now faces the challenge of transforming itself into something deeper and broader. Green politics is based on the recognition that we can't have a healthy economy, peace among nations, or a satisfying quality of life if we are trying to live and work within a degraded environment.

American politics has always revolved around the economy—with disastrous results for the environment and human welfare. Most Republicans and Democrats view the environment as just another issue—a special interest, one among many. As a result, the environment is ignored whenever it is politically expedient—which is most of the time. Conventional political analysts often claim that concern about the environment evaporates in the face of a nation's economic and other stresses.

But an intricate, delicate natural system cannot regularly be shunted aside without suffering considerable, even permanent damage. The earth's biological system supports our economy; it is literally our life-support system—hardly a special interest! With further bad news about global warming, the ozone hole, extinction of species, and toxic waste horrors, more and more people are beginning to realize this.

The seemingly insoluble nature of the country's economic and other problems has catalyzed many people's search for a more holistic, commonsensical approach to politics. This new thinking may begin to make itself felt at the polls in November—if not in the presidential election, then in many congressional, state, and local races. In the increasingly stale political atmosphere of 1992, these visionary green ideas coming from all corners of the nation as well as from Capitol Hill are a breath of fresh air.

In our study of proposed federal legislation, we uncovered bills that present a whole new way of seeing and relating to the world—ideas that challenge conventional notions of global security, economics, progress, science and technology, and community.

For example, some members of Congress are beginning to sense that an increasingly weakened biosphere poses a more serious threat to our individual and national security than the relative military and economic strength of other nations. Some of the legislation they have proposed reflects this shift in thinking. The bills range from those that would protect and preserve the global commons—rain forests, the atmosphere, outer space, Antarctica, and even the gene pool of the planet—to those that would begin to dismantle the U. S. military-industrial complex and move toward an equitable, sustainable peacetime economy.

In 1990, a number of legislators—including Gore, Sen. John Kerry (D-Mass.) and Rep. Wayne Owens (D-Utah)—proposed and pushed through legislation to "fully protect Antarctica as a global ecological commons." In 1991, President Bush, under heavy pressure, was eventually forced to sign this legislation as well as a global treaty banning commercial activity on the continent for another 50 years.

Far-reaching legislation to counter global warming and deterioration of the ozone layer, and to dramatically limit the gas emissions that are responsible for these potentially cataclysmic environmental effects, has been submitted by a handful of legislators including Gore and former Republican Rep. Claudine Schneider of Rhode Island.

Protecting the planet's gene pool has also gained the attention of Congress. Legislation has been introduced by Sen. Mark Hatfield (R-Ore.) that challenges the right of corporations and individuals to genetically engineer, patent, and own plants, animals, and microbes.

Legislation to rein in the U.S. military-industrial complex includes a congressional resolution to cut U.S. military spending by at least 50 percent by the year 2000 and dramatically cut U.S. military assistance and arms sales to developing nations. Bills introduced by Reps. Barbara boxer (D-Calif.), Ted Weiss (D-N.Y.), Sam Gejdenson (D-Conn.), and Nicholas Mavroules (D-Mass.) would ease the economic transition for companies, workers, and communities in the wake of cutbacks in military spending by requiring military contractors to establish special committees to plan for the transition, and by providing workers with economic assistance and retraining.

A bill sponsored by Hatfield and Rep. Andrew Jacobs (D-Ind.) would create a "peace tax fund" into which citizens who are conscientiously opposed to the military could pay their federal taxes; such funds would be used only to fund social and environmental protection programs.

In other areas too, the range and depth of green legislation being proposed is extraordinary and provocative and based on radical green values and ideas. In the area of animal rights, for example, one bill would allow any citizen or organization to file suit against the federal government on behalf of an individual animal in order to compel enforcement of the Animal Welfare Act, an animal-protection law. Implicit in the legislation is the revolutionary idea that individual animals have intrinsic value and inherent rights to exist and not be harmed. At one point, the bill had more than 68 co-sponsors in the House. Another animal-rights bill would require all federally funded school lunch programs to provide optional meatless meals for all students and teachers who are conscientiously opposed to eating meat.

In the area of foreign development aid, one green bill would require the U.S. government to dramatically increase the number of cash loans of between $50 and $300 to women and the poorest of the poor in developing nations to enable them to set up their own self-sustaining and environmentally sustainable businesses. Another bill would require the United States to promote and defend the rights of indigenous and tribal peoples throughout the world. These two pieces of green legislation represent radical departures from the goals and methods of current U.S. foreign aid programs and policies, which do not encourage self-reliance and sustainability.

These are just a few of the green ideas and practical approaches being discussed among legislators on Capitol Hill. Make no mistake—these lawmakers are not dyed-in-the-wool, self-conscious, ideological greens; but they are experimenting with new ideas about what constitutes security and quality of life. Unfortunately, green initiatives and progressive legislation are almost always ignored or go down to defeat in Congress because of a lack of broad-based support. Such legislation is usually supported by and lobbied for almost exclusively by the constituency group that is considered the "closest" to the issue at hand.

But as the idea of a comprehensive green politics—one that places the environment at the center of public life and plans economic and other activities around it—takes root among voters and elected officials, we are likely to see less fragmentation and more cooperation among various constituencies. Advocates of the environment, social justice, workers, women, family farmers, animal rights, peace, community empowerment, and numerous other groups and issues can find common ground in a green agenda.

Perhaps the only ingredient that's now missing for a national green movement is a sense of urgency. The forces of environmental backlash continue to press for the exploitation of the steadily weakening natural environment. So far, they are winning. The various constituencies that would make up the new green movement are acting as though they have all the time in the world to mobilize themselves.

Meanwhile, the short-lived presidential "candidacy" of H. Ross Perot gained surprising support among an increasingly alienated electorate in search of a new vision for the country. For these and millions of other Americans, the old political labels of "Republican/Democrat," "conservative/liberal," "right/left" that have long been used to define political debate are becoming increasingly irrelevant. That's because many issues of interest to American voters (and non-voters) transcend these old forms of classification.

A new, more relevant political spectrum is beginning to emerge. At one end are those who view their fellow human beings, other species, and the environment in strictly utilitarian terms—as resources to exploit for short-term material gain. At the opposite end of the spectrum are those who view all life on the earth as an interrelated community to which we are all indebted and for which we are all responsible.

Increasingly, political debate will be defined and shaped by looming global environmental threats and resource shortages; as a result we will see growing polarization between these two camps.

Among some groups in Congress, there is evidence that traditional political boundaries are becoming blurred and are beginning to reorganize around this new value system. For example, members of the two-year-old animal-rights caucus, Congressional Friends of Animals, which provides a base of support for animal-protection legislation in Congress, is bipartisan and includes a significant number of conservative Republicans as well as liberal Democrats.

If we act now to join forces under the green banner, support those legislators at all levels—federal, state, and local—who are trying to think green, aggressively lobby for the green legislation that is being proposed, and vote more greens (including ourselves) into public office, we could spawn a powerful new political force—one that could have a major impact on the nation and the world by the time another presidential election rolls around in 1996.

Themes, Issues, and Ideas

1. How would you describe Grunewald's perspective? Is she a convincing advocate of green politics? Why or why not?

2. What sort of person does Grunewald seem to be? Is she like anyone you know? How would you describe her politically?

3. How would you describe the moral tone of Grunewald's essay?

Writing Strategies and Techniques

1. Why does Grunewald begin her essay with quotations? Why are the quotes from anti-environmental voices?

2. Compare Grunewald's style with Hillary Clinton's (Chapter 4). Who is the better writer? Who is more persuasive? Why? Defend both the "policy-paper" style of Clinton and the journalistic style of Grunewald.

Suggestions for Writing

1. Write an essay predicting what a twenty-first century election would be like, given Grunewald's predictions.

2. Write an essay advocating the traditional two-party system as the best avenue for change.

Reforest the Earth!

Norman Myers

Suppose that those scientists are correct who suspect global disasters to be the result of the greenhouse effect described in the previous essay. What can be done to avoid or to limit those disasters? Norman Myers, a senior fellow for the World Wildlife Fund and an expert on environment and development, suggests a plan: "A worldwide campaign to reforest the earth . . . will improve the quality of our lives, stabilize rising temperatures, and buy time until we find solutions to the greenhouse effect." Myers proposes that for an average cost of $160 per acre we could undertake a program of reforestation that would greatly counter the negative symptoms of an "ailing world." Though the total costs are very high, Myers argues that the costs of not reforesting are even higher. This essay was first published in Omni *magazine, under the title "First Word."*

Throughout the drought-ridden summer of 1988, the world heard much about how the burning of fossil fuels causes the greenhouse effect (the rapid warming of the earth's atmosphere). We heard little about how the burning of tropical rain forests also contributes to the greenhouse effect. And still less do we hear about how reforestation of these tropics could help heal an ailing world.

The earth constantly maintains 700 billion metric tons of carbon dioxide (CO_2) in the atmosphere. Fossil fuels emit another 5.2 billion metric tons of CO_2 into the air each year, while the burning of tropical forests emits roughly 1.8 billion metric tons of CO_2—both contributing to a buildup of carbon dioxide that will soon trigger the greenhouse effect. The CO_2 gases trap the heat of the sun in the same way the glass of a greenhouse controls temperature for plants. If the gases become too concentrated, too much heat will collect, resulting in rising temperatures.

Of all the carbon dioxide spewed into the atmosphere, only about half accumulates in the skies while the rest disappears into oceans and lakes, vegetation and soil. So out of the 5.2 billion metric tons of CO_2 emitted from the burning of fossil fuels and the 1.8 billion metric tons released from the burning of rain forests each year, only 3.5 billion metric tons contributes to global warming.

In 1980, 36,000 square miles of forest were burned in the tropics. In 1987, 33,000 square miles of rain forest were burned in Brazilian Amazonia alone. By the year 2020 the figure for tropical-forest emissions of CO_2 could climb to another 5 billion metric tons. As a result, the CO_2 released into the atmosphere each year would rise to approximately 10.2 billion metric tons.

Replanting trees in the tropics could eventually offer a solution to the greenhouse effect. A tree absorbs carbon dioxide through photosynthesis. Plant enough trees (as many as 250 billion) and we could remove much of the additional CO_2 building up in the atmosphere. Nowhere in the world are conditions better for growing trees than in the tropics, where year-round warmth and moisture encourage rapid growth. To embark on a grand-scale tree-growing project in the tropics, however, would require as many as 20 governments in Latin America, Africa, and Asia to stop the rapid destruction of rain forests.

How many trees would we need to reforest the earth and stabilize the damage produced by global warming? One acre of a tropical plantation can absorb an annual average of four metric tons of atmospheric carbon. In order to soak up 1 billion metric tons of CO_2, we would have to plant 400,000 square miles of new tropical forests. To eliminate the buildup of 3.5 billion metric tons would require planting trees on 1.2 million square miles, an expanse roughly equivalent to all states east of the Mississippi.

Where can we find enough space to replant what isn't being otherwise utilized? In the humid tropics forests have been cut down in watershed regions where replanting is urgently needed to stop topsoil from eroding and to prevent flooding. Last year flooding devastated regions in Bangladesh, India, the Sudan, and Thailand. In lowland Southeast Asia deforested lands have degenerated into poor-quality scrub and brush or coarse grasslands, good for little apart from reforestation. In addition, tropical countries urgently need to increase forest cover to adequately expand their fuelwood and commercial timber supplies.

At an average cost of $160 per acre, reforesting the tropics would cost $120 billion. This may seem like a high figure, but the global community would be spared much higher greenhouse costs. According to the Environmental Protection Agency, a rise in sea level (just through heating of the ocean surface) would threaten the developed coastal regions of the eastern United States. To protect these shorelines, seawalls and tidal dams would have to be built at a cost of

$110 billion. To revamp dams and irrigation systems in the United States could cost an additional $23 billion. In comparison, the Department of Agriculture currently spends $200 million a year on flood-prevention programs. Further costs related to sealevel rise and disrupted agriculture in other parts of the world (lush, fertile cropland may turn into desert) would surely turn out to be similarly great.

The consequences of the greenhouse effect will be far-reaching and possibly even devastating. If the projections of experts come to pass in the next 50 years, the earth's temperatures will rise between 3° and 9°F. (In polar regions the temperatures may rise as much as 20°F). After a look at the consequences we face as a result of the greenhouse effect, reforesting the earth doesn't seem as outrageous as it might have at first. In fact, a program to plant billions of trees throughout the tropics now seems like a very sensible action.

Reforesting the earth is not the definitive solution to the warming trend of the greenhouse effect. It is only one way to bring the rising levels of carbon in the atmosphere under control. A worldwide campaign to reforest the earth, however, will improve the quality of our lives, stabilize rising temperatures, and buy time until we find additional solutions to the greenhouse effect.

Themes, Issues, and Ideas

1. Myers deals in staggering figures and, since the essay is not a formal scientific presentation, he does not list all the sources of those figures. But educated readers should try to avoid being staggered. Try to check his numbers—do they add up and divide properly? How else might they be presented? For example, how much per *tree* would Myers's program cost?

2. Why does Myers focus on the tropics for the location of his plan? Surely trees grow the world over. According to Myers, what makes the tropics such an attractive place for reforestation?

3. Myers says that the cooperation of twenty governments would be needed to stop the destruction of tropical rain forests. How and why might these governments argue *against* Myers's proposals?

Writing Strategies and Techniques

1. Myers alludes to experts, but does not quote any as the sources for his statistics. When do you think it is necessary to give precise citations in your writing, and when is it not? Explain your reasoning.

2. Alternative sources of fuel (for example, nuclear, solar) are not mentioned in the essay. Do you find this appropriate, given the nature of the essay?

Suggestions for Writing

1. When first reading the title, a reader might think Myers's program to be irrational, yet Myers himself concludes that "reforesting the earth doesn't seem as outrageous as it might have at first." Do you agree? Write a brief essay in which you analyze and demonstrate the strengths and weaknesses of Myers's essay as you see them.

2. How does one properly make a global proposal that includes such immense costs? Write an essay in which you argue the appropriateness of Myers's style to the importance of his context by analyzing particular examples.

MAKING CONNECTIONS

1. If the purpose of an essay is to persuade, who in this chapter does the best job? Does a descriptive, personal essay like Annie Dillard's "In the Jungle" affect you more than a formal statement like Al Gore's "Ecology: The New Sacred Agenda?"

2. The essays by Al Gore and Arthur C. Clarke in this chapter differ strongly in their images of the future—plenty versus disaster. Yet what can be learned from the two essayists as writers? Write an essay analyzing the different ways in which Arthur C. Clarke and Al Gore discuss a future neither can be truly sure about.

3. Norman Myers takes a somewhat different approach to environmental change than does Gore or, for that matter, Grunewald. Evaluate each of these authors on the practicality, sincerity, and potential usefulness of their ideas.

4. Many environmental problems have dramatic effects but obscure origins. Which of the authors in this chapter give you the best grasp on where environmental crises come from, as opposed to how they may be cured?

5. Many environmental problems are raised in this chapter, but which author seems to you the best at presenting a problem clearly and forcefully? Who is next best? Write an essay comparing the writers' expository strengths.

RHETORICAL
INDEX

ILLUSTRATION AND EXEMPLIFICATION

ANALOGY AND METAPHOR

PROCESS ANALYSIS

DESCRIPTION

NARRATION

ARGUMENT AND PERSUASION

INDEX
OF AUTHORS
AND TITLES

Credits continued from copyright page.

Angier, Natalie. "The Gene Dream," *American Health,* March 1989, Vol. 8, pp. 102–108. Reprinted by permission of the author.

Asimov, Isaac. "The Never-ending Fight," by Issac Asimov first appeared in the March/April 1989 issue of *The Humanist* and is reprinted with permission.

Bailey, Julie. "Jobs for Women in the Nineties," reprinted with permission from *Ms.* magazine, July 1988, pp. 74–79. Copyright 1988.

Carson, Rachel. "A Fable for Tomorrow," from *Silent Spring* by Rachel Carson. Copyright © 1962 by Rachel L. Carson, © renewed 1990 by Roger Christie. Reprinted by permission of Houghton Mifflin Co. All rights reserved.

Chandler, Tertius. "Education—Less of It!" *The College Board Review,* No. 144, Summer 1987, pp. 5–7, 24–35. Reprinted by permission of the author.

Chesterton, G. K. "A Defence of Skeletons," *The Defendant,* 1904, Mead and Company, London.

Clarke, Arthur C. "Ages of Plenty," from *Profiles of the Future* by Authur C. Clarke. Copyright © 1962, 1973, 1982, 1984 by Arthur C. Clarke. Reprinted by permission of Henry Holt and Company, Inc.

Cotts, Cynthia. "Xanax Panic: The Pushers in the Suites." This article is reprinted with permission from the August 31/September 7, 1992 issue of *The Nation* magazine, p. 208. © The Nation Company, Inc.

Dillard, Annie. "In the Jungle," excerpt from *Teaching a Stone to Talk* by Annie Dillard. Copyright © 1982 by Annie Dillard. Reprinted by permission of HarperCollins Publishers, Inc.

Ehrenreich, Barbara. "Ice-T . . . or is it Creative Freedom?" *Time,* July 20, 1992, p. 88. Copyright 1992 Time Inc. Reprinted by permission.

Eisenberg, Anne. "Imperial English: The Language of Science?" *Scientific American,* December 1992, p. 162. Reprinted with permission. Copyright © 1992 by Scientific American, Inc. All rights reserved.

Eisler, Riane. "Our Lost Heritage: New Facts on How God Became a Man" by Riane Eisler first appeared in the May/June 1985 issue of *The Humanist* and is reprinted with permission.

Falk, Richard. "The Surge to Democracy," reprinted by permission from *The Center* magazine, May/June 1987, Vol. 20, No. 3, pp. 44–46.

Fallows, Deborah. "Why Mothers Should Stay Home," reprinted with permission from *The Washington Monthly,* January 1982. Copyright by The Washington Monthly Company, 1611 Connecticut Avenue, NW, Washington DC 20009.

Fallows, James. "Japan: Playing by Different Rules," *The Atlantic,* September 1987, pp. 22–32. Reprinted by permission of the author.

Friedan, Betty. "The New Feminine Mystique," *McCall's* magazine, November 1991, p. 78. Reprinted by permission of Curtis Brown, Ltd. Copyright © 1991 by Betty Friedan.

Fuentes, Carlos. "The United States and Latin America," reprinted by permission from *The Center* magazine, May/June 1987, Vol. 20, No. 3, pp. 4–5.

Galarza, Ernesto. From *Barrio Boy* by Ernesto Galarza. © 1971 by the University of Notre Dame Press. Reprinted by permission.

Glazer, Nathan. "Some Very Modest Proposals for the Improvement of American Education," reprinted by permission of *Daedalus,* Journal of the American Academy of Arts and Sciences, from the issue entitled "Values, Resources and Politics in America's Schools," Fall 1984, Vol. 113, No. 4.

Gore, Al. "Ecology: The New Sacred Agenda," reprinted by permission from *New Perspectives Quarterly,* Winter 1992.

Gornick, Vivian. "Twice an Outsider," reprinted by permmssion from *Tikkun*, March 4, 1989. *Tikkun* is a bimonthly Jewish critique of Culture, Politics, and Society. Call 800-846-8575 for a subscription.

Grunewald, Carol. "Voting Green" by Carol Grunewald, reprinted from *Utne Reader*, September/October, 1992. Reprinted by permission of the author.

Harris, Louis. "2001: The World Our Students Will Enter," *The College Board Review* No. 150, Winter 1988–89, pp. 21–24, 34. Reprinted by permission of the author.

Haught, James. "The Code of the Universe" by James Haught first appeared in the September/October 1988 issue of *The Humanist* and is reprinted with permission.

hooks, bell. "Feminism—It's a Black Thang!" *Essence* magazine, July 1992, p. 124. Copyright 1992 by bell hooks. Reprinted by permission of the author.

Huxley, Aldous. "Liberty, Quality, Machinery," *Tomorrow and Tomorrow and Tomorrow* by Aldous Huxley. Copyright © 1953 by Aldous Huxley. Reprinted by permission of the Huxley Literary Estate.

Kapuscinski, Ryzsard. "America as a Collage," excerpted from *New Perspectives Quarterly* with permission, Summer 1988, pp. 39–42.

Kean, Patricia. "Blowing Up the Tracks," reprinted with permission from *The Washington Monthly*, January 1993. Copyright by The Washington Monthly Company, 1611 Connecticut Avenue NW, Washington, DC 20009.

Kennedy, John Fitzgerald. "Inaugural Address," February 6, 1961, *Weekly Compilation of Presidential Documents*.

King, Martin Luther, Jr. "I Have a Dream," reprinted by arrangement with the Heirs of the Estate of Martin Luther King, Jr., c/o Joan Daves Agency as agent for the proprietor. Copyright 1963 by Martin Luther King, Jr., copyright renewed 1991 by Coretta Scott King.

Kinsley, Michael. "Ice-T: Is the Issue Social Responsibility . . . ," *Time*, July 20, 1992, p. 88. Copyright 1992 Time Inc. Reprinted by permission.

Kluger, Jeffrey. "Body Doubles," reprinted by permission of *Omni*, August 1987, pp. 49–50, 106–109. © 1987, Omni Publications International, Ltd.

Lasch, Christopher. "Is Progress Obsolete?" *Time*, special "The Future" issue, Fall 1992. Copyright 1992 Time Inc. Reprinted by permission.

Lawren, Bill. "Apocalypse Now?" reprinted with permission from *Psychology Today* magazine, May 1989. Copyright © 1989. (Sussex Publishers, Inc.).

Lewis, Flora. "An Elephant in the Backyard," reprinted by permission from *New Perspectives Quarterly*, Fall 1991.

Magaziner, Ira and Clinton, Hillary Rodham. "Will America Choose High Skills or Low Wages?" *Educational Leadership*, March 1992, Vol. 49, No. 6, pp 10–14. Reprinted with permission of the Association for Supervision and Curriculum Development. Copyright © 1992 by the Association for Supervision and Curriculum Development. All rights reserved.

Malcolm X. Excerpts from "The Ballot or the Bullet," *Malcolm X Speaks*, pp. 25–26, 43–44. Reprinted by permission of Pathfinder Press. Copyright © 1965 & 1989 by Betty Shabazz and Pathfinder Press.

Miller, Mark Crispin. "Big Brother Is You, Watching," *Boxed In: The Culture of Television*, 1988, pp. 326–331. Reprinted by permission from Northwestern University Press.

Monaco, James. "Into the Nineties and Beyond: The Coming Revolution in Film and TV," *American Film*, January/February 1989, pp. 24–27. Reprinted by permission of the author.

Moyers, Bill. Excerpt from "Old News Is Good News," reprinted by permission from *New Perspectives Quarterly*, Fall 1992.

Myers, Norman. "Reforest the Earth!" *Omni*, May 1989, p. 8. Reprinted by permission of Omni, © 1989, Omni Publications International, Ltd.